A HISTORY OF THE JEWS IN
CHRISTIAN SPAIN

I

Yitzhak Baer

A HISTORY OF THE JEWS IN

CHRISTIAN SPAIN

Volume

I

from the Age of Reconquest to the Fourteenth Century

translated from the Hebrew
by Louis Schoffman

THE JEWISH PUBLICATION SOCIETY OF
AMERICA, PHILADELPHIA

1978-5738

PUBLISHER'S PREFACE

Yitzhak Baer's *Toledot haYehudim biSefarad haNotzrit* was hailed, immediately upon its publication, as an outstanding work in the history of the Jews in Spain and, indeed, of medieval Spain in general. But being written in Hebrew, it was accessible to only a relatively small number of readers outside of Israel. There was a manifest need for a translation into one of the more widely used languages. The Jewish Publication Society was proud to undertake this task.

The first draft of the translation was based on the first edition of the work, which appeared in two volumes (Am Oved, Tel Aviv, 1945). When the second edition appeared, somewhat revised and published in a single large volume (1959), the English translation was revised accordingly. This volume may, therefore, be regarded as a translation of the second edition. Here and there—principally in chapter VII of this book—the text has been slightly abridged, with the approval of the author. Elsewhere, on the other hand, principally in the notes, the translation contains material not found in either of the Hebrew editions but supplied by the author to the translator (e.g., pp. 384-8).

A point of major interest in the book is the author's frequent quotation, both in the text and in the notes, from Hebrew sources of Hispano-Jewish history, especially in the sections dealing with its social and economic aspects. These quotations, some of them quite long, cover a wide range of literature and include selections from rabbinic responsa, ethical treatises, works of mysticism and theology, polemics, poetry and other literary expressions of Jewish life. With very few exceptions, all such quotations are here translated into English for the first time.

The chapter divisions of the English translation differ slightly from those of the Hebrew original. The long chapter III of the first and second Hebrew editions is represented by chapters III, IV, V and VI of the translation. The first part of chapter IV of the Hebrew version is here included as chapter VII.

The translation of this book was an arduous task. Expert knowledge of Hebrew and English had to be supplemented with knowledge of Aramaic, in which some of the quotations are couched, and of both Arabic and Latin which left traces on Spanish Jewish life. Nor was this enough, since a translator of this book had to be fully conversant with both Spanish and Jewish history. Dr. Louis Schoffman, of Brooklyn College, possesses all these qualifications to an eminent degree. The Jewish Publication Society wishes to express to him its wholehearted thanks, as does the author, who checked on the translation and approved it.

Thanks are also due to Miss Lotte Levensohn who has prepared a preliminary draft of Part Two of the work. Chapter VII of this volume is based largely on her draft. The quotations, however, found in this chapter, and all the notes were translated by Dr. Schoffman.

Mr. Bernard Sandler prepared the index to this volume. It is limited to personal and place names; a complete index will appear at the end of Volume Two.

CONTENTS

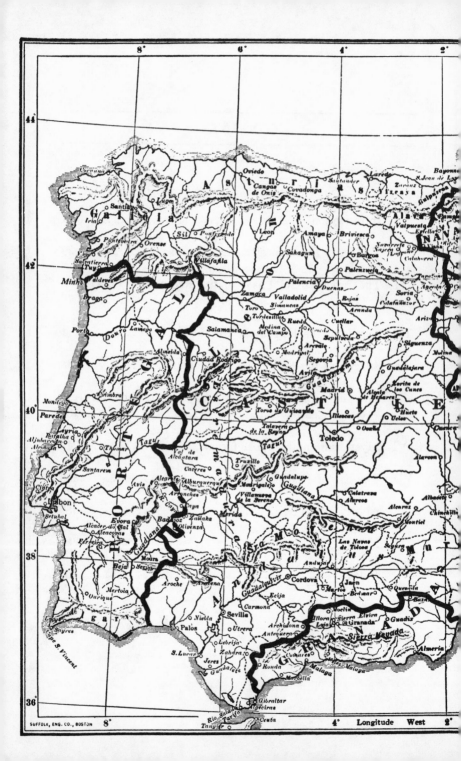

THE IBERIAN KINGDOMS
FROM 1250 TO 1450

SCALE OF MILES

0   50   100

Reproduced with the kind permission of
the Macmillan Company, New York, from
The Rise of the Spanish Empire
by R. B. Merriman

Greenwich   0°   Longitude   East   2°   from   Greenwich   4°   6°

INTRODUCTION

Jewish History, from its earliest beginnings to our own day, constitutes an organic unit. Each successive stage in its development reveals more fully the nature of the unique force guiding it, a force whose initial vitality is universally recognized and whose future course arouses widespread interest. Let this observation be the key to our study.

DEFINING OUR SUBJECT

The story of Jewish life in Christian Spain during the Middle Ages opens its second phase with the beginning of the Reconquest—that centuries-long war fought by the Christian Spaniards to recapture the Iberian peninsula from the Arabs—and ends with the completion of the Reconquest and the expulsion of the Jews from the entire peninsula. It is a story that occupies a distinguished place in the annals of our people, covering, as it does, a period which is virtually the only one in the entire history of the Diaspora—with the exception of modern times—that we are able to study in its entirety, throughout all the stages of rise and decline. Out of the great treasury of historical documents, preserved in the archives of Spain, we reconstruct the successive tiers of historical facts, and through the prism of the Hebrew literature written during this period we look into the minds of the bearers of that history. For they were men who were able—to the extent possible in those days—to grasp the meaning of their destiny and to give expression to the thoughts that filled their hearts. Modern historiography is inclined to regard the history of the Jews in Christian Spain as a sequel to the Golden Age of Hebrew and Judaeo-Arabic culture which preceded it; and, to be sure, the period with which we are concerned cannot be properly understood without reference to the former. Our period, however, differs from the one which preceded it in its specific political and religious problems. The contest between Judaism and Christianity, which the Middle Ages inherited from ancient times, took on here more poignant form than anywhere else.

History brought one of the most creative Jewish communities of the Diaspora into collaboration with one of the most gifted peoples of Christian Europe, the Spaniards. Far-reaching historical developments, affecting both groups, carried this association to dramatic heights and brought it to a tragic end. The war against their Moslem neighbors caused the Spaniards to become at once the most tolerant and the most fanatical people in medieval Christendom. The political objectives of the Reconquest opened up to the Jews broad opportunities for outwardly directed growth, but its religious motivation aroused the zeal of the Christians and subjected the internal religio-ethnic existence of the Jews to a severe trial.

The internal conflicts and external pressures, engendered by these conditions, are akin to the trials which beset our people today. The medieval Jew lived in a time midway between the original creative epoch of the national genius and the modern period of disintegration of traditional values. He entered the Middle Ages with a many-sided legacy which he himself had not created. The Jewish masses, for the most part, were not yet conscious of the difficulties inherent in such a condition. They did not yet feel bowed beneath the weight of a ponderous heritage, but still drew sustenance from those spiritual sources which had served as fountainheads of creativity for the preceding generations. Only occasionally were its ranks broken by individuals who, under the force of political and religious pressure from without, were led to desert their faith and their people. Eventually, the influences behind the political and religious oppression allied themselves more closely in a common destructive assault upon Judaism in Spain than they did in any other period of Jewish history. These external forces were assisted from within by a rationalism and scepticism which undermined tradition, the accepted ways of thinking, the logical bases for ritual practices, and the belief in the mission of Israel and the purpose and meaning of its Diaspora. Hellenic thought illuminated with its cold light the bitter battle for survival fought by Judaism against Christianity in Spain.

THE LINES OF DEVELOPMENT IN ANTIQUITY

The history of the Jews in Spain constitutes but one chapter in the comprehensive story which covers the period during which the Jews were caught between the two great religious and political powers, Christianity and Islam. During this entire long period, extending from the seventh to the eighteenth

3

centuries, all nations were committed to a social order founded upon political and religious tenets whose bases were accepted as beyond question. Christianity and Islam were the religions in power, and the Jews resided under their dominion as a subject people. The fate of our people depended upon the fortunes of the younger Christian and Moslem nations who entered upon the stage of history at a later date than the Jews, and borrowed heavily from earlier civilizations. Jewish history, however, though tied up with the histories of these nations, remained, nevertheless, distinguished from them by its antiquity and by its inner force, which still carries it forward. It is closer, fundamentally, to the histories of the peoples of Far Eastern Asia. Like them, the Jewish people preserved its heritage of national traditions in their original purity against that process of religious and cultural assimilation to which the peoples of Europe and the Near East succumbed during the decline of the Roman Empire and the period of the barbarian invasions. The historian, therefore, who would trace the subsequent history of our people, finds himself compelled to set down a few landmarks marking the course of our people's progress prior to its dispersal throughout Christendom.

In its earliest days the Jewish nation found itself in the midst of great powers and foreign cultures. It borrowed from them certain external forms, but remained ever conscious of the sharp contrasts that distinguished it from the other nations despite the latter's political might and cultural wealth. It had its own moral and theological outlook, regarding itself as intimately bound with God, who was the God of all mankind. It occupied, therefore, a unique position in the history of mankind. The consciousness of a bond between Israel and God determined and defined the position of the Jew among the nations, his relationship to his environment and his inner conduct. He raised himself above his environment by a life of holiness. Inwardly, Israelite society was founded upon the fundamental qualities of simplicity, brotherhood, and love.

4

"And ye shall be unto Me a kingdom of priests, and a holy nation" (Ex. 19. 6) imposed a regimen of pietism upon an entire nation. This historic world outlook, and the patterns of political and social life based upon it, grew out of a purely religious orientation. It had no scientific rationale and drew no distinction between ritual law and social precepts. Its teachings were intended primarily to introduce into the existing law the spirit of love for God and fellow man. But in the end, all these elements—historical, legal, ethical, and theological—fused into one mold, which impressed itself upon succeeding generations and compelled them to create a new society, unique in form and structure.

Such a society, founded upon the precepts of the Torah, was established by Ezra the Scribe. He jealously guarded the "sacred seed" from intermingling with the Gentiles and participating in their idolatrous practices. He restored the Holy Temple and revived Jewish national life on Jewish soil. But this renewed community remained under the tutelage of a foreign power, and the privileges which it was granted by the kings of Persia were substantially the same as those which the Jews throughout the Diaspora were wont to receive centuries later. The Hasmoneans, many generations after Ezra, saved their nation from betraying the Covenant by assimilating with the Greek civilization, and "while all the nations of the world lay prostrate before the idol, they remained standing erect like the palms." The heroism exhibited by this small group of pietists in Palestine remained a shining example for all succeeding ages; but when it came to implementing the structure of national life, differences arose in the interpretation of the hallowed traditions and the means of realizing them in life. Was the nation to be organized as a semi-Hellenized state, pursuing a realistic political course, or was it to constitute a theocratic national center under the aegis of foreign powers? Was it better to yield to the might of Rome or to wage a national war for the establishment of a "kingdom of

God"? Such are the main outlines, vastly rich in their implications, of the great, tragic, inner conflict which marked that
period in our history known as the Second Commonwealth, a
period which has come to serve as a symbol and a parable.

Palestine, with its Temple, pietist movements, and wealth
of sacred traditions, had around it, even during that period, a
widely dispersed Diaspora, exhibiting the fundamental characteristics of the Jewish dispersion of a later day—a Diaspora
with rights curtailed and living only on limited sufferance,
waiting for the Redeemer, defending itself against attackers,
and wrestling with a theoretical antisemitism which exploited
the obvious contradiction between the avowed mission of Israel
and his actual state of dependence. There already appeared,
in this environment, the type of Jew who betrayed his people
and scoffed at the ancestral tradition. But this type had not yet
become a conspicuous social phenomenon. The Judaeo-Hellenis-
tic literature, though couched in borrowed forms, was, nevertheless, fully nationalist and religious in content. It differed from
the polemic literature of the Middle Ages and of the modern
age of enlightenment in that it did not remain on the defensive
but set out to destroy paganism, to disseminate Jewish lore
among the Gentile nations, and to implant the pure virtues of
Israel in the hearts and homes of the depraved pagan masses.
It did not seek to disguise the inherent contradiction between
the religio-nationalist teachings of Israel and Graeco-Roman
culture. Together with the Palestinian center, the Diaspora
held to the messianic conception of history, which differs so
radically from the rationalist view of cause and effect in history upheld by the Greek philosophers. It shared with the
Palestinian center the belief in God, who "exercises His will"
in human history "whenever He will," who delivers His people from its suffering and its persecutors, directs the progress
of all mankind toward a predetermined goal, "changeth the
times and the seasons, removeth kings and setteth up kings"

until there shall arise "a kingdom which shall never be destroyed" (Dan. 2. 44).

The Pharisees

Select circles of pietists and sages—the Pharisees and the masters of the Mishna of the period following the destruction of the Second Temple—created that pattern of law and ritual observance which was to become the rule throughout the Diaspora. There is a marked similarity between the development of the Halakha and Aggada, down to the completion of the Talmud, and the growth of Christianity from its beginnings down to Augustine. From one common fountainhead, that is, Jewish life during the period of the Second Temple, flowed two separate streams, two complete and well-defined ways of life, which to this day characterize Judaism and Christianity. Without a knowledge of them it is impossible to understand Jewish life during the Middle Ages. Ordinary historical laws brought it about that the contributions of a small group, active during a limited period, achieved authoritative status among the Jews for ages to come. Yet more than historical accident was involved. The teachings of the Tannaim gave expression to the innate tendencies of their people, to national folk concepts, remote from Western ways of thinking. They collected and compiled the surviving memories of national freedom, of a natural life on native soil, of the Holy Temple, whence issued teaching and atonement for Israel and for all the world, of those days when the divine grace still rested on the nation. The Halakha and Aggada together offer a complete and well-defined way of life, strong enough to preserve the people which pursues it in the face of all the tempests of history. They are the products of a religious-nationalist vitality which glows in every statement and whose vigor interpenetrates every teaching. The teachings of Judaism by the sages of the Mishna, as a mythic, monotheistic folk religion, developed the theological and ethical elements of the Pentateuch, the Prophets, and the Psalms. Endowed with insight into the human heart, these masters took the spiritual values which were born and throve in so exalted an atmosphere and put them within the mental grasp of the simple man, the peasant, the laborer, and the petty bourgeois of European society to this day.

A people of farmers and townsmen, living on its own soil, formed the social background of the Mishna. The scholars were closely attached to their people. Their primary concern was the national and religious survival of Israel in a period of political stress and persecution. A number of the scholars were themselves artisans and earned their livelihood by the toil of their hands. The true democratic spirit of a pietist community prevailed in the academies. No distinction was made between rich and poor: in fact, the God of Israel "loves the poor." Humility and meekness were considered noble traits. "Let a man be ever of the persecuted and not of the perse-cutors, of the humiliated and not of the humiliators." A privi-leged position was accorded only to the prince of the house of David, the preservation of whose lineage and grandeur was regarded as a guarantee of the nation's own survival. The sages of the Mishna were fundamentally ascetics and their lore was ascetic. Their pure asceticism did not distinguish in quality between the observance of the ritual commandments, the pursuit of social justice, and the introspective purging of the heart. A savant like Rabbi Phineas ben Yair, so meticulous in his observance of the ritual law and the principles of equity, also outlined ten progressive steps of spiritual preparation by which one ascends to Piety (*Hasidut*) which, in turn, leads to Divine Inspiration and ultimately to Resurrection and the appearance of Elijah the Prophet, the herald of the Redemp-tion (Jerus. Talmud, *Shabbat*, I, 3, and *Shekalim*, III, 3; cf. Mishna Sota, IX, 15; cf. also Jerus. Talmud, *Demai*, I, 3; Babyl. Talmud, *Hullin*, 7a-7b; *Aboda Zara*, 20b). In some instances the scholar was identified with the popular saint who has the power to perform miracles and bring rainfall. Sometimes he appeared as a mystic, a master of recondite lore. Some, it was believed, were vouchsafed divine revelation through the medium of a heavenly voice or a personal visit from the Prophet Elijah. The sages of the Talmud moved in an atmosphere of miracles and many miraculous acts were credited to them. The precepts of the Law itself, to be sure, do not rest upon miracles or visions, but are founded upon tradition and the tried methods of biblical hermeneutics. But even the dialectic method of study bore a mytho-theological character. In spite of the temporary nature of the circumstances under which this Law was developed, and despite the danger of petrifaction to which all inherited tradition is exposed, this Law was destined to guide and preserve the people. The authors of the Mishna, in endowing the people of Israel with a wealth of law and precepts, did not intend to provide them with a guide for a prolonged Diaspora. They believed their own times to be close to the Messianic Age.

The growth of the Halakha paralleled in some ways the development of the Roman Law. The Jewish scholars collected the elements of positive law, both the fruits of the nation's own creative genius and some which bore the stamp of outside influences, analyzed them in the light of their underlying principles, and developed them further by applying the established methods of interpreting the Law. This collection, like the Roman Law, included laws which grew out of the specific conditions of a given period but remained in effect beyond it and were accepted by later generations, long after the conditions responsible for their origin had ceased to exist. True to the spirit of the Bible, the scholars of the Mishna laid down statutes and precepts inspired by love of God and fellow man. Many laws were based entirely upon this principle, such as the laws of charity—providing for the care of orphans, endowing indigent brides, being hospitable to strangers, comforting the sick, burying the dead, consoling the bereaved, redeeming captives, and similar benevolent deeds—which later formed the basis for Christian charity and for all the welfare institutions of European urban society. The same sages sought to instil this spirit into all of the statutory law. "He who would lead a life of piety," they taught, "must observe the laws of damages." Alongside the positive law, they set up guiding principles for a pietist way of life and laid down rules of virtuous conduct whose violation, though not punishable by the hand of man, called for retribution directly from Heaven. The legislation of the Mishna was meant to serve only as an interim code whose laws were to be given authoritative interpretation only in the Messianic Age. Thus, when the positive law failed to meet the requirements of their moral conscience, they refrained from making a decision, keeping the problem in abeyance by stating, "Let the matter rest until Elijah comes."

Talmudic jurisprudence never distinguished, as Roman Law did, between the civil and criminal law (*ius*) and the ritual law (*fas*). But their intuitive religious sense, which did not need the aid of Greek science, taught the rabbis to distinguish between "commandments written in the Bible, which, had they not been written, deserved to be inscribed—such as the prohibition of robbery, adultery, idolatry, blasphemy, and murder"—and ordinances, "which human passion and pagan thought question—such as the prohibitions against eating the swine's flesh and the wearing of garments of mixed fibers, and the provisions for levirate release (*halitza*), the purification of the leper, the rituals of the red heifer and the scapegoat." They distinguished between commandments whose observance is incumbent upon Israel alone and the "seven precepts of the descendants of Noah," obligatory for all mankind.

The teachings of the Tannaim represent a religious and nationalist reaction to pagan civilization, culture, and political power—the enemy and oppressor of Jewry. Hellenized Judaism learned from Hellenic culture to raise the banner of its teachings before the outside world in demonstrative and aggressive action. Even after the destruction of the Second Temple the

Jews continued to accept proselytes, though a contrary opinion —that converts are a painful sore to Israel—was also heard.

The authors of the Mishna sought to confine Jewish culture to the limits of the Halakha and Aggada. Every child and common artisan in Israel, they felt, possessed knowledge and learning enough to match the lore and science of the other nations. "Thou shalt not say," the sages admonished, "I have studied Jewish learning; I may now study the culture of the other nations." "Adopt not their institutions," they warned, "their theaters, circuses, and stadia." An entire tractate, *Aboda Zara,* was devoted to teaching, in great detail, how a Jew should guard against contact with idolatry and heresy, the latter including also the young Christian movement.

There were, besides, laws which grew out of the struggle for political and religious existence which the Jewish nation had to wage, even in its own land, against the foreign conqueror. These are the well-known statutes which were later exploited for their own ends by all sorts of antisemites and apologists. Included among them are certain laws, as, for example, those applying to informers, which continued to have practical application in the Jews' struggle for religious and national survival during the Middle Ages. In the conflict between Israel and Edom (Rome), the latter employed ruthless tactics. The emperors of pagan Rome continued in Palestine the campaign of persecution against Jews and Judaism initiated by Antiochus Epiphanes, while the Christian emperors found religious justification for their policy of oppression. Rome forbade the observance of the commandments of the faith, the study of Torah, the ordination of scholars, the sanctification of the new month, and the intercalation of the leap-year month. It exiled the scholars from the religious centers in Palestine, and dislodged the people from its ancestral home in Judaea. A new chapter was added then to the history of Jewish martyrology. The duty of martyrdom was then formulated in the words, "One must submit to death in prefer-

ence to apostasy." Those who were imbued with this spirit
clung with all their might to the national and religious centers
in the homeland. "I prefer a small conclave in Eretz Yisrael to
a large Sanhedrin abroad" (Jerus. Talmud, *Sanhedrin*, I, 2).
"It is better to dwell in the desert in Eretz Yisrael than in a
palace abroad" (Genesis Rabbah, 39). There could be no
compromise between the Jewish nation and the foreign power
in this struggle. In the teachings of the Palestinian scholars
one does not find the formula, evolved in Babylonia, stating
that "the law of the government is law unto us," nor does a
prayer for the welfare of the government exist in their liturgy
as in that of the western Diaspora. The Jews were in the end
compelled to concede, against their will, that "this nation
(*i.e.*, Rome) was granted dominion by Heaven"; and only in
the third century, for the first time, was a warning issued
not to revolt against the foreign powers. Talmudic Law does
not deal much with the details of the Jew's relationship to
the Gentile state and society, the very question to which the
Christians zealously devoted the greater part of their teachings
and precepts. Except for the laws regarding idolatry and the
injunction against restoring to Gentile courts of law, future
generations in the Diaspora remained without an authoritative
guide for the conduct of their relations with the people among
whom they lived.

Jewish circles voiced increasingly derogatory opinions of
pagan society. As against the dictum that the righteous of all
the nations merit salvation in the world to come, there are
other statements condemning the pagans to Hell, from which
the people of Israel are saved by virtue of their observance
of the commandments. Our sages were very careful not to
divide the universe into two spheres, the domain of God and
the realm of Satan, but their view of the kingdom of Edom
(*i.e.*, Rome) prepared the ground for Augustine's definition of
the conflict between the *civitas Dei* (city of God) and the
civitas diaboli (city of the devil). "Rabbi Judah spoke up

and said, 'How fine are the works of this nation (*i.e.*, Rome)!
They built forums, they constructed bridges, they erected
baths.' Rabbi Simeon son of Yohai replied and said, 'Whatever they built, they did so only for their own advantage.
They built forums in order to house harlots there, baths—to
refresh themselves in them, bridges—to collect tolls for them'"
(*Sabbath*, 33b). "Why is Edom called a villain (Heb. *naval*)?
Because he filled the world with villainy (Heb. *navlut*). He
erected temples of idolatry, brothels, theaters, and circuses"
(Midrash to Psalm 14). Other homilies express similar distrust
and suspicion of the pagan world.

The people of Israel was dispersed throughout the empire
of Edom. Already in the Palestinian Aggada the opinion was
current that the Jewish dispersion must cover the entire earth
and be subjected to the domination of all seventy nations. The
aggadic picture of the Diaspora was fitted into the frame of
the Roman Empire, which was said to be unable to exist without the Jewish dispersion just as the world cannot exist without
the winds. The Diaspora has a salvationist mission. "The Holy
One, blessed be He, dispersed the people of Israel among the
nations in order that they may acquire proselytes" (*Pesahim*,
87b), and that they may atone for the sins of all mankind.
Wherever Israel is exiled, it is accompanied by the Divine
Presence. The day of redemption was believed to be close at
hand, bringing with it the national and political rehabilitation
of the Jewish people and the salvation of humanity. Just as
the realization of the Jewish messianic ideal was inconceivable without the revival of the people's national life in its historic homeland, so it was equally impossible—in the opinion
of most authorities—to divorce from this concept the eschatology of universal salvation. The liturgy confirms this opinion
in texts such as these, "They shall all become one community,
doing Thy will wholeheartedly . . . ," and "Thou alone shalt
reign over all Thy works. . . ."

The foregoing are a few fundamental characteristics of the

laws and teachings which the Jews carried with them throughout the difficult days of the Middle Ages. Their code represented a complete, detailed, and well-ordered world outlook. Their attitude was conceived in an atmosphere of mythological thinking where care was taken not to couch religious ideals in rational terms or to express their relation to the practical world in matter-of-fact language. Therein lay their strength and also their weakness.[1]

Christianity, on the other hand, introduced the belief in a divine Messiah who had already appeared and in a Church whose function in history was to offer immediate salvation. Christianity borrowed from Judaism, not only its fundamental religious and ethical principles, but also its specific orientation to the world around it. Until the Roman Empire turned Christian, the position of Christianity with respect to the Empire and pagan society was similar to the position of Israel among the nations. Christianity succeeded in converting the Roman Empire, not only because it discarded the national and ritual elements of the teachings of the rabbis, but also because it presented the mythic elements common to both Judaism and Christianity in simple, rational terms, and related them to existing social and political conditions. From the time the two religions separated and until the end of the Middle Ages the rivalry between Judaism and Christianity did not revolve around fundamental differences of faith and ethics, but took the form of a contest between two divergent conceptions of human history and two conflicting approaches to the problem of salvation, each seeking to gain ascendancy over the other. Without a knowledge of these theoretical considerations it is impossible to understand the harsh fate which befell our people during the Middle Ages.

In the fourth century Christianity entered into an alliance with the Roman Empire, for all the latter's iniquities, in anticipation of the day when it would possess enough strength to inculcate the spirit of righteousness and divine justice into the institutions of the Gentiles. Fortified with this outlook, the Christian Church rose to a dominant position among the powers of the earth, whereas Israel remained alone, fulfilling the function of the "city of God" besieged by the wicked, surviving only by dint of its faith in God who can be trusted to fulfil His promise. The Christian Church, united with the Roman Empire, wiped out pagan worship, but it could not and dared not destroy Israel completely. "Slay them not, lest my people forget; make them wander to and fro by Thy power" (Psalms 59. 12). Slay not the Jews—Augustine, the foremost teacher of medieval Christianity, taught—lest the nations forget My teachings, but scatter them throughout the world. It is forbidden to kill the Jews. They are to be preserved so that they, who are the guardians of the Holy Scriptures, may attest to the truth of Christianity. They must, however, be dispersed throughout the world and subjugated politically, as it is written, "And the elder shall serve the younger" (Genesis 25. 23). Israel must ever be a wanderer and fugitive on earth, like Cain the fratricide, bearing a sign, so that anyone encountering him would not kill him. These teachings were applied in practice. The Roman emperors relegated the dispersed Jews to the position of second-class citizens with limited rights. They enacted laws to prevent the spread of Judaism. They oppressed the Jewish community in Palestine and abolished the official authority of the Patriarch. Christianity, thus, in doctrine and in deed, imposed upon Israel the sentence of *Galut* (dispersion).

THE JEWS OF SPAIN UNDER THE ROMANS AND THE VISIGOTHS

The beginnings of Jewish settlement in Spain, as in all lands of the Diaspora, early became the subject of legend. From the tenth century onward numerous accounts circulated concerning Jewish families as well as communities whose forebears were reputed to have been exiled from Judaea by Titus, or even by Nebuchadnezzar, and brought to Spain. These accounts were

15

interwoven with legends of prehistoric Spain—tales of mythical Spanish kings, like Hercules, Hispanus and Pyrrhus, participating in the first conquest of Jerusalem. Jews and Christians alike sought to associate their origins with the earliest and most hallowed traditions of mankind. Toward the end of the Middle Ages, the *conversos* (converted Jews) sought support from these legends in apologetic attempts to deny responsibility for the crucifixion of Jesus by proving that their ancestors had had no part in it. But originally the prevailing motive in the development of this legend was the conviction of the Spanish Jews that their descent from the tribe of Judah, exiled to Spain after the destruction of the First Temple, was responsible for their high level of culture. This tradition first gained currency in the tenth century in the days of the distinguished statesman, Hasdai ben Isaac ibn Shaprut. Older still was the identification of Spain with the biblical "Sefarad," in the interpretation of the verse of the Prophet Obadiah which speaks of "the captivity of Jerusalem that is in Sefarad." According to the exegete, the Prophet prophesied the destruction of Edom, identified as Rome, and the ingathering of the Diaspora, including the tribe which was exiled to the far end of the Roman Empire, namely, Spain. Such an interpretation could suggest itself to the exegete only at a time when the Roman Empire consisted principally of the lands around the Mediterranean, and when Spain was regarded as its remotest province. Such political and geographic allusions, therefore, must date back to the latter days of the Roman Empire, or, at the very latest, to the period of Visigothic rule in Spain. At this point legend already merges with historic fact.[1a]

The first Jews to settle in Spain were part of the ancient Diaspora which was dispersed throughout all corners of the Roman Empire. Already the apostle Paul intended to visit Spain, undoubtedly to establish contact with a Judaeo-Christian community in existence there. More specific information comes to us from the period following the alliance of the Christian

Church with the Roman State, when Christian fanatics set out to destroy the last remnants of Israel and its culture. Severus, bishop of Majorca, in a letter written in the year 418, gives an account of the forced conversion to Christianity of the Jews on the island of Minorca. Violent street fighting between Jews and Christians, incited by the bishop, broke out in the town of Magona, on that island. The synagogue was set on fire. The Jews encouraged one another to remember the Maccabean martyrs and to die for the Divine Law. The women especially excelled in deeds of heroism and self-sacrifice. A few men succeeded in hiding for several days in the forests and in ravines in the mountains, but their efforts to take to the sea and escape from the place of persecution failed. The most distinguished members of the community yielded to the pressure. Severus claims to have gained five hundred and forty Jewish souls on that small island.

The Jews of Magona, like their brethren throughout the western Diaspora, had constituted until then a distinct national and religious community. At the same time, until the new Christian legislation succeeded in disturbing the harmony, they had also taken part in the political life of the city, enjoying equal rights with all the other inhabitants. The head of the Jewish community was exempted from the onerous duties that went with a seat on the *Curia* (municipal council) and also held the highly honored and coveted position of *Defensor*. Many of the townsmen accepted his protection (*Patrocinium*). Another Jew bore the title *Comes Provinciae*. Most of the Jews were wealthy landowners. They bore Latin and Greek names for the most part, and only in a few cases Hebrew names. Many names, which later became famous because of the distinguished personalities who bore them, originated, no doubt, during this period (*e.g.*, קרשקש, Cresques = Crescens; ברפת, Perfet = Perfectus). The condition of the Jews on the Spanish mainland must have been similar to that on the island. We hear that, shortly before the aforesaid persecution, a number

17

of Jews fled from the mainland to the island to escape from the Visigoths, who were then sweeping across Spain. We see, therefore, that a sizable Jewish population lived in the Iberian peninsula prior to its conquest by the Germanic tribes. It is important to bear this fact in mind for an understanding of the later history of the Jews in Spain.[2]

The Visigothic conquerors did not at first introduce any changes in the status of the Jews. The legislation in force in the seventh century seems to indicate that ownership of land formed the basis of existence for the Jews as well as for the Goths and the Romans. The Jews cultivated their soil with their own hands or with the help of slaves. They held land in lease or rented it out under the prevailing terms of tenancy. Some served as stewards (*villici*) of estates owned by Christians. Of their town life we know very little. The Roman Municipal Law remained in force, but we do not know whether the social and economic position of the Jews living in towns remained the same. Only incidentally do we learn of Jews engaging in overseas commerce. One may conclude from existing sources, however, that the Jews concentrated primarily in the culturally advanced centers: the capital Toledo, the southern and eastern regions—the Andalusia and Catalonia of a later day—which lay along the Mediterranean coast, where we shall find most of the Jews living also during the Arabic and the second Christian periods. But there is no trace in Spain of the specific economic development of the Jews of the Middle Ages, whose beginnings were already in evidence among the Jews in the Frankish kingdom.

How the political differences, which arose in Spain following the Germanic invasions, affected the position of the Jews is not clear. In the civil courts Jews were judged according to Roman Law. Yet they were not regarded as full Roman citizens, since the provisions of the Theodosian Code, which curtailed Jewish rights in accordance with Christian teachings, were included in the first Visigothic code of law, the Lex

Romana Visigothorum, promulgated in the year 506, which defined the legal status of the Romans living in the Visigothic State. This code forbade Jews to hold public office, to intermarry with Christians, to build new synagogues, to own Christian slaves, to persecute apostates, etc. These provisions were not, however, always enforced.

In their outer forms of life the Jews were closer to the Romans than to the Visigoths, but religious fanaticism stood as a barrier between them. The Jews, it appears, were required to pay a special tax. In the larger cities they were organized into separate communities. The decrees issued against them during the later persecutions tell us something of their inner life. They observed the fundamental precepts of Jewish Law—circumcision, the Sabbath and festivals, dietary laws, marital laws and the laws pertaining to slaves. They read religious tracts, written most likely in Latin, to strengthen their faith.

In 589 the Visigothic king changed his Arian faith for the Roman Catholic and proceeded to oppress the Jews in the manner practiced throughout the Catholic world. A few years earlier, in 576, in the city of Arvernum (Clermont) in the neighboring Frankish kingdom, the local bishop, following a street battle between Jews and Christians, compelled the Jews to choose between baptism and expulsion. A little later, in 582, the Merovingian king, Chilperic, ordered all the Jews of his realm to be baptized. The Byzantine emperor, Heraclius, who still exercised jurisdiction over certain areas of Spain, followed his victory over the Persians and Jews in Palestine in 628 with an order to convert by force all the Jews throughout the provinces of his Empire, and the Merovingian Dagobert is said to have followed his example. Both Gaul and the Byzantine province of Africa provide us with information concerning the spiritual conflicts suffered by the forced converts. Throughout the Jewish world a generation of heroes and saints must have arisen then and saved Jewry from utter extinction.

In Spain the era of persecutions was opened by King Sisebut

with a decree issued in 612, a few months after he ascended the throne. He ordered all Christians freed from all relationships rendering them dependent upon Jews. The Jews were required to give up their Christian slaves and servants as well as their Christian tenants, together with the land the latter held in lease, and to transfer them to Christian control or set them free, without making their freedom conditional upon their observance of Judaism. A Jew who converted a Christian to Judaism was to suffer death and confiscation of property. Children of Christian female slaves by their Jewish masters were to be brought up as Christians. Jews who accepted Christianity were to retain their property. The clear purpose of the law was to prevent proselytization by Jews and to encourage their own conversion. Full enforcement of this law would have shaken the foundations of the economic life of the Jews. They were excluded from the natural social structure as it existed at the end of the Roman period. Under the new conditions, deprived of slaves and tenants, it became virtually impossible for them to cultivate or even own large estates.

A short time later Sisebut ordered the Jews either to accept Christianity or leave the country. The problem of forced converts, which was already a painful one throughout the Byzantine Empire, now began to unfold itself in Spain as a tragedy which was to last several generations. The royal decree could not with a single stroke extirpate from the hearts of the Jews the faith of their fathers; and the decree, it appears, was not fully enforced. In order to deal with the new situation, a council of the bishops of the realm met in Toledo in 633 and decreed that Jews shall not be converted by force, but that those already converted must remain Christians and must be prevented from practicing the Jewish faith. Their children shall be taken from them and brought up as Christians. The slaves they had circumcised shall be set free. The testimony of converts found practicing their old faith shall not be trusted. The marriage of a Jew and a Christian shall be invalid, unless the Jewish member accepted Christianity; children of such a union shall be brought up as Christians. Converts as well as Jews shall be excluded from public office. These laws struck not only the Jews but also the converts, who were suspected of remaining faithful to the religion of their fathers. Five years later a Church council forbade all non-Catholics to reside in the country. The converts were placed under strict episcopal supervision. They were not permitted to travel within the country without a permit signed by the local Church authorities. Every Jew was required to take an oath, according to a fixed formula, that he had given up Jewish law and practice. The penalty for relapsing varied, according to the seriousness of the offense, from religious penance to flogging, loss of a limb, confiscation of property, or burning at the stake.

The Church never did succeed in converting all the Jews in the country. It was simply unable to keep an eye on all of them. The nobility, still devoutly Arian in their faith and wavering in their loyalty to the crown, needed the services of the Jews and gave them refuge on their estates. Isidore, bishop of Seville, and Julian, bishop of Toledo, wrote polemic works against Judaism. But the Jews too had books to strengthen their faith, preaching the messianic hope supported by eschatological computations, and telling tales of a king of the tribe of Judah holding sway somewhere in the East.

A new but vain attempt to enforce the anti-Jewish legislation was made by King Ervig in 681. To the laws of his predecessors he added even more oppressive restrictions. Severe penalties were ordered for the evasion of baptism, the observance of Jewish precepts, religious instruction, and the distribution of tracts defending the Jewish faith and disparaging the Christian. Ervig also attempted to enforce at last Sisebut's decree releasing Christian slaves and tenants from Jewish control. He sought to remove the Jews from all public office and from the stewardship of large estates, and to take measures against the nobles who protected their Jewish retainers from clerical supervision. He further forbade professing Jews to enter seaports, lest they escape overseas, and to engage in business transactions with Christians. He exempted converts from the payment of taxes, and levied their burden upon the remaining Jews. He ordered that all the land and slaves acquired by Jews over a period of many years be taken over by the state treasury at a fixed price. At the Church council of Toledo in 694, serious political accusations were hurled against the Jews. It was charged that they not only sought to undermine the Church, but were also plotting to seize the crown, massacre the Catholics and destroy the country along with the people; that they were conspiring with "the Hebrews across the sea" for help in executing their plan. These accusations were inspired, no doubt, by the messianic agitation among the Jews and by their connections with the rebellious nobility. As punishment the council decreed that the property of all the Jews be confiscated, they themselves be impressed into slavery, and their lands turned over to their former slaves for cultivation.[3]

This conciliar decree of the year 694 constitutes the last authentic documentary evidence bearing upon the struggle between Judaism and Christianity in Visigothic Spain. The series of events which took place in Spain during the seventh century remained a symbol and example for the Christian fanatics of the latter Middle Ages. These events occurred in a historical, religious and social setting that was still of the ancient world. The last foundations of the Roman Empire had, however, already begun to crumble beneath the blows of the Arab conquerors.

Moslem Spain

In the year 711 the Arabs invaded Spain and in a victorious campaign of only a few years conquered the entire country.[4] According to a later tradition, the conquerors settled Jews in the cities of Cordova, Granada, Seville, Elvira and Toledo, or

22

turned their citadels over to Jews and Arabs. This tradition was utilized by Christian writers from the twelfth century on for anti-Jewish propaganda; they converted it into stories of Jewish treachery and conspiracy with the foreign invader. The original tradition does have a basis of truth. Settlements of Jewish merchants were established near Arab military garrisons also in other lands. In Spain the Arabs were able to make use of Jewish communities already there. It seems that at first the Arabs did not permit the growth of a large Jewish community in Cordova, capital of Andalusia, which soon became a caliphate independent of Bagdad, "for it was the seat of the Caliph, full of Moslems with a few Jews." Neighboring Lucena, however, later the seat of a famous academy which flourished until the twelfth century, is referred to in a responsum of Rabbi Natronai, Gaon of Sura (853), as "a city of many Jews . . . there is not a Gentile among you." Arab geographers of the tenth and twelfth centuries already call Granada and Tarragona "Jewish cities." It is safe to assume that Jewish merchants resided in many localities in the fortified sections of the city, sharing all the responsibilities and privileges of its defense, as they did later under Christian rule.

The Moslem tribesmen who came from the East did not quickly adapt themselves to the norms of city life. But the Arabs did not attempt to upset the social order that had existed in Spain prior to their invasion. They themselves formed only a thin ruling stratum. The Mozarabic Christians retained their language and customs, and their influence gave Arabic culture in Spain its individual character. The Christians and Jews who remained loyal to their faith enjoyed national and religious autonomy. Jews and Christians filled various offices at the court of the caliph and in the state administration, as they did in the caliphate of Bagdad. The Mohammedan rulers needed Jewish and Christian officials, since the Moslem tribesmen proved neither qualified nor trustworthy. Moslem religious fanaticism, which from time to time made the life of the Jews miserable, directed itself in the first half of the ninth century primarily against certain Christian groups, whose members would publicly blaspheme the dominant faith, thereby to earn the crown of martyrdom. The Jewish position was not seriously affected by these persecutions. The Christians complained that the caliphs delegated Moslems and Jews to be present at the sessions of Church councils.

Arabic Spain became a refuge for Jews. To the great chagrin of Christian Europe, a deacon of Alemannic descent by the name of Bodo went to Saragossa, embraced Judaism, took the name of Eleazar and married a Jewish girl (839). His writings in a messianic vein, denouncing Christianity, drew replies from Alvarus, a leader of the Christian zealots in Cordova. Both writers, remarkably enough, made use of the Talmud. Our earliest evidence of correspondence between the gaonim of Babylonia and Jewish scholars in Lucena and Barcelona—the latter city remained almost without interruption in Christian hands—dates back to this period. A well known legend has Rabbi Natronai Gaon make a miraculously rapid journey to Spain, spread learning there and return to Babylon as miraculously as he had gone.[5]

The invasions of the Germanic tribes in the west and the Arab conquests in the east and south destroyed the political and social foundations of the Roman Empire and of ancient civilization. As a result of this mighty upheaval both Jews and Christians were faced with new and ever-changing tasks. The forms of religious thought and action, which bore the stamp of the historical era during which they evolved, were now fixed for all time. The Catholic Church aspired to control human society by wielding the power of the sacraments, regardless of the changing world order. The Synagogue, for its part, learned to wait for divine intervention to bring about the reign of justice on earth. Judaism revealed its greatness and distinction through the collection of the traditions and precepts inherited from preceding generations. Its great wealth of law and lore was transmitted from generation to generation as a cultural treasure, well-ordered and authoritative, to cherish which was regarded as man's highest duty. The mythological and the rational elements of the tradition together continued to mold the character of the people. The gift of myth-weaving, rooted deep within the people's soul, wove tales of alluring charm round the people's sufferings; but the principal duty of the Jew on earth was to be the study of the Torah. And, as Torah came to permeate Jewish life ever more fully, its effect upon the spiritual, social and economic life became more and more pronounced.

As the Talmud became an ever more dominant factor in life, consideration was given time and again by certain groups within the people to the same problem which had troubled the Hellenistic Jews—the one rising out of the difficulty of reconciling the nationalist-mythical approach with the ways of rational philosophic thought. The rationalists saw no way other than to accept the Torah as handed down and to justify it, or, as was done at a later date, to elevate it to new heights of mysticism. Without the help of historical criticism, the medieval Jews were not capable of penetrating to the basic ideals given expression in Halakha and the Aggada and to set them up as guides in the conduct of their lives. At the beginning of this chapter we tried to indicate briefly the original aims of the authors of the Mishna. Since their day the aggadic and halakhic traditions had increased, but without their practical application growing apace. The rationalist line of thinking failed to recognize even the purest and most precious gems of tannaitic Aggada, while the Talmud, particularly the Babylonian, added tales of saints and miracles, as seen by the naive popular mind. The Halakha in Babylonia had developed along pilpulistic lines, foreign even to contemporary Palestinian scholars. ["'He has made me dwell in dark places' (Lamentations 3. 6)—that is the Babylonian Talmud" (*Sanh.* 24a).]

The Talmud, pursuing its own lines of reasoning, did not—as some modern scholars would have it—arrive at legal conclusions designed to prepare the people, living in the Diaspora, for a capitalistic order of society. The laws of the Talmud, whether ritual, civil, or criminal, were made to implement the theoretical bases of simple religious and moral ideals, not to circumvent them. The Karaites made a last attempt to discard the results of this late development and to direct the growth of the Halakha along less complicated lines. The Karaites did not differ fundamentally from the Rabbanites in their lines of thinking, which were nationalist and religious, inclining toward myth and ritualism and extreme asceticism. But the Talmud overcame all opposition. The latest layer of Jewish tradition became the dominant one through a process of historical development characteristic of that period. Only through the acceptance of the final form of the tradition was it possible to retain the uniform character of Judaism.

The acceptance of the law of the Babylonian Talmud by the communities of the Diaspora was not due to apathy on their part or to the failure of their own creative powers. It came rather as a result of a planned campaign by the academies of Babylonia to impose the authority of the Babylonian Talmud upon the entire Diaspora. To be sure, their religious and ethnic bonds had kept the scattered Jewish communities united even earlier, but their practices and customs had differed and even been at variance with some of the principles regarded by the authors of the Mishna as fundamental. The Diaspora had had no common tongue; teachers of the law were not to be found in western Europe; the law of the Mishna did not achieve full authority throughout the wide Diaspora until this very period which served as an area of transition from ancient times to the Middle Ages. The beginnings of the great change remain obscure, but its final results are clear and evident. A unifying revivalist movement, ascetic in character, swept over all the communities of the Diaspora. Contemporary parallels can be found in the developments of the other faiths—in the rise of Islam and in the history of the Church of Rome, following its alliance with the Frankish kingdom. Hebrew now supplanted Aramaic, Greek and Latin in the communal affairs of the Jews and even became the spoken tongue of wide circles. The calendar, fixed by computation, was accepted throughout the Diaspora. It was a process which led to the renewal and strengthening of the bonds between the western Diaspora and the academies in Palestine and Babylonia. Yet, at the same time, the Jewish communities in the west became self-reliant and independent of the east.

The historical development of a people is not guided by religion and precept alone. Such demands of the inner life sometimes clash with and are subject to conditions imposed by the world outside. In place of the old Roman Empire came the ruling policies of the Moslem powers, the Eastern Roman Empire of Byzantium, and the Western Roman Empire allied with the kingdom of the Franks, the kernel of the Europe of the future. This new political setting confronted Judaism with problems, both theoretical and practical, for which no satisfactory solutions were to be found in the original Halakha. The law of the Palestinian sages was based on the principle of legitimate opposition to the pagan enemy power. Talmudic Halakha did not appreciably modify this attitude. Only after the passing of the ancient world did there arise, openly and clearly, the problem of the relation of the Jews to the Gentile society and state and to the national states of Europe which came into being at a later date.

As long as the messianic ideal and the hope of redemption were kept alive, a certain consciousness of conflict between Israel and the dominant power was bound to persist. In practice, however, the Jews began to show signs of adapting themselves to life in Diaspora lands. The Christians, following Augustine's teachings, subjected the Jews to the status of slaves of the crown (*servi regis*).[6] Though this principle was

27

not clearly formulated and accepted until the twelfth century, it was nevertheless already put into practical effect from the transition period of Frankish rule on. The caliphs, to be sure, were unaware of this principle, but in practice they differed little from the Christians in their treatment of the Jews. Foreign rulers of all ranks were thus able to utilize Jews for their own personal ends. This in turn opened to the Jews the doors to outside society, within which it enabled them to gain for themselves social and economic positions.

The Jew of the Diaspora became the spiritual as well as material middleman. In Christian Europe he eventually became a professional moneylender. He became the loyal servant of the feudal lords, the financier, tax-collector and physician of the crown. The position of the Jews close to the court was widely regarded among them as a boon from God. The Jewish courtier was sent by divine Providence to be the defender of his people in time of need, and he was, moreover, permitted to pursue secular learning. Thus, in the very period when the Babylonian Talmud attained full authority, restrictions were relaxed in matters which had been strictly forbidden by the early pietists. Some modern scholars have come to accept such phenomena, which then appeared on the Jewish scene, as characteristic, whereas actually they were still in direct conflict with the pure ideals adhered to by the people and their spiritual leaders. Every succeeding generation saw the rise of reformers who sought to restore Judaism to its pristine state and to replace it on its original foundations.

The specific character of the revived Hebrew culture and the nature of its bearers became apparent, from the tenth century on, in Spain as in the other communities east and west: the rise of Hebrew culture was connected with external political factors. The Caliph Abd-ar-Rahman III (912-961), having suppressed the separatist political forces, established a unified and powerful kingdom whose high cultural level commanded the respect of all of Europe. This great power had only a few small Christian states in the north as neighbors—the kingdom of Leon which was for a time united with Navarre, the county of Barcelona and a few tiny principalities. The caliph's political power rested upon Slavic and Germanic slaves. Among his non-Moslem courtiers was Abu Yusuf Hasdai ibn Shaprut, the first Jewish personality in Spain whose life and work are known to us.

Hasdai's position was that of court physician; but he was also engaged in the translation of scientific works. Being well versed in languages, he served in a diplomatic capacity in negotiations with foreign rulers and thereby exercised an influence on foreign policy. He was thus the first to exercise functions which Jewish physicians performed at a later date in the courts of the Christian kings. In 956 Hasdai, on behalf of the caliph, received John, abbot of Gorze in Lorraine, the emissary of the German emperor, Otto I. In the same year Hasdai was sent to the Christian court of Leon to conclude a pact of friendship. In 958 he went on another diplomatic mission to Pamplona, capital of Navarre. Sancho, king of Leon and Navarre, had been expelled from Leon by the nobility and had fled to his grandmother, Tota, in Pamplona. Abd-ar-Rahman promised, through his Jewish emissary, to bring Sancho back to Leon, in return for the rights to ten fortresses. The Christian king, accompanied by his grandmother, was brought to Cordova in triumphal procession to undergo medical treatment by the Jewish physician. This event was celebrated in glowing verse by the two poet-protégés of Hasdai, Dunash ben Labrat and Menahem ben Saruk.

From Hasdai's letter to the king of the Khazars we learn of his duties as supervisor over the trade of foreign merchants, "whose commerce and affairs cannot be conducted except through my hand and at my command." It is quite possible that Hasdai was entrusted with the collection of port tolls and customs and with certain phases of the financial administration, as were Jews serving in similar capacities in Christian countries. There is, to be sure, room for doubt whether the famous letter of Hasdai to the king of the Khazars was actually written by him or at his command. But it is certain that the letter already circulated in Spain during the eleventh century and may have been written during the generation following Hasdai's death for nationalist and religious propaganda purposes.

Hasdai's career served as a model and precedent for the many Jewish statesmen who flourished in Spain during the five centuries following. In his own day, his position was looked upon as a guarantee of his people's survival. "When our God saw their affliction and toil, 'and none remaining shut up or left at large' (I Kings 21. 21), He caused me to be presented to the king, treated me with kindness and turned the king's heart toward me, not on account of my own virtues but because of His kindness and His covenant. The afflicted and depressed sheep thereby gathered strength in deliverance, and the hands of their oppressors were weakened. They were relieved of their affliction and their yoke was lightened, through the mercy of our Lord." Tradition also associates with the name of Hasdai and his times the beginnings of Hebrew literature in Spain, the establishment of new centers of learning independent of the authority of the gaonim of the East, and the awakening within this young community in Israel of a consciousness of its own political and cultural importance which entitled it to the position of leadership over the entire people.[7]

At the height of the caliphate's power the court at Cordova was almost the sole support of the oppressed Jewish population scattered throughout the land. In the beginning of the eleventh century, however, mighty Al-Andalus broke up into several small states. In Cordova as well as in Seville aristocratic republics were formed, which lasted until the family of the 'Abbadides seized sole power. Tyrants of pure Arab blood held sway in Saragossa and Valencia. Berber chieftains were in power in Malaga, Granada and Badajoz. Slavic generals ruled in Almeria, Denia and the Balearic islands. This pattern of republics and principalities resembled closely the political structure of Italy during the Renaissance. Both were characterized by a high level of culture in both the scientific and esthetic fields, by ways of thinking which reviewed critically all historical, political and religious phenomena, and by tyrannical methods of government, devoid of religious or moral conscience. In the north, small Christian states formed —Leon, Castile, Navarre, Aragon, Barcelona and others— peopled by a military yeomanry, with nascent urban centers. Despite their profoundly different culture, the latter states could not avoid being influenced by the civilization of their Arab neighbors. At the same time, the Christians had already begun their attacks against the Arabs, and some of their successful offensives carried them as far as the southern regions of Andalusia.

Jewish history in Spain was affected by these political developments. The capitals of the small Arab principalities became the centers of Jewish culture. In the courts of the princes, Jews rose to positions of eminence and influence. The fate of the Jewish communities was closely bound up with the political fortunes of these Jewish courtiers, whose personal rise or fall often carried with it the prosperity or ruin of their community. We obtain most of our knowledge of this period from contemporary Hebrew poetry, fostered and cultivated under the tutelage of the Jewish courtiers. From what we know of Jewish life and influence in Granada, and to a lesser degree in Saragossa, we are justified in taking the conditions there as typical of the other Arab states. Only in Cordova, which was ruled by a number of aristocratic families, were Jews consistently harassed. In Seville, a Jew-baiting cadi was in power for a while, but was eventually supplanted by a king who kept a Jewish astronomer at his court. It would not be correct to assert that the pure-blooded Arab princes excluded the Jews from their courts, whereas the semi-civilized Berbers and Slavs attracted them because they were unable to conduct the affairs of state without the help of cultured Jews. In reality the treatment accorded the Jews by the several states varied according to their political structures. In a republic headed by aristocratic families there was no room for Jewish statesmen. On the other hand, a monarch or other autocrat, the absolute ruler over an unfriendly native population, would attract to his service Jews —the perpetual "aliens"—on whose loyal support he could count in securing his regime. This phenomenon, in varying forms, manifested itself time and again also in the history of Christian Europe.

The foremost among the Jewish statesmen of that period was Samuel ha-Nagid.[8] Over a period of thirty years, marked by uninterrupted warfare, he conducted both the domestic and foreign affairs of the kingdom of Granada. At the same time he was a rabbinic scholar of note and an authority in Halakha. He rose to the defense of his people and his faith and engaged in a polemic with Ibn Hazm, one of the leading Moslem scholars of his day. Samuel occupies a unique position among the Hebrew poets in Spain. He sang not only of sacred faith and secular love, but also of ruthless war. Samuel was born in Cordova, where he became a wealthy merchant engaged in overseas commerce. During the political disorders which broke out in Cordova in 1013, Samuel, like many other Jews, fled and settled in Malaga. He was soon called to the service of Habbus, the king of Granada.

The account of Samuel's rise as given by Abraham ibn Daud, the Spanish-Jewish historian of the twelfth century, is well known. Samuel "was a merchant, and would sit in his store, which was adjacent to the palace of Ibn al-'Arif, the vizir of Habbus ben Makhsan, king of the Philistines (*i.e.*, Berbers) in Granada. The vizir's maid would request of

him that he write letters for her to her master the vizir. . . ."
His skill in letter writing was reponsible for his rise to high
office and for his becoming one of the king's foremost ministers.

One cannot take this legend literally and believe that
Samuel rose from poverty to prominence through pure chance.
He very likely brought considerable wealth with him to
Granada, which helped him pave his way. In his earliest poems,
which may have been written in Cordova, he expressed strong
ambition for great achievements. The road to the top was
not all straight and smooth. As a result of charges brought
against them, Samuel was removed, in 1020, from a post in
the local administration, and his father-in-law and nephew
were executed. Nevertheless we find him, a few years later,
vizir and *katib* (secretary) of king Habbus and Nagid over
all the Jews of the realm. After Habbus' death, his two sons
vied for the crown, each supported by a faction of the leading
politicians. The Jewish courtiers also took part in the quarrel,
on one side or the other. Finally, the elder son, Badis, came
out victorious, and with him Samuel, who had supported him
throughout. The Jewish members of the opposition fled to
Seville.

Samuel ha-Nagid's career from here on may be studied in
detail from his extant poetry. He continued until his death
in 1056 to direct the foreign affairs of the small kingdom.
Every year he accompanied the troops in the field on their
campaigns. Expansionist ambitions, characteristic of all the
small states in Spain, were the mainspring also of Samuel's
foreign policy. Yet it was all too conspicuous that a Jew was
directing the foreign affairs of Granada, a fact which was a
constant thorn in the side of the orthodox Moslems. Samuel,
on the other hand, regarded himself as designated by Providence to make Granada the defender of his people who were
being oppressed in neighboring states. The precarious position
of the Jews became apparent during the disturbances which
followed the death of Habbus. Ibn 'Abbas, the vizar of the

Slavic king of Almeria, hated the Jews. He circulated throughout the near-by states inflammatory tracts, attacking Samuel
ha-Nagid and all Jews. He demanded of Badis that he dis-
miss his Jewish vizir. A provocative visit by the king of
Almeria led to open warfare between his forces and those of
Granada. The king of Almeria fell in battle. Ibn 'Abbas was
brought to Granada in chains and executed there at Samuel's
command. The Nagid celebrated the victory in verses of
thanksgiving to God and wrote to the academies and scholars
in Palestine, Babylonia, Africa (Kairawan) and Egypt about
the Lord's great deeds.

The Jewish question also figured as a side issue in the wars
between Granada and Seville. Motadhid, the cadi of Seville,
was highly praised by the nationalist Arabs for leading the
fight against the Berbers, among whom Jewish influence was
strong. But Samuel saw in him the oppressor of the Jews in
his state. The wars that followed between Granada and Seville
were fought principally for the political hegemony of southern
Spain, and the details of the struggle are not important for
our account. There is no doubt, however, that the Jewish
vizir devoted his best energies to strengthening the position
of his master, the autocrat of Granada. From Samuel's poetry
it would appear that he was entirely absorbed in this world of
wars, uprisings, murders, intrigue and treachery.

In domestic affairs, Samuel did, as his enemies charged,
utilize every available means to get rid of opponents and
to elevate his friends. His poetic accounts of his military
experiences he dedicated for the most part to his son Joseph,
who was to succeed him. He would also send his paeans of
victory to the rabbis in Kairawan and Fostat (Egypt), to the
academies in Babylonia, to the exilarch in Bagdad, and especially to the leaders of the Jewish community in Jerusalem.
In a poem celebrating his victory over Seville in 1055, which
he sent to the Exilarch Hezekiah—whom he addresses as
"the prince of the noble community, which is the crown on

the head of the entire people," the scion of King David, who is destined to restore the monarchy in Israel—he defines the Providential relationship between himself and the exilarch in the following verse, "To you royalty and to me prophecy are vouchsafed; you and I alone are the divine sign on this earth." He fully believed that he was sent by Providence to defend Israel, the scattered sheep, humiliated and depressed, homeless and wandering, and to rescue the lambs from the mouths of the wolves. On the battlefield, the God of Israel fights for him and angels descend to his side. The patriarchs plead for him, "and out of their dust draw succor with ropes of prayer." Their intercession serves him in time of trial. Samuel believes that God deals justice on earth and is due to set the universe aright. The simple faith of his people and his own political ambitions are in perfect harmony. "I shall rise," he writes, "over the heights of death to eternal life and shall travel past Hades to Paradise." He knows that his work is abhorrent, that he is drowning in a sea of blood and is in need of atonement. He turns with longing to Zion, where residence is atonement for sin. He wants to live in the Holy Land and be purified there. He dreams of the era of the nation's youth which is to be restored when redemption comes.[9]

Samuel ha-Nagid was succeeded by his son Joseph. One Arab historian testifies that Joseph conducted the affairs of state with manifest energy, increased the country's wealth, saw to it that the state revenues were collected on time and appointed Jews to high public office. But much abuse was heaped upon him as well. Lately there have come to light the memoirs of Abdallah, the grandson of Badis, wherein the Jewish vizir is bitterly denounced. It was charged that Joseph had poisoned Balukin, the son of Badis; that during a drinking revel he had, with his own hand, killed one of the highest officials of the realm, a Jew of the opposing faction; that he had entered into a conspiracy to surrender the kingdom of Granada to the king of Almeria, in order to bolster up his own tottering position. Joseph's activities fed the hatred of the religious and nationalist fanatics among the Arabs. One of them, a certain Abu Ishak of Elvira, wrote inflammatory poems attacking Joseph, seeking to incite the populace against him. Thanks to the influence of the Jewish *katib*, they charged, the Jews rose from lowly station, from the state of shut-out dogs, which is their lot all over the world, to the position of masters. They divide the kingdom of Granada among themselves into districts, and everywhere one of the accursed Jews is master. They collect the taxes. They eat their fill and dress luxuriously. They slaughter their cattle in the Arab markets and leave to the non-Jews the meat ritually forbidden to themselves. Joseph built himself a palace of marble, equipped with fresh water fountains. The welfare of the Arabs is in his hands; and while they wait at his door, he scoffs at them and their religion. This vicious propaganda brought about the desired result. In 1066 Joseph was assassinated and many Jews were massacred along with him in the city of Granada and in other parts of the country. Only a few years later, however, Jews again were holding high office in Granada.[10]

Conditions similar to the above prevailed in the other principalities of Moslem Spain. The Jews acquired political skill and the technique of public administration; and they eventually brought their talents and experience to the courts of the Christian princes in the north. A fuller evaluation of this glorious period in Jewish history requires a thorough and comprehensive knowledge of Arabic civilization.[11] The Jews of Spain lived during this time in a part of the vast Mohammedan domain. Within this political and cultural sphere Palestine retained its natural place as the national and religious center of Jewry. Except for local differences, the level of civilization in the west and in the east was the same. Regular cultural and commercial intercourse between the

Jews of the east and the west united them into a homogeneous community, distinguished from the Jews living under Christian rule, even though they maintained business relations with the latter as well. Jewish communal leadership was in the hands of a small group of men of wealth and education who were influential at court. The Jewish court officials of this period, like those who served in similar capacity in the courts of Christian monarchs later on, were the owners of large estates and even entire villages. But the Jewish masses derived their livelihood from the cultivation of fields and orchards, from manufacture and handicraft.

The Hebrew poetry of this period reflects primarily the life of the upper classes, the bourgeoisie and courtiers, who enjoyed their life, tasted the pleasures of wine, women, palaces and gardens, and pursued the literary arts and the sciences. Traditional religiosity lived in harmony with secular culture. Boys and young men studied the Talmud and Hebrew grammar along with poetry and "Greek Wisdom." Political ambition, the passion for erotic experience, the desire for rational understanding penetrated the Jewish community, bringing disintegration and heresy on the one hand, and leading, on the other, to the refinement of the traditional religious concepts and to the strengthening of the national consciousness which acquired a modern political hue.

Jewish culture in Spain was guided by a line of thinking different from that of the authors of the Mishna and expressed itself in a way of life different from that of the pietists of German Jewry who died a martyr's death for their faith. And yet the Spanish Jews clung fast to those roots from which one can never entirely tear himself away. They created for their people a national-religious lyrical poetry of singular quality—new, yet old—and explained the meaning of their people's fate. The causes for these cultural achievements did not lie in external circumstances alone. Politically this period was not a "Golden Age" at all. The poetry of Solomon ibn

Gabirol and his contemporaries is full of plaints and laments over the people's state of subjugation and exile. Absolutism and tyranny mark the political practices of that age. The cultural activity fostered by the courtiers was allowed to flourish only through the neglect and the religious and moral laxity of the rulers, and not as a result of the definite policy of tolerance and individual freedom. In the south and in the north, both in Islam and in Christianity, nationalist and religious movements, primitive in character, were forming, which were due to make an end of the existing laxity. Nevertheless, the patterns of life developed in the small Moslem states already laid the foundations for Jewish existence in Spain under Christian rule.

I

THE EARLY RECONQUEST

---

*(From the End of the Eleventh to the Middle
of the Twelfth Centuries)*

THE JEWS IN NORTHERN SPAIN BEFORE THE RECONQUEST

While Jewish life in Mohammedan Spain was reaching its peak
of material and cultural development, the foundations of new
Jewish centers were being laid in the Christian territory to the
north.[1] A Jewish community was already in existence in Barcelona in the late Carolingian period. This community was in
contact with the Babylonian cultural centers. It is known to
have addressed questions to Rab Amram Gaon (869-887). A
Jew by the name of Judah, or Judacot, brought (876-877) news
from Barcelona to Emperor Charles the Bald and carried back
from the emperor's court ten pounds of silver for the bishop of
Barcelona for the repair of his church.[2]

When in 985 Barcelona was captured by Almanzor, the commander of the army of the caliph of Cordova, several Jews were killed in the battle and the count and countess of Barcelona later fell heir to their property. From this time on we have abundant evidence of Jewish ownership of landed property in Barcelona and its environs and throughout Catalonia.[3] The Jews bought, sold and exchanged parcels of land, leased them or rented them out under the terms of existing law. Most of the Jewish estates lay close to the city. The Jews did not buy land merely as an investment, but cultivated their fields and vineyards themselves, as was the case also in France and Germany. Both in southern France and in Catalonia we find villages and hamlets called "Jewish Village" (*villa judaica*), but whether they owed their names to their Jewish owners or Jewish inhabitants is not clear.[4] In any case, land was the basis of the economy and social position of the Jews. We hear a Jew pleading, like a man deeply rooted in the soil for generations, "I do not want my ancestral estate to fall into the hands of strangers."[5] There were no legal limitations on the acquisition of land by Jews. They held their land in allodial ownership or under lease. The same laws which governed the sale and lease of land among Christians applied also in transactions of this kind between Jews and Christians and even between Jews and ecclesiastical institutions.

The urban life of Barcelona began to flourish about this time, and the Jews were an integral part of it. By the end of the eleventh century a Jewish quarter (*callis iudaicus*), situated near the cathedral and the castle of the count, was in existence; and it remained in the same location until the destruction of the Jewish community in 1391.[6] Jewish shops and stalls were to be found, in the middle of the twelfth century, in the marketplace outside the city walls near the old fort.[7] The urban economy of Barcelona, benefiting Jews and Christians alike, continued to expand in even greater measure from this period on. Even before this date the sources mention Jewish tailors, shoemakers, gold and silver smiths. Wealthy Jews engaged in moneylending activities, extending loans to the counts of Barcelona among others. Jews were minting coins for these counts in the eleventh century, and some gold coins were named after the Jewish goldsmith who executed them.[8] A roster of the Jewish households of Barcelona, compiled in 1079, contains about sixty names, and the community at this time already had a long tradition behind it.

The texts of the distinctive Hebrew *shetarot* (legal instruments), in use in legal transactions between members of the community, formed the basis, in the beginning of the twelfth century, for the well-known treatise, *Sefer ha-Shetarot*, by Judah ben Barzilai al-Barceloni.[9] In legal transactions between a Jew and a Christian a Hebrew *shetar* would sometimes be drawn up and, where the matter was settled in a Spanish court of law, the Latin text would be followed by a summary in Hebrew with Hebrew signatures.

Privileges granted by the count to the Jews of Barcelona, regulating testimony and court procedure in legal suits between Jews and Christians, are mentioned for the first time in a document of the middle of the twelfth century, but there is reason to believe that their origin was of earlier date.[10] The Jewish privileges of the Carolingian era no doubt served as the prototype for Catalonia, as they did for the rest of Christian Europe. It must be assumed that the relation of the Jews to the local count was one of near-servitude. Only on this basis can we explain the acquisition by the count of the estates of the Jews killed in 985 and his confiscation, in 1022, of the property of a Jew who committed adultery with a married Christian woman. The Jew himself escaped death by conversion. The old Catalonian code of law, the *Usatges de Barcelona*, compiled between the years 1053 and 1071, clearly provides that the wergild to be paid for the killing or injury of a Jew is to be fixed arbitrarily by the count, which is not the treatment accorded to free men. The entire code reveals the influence of the contemporary reform propaganda emanating from Rome.[11] It is this influence, rather than prevailing custom, that is responsible for the enactment that a Christian should under no circumstances be required to swear to a Jew. Otherwise, the equality of Jews with Christians in bearing testimony in court remained. A Church council, which was convened in Gerona in 1068 by the papal legate Hugo Candidus, decreed that the Jews must pay the tithes for land bought from Christians. The roster of the Jews of Barcelona, of the year 1079, is especially significant. It is part of an overall agreement whereby two brothers, heirs to the county of Barcelona, divided the inheritance between them. Only the Jewish inhabitants are listed in the text, a fact which proves that the estate of the deceased count included, as one of its valuable assets, the special property rights over the Jews, whose relation to their ruler expressed itself in terms of personal vassalage rather than political allegiance.

Our information regarding the Jews living in the mountainous regions of old Aragon and Navarre is rather meager. In 1062 King Sancho Ramirez freed the inhabitants of Jaca, Jews and bakers excepted, from the obligation to grind their flour in the mills of the overlord. The Jews did not succeed in freeing themselves from this semi-servile obligation until some years later.[12] By the end of the eleventh century there were Jews living in Estella, Ruesta and Montclus. Mention is made, in the extant documents, of several commercial levies, tithes and fines paid by them. In Estella the Jews lived in the local citadel as well as in a nearby hamlet, and both communities paid an annual tax (*paria*) to the crown.[12a]

In Castile there were Jews living as early as the second half of the tenth century. The special rights that the count exercised over them indicate that their legal position was dependence of a special kind. The wergild (*caloña*) for the injury or death of a Jew went not to the injured or to the family of the victim, as was the practice among the Christians, but to the count. The wergild of Jews was generally higher than that of most of the Christian population. In one instance, in 974, the count yielded to the plea of the inhabitants of Castrojeriz, near Burgos, and allowed that the wergild of a Jew shall be no higher than that of a Christian peasant. In Najera a royal privilege of the early eleventh century set the wergild of a Jew at no higher than that of a knight (*infanzon*) or a priest. Other localities received similar privileges. Upon the death of King Sancho the Great, in 1035, the inhabitants of Castrojeriz overran the royal mansion in the nearby town of Mercatello, in the vicinity of Burgos, and killed four officials of the crown and sixty Jews, destroying the Jewish settlement in the vicinity of the royal palace. The other residents of the place were not harmed, but were merely compelled to move to Castrojeriz. The significance of the event is clear: a revolt against the crown strikes at the Jews, the property of the crown.[13]

The rights of the Jews were set forth in charters of privilege granted by the crown to the Jewish communities. The charter of the Jewish community of Najera served as a model for similar grants of privilege to other communities of Castile and Aragon in the early twelfth century. Everywhere, land was the basis of the Jewish economy, with only modest beginnings of commerce and handicraft. Such must have been the economic structure of the "new Jewish village" (*villa nova de iudeis*) near Burgos, where, according to a document of the year 1137, the king also owned an estate.[13a]

There exists early evidence of Jewish settlements in the western part of the Iberian peninsula as well. Coimbra, now in Portugal, was reconquered from the Arabs by Alfonso III of Leon (866-910) very early in his reign. In the year 900 there was a Jewish farm with a house and a vineyard on the outskirts of the city.[14] In the forties of the eleventh century a number of Jewish merchants, who dealt in silks, woolens and linen, were living on the estate of a noble in the vicinity of the famous monastery of Celanova in Galicia. On one occasion they were attacked and robbed by another knight, an enemy of their overlord.[14a] Both Latin and Hebrew documents, of the tenth century and later, speak of Jewish holdings of land around the city of Leon. The earliest laws of the kingdom (1017-1020) provide that if a free tenant wishes to sell a house he had built on land owned by someone else, the property is to be assessed and its price fixed by four assessors, two Christians and two Jews.[14b] The law thus presumes that the Jews and Christians in the rural communities have common interests and equal rights. About the same time we find the king of Leon confiscating the country estate of a Jew in punishment for an offense committed by the owner. Even while the caliphate of Cordova was still at the height of its prosperity, an active urban life developed in Leon around the royal court, but to what extent Jews participated in it as merchants is not known. The extant documents of the period record transactions involving land, and only incidentally is a Jewish shoemaker or goldsmith mentioned. But the Hebrew sources tell us that Leon had an organized Jewish community, whose scribes were well versed in Jewish law.[14c] The community paid a collective tax to the crown. It had its charter of privileges, which probably extended to the other Jews of the realm. In 1091, Alfonso VI, acting under pressure from his subjects, the nobility as well as the common people, whose support he needed in his campaign against the Almoravides, curtailed the rights of the Jews. Jews were thenceforth forbidden to bear witness against Christians. If a Jew and a Christian had a quarrel, "in the field or vineyard, in the street or market place, or inside a house," and they struck each other, the case was to be adjudged either by a jury of the lords of the realm, or by the court of the royal household, or by a court composed of the three highest prelates of the realm. If it was impossible to bring the case before any of these tribunals, the issue was to be decided by a duel between champions for the two litigants. The Christian, if he wanted to do so, could fight the duel himself, but the Jew had to appoint a champion. If the Jew was defeated, he paid a fine, half of which went to his adversary and half to the crown. If the Christian lost and paid a fine, the entire sum went to the crown. These changes, made in a time of emergency for the crown, affected the Jewish position adversely, but it may be assumed that in normal times those procedures of testimony applied which had been in force during the Carolingian period. In case a Jew sued a Christian for payment of a debt, or vice versa, the litigants were required to offer the testimony of one of the lords of the realm in support of their claim or take an oath. Jewish testimony was not acceptable. It is noteworthy that the Jew appears here as either a creditor or a debtor, and no mention is made of interest. The provision that the fine for assaulting a Jew shall be paid into the coffers of the crown reveals that here, as in the rest of the Christian territory, the Jew was regarded as a royal serf.[14d]

Thus we find small, scattered settlements of Jews in the north of Spain even before the Reconquest. Agriculture was their principal occupation, with a trend toward the urban occupations of commerce and handicraft. They lived in a territory dotted with numerous Benedictine monasteries, amid a warlike Christian population of peasants and knights, unaccustomed to a feudal order such as existed in France. The Jews were dependent for protection upon the kings and lords; and when this source of safety failed, they were exposed to attack from all quarters.

The political position and cultural level of the Jews in the north were different from those of their brethren in the Moslem south. But the borders between the various states were never closed. In the northeast, the centers of Judaeo-

Arabic culture—Saragossa, Tudela, Tortosa—lay close to the Jewish settlements under Christian rule, and a more lively traffic in cultural values must have been carried on across the frontiers than the existing sources reveal. The diplomatic missions of Hasdai ibn Shaprut to Navarre and Leon illustrate one means of contact between the communities of the south and the north. The policy pursued by the Christian princes in their treatment of the Jews prior to the Reconquest is not known to us in all its detail. To the extent to which the Jews suffered from Christian religious zeal, their persecution is to be attributed to the influence of the Christian reform movement carried into Spain in the sixties and seventies of the eleventh century by the legates of the papacy.

THE POLITICS OF THE CHRISTIAN PRINCES DURING THE EARLY RECONQUEST

Sweeping political, social and spiritual changes occurred in Europe about this time and profoundly affected the life of the Jews. After a period of exhaustion and passivity, the conflict between Christianity and Islam flared up anew both in the east and in the west. The Jewish people, caught between the two camps, entered a new era of martyrdom. When the crusaders conquered the Holy Land in 1099, they destroyed the Jewish communities they found there. The Jewish population of Palestine continued to dwindle and lost its position of importance among the Jews of the world. The centers of Jewish culture were transplanted to the west.

Equally fateful for the Jews was the struggle between the two faiths on Spanish soil. The more the small Moslem states weakened each other through internecine warfare, the greater waxed the zeal for reconquest among the Christian rulers. Until the middle of the eleventh century the Christian princes confined themselves to the exploitation for their own ends of the fraternal strife that rent the Moslems. In return for military aid to one or another of the warring states, they obtained political concessions and an opportunity to plunder Arab territories and exact heavy tribute from their rulers. But from about 1060 on the Christians descended upon the Moslem south with the aim of permanent conquest. Their victorious march was twice halted by a counterattack of Mohammedan tribes—the Almoravides in the eighties of the eleventh century, and the Almohades in the forties of the twelfth—who crossed over from North Africa and forced political unity and religious fanaticism upon the Arabs of Andalusia. The Almohades succeeded in completely stopping the Christian advance, which was not resumed until the early part of the thirteenth century. But the map of Spain had already undergone some fundamental changes during the first two or three generations of the struggle. Jewish life in Spain came out of these wars revitalized, but only after having suffered a period of disaster, the third in a series of catastrophies which befell our people on three fronts at once—in Palestine, the Rhineland, and Spain.

The warriors of the Spanish Reconquest were fired by the same fanaticism which animated the crusaders.[15] Contemporary Hebrew poetry tells of fierce religious warfare, of slaughter and compulsory conversion. The French knights who came to the aid of the Spaniards, were experienced in anti-Jewish excesses, and as early as 1066 had to be warned by Pope Alexander II to refrain from acts of violence against the Jews. The treatment of the Jews, however, soon came to be dictated by practical political needs. The Jews were during this period an important element in the founding of new cities throughout Europe. This is a known fact in the rise of cities in Germany; and the economic importance of the Jews in Spain was even greater. The political situation which confronted the Christian kings in the reconquered territories compelled them to employ Jews in important positions in the state organization. The Jewish population of Moslem Spain was numerically the largest in Europe. Whereas there were

47

good political reasons for forcing the Moslems out of Spain, it was found to be advantageous not to expel or destroy the Jews. Constant warfare left the land in ruins and it was necessary to repopulate the devastated areas and develop the commerce of the cities. Among the Christians, the burgher class, drawn from the military knighthood and the oppressed peasantry, grew very slowly. It was therefore essential to make use of the Jews who were already living in the cities. They were skilled in commerce and handicraft and were also able to advance the large sums needed for the conduct of war. It was but natural also that the experience the Jews had acquired in administration and diplomacy be utilized. The Christian kings needed secretaries proficient in Arabic. The Jews were familiar with the nature of the conquered territory and its administration and knew the language and customs of its inhabitants. In addition to these political considerations, the Christian kings were impressed by the highly developed civilization they found in the Arab lands and were inclined to seek advisers and aides brought up in this culture. Moreover, the Christian conquerors had before them the example of the Moslem rulers. In the small Arab kingdoms and principalities, to which the Christians fell heir, Jews had been employed as government officials and Jewish scientists had been attached to the courts of the princes. The prestige to be derived from brilliant literary and scientific achievements was a political asset not to be overlooked. All the above considerations prompted the Christian kings to befriend the Jews, the only ones who could be trusted to give faithful service without harboring any ulterior political ambitions. Neither the Moslems, who remained loyal to their national and religious interests, nor the Christian knights, who were always ready to rise against their liege, could be so trusted. The Jews, for their part, readily transferred their services to the new conquerors, whose power was rising. The moral standards of those days attached no particular stigma to such action, and even the knights changed their allegiance several times, serving, in turn, Christian kings and Arab princes.

Alfonso VI, king of Castile and Leon, "Emperor of all Spain," led the campaign against the small states of Al-Andalus and their allies, the Almoravides. Through combined military action and diplomatic stratagem he made himself master of Toledo in 1085.[16] Internal disunity added to outside pressure forced the last Arab ruler of Toledo to capitulate. The treaty of surrender guaranteed safe-conduct to the Moslems desiring to leave the city and protection to the lives and property of those who chose to remain. The Moslems retained possession of their mosques. They were required to turn over to the victors only the fortified parts of the city. These terms, however, were soon violated. The first archbishop of Toledo to be appointed after its reconquest was a monk from the famous monastery of Cluny. He attended the council of Clermont in 1095 and took an oath to go on a crusade to the Holy Land. The Pope, however, absolved him of his vow, because of his participation in the war against the infidel in Spain. Taking advantage of the king's absence and much to the latter's displeasure, the archbishop confiscated the leading Arab mosque in 1102 and dedicated it as a cathedral. During the two succeeding generations the Moslems were gradually forced to leave the city. By the middle of the twelfth century only a few of the poorest remained.

What terms were granted the Jews at the time of surrender we do not know, but something can be learned from later developments.[17] The existing documents place the Jewish quarter of Toledo, in the middle of the twelfth century, in the same location where we find it during the persecutions of 1391 and where it remained until the expulsion. It was virtually a town in itself, situated in the southwestern part of the city. The southern portion of it sloped down an incline to the bank of the Tagus river and included a fortress known as the Jews' Citadel; to the north the judería was bounded by the city wall. At a later date the judería of Toledo helped the king fortify his position against his enemies both within and without. The Jewish quarters of other cities at times served a similar purpose. Toledo had been regarded since the Visigothic period as the capital of all Spain, and it does not seem likely that the knighthood and the clergy who sought to restore to the city its hallowed position would allot so choice an area for Jewish settlement. Undoubtedly the Jews had lived in the same section under the Moslems, and the Christians only confirmed an established fact.

In Toledo, as in other cities, the ownership of real property kept changing continuously during the ensuing two generations. The king rewarded his retainers with grants of houses and land confiscated from the earlier inhabitants; estates already allotted were taken away from the original recipients and given to others. These changes were occasioned by economic needs and by the fluctuating political fortunes of the individuals affected. No doubt there were Jews, just as there were Christians, who left the city at the time of its surrender, or somewhat later, and whose estates were confiscated by the crown for the offense of treason or for other reasons.[18]

The Jewish population of Toledo grew with the influx of Jews who were brought in by the king from Old Castile as well as of some who fled from the Moslem states. Alfonso VI welcomed them all and often entrusted them with important state functions. As early as 1081, Pope Gregory VII warned Alfonso VI not to appoint Jews to positions of authority and command over Christians.[19] In 1086, Alfonso VI sent Jews to the courts of the Arab rulers of Seville and Valencia to collect tribute. A position of unusual importance was held by the *nasi*, Joseph Ferrizuel, surnamed Cidellus, the physician of Alfonso VI. He was the succor and support of Jews fleeing from the south to seek refuge in the north and often saved them also from attacks by Christians. His nephew, Solomon Ferrizuel, functioned in a similar capacity; he was sent on a diplomatic mission from Castile to Aragon, but was murdered upon his return to Toledo in 1108. Cidellus conducted the inner affairs of the Jewish community with a high hand. He expelled the Karaites "from all the citadels of Castile, except one small citadel, for he did not want to kill them." He owned houses and large estates, in and around Toledo, which were confiscated by the crown after his death. According to a late tradition, the Castilian nobles employed him as an intermediary in presenting to the king a proposal of marriage for his daughter Urraca. The proposal was not to the king's liking and Cidellus fell from favor. Actually Cidellus' name still appears among the signatures of several high dignitaries confirming a charter of immunities granted by Queen Urraca in June of 1110, a year after the death of Alfonso VI. This document is, incidentally, the only evidence of a Jew in such high station at that early date.[20]

The safety of the Jews could be secured only through the strong hand of the king and the influence of his Jewish officials. After the death of Alfonso VI, in June 1109, a general uprising broke out in Toledo, in the environs of Burgos and throughout Leon, marked by destruction of royal property and especially by murder and pillage of the Jews, the protégés of the crown. Many years later, Alfonso VII came to terms with the inhabitants of the localities where the disturbances had occurred and cancelled all fines and wergild due him for the murdered Jews. He further established that in the future the wergild of a Jew was to be the same as that of a peasant. In a special ordinance for the city of Toledo he provided that all suits between a Jew and a Christian, even when the Jew was the defendant, were to be tried only before a Christian judge, and not by a Jewish court. He revived, for the benefit of Toledo and its adjacent territory, a decree of an old Church council forbidding Jews and recent converts from holding any office which gave them authority over Christians.[21] The revival of this old anti-Jewish legislation had no immediate practical effect, except as an indication of a tendency current in certain circles. For the time being, not only the crown, but the Church hierarchy as well preferred to be guided by practical political necessity in their treatment of the Jews. The second archbishop of Toledo gave the Jews of Alcalá de Henares, which was under his jurisdiction, equal rights with the Christians.[22] He also established in Toledo a famous center for the translation of philosophic and scientific works from Arabic into Latin, and among the participating scholars was the Jewish astronomer, Johanan ibn Daud (Johannes Avendehut).

The policy toward the Jews pursued by the rulers of the northeastern part of the peninsula during the Reconquest can be traced through the documents in greater detail. Alfonso I of Aragon (*el Batallador*)—who for a time laid claim also to the throne of Castile and to the title of Emperor of all Spain —captured the city of Tudela on the Ebro river in 1115. We have the two pacts which the king concluded with the Moslem and Jewish inhabitants of the city in March 1115. They were originally drawn up in both Latin and Arabic, but only the Latin text has survived. The agreement with the Moslems follows the terms granted by the celebrated El Cid to the Mohammedans in Valencia in 1095. All the Moslems of the city who did not wish to leave the country were required to give up their houses and mosques inside the walls. They were granted a measure of religious and ethnic autonomy. Out of regard for the religious and national sentiments of the Moslems, Moorish captives were not to be brought into the city, and Jews were forbidden to purchase them as slaves. If a Jew should insult a Moslem by word or deed, he was to be punished. Jews were not to be given authority over Moslems or their property. One can readily see that the relations between the Jews and the Moslems were strained even before the fall of the city.[23]

From the second document we learn that many Jews fled the city during the siege or at the time of its capitulation.

These were allowed to return to their homes, and all the Jews were guaranteed possession of their houses and property. The Jews were required to pay to the Christian ruler the same taxes which they had paid the Arabs. In their civil and criminal litigation with Christians they were to enjoy the privileges of the Jews of Najera, the nearest city with a large Jewish community. This last provision shows that reciprocal influences brought about a striking similarity between the Jews living under Christian rule and those in Moslem territory: the legal status of the Jews of Najera, as defined by the Carolingian privileges, could be assumed without difficulty by Jews who had lived all along under Arab law. The prejudicial treatment of the Moslems as compared to the Jews stands out prominently. The latter were allowed to remain in their own quarter, while the former were expelled from the city.[24]

The Moslems in Saragossa capitulated to Alfonso I in 1118 under the same terms as Tudela.[25] The privileges granted the Jews have not been preserved. We know that the Aragonese king had dealings with a certain Eleazar of Saragossa, who appears either to have resided in the city prior to its reconquest or to have come up from the Moslem south to enter the service of the Christian conqueror. The judería of Saragossa remained until the expulsion inside the old Roman wall, which still marked the city's limits at the time of the Reconquest. Later, when the city's periphery was widened, the Jews were not required to change their domicile. The Moslems, however, had to leave the city proper following its capitulation and settle in the suburbs.

A great deal of detailed information is available for those regions which constituted the sphere of activity of the counts of Barcelona. Together with the kings of Castile and Aragon these counts formed the vanguard of the war against Islam and, like the former, had the assistance of Jews. The services rendered by the Jews of Barcelona to their count were not limited to moneylending. We find that, in 1104, Ramon Berenguer

III granted four Jews of Barcelona the exclusive right to transport Saracen captives by sea to Moslem Spain for ransom.[26]
A certain Jew, Joseph Cavaler of Barcelona, owned property
in Balaguer as early as 1090,[27] while the city, which did not
pass completely into Christian hands until some fifteen years
later, was still being fought over. An official document, issued
in 1121 in the name of Count Ramon Berenguer III, bears
the Hebrew signature of his Jewish bailiff Sheshet b. R.
Shelomo, whose Latin name is given as Perfet (Perfectus).
He is obviously the personage of whom Judah ibn Tibbon
wrote in his will to his son Samuel, "You know well that the
great men of our people attained fame and high rank only
through the writing of Arabic. You have seen that the Nagid,
of blessed memory, tells how he rose to high station by a
mastery thereof. . . . You see that the *Nasi* Rabbi Sheshet, of
blessed memory, by a knowledge thereof attained wealth and
honor in this land as well as in the Arab kingdom, cleared
himself of debt and made great expenditures for charity."
R. Sheshet was no doubt versed in Arabic culture and served
the count as secretary for Arabic correspondence, interpreter
and diplomatic emissary in negotiations with the Arabs. He
was at the same time also steward of the count's possessions.[28]
Abraham bar Hiyya, author of the *Sefer Megillat ha-Megalleh*
("The Scroll of the Revealer," a prediction of the advent of
the Messiah, based on astrological computations) and the
Hibbur ha-Meshiha we-ha-Tishboret (Treatise on Surveying and Geometry), probably held a similar position, serving
Alfonso I of Aragon and the counts of Barcelona as astronomer
and mathematician and helping them in the subdivision of
their territories.

The greatest of the counts of Barcelona was Ramon Berenguer IV (1131-1162), who united the county of Barcelona
with the kingdom of Aragon. The activities of his Jewish aides
are known to us in considerable detail. The same Eleazar of

Saragossa, who was associated with Alfonso I of Aragon, served Ramon Berenguer IV as steward of his household (*repositarius*). A Jew by the name of Zecri of Barbastro received an estate from the count as a reward for his services. Official documents of the county, dating from the forties of the twelfth century, bear the Hebrew signature of Judah son of Isaac; and in documents of the following decade the name of Shealtiel, son of the aforementioned Sheshet, appears, also in Hebrew. Some documents carry additional notes in Hebrew, in the hand of the count's officials. These records cover the count's private transactions, sales of land inside Barcelona requiring the count's approval, leases of ground near Gerona for the construction of stalls and workshops, and the like. The Jew who signed the document did so, not as the personal steward of the king, but as a state official. A large loan that the count had made from a wealthy Christian, to finance a campaign in southern France in 1162, was guaranteed by a number of bishops and abbots, four knights, and two Jews—the said Shealtiel and Abraham Alfaquim, the count's physician. In 1160, two years before his death, the count made a contract with the same physician covering the construction of a public bath in Barcelona, which Abraham undertook to build in a garden allotted for the purpose by the count. In return for his labors and investment, the physician and his heirs were to have a perpetual one-third interest in the income from the establishment. After completion of the building the count was to bear two-thirds of the cost of equipping the interior, and the physician one-third. The operation of the baths was to remain a monopoly of the Jewish physician, and no one else would be permitted to erect another bathhouse in Barcelona. The baths remained in the hands of Abraham's family until 1199, when they sold them to one of the prominent Christians of the city.[29]

In December 1148, Ramon Berenguer IV captured the city of Tortosa, at the mouth of the Ebro river. The concordat concluded at the time of the city's capitulation between the Christian count and the Jewish and Arab inhabitants is extant. The Jews of Tortosa, like those of Tudela, were forbidden to buy Moslem captives as slaves or to insult the Moors. But the clause prohibiting the appointment of Jewish officials with authority over Moslems was omitted. The reason for the omission can only be conjectured. It may be that there were no Jewish officials serving in this area, so that no actual problem existed, or that the count found it necessary, for some reason, to deviate in this instance from his established policy. The Jewish community of Tortosa had already become famous in Hebrew literature as early as the tenth century. However, it appears to have been destroyed in the course of the war, and the Christian conqueror sought to revive it. Ramon Berenguer IV accordingly allotted to the Jews a fortified area, situated between the Ebro and the seashore, for the construction of sixty dwellings. This area must have formed, under Arab rule, one of the principal quays of this thriving commercial center. A number of Genoese Italians, who participated in the conquest of the city, were also assigned a section of the port area for their settlement. In addition the Jews received from the count extensive grants of land, cultivated as gardens, vineyards, olive groves, and fig orchards, which had formerly belonged to Arabs. The count further promised the Jews that, should more of their coreligionists come to settle in Tortosa, additional houses would be made available to them. The Jews were exempted from the payment of taxes for the first four years following the capitulation of the city, and even thereafter they were not to be required to render any of the customary services either to the count or to any other authorities in Tortosa. No Moslem was to exercise authority over Jews. The privileges of the Jewish community of Barcelona were to be the guide in all legal matters involving Jews and Christians. Favorable conditions were thus created for the Jews to enable them to develop the city's overseas trade. But neither the city itself nor its Jewish community lived up to expectations. The city never achieved the hoped-for distinction as a center of maritime commerce. The Jewish community suffered from the outset from the division of authority within the city among the count of Barcelona and the other lords who had shared in its conquest. The latter were interested only in the immediate exploitation of the Jews and not in any long range economic policy.[30]

About a year later, in October 1149, the count of Barcelona, assisted by other knights, conquered Lerida. As elsewhere, stable conditions of property ownership and land settlement were only gradually achieved. We hear of a synagogue converted into a church in 1173. From the eighties on we find the Jewish quarter in a fortified portion of the city, and it may be assumed that it was also located there at the time of the city's reconquest. The Order of Knights Templar shared in the rule of the city. This Order was originally organized to go on a crusade to Palestine, but it found also in Spain ample opportunity for carrying on religious warfare and expanding the political influence of the organization. Jews were employed in its fiscal administration. In the years immediately following the conquest of Lerida, we find the commander of the Order permanently leasing to Jews some of the lands recently expropriated from the Arabs.

A Jew, by the name of Yahia (Jafia) ben David of Monzon, helped organize the administration of the district. He is the first Jew to be designated in official documents as "bailiff" (*baiulus*), that is, the steward of the king's private domain (*patrimonium*). Yahia served primarily Alfonso II (1162-1196) of Aragon, son of Ramon Berenguer IV. His signature, in Latin characters, appears on documents dealing with taxes and other fiscal matters, on writs of exemption from taxes, on the charters of newly established Christian villages; and we find him, too, approving leases and transfers of land. He signed an official document fixing the boundaries of the city of Lerida under Moslem rule. In all, he appears to have fulfilled an important function in the apportionment of the conquered territory. He was himself the beneficiary of extensive grants of land in the vicinity of Lerida. Alfonso II presented him with a workshop and a small house adjoining the royal palace in Lerida, with permission to rent them to whomever he desired, Christian, Jew, or Saracen. He also owned wine cellars in the Jewish citadel of Lerida.[31] Certain changes which the king instituted in the economic administration of the city finally brought about Yahia's dismissal, but the exact circumstances of this change in his status are not known.

The political conditions and policies which governed the transition of the Jews from Moslem to Christian rule stand out very clearly. But the personal reactions of the actors of this historic drama, as expressed in literature, admit of several interpretations. The *Poema del Cid,* written about 1140, reveals the mind of the Spanish knight. This celebrated champion of the Reconquest lost the favor of his liege, Alfonso VI, and decided to carry on the war against the Moslems on his own. Being without funds, he dispatches a trusted friend to Burgos to seek a loan from two Jewish merchants. The Christian knight's negotiations with the Jews are carried on in a friendly, informal atmosphere and he himself pockets a handsome commission for his pains. The Jews are most obsequious, mindful, naturally, of their own profit. But the reader feels instinctively that they are bound to be cheated in the end.[32] Some modern interpreters, Jews and Christians alike, have tried in vain to gloss over the anti-Jewish bias of this representative poem, a bias revealed not merely in the accounts of individual incidents, but also in the author's adherence to the popular conception of the Jew as the deceitful merchant, rather than the loyal political aide, the function which he undoubtedly exercised in the circles around the historic Cid. On the other hand, there is not a single word of religious fanaticism aimed at the Jews throughout this poem.

The *Poema del Cid* is the epic of the sober Spanish warrior
and statesman, the hero of the Reconquest; the French knights,
on the other hand, entered Spain as zealous crusaders. They
were accompanied by Benedictine monks, armed with an extensive literature of religious polemics directed against Judaism. From these fanatics Petrus Alfonsi (Moshe ha-
Sefardi) of Huesca received baptism in the presence of Alfonso
I of Aragon, the same king who concluded those favorable
pacts with the Jews of Tudela. The apostate immediately entered the fray by publishing a tract denouncing Judaism. Echoes
of this conflict are heard in contemporary Hebrew works.
Abraham bar Hiyya, in his *Megillat ha-Megalleh,* sought to
refute the currently accepted teachings of Jerome and Augustine, and to prove that the six epochs of the universe would
be completed only during the period of the crusades, and that
the visions of Daniel applied not to the times of Jesus of
Nazareth but to the wars presaging the advent of the Messiah,
then being waged before the eyes of his own contemporaries.[33]
Similar refutation of Christian teaching is to be found in the
contemporary commentary of Judah ben Barzilai al-Barceloni
to the *Sefer Yezirah.*

Intellectual Currents During the Reconquest

(*Moses ibn Ezra and Judah Halevi*)

The transition of Spanish Jewry from Moslem rule to Christian domination shook Jewish life deeply. Relatively few Jews
were able to utilize the changing situation to advantage, to circulate as traders between the warring camps, at times even
to traffic in human beings, and to engage in the ransoming of
captives, whether for profit or out of genuine humanitarian
and pious motives.[34] Later Arab historians speak—with obvious exaggeration—of large numbers of Jews fighting side by
side with the Christians in the great decisive battles.[35] To be
sure, there were even in the fourteenth century instances of

Jewish inhabitants of frontier towns going to battle against the Moslem enemy by the side of the local citizens' militia. But the fact of the matter is that Jewish participation in the conflict was limited to the defense of their own dwelling places and districts. They did not join either side, but remained throughout a harassed and suffering community caught between the two warring camps.

In the south of Spain the foundations of Jewish existence collapsed completely. The Almoravides made an end to the small states of Andalusia and to the easygoing and enlightened way of life which prevailed in the courts of their rulers. The Jewish position deteriorated correspondingly. To be sure, remnants of most of the Jewish communities, visited by destruction and pillage, did survive; and the heirs of the erstwhile ministers to the late princelings sought to purchase similar careers in the service of the vassals and officials of the Almoravides. But many Jewish courtiers of the old regimes were too deeply compromised and were compelled to flee. The fate of the Ibn Ezra family offers a characteristic example.[36] When, in 1090, Granada was captured by Ibn Tashufin, king of the Almoravides, and the Jewish community was destroyed, the members of that family lost their positions. Joseph ibn Ezra and his son Judah went to Toledo and rose there to high station. Isaac ibn Ezra also appears to have settled in Toledo. The name is found in local documents of the year 1118-1119. But he appears to have left the city shortly thereafter, perhaps as a result of disturbed conditions prevailing at the time throughout Castile, and he died in Lucena in 1121 a lonely man. Moses ibn Ezra, the celebrated poet—who had attained the courtier's rank "Sahib al-Shorta," and bore also the title of Rabbi, a man who could write erotic verse, sensual in quality, as well as religious poetry which inspired the pious of many a later generation—forfeited his position and wealth but did not succeed in fleeing as promptly as his brothers. In letters to friends he complains of the "perverseness of his contemporaries . . . who set snares for his life."

> I grieved not for the wealth that was plundered, I cared not that it had vanished and gone, I lamented not opulence come to an end, I felt not ill over servants deserting . . . I can only scoff at the works of fate and laugh at its pranks. Throughout my life I have known success; but my wealth took flight like a soaring eagle, all the toil of my hands took wing, and God's mighty hand thereby became manifest. But the tears flow from my eyes as I seek to overcome my grief over my loneliness in my native land, without a companion at my side. I am like a stranger sojourning therein, and I see no man about me of my family and kin.
> I remain in Granada, a city of declining bustle and splendor, like a stranger in the land, like a sparrow strayed from its nest, like a bird banished and driven; and amongst this generation, wayward and corrupt, there is no refuge for me; there remains no one to remember me and inquire after my welfare.[37]

The poet leaves no doubt that he blames one of his brothers for his bitter fate. Theirs are "wrongs such as have not been committed since the world came into being; merely hearing of them makes our ears tingle. . . .Yet, while I lie in the pit of fortune's fury, they dwell securely beneath its beneficent wing."[38] Finally, in 1095, Moses ibn Ezra also succeeded in escaping to Christian territory. Thenceforth, and until his death in 1135, he wandered from place to place throughout northern Spain. He speaks of his wanderings in several of his poems.

> I am weary of roaming about the world, measuring its expanse; and I am not yet done. . . .
> I walk with the beasts of the forest and I hover like a bird of prey over the peaks of mountains.

61

> My feet run about like lightning to the far ends of the
> earth, and I move from sea to sea.
> Journey follows journey, but I find no resting-place, no
> calm repose.[39]

The poet wandered mostly through the provinces of Castile.
In one of his beautiful poems he pours forth his soul's bitterness at the fate which brought him to one of the lonely castles
of this land of many castles (Castilla). It is possible that he
had Burgos in mind, the city which was itself sometimes referred to as "Castella." Speaking in the third person, the poet
laments:

> For him did Fate compel atop a castle climb, and
> there recluse-like on a roof-top dwell,
> To hear naught but the jackals wail or the
> ostrich moan.
> The eagle, eying him, his baldness spreads,
> and hearing him, rends his flesh.
> Fate set his lair among the stars and stretched
> a cloud beneath him,
> And commanded him to count the stars and to measure
> the arched sky.
> Woe to the land where no friend there be, to nod a head in
> condolence or to extend a hand in succor![40]

He was invited by the local authorities to settle in Estella,
where, at the time, a begining of autonomous urban life was
being made on the initiative of the king of Navarre. Judah
Halevi, seeking to dissuade him, wrote to him:

> Eloquent tongue! What wouldst thou among the tongue-
> tied?
> Why should the dew of Mount Hermon fall upon
> Gilboa?[40a]

Others too asked him in amazement:

> Would the light of the lofty spheres descend to a mere
> star (*stella*, Estella) and wish to mingle therewith?

To which the poet sadly replies:

> The star (Estella) you speak of, darkness hid its light.
> Were one to set his seat above it, he would still among the
>   lowly dwell.[40b]

Only a man like himself, sorely tried in the crucible of pain
and sorrow, would seek refuge in this habitat of fools, of
wolves, bears and lions, and of men cast in their image:

> Who are like the wolves that dwell in the desert,
>   never hearing the name of man.
> 'Tis far better to meet a bereaved bear or consort with a
>   lion than to have encounter with them.
> They turn light to darkness; how, then, can they
>   distinguish knave from noble?[41]

The poet's wealth, the key to a new and sound economic
position, was gone. The material and cultural conditions that
were offered him in several places failed to satisfy a man of
his refined tastes.[42] Throughout his wandering he longed for
his native land, "the most delightful of lands," for "Granada,
the glorious," for "the mountains of Senir (Sierra Nevada)."
It was his fate to be exiled from "luxurious mansions" and
to dwell among "barbarians, famished for lack of the bread of
reason, parched for dearth of the waters of faith . . . would-be
sages without wisdom, would-be seers without vision."[43] And
we hear a further complaint:

> Fortune has hurled me to a land where the lights of
>   my understanding dimmed
> And the stars of my reason were beclouded with the murk
>   of faltering knowledge and stammering speech.
> I have come to the iniquitous domain of a people
>   scorned by God and accursed by man,
> Amongst savages who love corruption and set an ambush
>   for the blood of the righteous and innocent.
> They have adopted their neighbors' ways, anxious to enter
>   their midst,

And mingling with them they share their deeds and are
now reckoned among their number.
Those nurtured, in their youth, in the gardens of truth,
hew, in old age, the wood of forests of folly.

That is to say, the Jews who emigrated from Andalusia to
the territories of the Christians soon assimilated the ways of
the latter, and just as they learned from them to turn forest
land into fertile fields and populous towns, so they also learned
to "hew the wood of the forests of folly," that is, to accept
their values.[44]

The experiences of Moses ibn Ezra were not unlike those
of many Italian humanists of the Renaissance. His was the
sad figure of a courtier, fallen from high station, seeking solace
in philosophy. There were, no doubt, others of this type to be
found in Spain of that day. Yet, on the whole, this class of
professional court officials, the characteristic product of the
Andalusian political pattern of small states, sought to continue
its accustomed way of life also under the Almoravides, or to
embark upon new but similar careers under the aegis of the
Christian conquerors. This latter transition was fraught with
consequences which contributed to the complexity of Jewish
life in Spain during the centuries that followed.

The social structure of the Jewish communities underwent
little change. Leadership was vested in a small aristocratic
upper stratum, whose members were men of rank and influence in the royal courts. These "nobles," "princes," and
"vizirs" are familiar to us through the flattering poems of
Moses ibn Ezra and Judah Halevi. Not in every case was the
lavish praise, couched in elegant verse, justified. But imbued
as they were with a simple religious and nationalist faith, even
such enlightened and broadly cultured men as these two poets
regarded every Jewish court functionary as a scion of the
house of David, extolled him as a prince of his people provi-
dentially delegated to serve as a guarantee of the approaching
redemption.

Of the political conditions prevailing in the courts of the Almoravides, we have only limited knowledge. In the Christian courts, however, there now began a period of steady advancement for the Jewish notables. Many of them proved to be dauntless defenders of their people and faith, but there were also those who turned their backs upon both. The wide intellectual gulf between the sophisticated culture of the aristocracy and the naive faith of the masses led eventually to open strife. The court dignitaries, orthodox and rational in their faith, regarded it as their duty to wipe out Karaite sectarianism. Long ago, under Moslem rule, the Karaites had been forced to withdraw to the border regions adjoining the Christian territories and eventually to seek refuge in the fortress towns of Castile. The relentless persecution by three generations of Jewish courtiers in the service of Alfonso VI, Alfonso VII and Alfonso VIII, overtook them there and succeeded in destroying the sect with the aid of the governing powers.[45]

The epoch-making events of those times shook the souls of the simple masses and the communal leaders alike. Spanish Jewry, to be sure was spared such martyrdom as was suffered by their pious brethren in Germany, who fervently offered their lives for their faith. But the life-and-death struggle between Christianity and Islam reawakened the dormant messianic hopes and, for the first time since the initial stages of the contest between the two great powers in the seventh century, revived interest in the ancient apocalyptic teachings. In the early years of the twelfth century a number of men gathered in Cordova for the purpose of determining the date and hastening the advent of the Messiah through astrological computations and nocturnal visions. They agreed upon a pious man by the name of Ibn Aryeh as the long awaited Messiah. The communal authorities, however, put an end to the movement. At the beginning of the Almohadic invasion, a Jew by the name of Moses al Dar'i travelled from Morocco to Lucena, the seat of the famous academy of Joseph ibn Megas, announcing throughout Andalusia as well as in Fez that the Messiah had already appeared. Some of his prophecies and portents seem to have come true. Finally, he stated that the Messiah would arrive on the first night of Passover and he advised the Jews to prepare for their journey to the Holy Land by selling all their property and borrowing heavily from the Moslems, thus observing to the letter the biblical verse, "And they despoiled the Egyptians." When his visions failed to materialize, the would-be prophet left for Palestine, where he died. "May his memory be blessed," says Maimonides, our authority for this account.[46] A number of years later, between 1126 and 1151, Johanan ibn Daud, mentioned earlier as one of the group of scholars called to Toledo by its archbishop, published an old apocalypse on the Final Struggle and circulated it widely as an account of events that would take place during the years 1179-1186. These prophecies created a stir among the Christians of Europe during the third crusade.[47] Close to 1129, Abraham bar Hiyya published his *Megillat ha-Megalleh*, wherein he expatiates on the signs of the coming redemption, which he saw in the attacks of the Turkish emir, Zenghi, upon the territories held by the crusaders.

Abraham bar Hiyya, while in the service of a Christian prince in Spain, showed great interest in developments in Palestine, but carefully refrained from touching upon events in his own country. This may have been due either to discretion or to a conviction that the final decision would come, not on Spanish soil, but in Palestine. He hoped for the fall of the Christian kingdom of Jerusalem, whose collapse would be the first step toward redemption. Abraham bar Hiyya had no love for the Arabs, but he nursed an even greater antagonism to the Christians, the latter having been the first "to claim title to the sacred dwelling and establish their house of worship therein," and "they defiled the Temple site, established upon it a house of their worship, set up therein the sculptured images of their folly, abolished the daily sacrifice in that they prevented the Jews from offering prayer on the Temple site. . . . For, since the day they gained control over the sanctuary, they have forbidden Jews to set foot therein, and not a single Jew is to be found in Jerusalem today." Thus wrote a Jewish scientist of that day, the author of a work on surveying (*Ha-Meshiha we-ha-Tishboret*), written to facilitate the measurement and distribution of the lands reconquered by the Christian princes in Spain. This was the social and spiritual environment in which there flourished a Jewish thinker who was equally conversant with the politics of the sober statesmen and the speculations and visions of the eschatologists, but who struck out on a new path and bequeathed to his generation a new meaning of its fate and destiny—Judah Halevi.

Judah Halevi[48] was born about the time Alfonso VI began his campaign against the Almoravides. He left Spain, with the intention of going to Palestine, a short while before the Almohades swept over southern Spain, bringing destruction to the Jewish communities in Andalusia. He spent part of his youth in the Christian north, and later travelled to the centers of classical Jewish culture in the south in pursuit of Jewish and general learning as well as for a taste of worldly pleasures. Political conditions compelled his return to the north, but he may later have made several other visits to the south. His poems seem to indicate that a trip across the border into enemy territory was not at all impossible. Wherever he happened to be, in the north or in the south—called east and west in his poems—he addressed, in verse, expression of friendship and flattery to the Jewish notables of the Moslem or Christian courts, sometimes in the hope of being rewarded with financial assistance, but primarily out of a genuine sense of social and intellectual kinship to those groups. The poet's formative years were spent among the Jewish circles close to the Castilian court. He appears to have practiced medicine in Toledo, ministering with his skill to its Christian conquerors. These circumstances account for his remarks in a letter to one of his friends:

> Thus I busy myself at an hour that is neither day nor night with the vanities of medicine. . . . The city is large and its inhabitants are giants and they are hard masters; and how can a slave please his masters other than by spending his days fulfilling their desires. . . . We heal Babel, but it is beyond healing.[49]

That he felt a warm attachment to the Jewish community of Toledo is attested even by these simple verses, indited on the occasion of the repair of the local synagogue in 1107,

> From God it issued for His people's sake. . . .
> He restored joy to all hearts with the restoration of the shrine,
> And sighs and grief now ceased.[50]

During the Christian Reconquest, when the rights of individuals and communities were subject to constant change, when both mosques and synagogues were either destroyed or turned into churches, the repair of the old synagogue inside the walls of Toledo, the restored Visigothic capital of Spain, could be regarded as something of a political victory.

Living in Toledo at the time was Joseph Ferrizuel, also known as Cidellus, who has been mentioned above as the physician of Alfonso VI. The personality of this influential courtier and his aid to his refugee coreligionists in the vicinity of Guadalajara, which had been reconquered along with Toledo in 1085, are celebrated in stately verse by Judah Halevi. The poet tells of Cidellus—and his account is corroborated by various Christian chroniclers—that "when the heads of the nation and the king assemble in council, they all defer to Joseph who is the eye of their grandeur." And referring to his efforts on behalf of his persecuted people, Halevi writes, "Through him the oppressive burden was lightened, for he strove and prevailed, and like a tower of might he stayed the people fleeing in ten directions." Like the sun he shone over the earth. With his appearance "the degraded people" was relieved of oppression, for "his roar set the princes trembling." The poem ends with benedictory verses in both Hebrew and Spanish.[51]

When the nephew of Cidellus, Solomon Ferrizuel, was about to return from a diplomatic mission to Aragon, Judah Halevi welcomed him back in the most delicate and sweetest verse to be found in the poet's rich treasury, veritably strewing his path with his most tender lyrical blossoms.[51a] But on this return journey, in 1108, Solomon met his death at the hands of political adversaries. The poet's grief and his fury against the assassins knew no restraint.

> Where shall the small flock and the diaspora in Spain
>   seek refuge, when you are no more. . . .
> Who will carry the lambs at his bosom and who will
>   unshackle the fetters of the imprisoned? . . .
> May dew never fall upon you, fields of Seir! . . .
> May God send a downpour of wrath upon the daughter
>   of Edom! . . .
> May He visit upon her, in retribution, bereavement and
>   widowhood; may He strike down her population along
>   with her idolatrous images![52]

It is as if the poet wished to awaken the ancient apocalyptic writers to portray the long foreseen destruction of the fourth world empire.

Judah Halevi personally witnessed the utter destruction of Jewish communities at the hands of the plundering Christian reconquerors; and he likewise saw streams of Jewish refugees fleeing before the sword of the Almoravides. As he recorded these events and expressed his own reactions to them in a series of poems, his own national consciousness intensified steadily until it attained its full fruition. The poet developed along with the political events of his day and became the seer of a decisive period in history—a prophet for his contemporaries and for the coming generations. Specific political events, alluded to in several of his poems, led the poet to a conviction and an outlook which are at once new and yet old. In one of his poems he describes the destruction of an entire Jewish community, and whoever is looking for a graphic portrayal of the tribulations of the Jews caught between the two warring camps in the wars of the Reconquest, should read his words.

> Between the hosts of Seir (Christians) and Kedar (Moslems), my host is lost; Israel's host vanishes. They wage their wars and we fall when they fall—thus it was ever in Israel. . . . In a city of merchant princes, among whom are threescore mighty men of the mighty men of Israel, when the angel tore the houses down, he did not then pass over the homes of the sons of Israel. From God issued the decree to destroy a mother city in Israel. . . . And on the day the city was taken by assault, the vengeance of the sons of Seir was wreaked upon Israel, and their streets were filled with the slain. Philistines (Berbers) retreat and Edomites (Christians) plunder, some in vehicles and some on horse. . . . The foes battle like savage beasts, the princes of Eliphaz (Christians) with the chieftains of Nebaioth (Moslems), and terrorized between them are the young lambs.[53]

In another poem, he reaches out beyond the immediate situation in Spain. The dove (Israel), borne of yore on the pinions of eagles, is now left "wandering through the forests, beset on all sides by those who lay snares," seeking to entice her away from her Lord. In Spain, Israel is caught between Edom and Ishmael and subjected to terror and plunder, while in the land of Israel the Temple site is in foreign hands, and no one knows when the end will come. In Spain again,

> The tender maidens were exiled from their homes, from their soft beds and peaceful havens, and scattered amid a people devoid of understanding, babbling in strange

tongues. Yet they kept the faith in which they were nurtured and refused to bow to idolatrous images.

And he concludes with the fearful question, "Is there no
end to the prophetically designated time?"[54]

Other poems emphasize, in lesser detail, the lot of Israel in
the crucial struggle between Edom and Ishmael. In some, the
poet stresses the oppression by Ishmael, and in others the
cruelty of Edom—depending, probably, upon where the author
lived at the time of writing. It appears that in the main
the poet's observations were made from the Christian side of
the peninsula. Very frequently his vision encompasses also the
sacred Temple site which was under the dominion of the
crusaders.

> Forget not Edom, the yoke of whose oppression is so
> bitter and harsh. . . . Remember the day he drove into
> exile men of prominence and simple folk, without leaving
> even a dog in my home. . . . Drive from the abode of
> peace the lion's whelps, gathered to devour the weak
> lamb.[55]

The same motifs are variously interwoven in Judah Halevi's
poetry—mourning over the departure of God's near presence,
the political conditions in Spain, the conquest of Jerusalem
by the crusaders, and the question, "How long?" He follows
the traditional patterns of poetry on the *Galut* theme; but he
introduces a note of deeper realism into his description of
the present and a more concrete formulation of the hopes
for the future.[56] In the wars of his age and the suffering they
brought he saw the birth throes of the Messianic Age. Once
he even foretold the appearance of the Messiah in the year
1130; this was expressed in a short poem written after the
assumption by Alfonso VII of the title "Emperor of all Spain,"
when the hopes of victory flared up anew among the Christians and messianic strivings ran high among the Jews both
in the north and the south of the peninsula.[57] But it was not

only in an occasional mood that Judah Halevi caught the messianic fever of his generation; most of his poems which recount the trials and tribulations of the *Galut* end on the popular apocalyptic note. Thus the prospect of redemption, which is traditionally an integral part of the *Galut* poetry, frequently became politically inspired and presented, in line with the poet's personality, an original approach and a concrete political line of thinking. Edom, in his victorious march, was destroying the Jewish communities. The Jewish courtiers, however, succeeded in curbing the fury of the Christian knights and saving the Jews of Andalusia who sought refuge in the territory held by the Christians. For a time, therefore, the poet heaped lavish praise upon the Jewish statesmen of his time. But these encomiums finally ceased. His thinking took a new turn. It had become clear to him that the efforts of his friends to secure for their fellow Jews a new haven in the Christian states were futile.

> Lord, show the hand of Thy favor to those who trust in Thee . . . for the hand of the redeemers is too weak to redeem me. And, I pray, may my paths before the Lord be firm and true, perchance He will see how powerless are all my (would-be) saviors. For the son who but yesterday was a prince is now enslaved, and his abode is in the hands of every foe. . . . I am weary of seeing myself pursued and overtaken by a fate relentlessly hostile even to my surviving remnant. . . . Behold, the son of my handmaiden (Ishmael—the Arabs) hates me furiously; and though we continue pleading with Esau, he continues to devour us.[58]

The inner crisis in the life of Judah Halevi, to which scholars have already called attention, was brought about, not merely by his new and critical attitude toward philosophy and worldly pleasures, but by a wholehearted and total revolt against the social order which had become deeply rooted in Jewish communal life during the "Golden [Arab] Age." Judah

Halevi discounted the activities of the Jewish notables which formed the basis for the society and culture of the courtier class and upon which depended, according to the then prevailing view, the survival of the Jewish Diaspora. Friends who sought to persuade him to remain in Spain by pointing to the well-being attainable in the princely courts, were rebuked with a curt reply, "They're drunk."

> How can one be made happy in the service of kings if it is like idol-worship in his eyes? Is it good for a pure and righteous man to be led about, like a captive bird in the hands of youngsters, chained to the service of Philistines (Berbers), Ishmaelites, and Hittites (Christians)? They are strange gods that strive to turn his heart to seek their favor, forsaking the will of God, to betray the Creator and worship mere creatures.[59]

These words must be taken not merely as a confession of personal disillusionment, but as a protest against the order of things prevailing in Spain. In two places in his *Book of the Kusari*, Judah Halevi defended the Jewish aristocrats of his day. Even if they are not very pious, he said, they are to be commended for not turning their backs upon their people and faith. But, in departing from them, instead of poems of adulation like "The Enchanting One" *(Ba 'alat Keshafim)*, he wrote,

> Turn your cheeks to the pluckers and shield not your face from being spat upon.

And he called to his friends,

> Ye doves in flight through a pit-strewn wilderness, Arise; there is no rest for you here, while your home is deserted.[60]

Judah Halevi's philosophic treatise, like his poetry, is the product of his age, the period of the Reconquest and the Crusades. The great historic struggle between Christianity and

Islam forms the background for the book and serves as the underlying premise in all its discussions. The *Kusari* seeks to prove that not the aforesaid world powers but Israel and his Torah are God's select, and that to Israel was vouchsafed the promise of an heirloom in heaven as well as on earth—in the Land of Israel. It declares war as well on the philosophic rationalism which was undermining the traditional faith in the aristocratic Jewish circles of Spain. The *Kusari* differs from earlier as well as later works which sought to harmonize the Jewish religious traditions with philosophy. The other apologist thinkers would begin with a consideration of certain metaphysical problems and then proceed to derive the tenets of Judaism, as it were, from established philosophic axioms. Judah Halevi categorically rejects this approach. He lays down as his basic premise the inherited traditions regarding the divine selection of Israel and the verification of this selection in the evolution of history. This theological-monotheistic view of history is in direct contradiction to the concept of causality in history, then current in the rationalist circles trained in the Greek and Arab sciences. The development of human history was, according to Judah Halevi, preordained by "God who does His will when He will, and not by nature, or by the stars, or by magic, or by accident" (*Kusari*, I, 83).

The purpose of the book, its general content and many of its details, as well as its literary form, recall the classical apologetic works of the Hellenistic Jews and early Christians in their polemics against paganism. It bears a striking similarity to Augustine's *City of God:* it is quite possible that Judah Halevi read this classic work himself or learned of it through his discussions with Christians. The arguments of his adversaries served only to revitalize within Judah's own mind those historic Jewish teachings which had already lost their hold on the minds of many of his contemporaries. There is nothing fundamentally new in Halevi's philosophy concerning the mission of his suffering people, surrounded by hostile nations, yet tied with bonds everlasting to its ancestral land and its divine law. It is an old lore, developed into a well-integrated system by its original propounders and faithfully cherished by subsequent generations. It had infused into the people its life's breath and led it on to the stage of history. The sages of the Mishna gave it authoritative formulation. In Germany and France, Jewish scholars made wholehearted adherence to it the guiding principle of Jewish life. But to his rationalist contemporaries in Spain, Judah Halevi had to prove that their historic faith was still valid despite the critique of philosophy, and, what is more, that its validity may be established with the help of rationalist science.

Not in every respect was the attempt successful. Like his predecessors, the Hellenistic apologists, Halevi did not avoid lapsing into banalities as he sought to explain the divine commandments rationally. In order to establish the rather naive concept of the select nation, he developed a theory of spiritual superiority which placed Israel on a plane above that of the other nations—this despite his broad humanism which even kept him from ending his treatise on the eschatological note which is so vital a part of his nationalist poetry.

Only where the apologist yields to the poet and seer in him, is Judah Halevi's original contribution apparent. He carried the traditional conception of Jewish history out of its original setting—the old Roman Empire—and adapted it to the contemporary scene of dynamic political developments in Europe and the Near East. This gave him a deeper understanding of the meaning of his nation's suffering. Here, too, the artistry of his great poetic work in prose is revealed. On four different occasions in the *Kusari* we find the same problem presented and the same contradiction brought out, each time in different form. Part One relates the past history of Israel and stresses the nation's selection as God's Chosen; yet this glorious account does not omit mention of the degradation and oppression suffered by the people in the present. Part Two extols

Israel's Constitution and the organic sources of its sanctity
—the divine attribute of prophecy, vouchsafed only to the
Chosen People, the land of Israel, the sacrificial offerings, the
Torah, and the Hebrew tongue—and together with this he
offers a picture of the nation's present state as a body without
head or heart, not even a whole body, only scattered limbs.
In Part Three, describing "the way of the pious man among
us," Judah presents an idealized picture of the pious Jew
who has within his own heart reconciled this contradiction,
cited here for the third time: "when his mind is disturbed
by the length of the exile, the dispersion of his people, its
degradation and decline." And finally, Part Four, contains
the exposition concerning the divine light that shone upon
Israel, countered by the crushing argument that "the light
whereof you speak has set, and it does not seem likely that
it will ever reappear"; and the comforting parable of the seed
is introduced, allegorizing the mission of Israel in the Diaspora.
Judah Halevi wanted to lead the proud and enlightened Jewish courtiers of his day to recognize the worth of their own
people and to give them an understanding of its unique position in the broader framework of the history of mankind.
This conflict between the wide external, secular world and
the inner light concentrated within the heart of the small
persecuted people, manifests itself prominently throughout
the course of Jewish history in Spain, from the beginning of
the Reconquest to the emergence of the Marrano problem on
the eve of the final expulsion.[61]

A short time after Judah Halevi's pilgrimage to Palestine,
in the forties of the twelfth century, the Almohades invaded
Spain and brought destruction to the Jewish communities of
Andalusia. The Jews who survived the sword were compelled
to renounce their faith publicly. Some time later they were
permitted to return to their faith, but the south of Spain did
not again play an important role in Jewish life on the peninsula until it too passed under Christian domination. Many

76

Jews, including the family of Moses Maimonides, fled to the east; but a far greater number sought refuge in northern Spain, in Christian territory. As in the reign of Alfonso VI, these Jews found a savior in Castile, this time in the person of Judah ibn Ezra, a member of the illustrious family who had, at an earlier date, immigrated from Granada. This Judah was the collector of revenues (*almoxarife*) of the king-emperor Alfonso VII. In 1147 he was placed in charge of the frontier fortress of Calatrava, where he appears to have served as coordinator of supplies for the troops fighting the Moslems, and he made this town a "city of refuge for the exiled." Abraham ibn Daud relates that he liberated the Jewish refugees fleeing from the sword of the Almohades and brought them to safety in Toledo. We are told also that later "the king sent for him and made him master of his household and ruler of his entire domain," meaning that the king appointed him head of the central administration of the realm. Judah ibn Ezra's activities were in many ways similar to those of his predecessor, Cidellus, and, like the latter, he, with the aid of the crown, relentlessly persecuted the Karaites.[62]

II

THE INTERMEDIATE PHASE OF THE RECONQUEST (1150-1230)

The Jews who fled from southern Spain to find refuge in the north were hardly aware that they were laying the foundations of communities destined to survive for many generations. For a while, following the conquest of Palestine by Saladin, the messianic hopes which were smouldering all through the Crusading Era, flared up anew. But these were again doomed to disappointment, and the Diaspora in the west continued its independent development. The Jews proved themselves to be a valuable colonizing agent in the flourishing Christian states of Spain, as the use which the Christian rulers made of them in the organization of the reconquered cities well proves. Following are a few additional facts, not directly connected with the war, pertinent to this subject.

In their social-economic structure the Jews differed from both the Christian and the Moslem populations. They were not yet entirely removed from the soil, but their attachment to it was not of the same nature as that of their neighbors, who were, for the most part, peasants. In Aragon and Navarre —as twelfth century laws indicate[1]—Jews as well as Moslems cultivated crown lands, paying a rental in produce.[2] There also existed Jewish communities, unconnected with any Christian town, and independent of any manor, castle, or church.[3] These may not have been exclusively agricultural settlements, but they mark, at the very least, attempts on part of the Jews to create for themselves autonomous communities and a balanced economy. Jews established themselves also in other parts of the country as farmers who engaged in handicraft and commerce as well. They thus fall into that social class which laid the foundations of urban life in Europe.

Generally speaking, the conditions encountered by the Spanish Jews in the urban centers were similar to those which helped the growth of Jewish communities in the cities of Germany and the rest of northern Europe. There were, however, many differences of detail. In the episcopal city of Barcelona the Jewish quarter lay in the center of the walled part of town, below the castle of the count, not far from the cathedral, like similar quarters in many a German city. In Toledo, on the other hand, the Jews occupied a fortress situated on the slopes above the Tagus river, inside the city walls. Their quarter covered a wide area and was virtually a city in itself. In addition, some Jews owned stalls and dwellings in the business district of the city. In Tudela, Navarre, the Jewish quarter was moved to the citadel in 1170. The king promised to keep its walls in repair, and the Jews, in turn, were to defend the citadel against the king's enemies. They were also given express permission to utilize the fortifications

79

in defending themselves against possible mob violence and they were not to be held responsible for injuries or death suffered by the attackers in the event of such an assault. The following year, the Jews of Funes were transferred to the local citadel under the same terms, including the same responsibilities and privileges. The king even made the community a gift of a tract of land outside the citadel, for cultivation by its members.[4] It was not until the first half of the twelfth century that the Jews of Burgos moved into the famous citadel where El Cid—according to the epic—found the Jewish merchants who lent him the money to carry on his campaign.[5] The like happened in the south Castilian border town of Zorita, reconquered in 1085. In 1156, Alfonso VII turned its citadel over to Mozarab settlers from Aragon. This experiment was unsuccessful, and in 1174 the fortress was given to the Order of Calatrava. In 1180 a new Christian settlement was begun alongside the fort, and several Jews took up residence there. A few years later the Jews were moved into the fort, while the Christians remained outside in the open country. In 1215 King Henry I absolved the Jews of Zorita from further payment of taxes as a reward for the service they had rendered his father, Alfonso VIII, by advancing him large sums of money, as well as for the service they were still rendering the crown by holding the fortress of Zorita.[6]

The settlement of Jews in fortresses was thus a common thing in Spain. As early as the eleventh century they were used to garrison forts throughout Leon and they were still employed in the same capacity in Aragon at a later date. Inside their fortified quarters the Jews enjoyed complete autonomy. Royal officials were permitted to enter them only under special circumstances. According to a law still in force in Burgos in the thirteenth century, whenever the royal law enforcement officer (*merino*) wished to enter the Jewish citadel in search of criminals hiding there, the Jews were required to hand over to him the keys to the gates and to assist him in his mission. Whoever aided the escape of a criminal by opening the gates to him was liable to a fine. Likewise, when the royal tax collector (*portero*) came to the citadel to collect the revenues due from the community, he was to receive the keys upon request, so that he might lock the inhabitants in until full payment was made.[6a] Such provisions exposed the Jews to maltreatment, and it was often found necessary to give them special assurances that they would not be locked inside their quarters, and that their freedom to come and go as need arose would not be curtailed. These strongholds gave their occupants the protection they needed both as merchants and as Jews and, at the same time, the Jews rendered the king a service by defending these positions against foreign assault and domestic insurrection.

The contribution of the Jews to the development of an urban economy in Spain is quite clear. New Jewish communities came into being and old ones were revived in a manner similar to the rise of the Christian municipalities. Sometimes, a Jewish community was organized independently, aiming at economic self-sufficiency, and at other times the Jews participated from the outset in the economic life of a Christian city. Upon the conquest of an old city or the founding of a new one, the Jews were usually assigned plots of ground for the construction of dwellings, workshops and stalls, as well as for cultivation.[7] Detailed records of many such grants in Aragon and Catalonia are extant. The process continued into the thirteenth century. A Hebrew contract from Barcelona, dated 1165, confirms the following transaction: Preciosa daughter of Nathan bar Isaac, her husband Nathan bar David, and the latter's brother Isaac, sold to Isaac bar Judah "the stall which we have in the market place, which had belonged to our father . . . who sat and did business therein all his life." Mentioned as adjoining this stall are "the shop of the Christian, Julian the shoemaker, on the one side, the old city tower on the other side, the stall that had belonged to Jacob bar Solomon on the third, and the street on the fourth side."[8] Jewish officials of the count approved the construction and sale of stores in the market places of Barcelona and Gerona, and probably pursued some business or craft in those markets themselves. The royal bailiff Jafia (Yahia) had a workshop in Lerida.[8a]

Several documents describe Jewish participation in the economic development of Huesca. In 1170 two Jews contracted to build a series of stalls for the bishop of the city. The bishop undertook to provide the materials and some supervisory personnel. The Jewish contractors were to receive two of the stalls in perpetual lease.[8b] In 1190 a group of Jews, men of means and social station, joined in a cooperative enterprise. They received from Queen Sancha, consort of Alfonso II of Aragon, a garden plot in the business district of Huesca with permission to build for themselves houses there. This garden was the property of the convent of Sigena, and the nuns consented to the transfer in return for an annual tax from the Jews. Included in the group were Don Solomon Alfaol, a physician, and Don David ibn Aldaian, who is mentioned elsewhere as the *alfaquim* of Alfonso II. Of interest, likewise, is the designation of one of the group as a *tannador*, that is, a harpist. Several distinguished personalities are signed as witnesses to the royal grant—namely, Joseph, a physician, apparently the personal physician of the queen; Eleazar, the steward of the royal household; and Joshua ibn Shaprut, a landowner of Huesca—indicating that this was no ordinary venture and that these personages were very much interested in its success.[9] In 1218 the monastery of Montearagon gave Joseph ben Moses ibn Baruch, in return for services rendered, a stall in Huesca, on condition that it revert to the monastery after the death of Joseph's immediate heirs. A few years earlier the same Joseph had leased from the monastery a field in the vicinity of Huesca, at an annual rental of a pound and a half of pepper.[10]

We find Jews living on Church land under similar conditions also in Castile and Navarre, but we do not know precisely what economic function they fulfilled. In some cities the Jews had special rights in the *alcaiceria*, a kind of fortified bazaar, such as may still be seen in Jerusalem and other cities of the Near East. Thus, according to certain Spanish codes of law, it was forbidden to take as surety any merchandise that a Jew might have in the *alcaiceria*, nor was a Jewish merchant who had his stall in the *alcaiceria* required to answer to the charge of buying stolen goods, if he had bought the merchandise in question in this stall. Trials between Jews and Christians were sometimes held in the *alcaiceria* rather than in the synagogue.[11] In Tudela, from the latter part of the thirteenth century, the Jewish community held the *alcaiceria* and the shops of the silversmiths and shoemakers in lease from the crown.[12] The occupants of these shops were, of course, all Jews. These arrangements must have originated during the Reconquest, or even earlier.

Many of the Jews who settled in the cities, under the protection of the Christian rulers, had been brought up in an Arab environment, and some continued to speak Arabic. They were frequently joined by immigrants from southern France. The founders of new cities invited Jews to settle in them, just as they invited Christians, both native and foreign. The terms of settlement were worked out through negotiations on an individual or group basis. When Moses ibn Ezra took up residence in distant Estella,[13] his friends, and even he himself, expressed serious concern. But it must be assumed that the poet had assured for himself a secure existence there by agreement with the local ruler, as was customary in those days. The king of Navarre had established a colony of Frenchmen in Estella in 1090, and three years later Jews were already living in its citadel and in a nearby village. The privileges of the Jews of Estella were famous, and the city seems to have held a great attraction for the Jews of the neighboring countries despite the many changes of fortune suffered by the local community.[14] A short time after the death of Moses ibn Ezra, R. Moses ha-Parnas, a member of an illustrious family of Narbonne, moved to Estella, "driven by informers. He enjoyed the favor of the king, became very successful, and died there."[15]

Some of the new settlers brought money to help them reestablish themselves. Others, having lost their fortunes in the political upheavals, had to rely upon their talents and their ability to adjust quickly to new circumstances in order to secure the patronage of the Christian princes. Modern historians, who are inclined to be impressed by the remarkable energy of the medieval city-builders and creators of urban economies, would do well to take notice of the Andalusian Jews, whose world had collapsed about them, but who nevertheless, mustered sufficient courage and strength to acquire new positions under difficult conditions. Not only did they succeed in saving themselves, but they helped organize states and build cities. This sheds new light on the economic history of the Jews. Biased historians have wrongly accused the Jews of failing to participate in the development of urban economy in Europe during the transition from itinerant trading to commerce and industry in fixed establishments. These accusations stem from an inadequate knowledge of the economic history of the Jews in northern Europe. The truth of the matter is that it is possible to find even there evidence of a desire on part of the Jews to participate in the new developments; but the dispersion of the Jewish population, and the unceasing persecutions and repeated spoliations which it suffered, forced it into the restricted and distasteful pursuit of moneylending. Even in Spain, beginning with the thirteenth century, there were forces which tended to restrict the economic activities of the Jews. As the Spanish kings began to copy the policies of the kings of France and England toward the Jews, the Spanish Jew started to approach, sociologically speaking, the German Jewish type. The process, however, which turned the Jew into a professional moneylender had not yet been completed by the end of the twelfth century, and in Spain moneylending never did become a principal or characteristic Jewish occupation.

The Jews were legally the property of the rulers of the land, its kings and princes. In some cases, other temporal and ecclesiastical authorities were given the right to keep Jews, settle them on their land, collect taxes from them, and utilize their services. During the twelfth century, especially in Aragon, the military Orders of the Knights Hospitalers and the Knights Templar, who supported the counts of Barcelona and the kings of Aragon in the Reconquest, acquired such special rights over Jews. But generally speaking, the Jews in Spain, as in all of Christian Europe, were regarded as the personal property of the king. This principle followed directly from the teaching of the Church Fathers that the Jews were doomed to eternal servitude. A clear formulation of it is given in the municipal charter (*fuero*) of Teruel, of the year 1176, which served as a model for other cities in Aragon and Castile: "The Jews are the slaves of the crown and belong exclusively to the royal treasury."[16] This theory had practical application. Whereas Moslem captives of war were sold as slaves, Jewish captives were not. Instead, the Jewish communities were permitted to ransom them.[17] Religious as well as sociological considerations made a special status for the Jews imperative. The Khazar interlocutor of Judah Halevi's philosophic dialogue observed correctly that

> God has a secret purpose in preserving you, and he has
> made the Sabbaths and the festivals the strongest means
> of preserving your integrity and dignity. For the nations
> would certainly have broken you up and made you their

slaves because of your intelligence and clarity of thought, or they would have made you their warriors, were it not for these festivals which you observe so conscientiously.[18]

The legal dependence of the Jews upon the king was a decisive factor in determining their social position. That they were fully aware of it even at a much later date is indicated by the statement that,

> Divine Providence bestowed this favor upon us, so that we would not be sold as slaves by our enemies, who would traffic in us and hold us in perpetual bondage as they do to Negroes and other peoples. We remain in the hands of the kings of the earth and are slaves to kings and not to slaves. So was it in Egypt, and so has it also been throughout this long exile of ours. The Jews in all the lands of their dispersion are the property of the kings and princes, the lords of the land.[19]

In the affairs of everyday life this vassalage was barely felt. In the new cities which sprang up during the Reconquest the principle of equal rights for all inhabitants—Christians, Jews and Moslems—usually prevailed.[20] These rights were granted to them as members of religious and national groups rather than as citizens of one common country. The individual communities remained separate political entities. A special government official supervised the affairs of the Jewish aljama (*i.e.*, community). The aljama paid its special taxes directly to the royal treasury and enjoyed administrative and judicial autonomy. Its specific rights were embodied in charters which were issued to some Jewish communities as early as the eleventh century. The number of such charters still extant, dating back to the twelfth century and later, is quite large. The oldest charters merely defined the juridical relations between Jews and Christians and between Jews and Moslems. Such provisions were often included also in the municipal charters (*fueros*) of various localities. The rights of the Jews in Spain, as in the rest of Europe, are a development from the Jewish privileges of the Carolingian period. They are based on the premise that the Jewish community is a separate political body, distinct from the Christian burgher and peasant estates. The principle of equal rights, stressed in the *fueros*, applied in practice only to economic matters as governed by civil law. It did not everywhere apply to matters of criminal jurisdiction, such as assault and homicide. Political and social equality was not even implied. That was a privilege, rarely attained even by Jews close to the royal court. In isolated instances, all elements of the population became aware of the existence of common interests, but only the respective communities, not the individuals in them, were equal in status. The laws governing judicial procedure point up this fact very clearly.

In a lawsuit between a Jew and a Christian each of the litigants was required to support his claim through the joint testimony of members of both communities. Likewise, judicial authority in such cases was, according to the widely copied *fuero* of Teruel, vested in a court of arbitration, composed of one Jew and one Christian, chosen by the litigants. Appeals from its decisions could be taken to a higher court of arbitration consisting of two Jews and two Christians.[20a] Each community had its own executive officer to carry out the decisions of the courts. He could secure the claims adjudged his side by impounding the property of the opponent. The city judge (*judex*) performed this function for the Christians, and a constable who was called by an Arabic name, *albedin* or *alvedi*, performed it for the Jews. This officer still functioned at a later date in many aljamas in Aragon and Castile.[21] If the plaintiff won his case and could not compel the defendant to abide by the court's decision, either the *judex* or the *albedin* was empowered to arrest the defendant, be he Jew or Christian, and turn him over to the plaintiff. If the plaintiff was Jewish, the entire Christian community could be held responsible for the satisfaction of his claim, and vice versa.[22] However, the merchandise that a Jew had in the *alcaiceria* could not be touched. No trials were held either on the Christian or the Jewish Sabbaths and holidays. According to some of the law codes, a Hebrew *shetar* (promissory note) could be admitted as evidence against a Jewish debtor,[23] and such was actually the practice until a very late date.

There was considerable diversity among the several *fueros* regarding the application of the Jewish oath and its exact text. The formulae of these oaths dated back to the gaonic period and, being of Jewish origin, there was at first nothing in them degrading to the Jew. But the very fact that the text of the oath is given in the law codes is evidence of mutual mistrust between the two communities. The Jews were interested in reducing the number of anathemas and curses in these oaths, whereas the Christians wanted to make them all the more strict.[24]

An accepted method of that day for deciding a dispute was the duel; but the laws provided that it was not to be resorted to in suits between Jews and Christians.[25] This exception may have been motivated by a desire to limit the rights of the Jews, although it may well be assumed that the Jews themselves were averse to a procedure so foreign to the spirit of Judaism. Merchants in general were reluctant to trust their cause to so irrational a judicial method. The bearing of arms was still common among the Jews of Spain at this time and, as previously shown, the Jews at times fought in defense of their cities. Jews were sometimes exempted by law from military service.[26] But also the Christian burghers and merchants sought to reduce their military obligations. No doubt the Jews in Spain, as in other countries, showed little inclination to military activity, a characteristic distinguishing them from the Christians.

Differences in status between Jew and Christian appear in the payment of wergild (*caloña*) for injury and murder. The wergild of a Christian was payable to himself or to his family.

The wergild of a Jew was paid to his master, the king. The amount of a Jew's wergild was everywhere determined by political considerations. The king and the Jews were interested in keeping it high; the Christian knight, burgher and peasant sought to reduce it. Hence the wide disparity on this subject in the *fueros*.[27] The matter was one of great importance. The king often took severe measures to protect his Jewish protégés. The troubadour Bertran de Born complained that one of his friends had been "sold" to the Jews by Alfonso II of Aragon. This friend and another had quarrelled with a group of Jews and killed one of them. The Jews asked the king to surrender the murderers to them, offering him a sum of money. The king yielded to their request and the murderers were burned by the Jews on Christmas Day—so goes the troubadour's tale.[28] The king might impose a collective fine upon a locality where Jews were murdered. To this period belong the laws which hold the entire city, in whose environs a Jew was found slain, responsible for the murder.[29] Conversely, every rebellion against the crown brought with it outbreaks of violence against the Jews. We mentioned earlier the disturbances which followed the death of Alfonso VI. A revolt likewise broke out in Leon in 1230, upon the death of Alfonso IX, and all the Jewish communities of the kingdom were destroyed.[30] When Toledo was threatened by the Almohades, in the late twelfth and early thirteenth centuries, the Christian forces, fired by crusading zeal, attacked the Jews, in spite of the latter's participation in the defense of the city.[31]

In the early charters the Jew appears as a merchant and man of wealth, not as a professional moneylender. Jews and Christians figure alike as both creditors and debtors.[32] Only toward the end of our period do the laws begin to treat the Jews as a special group permitted to take interest from Christians. They also regulate the rate of interest, the placing of collateral security, and the evidence required in lawsuits arising from loans.[33] Certain provisions of the early *fueros*,

89

such as the one prescribing death by fire for carnal relations
between a Christian woman and a Jew or a Moor, or another
which assigns each of the separate communities a different
time for using the municipal baths, give evidence of rising
religious and racial tension.[34] Beginning with the latter part
of the twelfth century, a growing tendency to restrict the
rights of the Jews appears in the *fueros,* especially those of
the kingdom of Leon.[35] The impression is gained that in certain regions the principle of equality was disappearing. The
Christian municipality now becomes the controlling authority
and it takes the Jews under its protection, as in contemporary
Germany. The king is still the supreme overlord and the Jews
continue to pay him their annual tax, not directly into the
royal treasury, however, but through the city officials. In
addition, the Jews are now also required to pay a real estate
tax into the municipal treasury, "as if they were citizens
(*vezinos*)." The Spanish cities never attained any considerable
degree of autonomy, and therefore did not, as a general rule,
succeed in gaining complete authority over the Jews. They
strove toward that end, however, ever more strongly during
the ensuing period.

SOCIAL AND SPIRITUAL CONFLICTS WITHIN THE COMMUNITIES

We know little of the inner life of the Jewish communities
at this stage. The Jews of northern Spain enjoyed sound
economic conditions, which gave them every opportunity to
develop their native talents, but they possessed neither the
high level of secular culture of Andalusian Jewry nor the
traditional learning cultivated in the talmudical academies of
France. We have seen the attitude of Moses ibn Ezra toward
the "barbarians" of the north. Above this Jewish population,
primitive in its way of life, there now rose in Toledo, Saragossa, Barcelona, and other large centers, a small but influential intellectual aristocracy, high in the favor of the court.
The two strata of the population were to merge eventually,

but as yet they were different and apart. In Toledo there were the families of Ibn Ezra, Ibn Shoshan, Alfakhar, Halevi Abulafia, Ibn Zadok and a few others.[36] They were the acknowledged leaders, not only in Toledo, but in all Castile. They farmed the state revenues, went on diplomatic missions to the Arabs, and in their rise or fall carried their communities with them. In Barcelona and Saragossa the families of Sheshet (Perfet), Benveniste (Bene venisti), and Eleazar were dominant.[37]

One of the most famous Jews in Spain in the second half of the twelfth century was Sheshet ben Isaac Benveniste, who was *alfaquim* (physician) and bailiff to Alfonso II and Pedro II of Aragon. His home was in Saragossa and later in Barcelona, but his activities extended to numerous other places. He sometimes accompanied the king on trips abroad. He and his brother Benveniste owned urban and rural property throughout Aragon and Catalonia and were the beneficiaries of certain state revenues. They were exempted from the payment of tolls on rivers or on land and they were removed from the jurisdiction of the local authorities, both Jewish and Christian. Both brothers were celebrated among the Jews as scholars, poets and patrons of learning. Their fame spread far and wide. A Jew of Mayence, Germany, travelled to Barcelona to be treated for an ailment by Sheshet. In the year 1200, Benveniste was sent by Pedro II on a mission to the king of Morocco. The journey was financed by a loan borrowed from a Christian. The original deed of this loan, which is still extant, bears the signatures of King Pedro, his mother, Dowager-Queen Sancha, several Christian functionaries of the court, and signatures, in Hebrew, of Benveniste and two other Jews.

Jews in such high positions were removed from the jurisdiction of local administrative and judicial authorities, which, in effect, conferred upon them the legal status of the highest nobility of the realm. Their signatures on state documents, alongside the signatures of the king, prelates and other dignitaries, testify to their high rank. Like the knights who distinguished themselves in war, they were the recipients of generous grants of land along with political privileges. Alfonso VIII of Castile gave his *almoxarife*, Abu Omar Joseph ibn Shoshan, a gift of an estate near Toledo with the privilege of "immunity," which meant exemption from taxes and freedom from invasion of his property by state officials.[37a] The notaries of Toledo designate these Jewish notables by the florid Arabic titles usually reserved for prelates and knights, an indication of the esteem in which they were held.

The Jewish courtiers enjoyed a special status in the Jewish community as well. Because of their success at court, Davidic lineage was ascribed to them, the title *Nasi* bestowed upon them, and they were allowed whatever special privileges they arrogated to themselves. Some of them were exempted by the crown from the jurisdiction of the aljamas, and were subject neither to its taxation, judicial power, ordinances or bans. Several families of Aragonese Jews, descendants of men who distinguished themselves in the service of a military Order or a monastery, still enjoyed, several generations later, an inherited status as "free Jews" in their communities.[38] A favorite way of rewarding a faithful Jewish official was to assign him an income from the slaughterhouse of his community. The first recorded instance of such a grant is the one made by Count Ramon Bereguer IV of Barcelona, who ordered that his steward, Eleazar, receive two pounds of meat daily from the Jewish slaughterhouse of Saragossa. Similar levies upon the aljama were imposed from time to time for the benefit of other favored Jews.[39]

These unique prerogatives, which continued to be exercised for generations by the descendants of the original recipients, became a burden upon the aljamas. In 1281 this custom aroused the indignation of the moralist and mystic Isaac ibn Sahula of Guadalajara, who, in his work *Meshal ha-Kadmoni*

(Parable of the Ancient),[40] lists among those who merit no share in the world-to-come:

> the communal warden who rules high-handedly in the manner of Jeroboam, his associates and followers, who appoint the butchers, sell ritually unfit fats, and love goblets of wine. And when the slaughterers slaughter an animal, the butcher has to summon them. May the wrath of God fall upon them there, when the one claims before the judge, "This portion is mine," with his friend standing by, and they weigh him also a choice cut.

A democratic movement within the Jewish communities, seeking to abolish the special status of this aristocratic group, arose early in the thirteenth century. In 1212 the aljama of Huesca complained to Pedro II of Aragon that it suffered a loss of prestige and excessive burdens through the withdrawal of local Jews from its jurisdiction. The king was sympathetic and proceeded to right the wrong. He cancelled all deeds of exemption issued by him or by his predecessors and restored the "free" Jews to the jurisdiction of the aljama, making them liable to all communal obligations. What is more, the king decreed that, should any Jew thereafter seek the protection of a Church institution in order to escape the authority of the aljama, his person and property shall be forfeit to the crown and the aljama may force its will upon him through the ban, the impounding of his property, and other means of compulsion at its disposal, "and, if you wish, you may fall upon him and stone him to death," paying only his wergild of 1,000 *sueldos* to the crown. Punishment of the last sort has no basis in Jewish tradition, and is not analogous to the treatment of informers with whom we shall deal later on. What we have here is a relic of the primitive custom, in vogue in the young Spanish towns, whereby the townsmen wreaked their vengeance upon anyone who dared circumvent communal authority.[41]

It is not difficult to define sociologically the type of Jew who was reluctant to submit to the organized authority of his community. Several of the men mentioned in the above document were among the group who settled in Huesca in 1190 under the protection of the convent of Sigena. One of them bore the title "Sahib al-Shorta." They belonged to that well-educated class which still cultivated Arabic culture and at the same time participated on a grand scale in the economic development of the country. A wide gulf of political, social and cultural differences separated them from the Jewish masses.

One finds allusions to this situation in *Divre ha-Alah we-ha-Niddui* (The Words of the Curse and the Ban), of Judah ben Isaac ibn Sabbatai.[42] This poet moved in aristocratic Jewish circles in Toledo and later in Saragossa. He composed a work eulogizing the scholars, poets and notables who came to the aid of their people in time of stress, and included in it an account of the exploits of "the five kings of Spain." He seems to have been the first Jew to interest himself in the chronicles of the Spanish rulers and was impressed by their achievements. This fact, along with some of the book's contents were enough to cause pious Jews of Saragossa to declare it a work of heresy. "Vicious foxes and scorpions . . . stupid and heartless folk" excommunicated the author and publicly burned his book in the courtyard of the synagogue. The poet retorted with an incisive satire, reviling his prosecutors and accusing them in turn of intimacy with their slave girls, of informing, of tax evasion and like crimes. There is no way of telling whether there was any basis to these charges. Undoubtedly, the traditionalists, whom the poet calls "men of folly," made up the great majority of the Jewish population.

About this time also a certain Samuel Benveniste stirred up a revolt in the community of Barcelona. He defied the family of the *nesiim* and denounced the synagogue regulations which had been laid down by the late *nasi*, Sheshet ben

Benveniste, by authority of powers granted him by the crown.
It was said also that he spoke irreverently of Rashi and
in his discourses made light of tradition. R. Machir ben
Sheshet, one of the last of the *nesiim*, took the matter to the
rabbis of Provence, among whom was R. David Kamhi. They
imposed penance upon the offender and sentenced him to go
to the nearby communities of Gerona and Tarragona, there
to confess his sin and suffer the lash.[43] The *nesiim*, who wielded
great authority in Barcelona, Toledo and other communities,
maintained their positions, both within their communities as
well as in their dealings with outside powers, by virtue of
their wealth and culture.

> Culture and wealth [wrote Judah ibn Sabbatai in a work
> dedicated to R. Todros Halevi of Toledo] are the leaders
> of the generation. Possessions and honor precede them
> when they venture forth. Both are of equal worth, and
> each pursues the course it deems best and suits its char-
> acter most. The one says, "I have found it," and the
> other claims, "I have found it." The one says, "It is all
> mine," and the other asserts, "It is all mine." But it is
> evident without doubt that division is not the law here.
> For it is clear to every seer and prophet that each needs
> the other, neither being sufficient by itself.[44]

A further study of the writings of Judah ibn Sabbatai and
his colleagues, Judah al-Harizi and Joseph ibn Zabara, may
help to delineate the character of this period more sharply.

R. Todros Halevi and his kinsman, Joseph ibn Alfakhar,
carried to a successful conclusion the religious purge begun by
Cidellus and continued by Judah ibn Ezra. With the help
of the crown, they drove the remnants of the Karaites out
of their last refuge in the fortresses of Castile.[45] But while
they thus prided themselves on preserving the purity of the
orthodox faith, members of their own circle and even of their
own family were accused by the religious zealots, and it seems
with good reason, of harboring even more dangerous heretical

beliefs. The rift between the ancestral religion and the rationalism of the prominent men of the day was becoming more pronounced. It broke into the open in the early part of the thirteenth century in the Maimunist controversy, which cast a deep shadow over a long period of the history of the Jews in Spain.

THE MAIMUNIST CONTROVERSY

Rabbi Moses ben Maimun, "the marvel of his generation," "who calmed the tempestuous seas of doubt," was recognized during his own lifetime as sent by Providence to be the true guide of his people, to harmonize the faith of the fathers with the thinking of their sons, and "to restore glory and grandeur to its pristine abode, to the select of mankind . . . making them a unique nation on earth." His very personality allayed all fears for the nation's survival. Generations later, in times of persecutions and forced conversions, the wavering found solace in his *Epistle to Yemen*, wherein he reviews the three long epochs in the history of Jewish persecution in order to strengthen the faith in redemption. He sought to revive *semikha* (ordination of rabbis and judges) which had lapsed shortly before his time, on the eve of the crusades. He was one of the firmest believers in the divine selection of Israel and in his people's ultimate redemption. But in his attempt to weld religion with philosophy, Maimonides was no more successful than his predecessors. He started out to save Judaism from the undermining effects of philosophic rationalism, and wound up by giving reason primacy over tradition. He had the courage to put the living Oral Law into the framework of a code, and he sought to find a rational basis for the commandments. The talmudic *aggadot*, and the references to *Ma'ase Bereshit* (Mystery of Creation) and *Ma'ase Merkaba* (Mystery of the Divine Throne-Chariot in the vision of Ezekiel) he took to be allegories. He gave the messianic belief a prominent place among his "Thirteen Articles of Faith," and thus contributed more than any other teacher of the Middle Ages to strengthening the people's hope for redemption. But he divorced his eschatology from the messianic ideal and gave the concept of Resurrection an unorthodox interpretation. The compromise that Maimonides effected between the popular religion and the demands of reason and science was accepted by the religious Jewish intellectuals of southern Europe as the only solution to their spiritual conflict. It was especially welcome to the learned of southern France who cultivated both the Talmud and the sciences, and to the polished aristocrats of Spain who let their reason and natural instincts guide their lives. There were many, it would seem, in Spain, who found in Maimonidean philosophy convenient support for their extreme liberalism. These men accepted only a faith of reason and rejected the popular beliefs. They put rational understanding ahead of the observance of the commandments and denied the value of talmudic *aggadot*.

Hispano-Jewish society was divided into an aristocracy pampered by the elegance of wealth and Arabic culture, and the backward masses, primitive in their outlook and way of life. Spanish Jewry's contacts with eastern Jewry were growing progressively weaker during the second half of the twelfth century; instead, the social and religious patterns developed by the Jews of France and Germany were beginning to infiltrate into Spain. R. Gershom, "Light of the Exile," Rashi, R. Jacob ben Meir (Rabbenu Tam), and their contemporaries had founded shrines of Palestinian learning both in the new commercial centers and in remote forest retreats of central Europe. They had created a new homeland for the social and religious ideals of our sages, on a soil that offered only limited economic opportunities. They had taught their communities to die a martyr's death in time of trial. The talmudical academies which they had founded were able to give the Jews of the small communities of Europe farther north a more homogeneous education and to inspire them with a more harmonious spirit than was possible in the turbulent atmosphere of the south, so full of conflicts and contradictions. To be sure, the face of even these small French and German communities presented a richer variety of social and cultural facets than we are inclined to think. Small as they were, these communities seethed with the same social ferment which rocked the Christian municipalities then struggling toward autonomy. The eve of the twelfth century saw the appearance in the German *kehillot* of an oligarchy which leaned toward secularization and the restriction of the rights of the poor. In reaction to these trends, both north and south European Jewry were swept by new popular currents whose similarity to contemporary Christian movements cannot be denied, the parallels and analogies being all too obvious. This unrest affected both social forms and religious thought.

At the very time that philosophy, in the Jewish camp, began to undermine or even to sidetrack the mythic and ritualistic framework of Judaism, the dominant Augustinian theology of the Church sought a compromise with Aristotelian philosophy, relying heavily in the attempt upon Jewish thinkers, notably Maimonides. The Church at this time felt compelled to embark upon a ruthless crusade against the neo-gnostic sects of Languedoc. It was eventually assisted therein by a new type of humble friar, men who themselves at one time had been close to heresy, who now travelled from land to land preaching a return to the religion of poverty of the Gospels and a new spiritual life. The work of Francis of Assisi and his followers in Christian society was paralleled by the efforts of R. Judah he-Hasid (the Saint) and his disciples among the Jews. The pietists of Germany, like their forefathers who had founded the communities and academies in the Rhineland, still drew vigor from the vitalizing fountains of talmudic lore. And even though they were influenced by theological ideas and popular beliefs current among their Christian neighbors, these simple men understood the fundamental principles of the lore of our sages better than any other generation in the history of the Diaspora. They did not seek to set aside the accepted methods of study and the established Halakha, but rather to make its day-to-day application more strict, conforming to the judgments of the "Celestial Tribunal," before which no legal quibbling avails, no partiality exists, social and economic inequalities vanish, and absolute equality prevails, as it prevailed at the inception of the universe, when God first created man.[46]

Even more explosive potentially was the lore of the mystics which had its origin in Languedoc (better known in Jewish literature as "Provence"), and thence spread to Spain in the beginning of the thirteenth century. While primarily theoretical in character, it contained by implication certain social objectives, as will appear later. Its gnostic-dualist element was at variance with the teachings of the sages of the Mishna who combatted all forms of religious dualism and sought to keep the mysteries of the universe secret. Parallel lines of development can be traced in the growth of Cabalism and the rise of the neo-Manichean Catharist movement in Christianity. They differ, however, in their impact upon the religious society from which each sprang. The Christian Church, with philosophy as an ally, declared war unto death against the heresy, so that the latter's influence upon established thought came to be only indirect. In Judaism the alignment was different. Basically, the cabalistic lines of thinking were akin to the mythologically colored outlook of those generations which had given Judaism its authoritative formulation. This new lore, therefore, fused successfully with the faith of the ancients and gave it strength and support in its struggle against the undermining influences of philosophic rationalism. The aims of the Church were something separate and apart from the everyday needs of the European population, so that, despite the theological controversies, the nations of Europe continued their normal political development. But the religious conflict within the Jewish people touched the very basis of Jewish survival in the Diaspora. Philosophic rationalism did not content itself with questioning the value of many of the laws and legends. It negated the very meaning and purpose of the *Galut* by denying the value of the nation's suffering in exile and of its survival in spite of its tribulations, even while it failed to seek a political solution—which, to be sure, did not enter anyone's mind in those days. It thus prepared the ground for the apostasy of later generations. Out of these fundamental differences grew the internal conflicts which plagued Spanish Jewry for three hundred years, to the ultimate profit of Christian propaganda.

The opposition to Maimonides in Spain began while the sage was still alive. His writings were severely criticized by Meir ben Todros Halevi Abulafia, one of the leaders of the Jewish community of Toledo.[47] On the other hand, Maimonides found an able champion in the *nasi*, R. Sheshet of Barcelona, whose great political influence has already been noted. In a letter which he wrote in the course of the controversy, Sheshet pointed with pride to his knowledge of world history and referred to his contacts with one of the scholars attached to the court of the king of Morocco. He ridiculed the judges of the Castilian communities who were wont to sit in trial and pronounce judgment singly, without fear of being challenged by anyone, because of the widespread ignorance. But now that the Code of Maimonides had arrived in Spain, their decisions were no longer above question, for anyone could open the book and dispute the law with the judge. He severely censured his adversary, and called him a fool who construed the concept of Resurrection literally. This Jewish statesman was surely in practice a loyal son of his people, but intellectually he had become estranged from them. His own faith was based principally upon the empirically derived laws of nature and of history.

Meir Halevi Abulafia sought to enlist the support of the

French rabbis for his plan to place the writings of Maimonides under the ban; but the reactions to his suggestions ranged from extreme caution to blunt rebuff. The deteriorated political situation may have been responsible. In 1182 the Jews had been expelled from the then tiny kingdom of France. It was the first instance of an expulsion from an entire state, no matter how small. They were permitted to return a short time later, but remained continuously harassed by the baronage, the clergy, and the populace which could easily be incited to violence by the charge of ritual murder. The French theologians revived the Augustinian theory that the Jews were condemned to remain in perpetual bondage to the Christian kings, and Pope Innocent III gave it the sanction of official doctrine in his bulls and letters. The centers of Jewish culture in Languedoc were caught in the crusade against the heretics and suffered heavily. From the Fourth Lateran Council, convened in Rome by Innocent III in 1215, issued strict decrees against the Jews. They were not permitted to charge excessive interest on loans, they were to be distinguished from Christians in their dress, and they were not to exercise authority over Christians. Converts were to be kept under surveillance lest they relapse into their old faith. Gregory IX, who continued the fight against heresy, also directed his attacks against the Jews. The integrity of the Christian faith was especially endangered by the propaganda which Jews carried on among converts and by the rationalist approach to religion, disseminated by the Jewish intellectuals. The center of all this tension was Languedoc, the land of inveterate heresy, and its capital, Montpellier.

The fire of religious controversy broke out in Montpellier in 1232 or somewhat earlier, and soon spread to the Jewish communities of southern France and Spain.[48] Quite suddenly reports began to circulate about liberal-minded Jews who ridiculed the words of the sages, scoffed at commandments, and, relying upon the authority of Maimonides, interpreted the legends of the Talmud allegorically. A distinguished talmudic scholar, by the name of Rabbi Solomon ben Abraham of Montpellier, and two of his disciples, R. Jonah Gerondi, who was to gain fame later on, and David ben Saul, issued a protest against the liberal opinions current in intellectual circles in Narbonne, Beziers and Lunel. "They rose against us," the liberals complained, "to libel us wickedly, turn popular feeling against us, to lash and disgrace us."[49] The anti-Maimunists enlisted the support of the rabbis of northern France, who put the writings of Maimonides and all secular learning under a ban. Whether this ban contained calumnies of Maimonides himself, as the Maimunists claimed, is not certain. The ban of the French rabbis, the *Tossafists,* was met with a counter-ban by the admirers of Maimonides, and both parties turned to Spain to seek adherents to their cause.

In Spain, where social antagonisms influenced religious thinking, the differences were even sharper than in Languedoc. The man most sympathetic to the cause of the zealots of Montpellier was Rabbi Moses ben Nahman (Nahmanides) of Gerona. His personality was the product of diverse influences: the Spanish cultural background, French talmudism, German pietism, the mysticism of the Cabala, and an acquaintance with Christian theological writings. He was the scion of an aristocratic family of Gerona. One of his few extant poems,[50] which may be taken as a personal confession, reveals that the youth of this mystic and ascetic had been spent in the full enjoyment of life in an environment not unlike that of the Christian urban society of southern Europe, in which the songs of the troubadours, the lore of the gnostics, and the preaching of the ascetics all found a hearing. This type of life is reflected more fully in the poetry of the friend and admirer of Nahmanides, Meshullam ben Solomon da Piera. Nahmanides was at this time in the prime of life and was looked up to by his teachers and colleagues in Gerona as their leader and the man summoned by Providence to be the champion of tradition. He identified himself unequivocally at the very outset with the position taken by the zealots of Montpellier, but his tactics were different.

He addressed a letter[51] to the aljamas of Aragon, Navarre and Castile, reminding their leaders of their duty to guard the scattered flock of Israel against foreign influences, "to bring back those who have strayed and strengthen the enfeebled," and if need be "use the shepherd's rod." The integrity of the Jewish religion sustained Israel in exile to this day. "Wholehearted faith shields us from sin so that we perish not." But now a spark has kindled which threatens to flare into an all-consuming fire. "We suffer in silence, lying on a bed of pain, for smoke rises from the earth like the smoke of a kiln." He therefore admonishes "the princes of Aragon, the nobles of Navarre, and the notables of Castile," to offer counsel that would restore peace in the land. For the Maimunists, "seducers into sin," have already begun to circulate their "glib writings" in Spain. They wrap themselves in the mantle of the pious, but are really hypocrites, "a rebellious sect, feigning piety to ensnare souls." If the rabbis of France slandered Maimonides, Rabbi Solomon of Montpellier is not responsible.

The aim of this letter was to restrain the Spanish communities from taking steps against the traditionalists of Montpellier. It seems, however, that Nahmanides sent a second letter in which he presented also a positive program to the Spanish aljamas. This is evident from a letter he wrote to the rabbis of France.[52] Nahmanides begins this letter to his northern colleagues with a reverent salutation and proceeds to protest against the ban which they had imposed upon anyone who read the *More Nebukhim* (Guide of the Perplexed) and the *Sefer ha-Madda'* ("Book of Knowledge," the first book of Maimonides' Code, containing some of his philosophic ideas). He defends Maimonides, "who erected a talmudic stronghold, a tower of strength to the Lord and a shrine for the ignorant masses, who breach the fences." "Throughout the Diaspora, in Spain and the west, in Palestine and the east, he was regarded as a great savior. He recalled many who had strayed from the faith." Whatever Maimonides wrote was intended to uphold the faith and was meant, not for the Jews of France, but for Jews of the southern lands who are consumed by the sword of freethinking and apostasy.

> May you, Sirs, be spared a pain such as ours; for the sons have strayed from their father's table and have contaminated themselves with the food and wine of the Gentiles; they mingled among the nations and learned their ways. Even the sword of apostasy is active, alas, in the captivity of Israel in Spain. Men in the royal service have been permitted to study Greek science, to learn the art of healing and the science of measurement, and all the other sciences and their application, so that they may earn their livelihood in the courts and palaces of the kings.

Maimonides had used his influence to drive the Karaites from the Egyptian court. The Yemenite Jews mention the name of Moses ben Maimun in the *Kaddish*. What will they say when they hear of the ban pronounced by the French rabbis? The affair is liable to lead to a schism in the ranks of Jewry. "The Torah would be divided into two Torahs and all Israel into two sects." Nahmanides therefore suggested that a detailed program be drawn up, with the consent of the several communities and the concurrence of Maimonides' son, R. Abraham, who resided in Egypt, a program adapted to the times and to local needs, setting forth a graded plan for the study of secular learning.

Nahmanides' intentions are clear. He hoped to free his people from the embrace of the outside world and the lure of its culture and royal favors, and to lead it back to the "four ells" of Jewish law and lore. But Nahmanides was a realist. He took existing conditions into account and sought to remedy them gradually. Had his plan been adopted it would not only have changed the program of education but would have revolutionized completely the entire pattern of life of the Spanish diaspora, and many of the differences that divided eastern Jewry from that of the west and the Jews in the north from their brethren in the south would have disappeared. It was a great and noble plan, but its realization depended upon the cooperation of all the Jewish communities.

In the summer of 1232, the Aragonese aljamas—Saragossa, Huesca, Monzon, Calatayud and Lerida—proclaimed the ban against R. Solomon of Montpellier and his associates in reprisal for their excommunication of those who read the *Guide* or the *Book of Knowledge,* or pursued secular studies. Among the signatories of the Aragonese proclamation were members of the leading families of that day. The first to sign was Bahye Alconstantini, whose public career will be treated in a later chapter.[53] Most of the Catalonian aljamas, it seems, identified themselves with the ban,[54] since the Sheshet family exercised decisive influence over the communities of the province. Nahmanides and his sympathizers stood alone in the northeastern part of the peninsula. Nahmanides himself, in a letter written about this time, unfolds the social background of this conflict between the traditionalists and the Jewish courtiers.[55] He tells the story that on one occasion he failed to protest against the arrogance of "the haughty of Barcelona (a reference to the Sheshet family) and the Ishmaelites (*i.e.,* the Alconstantini family) of the court," and was punished for it.

The Alconstantini family, like its predecessors at court, claimed the prerogatives of *nesiim* and obtained from the king a writ investing them with supreme rabbinical and judicial authority over all the aljamas of Aragon. After a while, they fell out of favor as a result, probably, of a new turn of political events. The Jewish population then lodged complaints against them before James I, and the latter sought the advice of Nahmanides. Nahmanides provided the king with a definition of the office of *nasi* in Israel and stated that "it has been our custom from time immemorial that fathers can bequeath to their sons only portions of which they are worthy." He thus declared his opposition to the political prerogatives assumed by the *nesiim,* which hitherto had gone unchallenged. The office of *nasi* (in the sense of tracing descent from the Davidic dynasty) had already lost its splendor by that time, as is evident from an opinion expressed by R. Abraham, son of Maimonides, whose views were similar to those of Nahmanides.[56] Nahmanides exposed the misdeeds of the powerful courtiers, calling them

> men of unclean reputation, full of confusion, guilty of vile sins. Why [he asked] is our generation different from all others, that in our time sinners are abetted and men suspected of immorality are invested with authority and honors. The community is sold, for nothing, to men who do not pray, recite no grace over their meals, are not careful with their bread and wine, and secretly even desecrate the Sabbath—veritable Ishmaelites.

A similar situation existed also in Castile.

R. Meir Halevi Abulafia of Toledo, who had risen to defend tradition a generation earlier, now addressed a reply to Nahmanides.[57] He praised R. Solomon of Montpellier as "the stem of faith, the well of wisdom and understanding." His opinion of the new rationalism had not changed; but the older man evades Nahmanides' request "to defend zealously the honor of our Torah and our teachers and to be in accord with the rabbis of France." He points to the situation in Toledo. "You have heard and know that I too am surrounded by thorns and nettles and dwell among scorpions." Even before the *Guide of the Perplexed* had reached there, "some of the people turned their wayward and rebellious hearts away from religion." The great wars between the Christian kings and the desert tribes who invaded the peninsula from Africa did not make them repent. "Even when they saw the tents of Cushan (that is, the African tribes) and the sword of Dishon and Dishan (that is, the Christians), and smoke rising from the earth like the smoke of a kiln, the people neither repented their ways nor turned back, neither listened to instruction nor embraced faith." R. Meir had more in mind than theoretical heresies that may have been discussed among scholars, as the next chapter will show. He had before his eyes an aristocracy which cultivated philosophy, not as a means to a higher spiritual life, but as a convenient rationalization for a life of pleasure. It was that same society upon which Judah Halevi had turned his back in his day, and which had learned nothing from the catastrophic events. We can sympathize with R. Meir who asks, "How can a man who is powerless to reform his own community reprove others far away?" In vain had he himself risen zealously to defend the faith thirty years earlier when he had seen "that the traditional belief in Resurrection was disappearing among the dwellers of towns unfortified (by faith) and wanton cities." It was the bitter outpouring of the soul of a man who had early appraised the situation correctly, but had found no support in his struggle.

About half a year after the Aragonese aljamas had published their ban, R. David Kamhi set out from his home in Narbonne for Toledo to try to prevail upon the elders of that community to underwrite the ban proclaimed by the Maimunists. Detained by illness at Avila, he dispatched a letter outlining his position to the physician Judah ben Joseph Alfakhar, one of the leaders of the Toledo community.[58] Kamhi apparently turned to him as the one among the elders of the community whom he regarded as his intellectual kin. But Kamhi had misjudged both the character of the men and the conditions in Toledo and in Spain generally. He could not, therefore, understand the blunt rebuff which he received. Alfakhar told him in his reply, "You regard the *Guide* as your teacher and guide; but among us it serves as a pretext for the wayward and defiant." "Why, then, do you sin by making of the *Guide* a new Law?" The Maimunists will eventually lead the Jews to apostasy. "They will lead the hearts of the Israelites astray so that they will seek to forswear their faith."

Similar in tone was the letter which R. Joseph ben Todros Halevi,[59] the brother of R. Meir, wrote somewhat later to the scholars of Provence, calling attention to the wide disparity between the teachings of Maimonides and the preachings of those who presume to be his disciples, "the rabble, every one of whom considers himself a philosopher . . . so that he might profane the sacred and absolve himself of the duties of prayer and *tefillin*." Now they have sent R. David Kamhi to Spain, "to seduce the dwellers of unfortified towns and wanton cities, and to provoke strife." "But I and all who are solicitous for the word of the Lord, sanctified the name of the Lord before the elders of our people and we dealt with him (that is, Kamhi) according to the decree of our teachers in France, until my father-in-law, R. Nathan, drove him from the city." According to R. Joseph, there were two types of people who held fast to the *Guide*.

> One group are the hypocrites who falsify the Law and secretly transgress it; who bow their heads like a reed; who put on righteousness, but it does not clothe them. The other group are the wealthy, engaged in pursuit of pleasure, who move the boundaries of the world. They are sinners and seducers, who chatter and prattle, who grow fat and arrogant, who force the poor off the road, who forsake the paths of equity and neglect the Torah in opulence.

These are harsh words, but they are amply borne out by documents written some three decades later, whose testimony undoubtedly applies to this period as well. The letters of both R. Joseph and R. Meir bear witness to the social conflicts existing within the Jewish community of Toledo.

The letters of these anti-Maimunists did not reflect the opinions of the majority. R. Joseph ben Todros found it necessary to stress the fact that the letters of approval that R. David Kamhi carried back from Toledo to Narbonne, "had not been approved by the *kahal* nor had they been written and signed with the knowledge of the rabbis." Apparently there must have been some in Toledo who openly subscribed to the ban against R. Solomon of Montpellier; and the brothers, R. Meir and R. Joseph Halevi, and R. Judah Alfakhar had great difficulty in opposing them.

The social and religious conflict did not reach its full denouement at this stage. We have only scant information concerning the end of the controversy in Montpellier, and even that is of questionable reliability.[60] According to a tradition that stems from Maimunist sources, R. Solomon and his followers invited the Franciscans and the Dominicans and even the papal legate himself to intervene in the matter and, as a result, the *Guide* and the *Book of Knowledge* were condemned by an ecclesiastical tribunal and publicly consigned to the flames. The papal legate, Cardinal Romanus, was in Montpellier at this time, directing the campaign of extermination against the Catharist heresy. Also, the aforesaid monastic orders were in 1233 empowered to proceed with the inquisition of heresy. It stands to reason that the newly created Inquisition wanted to look into Jewish religious matters, as it was wont to do later on. Canon Law, to be sure, did not give the Inquisition the right to interfere in internal Jewish affairs, but this was overlooked where there existed a danger of Jewish influence upon the Christian population. It is quite likely that the *Guide* was brought before a tribunal of the Church and certain passages in it were found to border on heresy. But it is inconceivable that the entire book was condemned and burned, since only a short time later the Church utilized the work in support of its own doctrines. The controversy among the Jews may have caused the Church to examine the controversial *aggadot* of the Talmud and finally order its destruction. The information which has reached us is full of contradictions and of partisan prejudice and it is impossible to determine what actually happened. One thing, however, is certain. The controversy in the Jewish camp opened the door to Inquisitional intervention in internal Jewish affairs. Whether the Maimunists or their adversaries were responsible for it we do not know. Neither side, it seems, had any scruples about turning to the Church for aid in suppressing the ideas which it regarded as heretical. So much for what happened in France. As for Spain, this controversy uncovered the first symptoms of the deep social and religious ferment which will be treated in the chapters to follow.

III

CASTILE AT THE END OF
THE RECONQUEST

The Jews in the Reconquered Andalusian Cities

The Castilian kings, Ferdinand III (1217-1252) and Alfonso
X (1252-1284), and the Aragonese James I (1213-1276) completed the work of the Reconquest. James I captured the
Balearic islands in the years 1224-1233, recovered Valencia in
1238 and Jativa in 1244. Ferdinand III reconquered most of
the Andalusian cities: Cordova fell in 1236, Murcia in 1241,
Jaen in 1246, and Seville in 1248. Alfonso X completed the
work of his father. During the course of these campaigns Jews
were again entrusted with tasks such as they had carried out
during the early Reconquest. In Aragon, whose rich archives
are well preserved, the treatment of the Jews can be studied

more fully than in Castile, whose records are incomplete and scattered. The unique character of Spain and of Spanish Jewry is, however, best traceable in the central portion of the peninsula, where Arabic influence did not cease, rather than in Aragon, or in Catalonia, which was closest to Rome and Paris, the two capitals of Latin Christianity. We, therefore, consider it proper to begin this chapter with the history of the Jews in Castile.

We have no detailed information on the Jewish policy of Ferdinand III. We know only that he granted the Jews some privileges, promulgated laws of a religious nature unfavorable to them, and employed Jews in his service. He no doubt adopted in the conquered Andalusian cities the same policy which was pursued by his successor and by the king of Aragon. Like their forerunners of the early Reconquest these kings utilized the counsel and assistance of able and well-to-do Jews and assigned them the task of resettling the destroyed areas and the cities which had been evacuated by the Moslems. In Seville, as earlier in Cordova,[1] Ferdinand III allowed the Jews to remain in their old quarter in the center of the city, near the cathedral, which had been converted from a mosque. He died before the distribution of the confiscated properties in Seville was completed; and final disposition was left to his son, Alfonso X. The latter dealt harshly with the Arabs and befriended the Jews. Jewish officials of the court—*almoxarifes, alfaquims,* ambassadors (*mandaderos*), astronomers and one secretary (*escrivano*)—received houses, vineyards, olive groves, fields and mills in and around Seville. These grants were made in perpetuity and the recipients exercised absolute control over their property. They were required only to pay specified taxes and to see to it that the houses they received were inhabited. Most of the beneficiaries were former residents of Toledo.

While the king was as generous in bestowing favors upon his Jewish courtiers as he was in rewarding the knights who fought at his side in battle, he was in this instance motivated primarily by his desire to resettle the depopulated city. Those who remained in the city after its reconquest were well-treated. One of them, Joseph Sabbatai (Rabi Yuçaf Çabaçay)—who is also mentioned in a contemporary collection of Hebrew poetry—received from Alfonso X in 1255 a writ confirming the property rights "which he had enjoyed under the Moors" over a stall opposite the cathedral, "behind the stalls of the Jewish money-changers." Whereas all the mosques throughout the rest of the city were converted into churches, the Jews were allowed to retain the three mosques located within the judería and convert them into synagogues, an act which violated Canon Law.[2] Later documents show that the Jews contributed actively to the economic rehabilitation of both Cordova and Seville. In some instances, also, Jewish residents of the reconquered Andalusian cities entered royal service and moved to Toledo, as others had done before them during the earlier stages of the Reconquest.

A comprehensive document of 1266, detailing the apportionment of property in Jerez de la Frontera, lists ninety buildings that were assigned to Jews. Again, most of the beneficiaries were Jewish court officials, residents of Toledo and other Castilian cities, some of whom also received properties in Seville. A few are described as *ballesteros,* which in the usage of the time meant mounted bowmen employed as military scouts, guards, or police. Of the latter, some received houses in the Jewish quarter, while others were settled among the rest of the *ballesteros.* This is further evidence of Jewish military participation in the Reconquest.

Among the Jews listed were also old residents of the city who had lived there before it was captured by the Christians. Some of them were deprived of their houses, while others, who received houses, lost them later. Some of the Jews suffered during the conquest of the city and the Moslem revolt which followed. One householder was deprived of his house because he failed to occupy it, and it was given to another Jew, "for being a good man and good citizen." Later, the original owner brought an order bearing the royal seal, restoring the house to him, and it remained in his possession thereafter. Among the home owners were also artisans. The aforementioned document indicates that Jerez de la Frontera had a well-established Jewish quarter, with synagogues and other communal institutions, even before the Reconquest, and, as almost everywhere else, there were Christians residing inside the judería and Jews outside it.[3]

In 1272, the Jews of Murcia were assigned their own quarter, probably the same one in which they had lived under Moslem rule. Here they were expressively forbidden by Alfonso X to reside among the Christians; this is the first evidence of increasing religious pressure upon state colonization policy.[4] At nearby Orihuela, a Jew is reported to have fallen in battle, fighting for the Castilian cause.[5]

We haven't sufficient information for a detailed description of the Jewish factor in the Castilian colonization policy. The listings in the *repartimientos* (bills of apportionment) of extensive Jewish landed possessions record, in part, a distribution of property which had existed under the Arabs. While the Moslem nobility, though not the peasantry, were completely expropriated by the conquerors, the Jews received the same treatment as the Christians. Jewish holdings of land in Andalusia appear to have increased during the thirteenth and fourteenth centuries, not only through the constant additions to their possessions made by the influential Jewish courtiers, whose estates were in any case usually confiscated by the crown after their death, but also through the more modest but more permanent acquisitions by small landowners. Jews also acquired urban real estate through the construction of dwellings, stores and workshops. The Christian burghers regarded the Jewish policy of the monarch with disfavor. Several Andalusian municipalities, such as Cordova, Carmona, Alicante, Seville and finally Murcia, even succeeded in wresting from the king the privileges, first obtained by the city of Toledo in 1118, which restricted the rights of the Jews. But the king made it clear that the provision forbidding Jews to hold state positions would not apply to the office of *almoxarife*. Only the Christian municipal judge was permitted to pass judgment in a lawsuit between a Jew and a Christian. In Murcia, however, this provision did not apply where the *almoxarife*, who might be a Jew, sued to collect taxes.[6] These local privileges were not always put into effect, be it in Toledo or in Andalusia. But other forces, more far-reaching, were building up, which were to neutralize the benefits to the Jews of the favorable royal policy.

ALFONSO X's LEGISLATION AND THE JEWS

In the middle of the thirteenth century the legal systems of all the Christian states of Europe, Castile and Aragon included, underwent considerable change. In line with the prevalent tendency, Alfonso X sought to limit the force of the special privileges of individuals and municipalities, which formed until that time the basis of the juridical system in Castile, and to replace them with a national system of law, uniformly binding upon all elements of the population. The influences of both Roman and Canon Law are discernible in the legal compilations of the time, whether prepared under royal auspices or privately edited, as well as in individual enactments. As far as the Jews were concerned, this legislation aimed at once to apply the Canon Law to them and at the same time allow them a certain measure of humane consideration in the spirit of Roman Law. It sought to abolish the contradictory privileges of the Christian municipalities and the Jewish aljamas. For a long time these remained purely theoretical objectives. The aljamas retained their status as separate political bodies, distinct from the municipalities and in possession of special privileges. From without, the influence of Church legislation, as formulated by Pope Innocent III and his successors, made

115

itself felt. The decrees of the Fourth Lateran Council became the subject of negotiations in Castile early in the reign of Ferdinand III. The Jews were required to pay to the Church the tithe for their land and to wear distinctive clothes or even a special badge.[7]

At the very beginning of his reign, Alfonso X enacted legislation regulating the life of the Christian estates in Castile. He restricted the display of luxury and even went so far as to fix the appropriate garb for each estate. For the Jews extreme simplicity in dress and adornment was ordered.[8] He sought by law to prevent Christians from consorting with Jews and thus exposing themselves to Jewish religious propaganda. In the spirit of the Justinian Code he limited the civil rights of Jews, Moslems and heretics, forbidding them to be the heirs of orthodox Christians, or to serve as their attorneys and executors of their wills.

The spirit of the Church permeates the famous code of law associated with the name of Alfonso X, *Las Siete Partidas*. This code did not go into effect until the middle of the fourteenth century, and its legislation affecting the Jews never carried much weight. It does, however, reflect the ideological currents working upon the mind of the monarch. The code confirms the Church legislation concerning the Jews. It denies them the right to hold public office and forbids Christians to accept medical treatment from Jews. It carries prejudice even further and prescribes a special judicial procedure for cases of the blood libel, to which the king and his jurists gave credence despite its denunciation by Pope Innocent IV. At the same time the code accords a certain measure of humane treatment to the Jews. It forbids breaking into and robbing a synagogue, "for a synagogue is a house where the name of God is praised." The Jewish Sabbaths and holidays are to be respected in accordance with the time-honored privileges of the Jews.[8a] Of greater practical importance were other laws, not included in the *Partidas*.[9] The legal rate of interest on loans extended by Jews to Christians was fixed at thirty-three and one-third per cent (33⅓%). The Christian estates sought to have abrogated the privileges of the Jews whereby they were able to place their Christian debtors who defaulted on their payments under arrest while they themselves remained immune against such arrest, and also their right, in litigation over money with Christians, to carry their appeals directly to the tribunal of the royal court. These privileges remained a constant source of contention as late as the second half of the fourteenth century.

Alfonso X also fixed the formula of the Jewish oath, a rather enlightened one for the time, and included it in the official law codes. In some of the lesser codes, having only local force, he yielded to the requests of the Christian estates and modified the penalties in criminal cases between Jews and Christians. But the desire of the jurists to abolish the wergild for injury and murder and substitute a state imposed penalty for personal monetary compensation met with the opposition of the Christian population wherever the change tended to favor the Jews.[10] A uniform legal system for the entire country, equally binding upon all its inhabitants, was still a long way off. The municipal *fueros* and the oft-confirmed privileges of the Jews were in frequent contradiction to the new codes. The Castilian crown had an interest, after all, in protecting the life and property of the Jews and especially their loan operations.

The canon of the Church which forbade its adherents to take interest on loans from fellow Christians began to be enforced in Spain in the thirteenth century, and only then did moneylending become a Jewish specialty. The social-economic aspects of this phenomenon will be treated later on. At this point we want to point out the influence of the problem thus created upon state policy and legislation affecting the Jews. Agitation motivated by religious and racial bias exaggerated the problem beyond its real importance. The interests affected were primarily those of the few capitalists in control of public

117

credit. The loan business of the Jews residing in small towns and villages could scarcely have had any influence upon the economy of the country generally. But the constant harping upon this question by the Cortes from the middle of the thirteenth century on made it appear the very crux of the Jewish position in the state and in Christian society. The legislation on the subject changed, therefore, in accordance with the fluctuations of the political balance, which sometimes favored the Jews and at other times affected them adversely. On the one side was the demand to fix the interest rate by law, with guarantees for its strict enforcement—though in a more moderate manner than was done in Aragon—while, on the other hand, the state assisted the Jews in the collection of their debts through the assignment thereto of special constables (*porteros, entregadores*), who undoubtedly deducted a certain percentage for the state and for their own benefit. This procedure was still new in the reign of Ferdinand III. It was improved and perfected as time went on.[11]

ALFONSO X AND THE JEWISH COMMUNITIES

Alfonso X encouraged the growth of Jewish communal autonomy. The aljamas possessed extensive criminal jurisdiction and they must have received the authorization for it from the earlier rulers of Castile.[12] Even during the reaction which set in toward the end of his reign, Alfonso X did not in any way limit this right. The administrative officers (Hebrew *mukademin*, Spanish *adelantados*), the "elders" and rabbis of the Jewish communities, adjudged disputes between Jews, but with the right of appeal to the king's tribunal granted to each of the litigants. The king reserved the right to intervene directly in lawsuits between Jews and refer them to his tribunal. The *alcaldes* (judges) of the palace court, however, had to have the *mukademin* and rabbis sit with them to advise them in rendering a decision. The Jewish judges dispensed justice according to the laws of the Torah and the decisions of contemporary talmudic authorities.[12a] The king might appoint, in a given locality or province, a superior "elder" whose duty it was to supervise all Jewish judicial matters in that area. In state documents, from the reign of Alfonso X on, the title *el rab* appears, to designate, very likely, crown-appointed chief rabbis or justices who enjoyed great social and political prestige.

Such a position was held by (*el rab Don Todros*) Rabbi Todros ben Joseph Halevi Abulafia, who is glorified in contemporary Hebrew literature as the "prince of the Spanish diaspora."[13] He was a member of an aristocratic family of Toledo, distinguished for its wealth, learning and piety. He knew the ways of the court and could turn out verses in courtly style. But as a mystic and an ascetic who practiced what he preached, he personified the very antithesis of the current tendency among Jewish courtiers to assimilate the ways of the Christian knighthood and the licentiousness of the royal court. He enjoyed the confidence of Alfonso and his consort, Violante. He and his son Joseph were among the recipients of houses and estates in Seville and Jerez de la Frontera. In 1275 he accompanied the king and queen on a journey to France. R. Todros remained in Perpignan with the queen, while the king proceeded to Beaucaire to meet Pope Gregory X for a discussion of international affairs. We learn about this incident through R. Todros' meeting in Perpignan with the poet Abraham Bedersi and from their subsequent exchange of verses. The poet, unfortunately, does not indicate R. Todros' official position which made it necessary for him to be in the queen's retinue. Possibly he was her personal physician, although neither the Castilian documents nor the Hebrew sources mention him as a physician. At court he was recognized as the chief rabbi and justice of all the Jews of the realm. The man chosen by the king to head all the Jews of his kingdom was by far the most worthy of this honor. Alfonso X evidently was interested in permitting the Jews to order their inner life in accordance with their own cherished aims and traditions.

JEWISH COURTIERS AND THEIR ADMINISTRATIVE POSITIONS

The friendly relations between Alfonso X, the Wise, and the Jews extended beyond the realm of politics. The king, himself a scholar and patron of learning, extended to Jewish scholars a hospitality not to be found in the courts of any of his contemporaries and surpassing even that of the Hohenstaufen Emperor Frederick II, whose association with learned Jews was far less permanent. Participating in the preparation of the famous Alfonsine astronomical tables were R. Isaac ibn Cid, the *hazzan* of the Toledo synagogue, and R. Judah ben Moses ha-Kohen. The latter, also known as Don Judah Mosca, was rewarded with some property in Jerez de la Frontera. Other Jews served the monarch as *alfaquims* and interpreters.[14] A son of Nahmanides was in the service of the Castilian court.[15] A German-Jewish cabalist, R. Abraham of Cologne, made his way into Alfonso's circle.[16] A versatile aggregation of Jewish scholars and scientists thus surrounded the learned king.

Our interest centers chiefly about those Jews who served the crown in administrative and diplomatic posts. Whereas in Aragon, Jews were being effectively forced out of these positions by the end of the thirteenth century, the social and political character of Castile permitted Jews to function in these capacities through the thirteenth and fourteenth centuries. The Castilian state represented a strange blend of the traditions of the Arab princely courts, the institutions of agrarian feudalism, and the fundamentals of Christian piety. The state administration lay principally in the hands of the higher clergy and nobility. Alongside them there grew up a class of knights of humble birth and of merchants who for one reason or another gained the favor of the king or one of the infantes. Competing interests filled the court with rivalry and intrigue. The fiscal administration was entrusted to men with commercial experience.

A nephew of Alfonso the Wise, the Infante Don Juan Manuel, a hero of the Reconquest and a writer gifted with delicacy and perception, gives an accurate account of the functions reserved for men of humble birth in the government of an aristocratic kingdom. Men of the merchant class, he says, are preferred for the administration of finances, for their sensibilities need not be respected like those of the nobility. An accounting may be demanded of them, and, where malpractices are discovered, punishment may be inflicted upon their person and property without hesitation.[17] But the Christian third estate offered few qualified candidates. The Castilian urban population, unlike its counterpart in Aragon, remained closely attached to the ways of life of the knighthood and peasantry whence it sprang, and took a greater interest in the pursuit of the war against the infidel than in the development of commerce. It could not, therefore, supply public servants for the fiscal organization in sufficient number, and Jews had to be called in to fill its posts. The Jews obviously could not be used to staff the military command and the higher courts; but they were to be found in almost all the other departments of the government. Their diplomatic and fiscal duties frequently required them to draw up treaties with foreign governments, principally Arab, and to sign royal decrees governing the constantly expanding economic and financial administration. Already in the reign of Alfonso X some Jews bore the title of royal secretary—an office which carried with it a variety of hard-to-define duties—and their number increased throughout the fourteenth century. The physician-in-ordinary to the king occupied a post of great political significance. In Portugal he was entitled to a seat on the crown council. In Castile, and at times even in Aragon, Jewish court physicians exercised an influence upon state affairs. Alfonso X had a number of Jewish physicians among his trusted advisers. In the diplomatic service Jews were to be entrusted, according to Don Juan Manuel, only with certain specified missions, that is, those involving negotiations with the Moslems, and these too not without proper precautions.

For an accurate description of the services rendered by Jews to the state one can rely neither upon legal compilations nor upon the works of the Christian moralists and chroniclers who, insofar as they could, passed over these Jewish contributions in silence. Their silence, however, is eloquently contradicted by the facts. The Jewish officials of Alfonso X performed functions similar to those carried out by the Jews who, in the midst of the unsettled conditions of the twelfth century, directed the financial affairs of the Christian conquerors and their economic and diplomatic relations with their Moslem vassals. Yet the functionaries of Alfonso's court resembled more closely the modern type of financial administrator and economic policy-maker. To be sure, attempts to introduce a rational fiscal administration were still tied to a policy of economic exploitation. But it is to be hoped that further studies into the manner in which Hellenist-Arabic administrative procedures were transmitted by way of Spain to the other European countries, they will reveal the contributions of the Jewish *almoxarifes* of Castile to this development. A handful of Jews, mostly residents of Toledo, together with a few Christians, organized the administration of taxes and other finance for the entire kingdom. They made all the necessary expenditures out of the royal treasury. They paid the salaries of the knights, supplied food, clothing and arms to the armies in the field, and took care of the needs of the royal household. They undoubtedly also exerted an influence upon economic legislation.

The relations of the prelates and the grandees to the Jews was generally the same as that of the king. Juan, bishop of Burgos and chancellor of Ferdinand III, entered into business relations with a Jewish physician and several Jewish financiers. The master of the Order of Santiago entrusted the management of the Order's vast domains to Jews.[18] Such cases were undoubtedly far more numerous than our incomplete documentary sources reveal. The petty nobility, however, proved far less friendly. The troubadours in their songs voiced bitter complaints against Jewish fiscal agents who, it was charged, deprived the knights of their just pay.[19]

The Jewish financiers and intellectuals, together with the members of the Church hierarchy and the feudal baronage who composed the royal retinue, lent the court—always on the move, never bound to a fixed residence—its colorful character. The work of the Moslems at court, unlike that of the Jews, was confined to specialized scientific endeavors. The Jewish courtiers readily assimilated the ways of knighthood, maintained amicable relations with the other court circles, and took part in the unceasing rivalry for royal favor. Their sycophantic verse in the Hebrew and vernacular tongues fell upon the susceptible ears of the "poet-king." In the tradition of Judah Halevi's day, they also honored one another with encomia couched in florid verse. Between the Jewish notables and their coreligionists dependent upon them a relationship developed similar to the one existing between the feudal barons and their retainers, the knights and troubadours.

The poet Todros ben Judah Halevi,[20] one of the younger members of the courtier set, left us a vivid portrayal of the life of the Jewish aristocracy in the reign of Alfonso X. His own career at court began auspiciously, under the aegis of powerful patrons, some time after 1270. The state of political affairs at the time is reflected in his poetry. The external security and inner integrity of the Jewish communities depended even now, as it had in the small principalities of the eleventh and twelfth centuries, upon the political fortunes of the notables who stood at their head. Thus, when the *almoxarife* Don Meir ibn Shoshan returned from a diplomatic mission to Morocco—probably in 1276, when a truce was signed between Castile and Morocco after years of warfare—the young poet cried out in exultation, "The sighs are gone—relief has come!"

> The evil days are over, and gone are the years when tyrants oppressed,
> When villains amassed riches and arrant rogues great wealth possessed,
> When asses, fit to carry straw or fodder, went laden with precious gold,
> When boors and sinners were exalted and fatuous knaves grew bold,
> When the nobles of the earth were humbled low, and fools the starry heights attained.
> Today, your enemies are in their own fetters bound and their princes are in irons chained.[21]

The most powerful of the court Jews during the early part of our period was Don Solomon ibn Zadok of Toledo, who is called Don Çulema in the Castilian documents.[22] During the reign of Ferdinand III he was entrusted with the collection of tribute from the king of Granada. Under Alfonso X he served as ambassador (*mandadero*) and chief collector of revenues (*almoxarife mayor*). He was highly respected within his own community for his generous endowment of synagogues and charitable institutions. Young Todros Halevi lavished upon him such high praise as had not been accorded to any Jewish notable since the days of Judah Halevi and Moses ibn Ezra. When Solomon died, in 1273, all of his property in Seville, Carmona and Ecija, consisting of houses, vineyards, olive groves and warehouses full of goods, was confiscated by the king and donated to the cathedral of Seville. He undoubtedly also left some property in his native Toledo.

Todros Halevi's own patron at court was Solomon's son, Don Isaac ibn Zadok, who was called in Castilian Don Çag de la Maleha.[23] A journey through Castile, in the company of his patron, is described by the poet in exaggerated metaphors.

And it happened in the dear and delightful days of our youth, when this noble (Don Isaac) was "prince and commander of nations," that we travelled through the vineyard country, boldly for all to see, accompanied by a large retinue of wealthy, worthy and wise men. We made a tour of all the Castilian ports. Time was kind to us and the days were pleasant and free from fear. . . .

When we passed through the salt marshes, they turned gold mines for us. We travelled pretentiously, in regal style, over hill and mount. . . . We went a-dancing, holding hands with fair and well-born maidens. . . . Gifts came pouring in from all sides . . . great revenue, and tribute in endless flow. . . . Then we embarked upon the sea in a ship and my heart was trembling with fear. But the old man was like a father to me and showed me great love and compassion. He praised the Lord at the sea's shore and prayed to God, whose works are awe-inspiring. And when the noble lady, her eyes deep blue, not with eye-tint but with native charm, sat in our company, there was naught but song and cheer. . . . When we returned we were met by the lords of Edom, in the service of his exalted office.[24]

Todros Halevi also comments on the decrees of Alfonso X, fixing prices and placing restrictions upon luxurious living. These laws, which were prompted by the country's economic needs and by the monarch's own religious and moral scruples, often missed their mark and caused discontent among his subjects. The coinage was also devaluated twice during Alfonso's reign, to the great dissatisfaction of both Jews and Christians. The Jews were directly involved in these experiments, either as the economic advisers or the victims of this legislation. Our poet satirizes the royal policy in a semi-jocular vein,

When the king commanded his subjects all
That every thing, whether large or small,
For half its worth be sold to all,

> The merchants and traders in dread
> Before the royal inspectors fled;
> The king and court in rags went dressed,
> No better than the poor oppressed;
> The grandees sought but could not find
> A pigeon or dove, or food of any kind.[25]

The chronicler of Alfonso X relates that the Christian population was bitter over these laws, which undoubtedly also failed to please the wealthy Jews of Toledo. Don Çag de Maleha was authorized to grant exemptions from the regulations. For a time he directed all economic matters that went through the royal chancellery. "He clothed one of his friends in purple and finery of all sorts, gave him delicacies to eat and let him ride in chariots and on steeds." The poet, who was the beneficiary of Don Isaac's liberality, thanks him profusely and extols him as the savior of his generation. "The troubles are gone . . . sighs have turned into smiles . . . for the Lord remembered the affliction of his people and sent the noble Isaac to be the mainstay of the communities." On this and other occasions the poet appeals to the influential courtier for special privileges, clothes, food, or a mule for riding. He complains of his rivals who have turned his patron's heart against him, and he reminds Don Isaac of the happy days they spent together.

Don Isaac's good fortune came to an abrupt end.[26] The king ordered his arrest and imposed an exorbitant tax on all the Jews of the kingdom. The continuous unrest of the feudal nobility since the year 1270 was largely responsible for this drastic turn of events. The nobles demanded the abolition of the harbor tolls and of the special imposts (*servicios*). One of the rebellious grandees, Don Nuño de Lara, claimed the salt concession held by Don Isaac. One of the Jewish court astronomers, Don Abraham Alfaquim, was captured by the rebels and held as a hostage. Only after the suppression of the uprising by the king in 1275 were the Jewish officials restored to power at court. Later that year Alfonso X travelled to Beaucaire to meet the pope and renounce his claims to the crown of the Holy Roman Empire; that was the occasion when the queen's retinue included the venerable Rabbi Todros Abulafia and several other Jews.

The Castilian kingdom was still involved in war with the Moslems to the south; and danger threatened likewise from the north, from France. This was the situation which must have moved Alfonso X to enter into some far-reaching financial agreements with several Jewish capitalists, late in 1276 and early in 1277.[27] The leader of the group was again Don Çag de la Maleha. He farmed from the crown the collection of all tax arrears of the entire kingdom, with the exception of the southern provinces, that had accumulated over the preceding twenty years. All the tax registers for those years were turned over to him for audit. Together with a Christian merchant and Don Abraham ibn Shoshan, son-in-law of the *almoxarife* Don Meir, he farmed the entire current tax on livestock and the fines for encroachment upon the privileges of the shepherds' guild, which later developed into the famous *Mesta*. Two sons of Don Meir ibn Shoshan, Isaac and Joseph, farmed the arrears of the livestock tax. They likewise undertook to secure the return of the wages paid out to knights derelict in their military duties; to retrieve the funds of the local administrations which had been embezzled, or unlawfully expended, or improperly withheld from the crown; and to collect all the unpaid fines of the past twenty years for violations of royal edicts or the forfeit clauses of private contracts. Isaac ibn Shoshan also undertook the collection of all fines for evasion of the export-and-import regulations and the laws governing the disposition of ownerless property, as well as the penalties for violations of royally granted privileges.

These contracts, which were preserved by chance, tell us a great deal about the fiscal administration of Castile. The practice of farming state revenues to individuals was borrowed, apparently, from the Moslem states. The revenue farmers were wealthy merchants, for the most part Jews. Transactions like the above were not unique in the administration of a medieval state. Such measures were resorted to as a means of enforcing long-neglected laws, of revitalizing a decrepit fiscal administration, and, most important, of refilling an empty treasury. There was naturally great resentment among those directly affected by such measures; and when Jews were invested with wide authority, as in this case, the complaints were loud and long. The above venture came to an end in the accustomed manner. A few months after their conclusion the contracts were all cancelled and we don't know whether the contractors even managed to recover the sums they had advanced to the crown. The cancellation of the agreements is not to be taken, however, as a change of royal policy regarding the employment of Jews in the state administration. The fall of Don Çag de la Maleha came later as a result of the struggle between Alfonso X and his son Sancho.

In attracting Jews to the service of the court, Alfonso X pursued the traditional state policy which served the best interests of the country. His personal attitude toward the Jews changed several times. After a frivolous youth, during which he composed merry ballads in troubadour style, he turned serious and wrote the *Cantigas de Santa Maria,* a collection of legends full of fanaticism and bigotry.[28] His legislation shows the same turn of mind. Whether he sponsored missionary work among the Jews, as did his neighbor, James I of Aragon, is not certain, but several known instances of conversion had his blessing and support. The Inquisition, which functioned in Languedoc and Aragon, had not yet been established in Castile, but Dominican and Franciscan chapters existed in every city. It was unavoidable that disputations should take place between the friars and qualified Jews, and contemporary Hebrew literature records their occurrence.[29] Primitive Castile, the western frontier of the Diaspora, was at this time the center of cabalist learning. The eschatological teachings and their leaven of mysticism were influenced by the political and religious oppression suffered under Alfonso X. We are unable, unfortunately, to trace in detail the causes of the vacillating Castilian policy affecting the Jews. The religious leaders of this period, both Jewish and Christian, remained anoymous for the most part. Only a very small fraction of the documents pertaining either to the Jews or to their opponents survive. But these are not the only difficulties. In Aragon it is possible to isolate the objective factors which determined the fate of the Jews. In Castile, however, in addition to the various objective factors—practical politics, religious interests, and class tensions—certain subjective factors often proved decisive, namely, the whims and vagaries of the king's mind.

EXECUTIONS AND IMPRISONMENTS

The sinister side of Alfonso's character was revealed toward the end of his reign, after his imperial ambitions involved his kingdom in the remote politics of the Holy Roman Empire, and later, when he was confronted with an uprising of the nobility and the rebellion of his son Sancho. The treatment of the Jews in the other European countries did not go unnoticed in Spain. Twice during this period the Jews were expelled from France. In England class interests and religio-ascetic tendencies were preparing the ground for their ultimate expulsion. Conditions in Spain had not yet reached this stage; yet a personal caprice of Alfonso X brought down upon the heads of the Castilian Jews the first catastrophic blow whose consequences are known to us in detail.[30]

In 1278, Don Çag de la Maleha, as the head tax-farmer of Leon and Castile, was ordered to forward a sum of money to the army and navy besieging Algeciras. But the Infante Sancho got hold of the money and diverted it to his own ends, and the forces before Algeciras found themselves in dire straits.

The king, in a vindictive mood, imprisoned all the Jewish tax-farmers in 1279. One of them saved his life through conversion. Another, apparently an intimate of Sancho, was dragged to death through the streets of Seville, past the monastery where the infante had taken up residence. Don Çag was hanged. Then, one Sabbath day in January 1281, the king had all the Jews arrested in their synagogues, and did not release them until they agreed to pay him 4,380,000 gold *maravedis*, a sum twice the annual tribute of the Castilian aljamas. Alfonso X thus followed the example set by Philip II of France a century earlier. Many of the leading Jews were kept in prison for several months, where they were subjected to torture and attempts to convert them. We don't know what took place elsewhere, but the Jewish community of Toledo was demolished, like "Sodom and Gomorrah." Only the now aged Rabbi Todros Abulafia remained free, and he did his utmost to secure the release of the prisoners. But he died shortly after 1281, and his son Joseph retired to Talavera, a small community south of Toledo, where he kept aloof from politics for the rest of his life and devoted himself to the maintenance of cabalist scholars. Todros Halevi, the poet, wandered about after his release, going first to Aragon and then to the south, returning to Castile in the reign of Sancho IV. The Jewish court set, now torn by inner intrigue and mutual vilification, was on the verge of utter ruin.

SANCHO IV AND THE OPPOSITION OF THE ESTATES

The last three years of Alfonso's reign were marred by civil war and we don't know how the Jews fared under those circumstances. Under Sancho IV (1284-1295) the Jewish notables regained their influence at court.[31] The military program undertaken by the new king made their services indispensable. Throughout his short reign Sancho IV had to suppress a rebellious nobility; he ended his reign with a victorious campaign against the king of Morocco. The extant documents of this period deal with the activities of certain Jews at court or in the state administration; but they tell us very little about the relations of the crown to the Jewish communities. The few decrees that do concern them deal with differences that arose between Jews and various municipalities or ecclesiastical institutions, and throw little light on conditions within the aljamas. Certain decrees promulgated by Sancho IV at sessions of the Cortes bespeak the pressure brought to bear upon him by the estates rather than the king's own attitude. In 1286 the Cortes demanded the removal of the special, crown-appointed judges (*alcaldes apartados*) who decided suits between a Jew and a Christian. They wished to subject the Jews in such cases to the authority of the local magistrates whose appointment generally lay in the hands of the municipalities. They also sought to abolish the Jewish privileges regarding testimony in such lawsuits. But these demands led to no actual changes as yet. We do know that the Jews bore a heavy burden of taxation. In the small towns in the western part of the country it sometimes happened that the Jews scattered at the approach of the tax collector.[32] The tax registers for the years 1290-1291, listing both the regular annual tax and the surtax (*servicio*) paid by the respective aljamas, show the sums to have remained constant. The economic condition of the individual aljamas also appears to have been taken into consideration. But on top of these regular taxes, additional special levies were exacted from the Jews.

During the reign of Sancho IV, no less than under his predecessor, the state administration was conducted largely by Jews of Toledo. In place of the men who had lost their position during the reaction toward the end of Alfonso's reign came others of the same families as well as some newcomers. The leading personality at this time was Don Abraham el Barchilon, a native of Toledo.[33] He is first mentioned as paymaster of the knights and the court personnel, and as purchaser of cloth for the court. Also the accounts of the local

131

tax-gatherers were submitted to him. Other Jews worked under his direction as tax-farmers and purveyors of supplies. Among them was Abraham ibn Shoshan,[34] already mentioned as one of the leading court Jews of the preceding reign. He was a learned talmudist, and his dicta and commentaries are quoted in contemporary Hebrew literature. Throughout his long life he was held in reverence by the Jewish community of Toledo. During Sancho's reign he served as the *almoxarife* of the queen. On one occasion he was assigned an even more important task. The Cortes of Palencia, in December 1286, decided upon the restoration to the crown of all the property and rights it had given up during the civil war, and Abraham ibn Shoshan was at first charged with the execution of this vast project. But the fiscal reforms at the time went even farther. In June 1287, upon the recommendation of the powerful Count Lope de Haro, the *mayordomo mayor,* the king and Don Abraham el Barchilon entered into a series of agreements as sweeping as those concluded by Alfonso X with Don Çag de la Maleha in 1276.[35] El Barchilon secured from Don Sancho a two-year lease of the principal sources of revenue of the state, first and foremost among them being the crown's prerogative to mint the gold coin of the entire realm. The agreement also embraced: the taxes on livestock; the collection of the debts of Jewish creditors; the disposition of ownerless property; the receipts of a variety of fines and penalties imposed for violation of the economic and fiscal regulations; the export duties; the income of the royal chancellery; the export of mercury; the right to examine the accounts of the earlier tax-farmers; and the collection of all arrears of payments due the crown. In addition, El Barchilon also farmed some salt mines, all the revenues of the *Frontera* (a territory bordering on the kingdom of Granada), as well as the revenues of the *almoxarifadgos* of Toledo and Murcia. El Barchilon thus concentrated in his hand control over the central fiscal administration as well as over some of the local ones. The impression one gains from these agreements is that we have here not merely an emergency measure for eliminating a deficit in the royal treasury, but a serious attempt to introduce thoroughgoing reforms into the state administration. Still another task, one of extreme political significance, was entrusted to El Barchilon: he took over the administration of the program to restore to the crown the domains alienated from it. He was empowered to come to terms with the holders of former royal estates, to issue permits for their sale, and to retain some of them for himself, tax-free. In several documents of the years 1287-1288, El Barchilon renounces, on behalf of the king, all claims to former crown property held by a number of churches and monasteries. These documents were drawn up in the royal chancellery and bear the signature of El Barchilon in Hebrew. On their backs are notes in Hebrew, made, no doubt, by Jewish secretaries of the chancellery.

The investment of a Jew with such broad powers naturally caused resentment among the higher nobility and clergy who were required to give up considerable property upon El Barchilon's decision. In July and August 1288 all the above agreements were cancelled at the demand of the Cortes. However, the opposition of the Cortes was directed against the initiator of these agreements, Count Lope de Haro, who was deposed from his high office and executed; it did not touch El Barchilon personally. The latter continued to perform his administrative duties and in 1290 again farmed the right to obtain the return of alienated crown property, this time in partnership with Todros Halevi.

Todros ben Judah Halevi, the courtier and poet, who together with the other court Jews had felt the wrath of Alfonso's old age, had gone into exile after his release from prison. He returned a penitent man, and for a time lived in pious retirement in Toledo. But he could not long resist the lure of wealth and political activity.[36] The details of his second public career are not known. In 1289 he already held a post in the financial administration. In the years 1292-1294 he

headed a company which farmed the port tolls, the income of
the royal chancellery, and other revenues. His company exercised supervision over all the state finances and could demand
an accounting from officials throughout the country. Sancho
IV, who was pressing his campaign against the king of
Morocco and had taken Tarifa, was constrained to rely
greatly on his Jewish public servants.

The poetry which Todros Halevi wrote after his return to
royal grace bears unflattering testimony to the character of
the court Jews. His own rise and the fall of his rivals the
poet regards as acts of Providence. He thanks the Lord as he
climbs the ladder of success rung by rung. When he received
the news of his recall to court he noted in his diary,

> A call rings in my ear:
> Cóme, the Lord's kindness hear.
> Trustingly, upon it I rely
> And hope to behold it with my eye.
> God, for Thy sake, be gracious unto me,
> For all my thoughts center upon Thee.

When he learned that his patent of appointment and his
contracts were in the chancellery awaiting signature, he cried
out jubilantly,

> Now, with the help of God, the Rock eternal,
> My writs shall be signed and sealed . . .
> His kindness will fill my chambers with riches
> And fate will direct wealth into my home.

Before he went for an audience with the king, he offered
a prayer:

> Before I go to one of flesh and blood, I shall praise
>   God . . . .
> That He might turn to my will the heart of king, grandee,
>   and noble.
>
> May my liege command his vassals
> All their property into my lap to offer;

> Let them come to me from every side
> Until, behold, each man's purse is in my coffer.

> May I find favor, kindness, and compassion in the eyes
> of my liege . . .
> That he may entrust his affairs to me and elevate me,
> And speak no word but through my tongue.

One of the most influential figures at court and in the chancellery, and the one directly concerned with the signing of Todros' patents, was Maestre Gonçalo, abbot of Arvas. We can readily understand why the poet directed at him the following invective epigram,

> The foe who hardened his heart,
> Plagued be he for his part.
> Who has been uprooted?—"The abbot."
> Destroyed and damned be he
> And call him may we,
> "The lost and gone, late abbot."[37]

In May 1293, Sancho IV acceded to the demand of the Cortes that Jews be excluded from the business of tax-farming. He could not, however, allow himself to enforce such a decision at this time. Of somewhat greater practical importance was another concession made by the king at the same session of the Cortes, in abrogating the special privileges favoring the Jews in their moneylending activities. The special collectors of Jewish debts (*porteros de los judios*) were to be abolished, and collection made by the officials regularly exercising such jurisdiction, namely, the *merinos mayores* of the crown and the *alcaldes* of the cities. But even this question remained unsettled for several generations to come. Certain legislation of Alfonso X was renewed. A new regulation provided that thereafter promissory notes would become invalid six years after date. Characteristic of the mood of the Cortes was its demand that Jews and Moslems be forbidden to acquire land either through purchase or through foreclosure, alleging that transfer of land to Jewish ownership resulted in a loss of revenue to the royal treasury. The king not only granted this request and forbade Jews and Moslems to purchase land from Christians, but even ordered them to sell any real estate previously acquired, exception being made only in the case of dwellings. Earlier, in 1288, Sancho IV had forbidden the Jews of Valladolid to buy land in the environs of their city, adding as a reason that, "You know very well that you pay taxes only for movable property." However, none of the aforesaid laws was fully applied in practice, nor were their details ever worked out with sufficient clarity to make their application possible. They are important only insofar as they reveal the interests and aims of those who projected them.[38]

Despite the persistent demands of the Cortes to eliminate Jews from positions of influence in the conduct of the state, Jewish officials continued to serve Sancho IV even as they had served his predecessors. The same men often served both as stewards of the personal finances of the royal family and as high-ranking officers of the central or provincial fiscal administrations. At times they exercised control over the entire national economy. But such authority was never of long duration. Political careers, whether Jewish or Christian, had little permanence in those days. Most of the Jewish functionaries were, as theretofore, natives of Toledo; Others came from the provinces: for example Don Judah (Abravanel) of Cordova, Don Samuel de Belorado, Don Joseph de Avila, Isaac de Faro, and Moses ibn Turiel in Murcia.[39] As ever, Jews were sent as ambassadors to the Moslem courts.[40]

Several Jewish physicians are mentioned in the accounts of the royal chancellery. Especially noted were the physicians of the Ibn Wakar family, Isaac and Abraham, to whose ability and integrity the Infante Don Juan Manuel paid high tribute many years later.[41] Todros Halevi likewise erected a lasting memorial to them in his poetry. One of them is prob-

ably the addressee of the following lovely verses to a friend
about to set out on a journey,

> In thee I found comfort and repose;
> My brother, God speed thee right!
> Who will remain, when thou hast departed,
> To befriend me, lend me might?
> To my ailing spirit thou art strength.
> To my pining heart—the soul's delight.[42]

Todros Halevi seems to have felt a genuine personal attachment to King Sancho IV. The few verses which the poet dedicated to him give the impression of greater sincerity than is
to be found in all the flowery encomia he lavished in his
youth upon Alfonso X. When Sancho IV came down with the
sickness of which he died, Todros wrote,

> Why doth man strain to amass knowledge?
> Is divine oracle (*Ephod*) more valid and necromancy
> vain?
> My king's suffering a faithful sign is
> That he who addeth knowledge addeth pain.

The Infante Don Juan Manuel described in simple yet
touching words the last hours of his king and cousin. The
infante, a young boy at the time, together with the abbot of
Arvas, Todros' rival, and Isaac and Abraham ibn Wakar, the
king's physicians, received from the lips of the dying monarch
his last will and testament. After Sancho died, on the twenty-
fifth of April 1295, Todros Halevi indited the following lines,

> They all cried, the year the king died
> "The ruler gone, can we survive?"
> But I said, when the king was dead,
> "God is my strength, through Him I thrive."

It was apparently feared that the king's death exposed the
Jews of Castile to violence and disaster. And, indeed, the
events which followed in the year of his death turned the
minds of the Castilian Jews to thoughts of penitence and
redemption.[43]

IV

ARAGON AT THE END OF
THE RECONQUEST

THE CONQUESTS OF JAMES I AND THE JEWS AS A FACTOR IN POLITICS AND COLONIZATION

The traditions of the glorious days of the early Reconquest, including the liberal policy toward the Jews, were carefully cultivated by James I (1213-1276), the Conqueror. After his accession to the throne, the young ruler retained in his service members of the same Jewish courtier set which had served his predecessors, Alfonso II and Pedro II.[1] With the resumption of the Reconquest the influence of these men increased. During the expedition against Majorca in 1229-1232 and in the negotiations with the Moslems which followed the surrender of the island, James I had the assistance of two Jewish interpreters of Saragossa, the brothers Bahye and Solomon

Alconstantini. Bahye performed similar duties during the siege of Jativa. He also took part in the negotiations which led to the surrender of Elche and Murcia in 1265-1266, when James I came to the aid of his son-in-law, Alfonso X of Castile, and suppressed the revolt of the semi-autonomous Moorish ruler of the province of Murcia. During this campaign Bahye was assisted by Astrug Bonsenyor, who acted as secretary for Arabic documents.

Jewish participation in the Reconquest, now as during its earlier stages, was not limited to the diplomatic service. They again helped apportion the conquered lands. The *repartimiento* of that section of Majorca which fell to Count Nuño Sanchez of Roussillon, the king's uncle, names the Jew Astrug as an assistant to the procurator in charge of land grants and resettlement in the city of Majorca. We find there awards to several Jews of dwellings, workshops and parcels of land, both inside the city walls and in the surrounding countryside. Among the recipients was Samuel Benveniste, the *alfaquim* of the count. Some of the Jews who settled in Majorca were former residents of Marseilles and other cities of southern France. The citizens of Marseilles had rendered valuable aid in the conquest of the island and were given priority in the distribution of its land. Many of the former residents of the island were banished; but while the list of the expropriated contains many Moslem names, it mentions only a few Jews.

The *repartimiento* of Valencia of the year 1238 contains a number of interesting details. The distribution of the confiscated land was in keeping with the policy followed later on by the Castilian kings in reconquered Andalusia. The Jewish courtiers, like the Christian knights, were rewarded with houses and estates in and around the city. In order to rebuild and resettle the depopulated city, the beneficiaries of these grants were required either to settle in the city themselves or to provide for the settlement therein of other Jews. Among the recipients were several royal *alfaquims*, including the aforesaid Bahye and Solomon Alconstantini and other members of their family. Included also was Solomon Bonafos, who is none other than the royal bailiff (*baiulus*) of Catalonia whose Hebrew signature appears on crown documents of the fourth and fifth decades of the thirteenth century. Other Jews, otherwise unknown, came to settle in Valencia from Barcelona, Gerona, Saragossa, Alagon, Lerida, Huesca, and other places, just as groups of Christians came to settle there from all over Aragon and Catalonia, even establishing separate quarters for the immigrants from each city.

Altogether a hundred and four Jews are listed as the recipients of houses and land in Valencia. Among those who settled in the environs of the city and the surrounding villages the number of Jews is smaller, but then the available registers are not complete. On the other hand, the number of Jews whose property was confiscated is larger here than anywhere else. One of the latter was Joseph Almeredi, who may possibly be identified as the Hebrew poet who later was a resident of Saragossa and served as physician to James I during the last years of the king's life. But if we can draw any conclusion from the Jewish names we meet there later on, the greater part of the native Jewish residents of Valencia remained undisturbed, They even retained their own quarter inside the city walls. The Moors, on the other hand, were expelled from the city. Most of them left the country, and those who remained had to settle outside the city walls. In general the Moslems remained only in the country districts, in a state of partial serfdom.[2]

James the Conqueror maintained throughout his reign a policy of colonization favorable to the Jews. The Jews of Valencia received from the king in 1239 and again in 1244 charters of privilege, guaranteeing them the rights of the aljamas of Saragossa and Barcelona.[3] In 1261 James I confirmed the rights of the Jews in Valencia to buy both urban and rural real estate from any inhabitants of the land, including the nobility and the clergy—an unusual privilege for the time, since it was forbidden, in general, to transfer land from one estate to another. Moorish tenants living on Jewish land were exempted from the special tax required of all Moslem farmers. In 1273 the king confirmed the old boundaries of the judería of Valencia and assured its residents that they would not be moved to another quarter. They were also permitted to buy up any Christian-owned houses within the judería.

In Jativa, the judería was restored after the reconquest of the city, and in 1274 the local Jews received a new charter containing various privileges, including tax exemption for new residents for a period of five years.[4] Among those who answered the call for new settlers was a certain Isaac ibn Janah of Toledo. In 1264 James I promised any Jews who would come to settle in Morella, in the province of Valencia, the rights of the *fuero* of Valencia. A Jewish quarter was established inside the city wall, and the settlers were exempted from taxes for a full year.[5] Transfers of land to both native Jews and new arrivals in the province of Valencia were regularly approved by James I. Both during his reign and that of his successor, Pedro III, Jewish officials increased their wealth in this fashion.[6] They acquired vast estates with allodial rights. It is reasonable to assume, however, that in some cases these had been Jewish possessions also during Moslem rule. Conditions were not quite as favorable for Jewish expansion elsewhere in the kingdom, but the royal policy was on the whole the same throughout.

The Jews of Majorca also received charters of privilege from James I.[7] Twice they were reassured that their quarter would not be moved to another location. The use of Moorish slaves was a vital necessity to the Jews of the island engaged in agriculture, and they petitioned the king to halt the Christian proselytizing activity among the slaves, which resulted in their loss to their Jewish masters. In 1252 James I ordered that Moorish slaves who sought baptism at any time other than the major Christian holidays—Easter, Whitsunday, and Christmas—pay to the royal bailiff the rather high sum of twelve *morabotins*. In 1269 the king added another provision, ordering that slaves entering a church and requesting baptism should be made to wait, in the church, several days before receiving the sacrament—perhaps to allow time for negotiations with their masters. A slave so baptized did not gain his freedom, but became the property of the crown.

In 1247, at the close of a specific phase of the Reconquest, a proclamation was issued extending royal protection to all Jews who would come, overland or by sea, to settle in Majorca, Catalonia, or Valencia.[8] A number of Jews from Sidjilmassa, in the kingdom of Fez, were included by name. About the same time the king granted all the aljamas of the kingdom exemption from the payment of inland customs.[9]

James I also took steps to rehabilitate the Jewish community of Perpignan in the county of Roussillon, which belonged to the crown of Aragon at the time.[10] In 1243 the Jews there were given a parcel of land, in free and full ownership, to settle on. All through his life the king showed great concern for the well-being of this, in the words of the poet Abraham Bedersi, "choice vineyard, which his right hand had planted" in the charged atmosphere, rife with religious tensions, of southern France. He also sought to attract Jews to the part of Montpellier under his jurisdiction.[11]

Following the example of his predecessors, he garrisoned frontier strongholds with Jews. In 1259 the Jews of Uncastillo were moved from the open town into the citadel, and given a three to four year exemption from taxes. The royal *alcaid* was forbidden to enter the fort or to interfere with the delivery of victuals to its occupants. Any Jew facing court action was required to appear in town of his own accord to post bail.[12] Also in Egea and Barbastro the Jews occupied the citadel.

In Calatayud, the Jews obtained permission to enlarge their fortified quarters.[13]

In Barcelona, however, the opportunities afforded the Jews for the expansion of their quarter were rather limited. James I issued but few permits for the construction of synagogues and the repair of cemeteries. Obviously, the motives which governed the treatment of the Jews in Catalonia, socially and economically the most advanced part of the kingdom and the center of the Church's power, were different from those which determined the policy in Aragon, where conditions resembled those of neighboring Castile, or in the reconquered southern territories devastated by war. Along with his encouragement of new colonization, James I also promoted the commercial development of the aljamas, by granting privileges for trade in grain, oil and cattle, and authorizing Jews to open stores in the cities. The consequences of this policy will be discussed later. The tax load was heavy, but the king several times remitted a portion of the tax of aljamas impoverished as a result of fires, drought, or similar disasters.[14]

James I took great interest also in the inner life of the Jewish communities. He issued charters regulating the election of magistrates and rabbis, the tax assessments, the administration of justice, and the general religious and moral conduct of their members. He gave them the right to punish offenders by fine, ban, flagellation, and expulsion. As far as we know definitely, only a very few communities, and those only in Aragon proper, were also invested with capital jurisdiction at this time, but it may be assumed that these were not isolated instances.[15] In the Aragonese kingdom, Church influence apparently prevented the granting to the aljamas of such wide jurisdiction as they enjoyed in Castile.

There were occasions when James I also intervened in Jewish communal matters. We have seen how in 1232, acting upon the advice of Nahmanides, he rejected the claim of the Alconstantini family to the rank of *nasi* and the chief judgeship over all Aragonese Jewry. He took a similar stand in 1271, at the request of his bailiff, Judah de Cavalleria. In general, however, he refrained from interfering with communal autonomy. At the same time, he would personally render a decision, in lawsuits involving dower and inheritance rights among Jews, more frequently than he did in similar Christian cases. He may have been motivated in this by the crown's stake in Jewish wealth, or by a personal interest in Jewish Law. In 1259 he gave a Jew of Montpellier permission to marry a second wife despite the opposition of the communal leaders who argued that the man's action violated Jewish Law and custom.[16] James I maintained contacts with Jews of many walks and counted among his friends, not only financiers and state officials, but also physicians and so saintly a personality as Nahmanides.

Jewish Officials

In 1228 James I, influenced by his clerical advisers, promulgated a series of anti-Jewish laws, among them one forbidding Jews to hold such public office as permitted them to exercise judicial or penal authority over Christians. His practice, however, shows that James I never felt bound by this legislation. Like his predecessors, he appointed Jews to the office of bailiff (*baiulus, baile;* Heb. *gizbar*), which involved stewardship of the *patrimonio real*, a very broad and inclusive term, and there was no sharp line drawn in those days between administrative and jurisdictional functions. Very early in his reign a Jew by the name of Bondia was *repositarius* of Aragon, and another, Abraham ben Saadia, was *repositarius* in Saragossa. A member of the Sheshet family was bailiff in Barcelona. Earlier we mentioned Solomon Bonafos, bailiff of Barcelona, and several other Jewish officials, who were the beneficiaries of royal bounty during the Reconquest.[17]

A detailed study of Jewish participation in the state administration from the year 1257 on is made possible by the preservation in the Aragonese archives of voluminous registers containing copies of all correspondence that went through the royal chancellery after that date. The situation at this time was different from the one prevailing a century earlier when Jews, trained in statecraft in the courts of the Arab princes, could offer the Christian conquerors talent and experience which the Christian knight and ecclesiastic lacked. In the middle of the thirteenth century a Christian burgher class came to the fore in Aragon. Jews still managed to rise to high office by the same means as the Christians. Merchants who advanced money to the crown, and had their loans guaranteed by a mortgage over certain crown revenues, became in the end the administrators of these revenues, or else, they literally bought a bailiwick (*baiulia*) for a sum paid in advance and then proceeded to recover their investment plus a handsome profit out of the taxes they were authorized to collect. In this way textile merchants and horse traders often rose to become state officials and in some instances even admirals of the fleet.[18]

Of the Jews in royal service at this time the most influential by far was Judah aben Lavi de la Cavalleria.[19] The family derived the surname "de la Cavalleria" from the fact that one of its ancestors at one time enjoyed the protection of the Order of Knights Templar. From 1257 on Judah appears as bailiff of Saragossa. In 1260 he was authorized to collect all the state revenues and to make all the necessary expenditures on behalf of the crown. All the bailiffs in the kingdom were required to turn over to him or his deputy all their collected monies along with their accounts. He had the right to discharge incompetent officials and appoint others in their stead. He was accountable directly to the royal chancellery. In 1263 Judah made available to the king a large sum of money to outfit a fleet against the Moslems and during the subsequent campaign against Murcia provided the means which enabled the king to garrison the border strongholds of Valencia with sufficient troops. He advanced the king money for his military and political needs on several other occasions. He finally became bailiff of the province of Valencia, where he acquired land and herds of sheep. He was a man of influence also in his own Jewish community of Saragossa. This brought him into conflict with the aristocratic Alconstantini family, which, as we have seen, aspired to authority not only in Saragossa but over all the Aragonese aljamas.

During the latter part of James' reign, Benveniste de Porta (died 1268) appears as one of the most prominent person-alities in Catalonia. He served as bailiff of Barcelona and sometimes also of Gerona, Perpignan and Lerida. He also leased the mint at Barcelona.[20] Astrug Jacob Xixon served as bailiff of Tortosa and nearby localities and in parts of the kingdom of Valencia north of the Jucar river. In the city of Valencia he owned a bakery, flour mills and baths.[21] A native of Valencia, Vives ben Joseph ibn Vives, was in charge of a number of rural bailiwicks in that kingdom.[22] He also had command of the royal citadel in the city of Valencia and directed its defense during the Moslem uprisings in 1271 and 1280.

A number of other Jews served the crown in a variety of administrative posts. Yet even during the reign of James I the first symptoms of a growing tendency to eliminate Jews from public office could be noticed. In Catalonia, Jewish par-ticipation in the public administration increased remarkably up to the middle of the thirteenth century, but thereafter it declined steadily. Benveniste de Porta was the last Jewish official in Barcelona. In Aragon Jewish influence remained undiminished and even spread to the kingdom of Valencia, royal assurances to the contrary, given to the citizens of Valencia in 1251, notwithstanding. This new territory, popu-lated predominantly by Moslems, was in need of colonizing initiative, and the services of Jews could not yet be dispensed with. But during the reign of James' successor, Pedro III, the forces which eventually brought about the exclusion of Jews from public office became more powerful and more effective.

RELIGIOUS AND LEGISLATIVE POLICIES AND THEIR EFFECT ON THE JEWS

The public careers of the Jewish functionaries, brilliant though they were, nevertheless represent only isolated instances of individual Jews rising above the generally modest station of their coreligionists. In our previous discussion we defined the conflicting forces which shaped policy toward the Jews, namely, the needs and objectives of the Reconquest and a rising tide of anti-Jewish feeling. The influence of the latter is clearly apparent in the legislation of James I. Geographically and spiritually Aragon was very close to Languedoc, the classic land of the Inquisition and the persecution of heretics. When the reform movement launched by Innocent III and carried forward by Gregory IX reached Spain, its was given practical effect in Aragon by the Dominican confessor to the king, Raymond de Peñaforte, and by his associates. As early as 1228, at a conclave of the highest temporal and ecclesiastical lords of the realm, James I issued a series of decrees affecting the Jews. He fixed the rate of interest Jews were permitted to take from Christians at twenty per cent, which was the current rate at the time also among the Florentine merchants. He also decreed that a Jewish creditor could not collect a debt on the strength of his oath alone, but was required to produce a note or witnesses. At the same session Jews were forbidden to hold public office and to employ Christian women as servants.[23] The papal legate had a hand in the preparation of these decrees. In 1235, a council of the prelates of the kingdom, which met at Tarragona under the presidency of James I, confirmed the interest rate set for Jews in 1228. (Christians were at that time still permitted to take interest at the rate of twelve

147

per cent.) A Jew who charged above the legal rate was liable to confiscation of property and the loss of his liberty. A Jew who accepted Islam or a Moslem who converted to Judaism was also to be deprived of his liberty.[24]

A few years later, at the Cortes of Gerona in 1241, further provisions governing the Jewish interest rate were enacted.[25] The language of this legislation breathes hatred and mistrust of the Jews and repeatedly charges them with avarice. The Christians, it is alleged, have cleansed themselves of the sin of usury, but the Jews still persist in it. However, since the Christians have to resort to Jewish moneylenders and the evil cannot, therefore, be completely eradicated, Jewish greed must, at least, be bridled. The interest rate was therefore set at four *denarii* per pound per month, the equivalent of twenty per cent per annum. But the annual increment of the loan due to interest was not to exceed one-sixth of the principal. In order to prevent subterfuge on part of the Jews, every Jewish moneylender was required to swear compliance with the law before the local royal representative. The town notary was to keep a list of all the Jews who took the oath and was permitted to draw up promissory notes only for the money-lenders on his list. Before the note was signed the creditor was again required to swear that he did not in any way circumvent the law. A notary who failed to take all the prescribed precautions was subject to dismissal. A Jew found guilty of evading the law was to lose the debt entirely. The Jew was to take the oath, not in the synagogue, as was customary hitherto, but before a Christian tribunal. The text of the oath was to be full of anathemas irritating to the Jews. In line with the contemporary tendency toward legal uniformity, James I published a comprehensive code for his entire kingdom.[26] The sections dealing with the Jews were borrowed, in part, from the laws already in force in Aragon and in the adjacent parts of Castile and Navarre. The decree of 1241 setting the interest rate for Jews and the text of the oath to be taken in connection with it were now confirmed as the general law.

Later we shall discuss the economic importance of loans and interest; at this point the laws cited serve only as landmarks in the growth of anti-Jewishness in Spain and its political effects. To be sure, the charge that the Jews were evading the moneylending regulations was not always pure libel. But the question of usury involved not so much an economic as a theological principle repeatedly harped upon by Christian preachers, thus adding fuel to the fire of religious fanaticism. Characteristic of the mounting tide of bigotry were the miracle tales which were circulated in Saragossa in 1250 concerning a Christian boy allegedly murdered by Jews—the first instance of the blood libel on Spanish soil.[27] No doubt religious and national differences had created a barrier between Jews and Christians also during the early Reconquest; but the blood libel, an invention of the barbaric imaginations of northern Europe, was not imported into Spain until this late date. The persecutions in France also cast their shadow upon Aragon. The vilification of the Jewish character in the aforementioned edict of 1241 was inspired by the denunciation and trial of the Talmud in France. In 1254, after Louis IX of France returned from his crusade, he ordered the expulsion of all Jews from his domains and the cancellation of all their loans. On October 6 of the same year James I confiscated for the crown all the outstanding Jewish debts, as an act of piety "for the salvation of our soul and the souls of our forebears," and as punishment for Jewish violations of royal edicts.[28] Yet in the years which followed he seemed to have had no fixed policy concerning loans and interest. At one time he would grant concessions to the Jewish moneylenders, in total disregard of the interests of the debtors and of his own decrees on the subject, and at another time he would insist upon the strict execution of the law, to the loss of the Jewish creditors. He might on one occasion grant a

general moratorium on all loans and soon thereafter promise
the aljamas not to grant any further moratoria for a specified
time. The reaction of the Christian population to such grants
can be seen in an incident which took place in Monzon sometime after 1260. When the local Jews obtained a royal patent
facilitating the collection of their debts, the Christian inhabitants threatened to raze the judería unless the royal rescript
was extended to cover the entire country and not their city
alone. Armed bands invaded the Jewish quarter. The local
commander of the Knights Templar came down from the
castle to defend the Jews, but had to stand by helpless. The
attackers drove a Jewish tailor out of his workshop, wounded
a number of other Jews, and announced that henceforth they
would not permit Jewish artisans to live and work in their
midst.[29]

Religious Disputations and their Consequences

More fateful for the future of the Jews was the religious
agitation carried from France into Spain by the mendicant
friars. The latter sought to extend their prosecution of heresy
to cover the Jews. The religious conflict which rent the Jewish
communities since 1232 appears to have provided the Church
with an occasion for looking into the Jewish books. The
demand for it, which came from the French scholastics and
the teachers of the University of Paris, was soon echoed all
over Europe, and deeply affected the course of the religious
conflict in Spain. Early Christianity had grown and developed
as a protest against the Pharisaic teachings and the Law and
lore of the Mishna and the Talmud, in short, against all of
the Oral Law. But the established Church began to take
cognizance of the Talmud as a written work only in the
thirteenth century. Nicholas Donin, an apostate, who prior to
his conversion had been excommunicated by the French communities for denying the validity of the Oral Law, denounced
the Talmud to Pope Gregory IX and provided the ecclesi-

astical tribunals with excerpts from the Talmud for examination. In June 1239 the pope addressed letters to the prelates and friars, and to the kings of France, England and the Iberian peninsula—Germany and Italy seem to have been left out due to the strained relations existing between the pope and the Emperor Frederick II—directing that on Saturday morning, March 3, 1240, when all the Jews would be in the synagogues, all the Jewish books be seized and turned over to the Dominicans and Franciscans for examination. As far as is known, the order was carried out only in Paris. The leading rabbis of France, headed by Rabbi Yehiel of Paris, were summoned for a hearing, and after long investigation and argument the Talmud was condemned to be burned. Volumes of the Talmud were consigned to the flames on several occasions in various places, until Pope Innocent IV stopped its destruction in answer to the pleas of the Jewish leaders that the Talmud was essential to the practice of their faith, which enjoyed the status of a tolerated religion. The accusations hurled at the Talmud by the Christian inquisitors at the instigation of Donin were substantially the same as those levelled against it by the Karaites. They insisted that the Talmud was the pure invention of the minds of its authors, who had set up their own law alongside the Law of Moses, that its Aggada was full of heresy and blasphemy and much of its halakhic material violated all logic and morality. But the Christian detractors of the Talmud charged further that the work contained derogatory references to Jesus and the Christians. They proceeded to censure the Jews for their moral behavior and their attitude toward Christians. The first attacks upon the *Kol Nidre* prayer were heard in this connection. In the end Innocent IV ordered the remaining copies of the Talmud returned to the Jews after all the objectionable passages had been expunged.[30]

In the early 1240s the mendicant friars in Aragon embarked on an intensive missionary campaign, and the Jews and Moslems were compelled to attend their sermons.[31] In a short polemic work which appeared about this time, the author, R. Jacob of Venice, rebukes a certain convert who spread calumnies concerning the Jewish prayers, sought to foment hatred against the Talmud and to stir up trouble over the usury problem, and tried to compel Jews to listen to Christian sermons.[32] We find in this little book the first mention of the disinterment of the bones of deceased Jews, who were, no doubt, posthumously accused of heresy. The friars adopted new tactics in their efforts to convert the Jews. They turned from condemnation and libel of the Talmud to drawing upon it for support of Christian doctrine. The *aggadot* of the Talmud, they contended, contain implicit corroboration of Christian teachings, but the rabbis, through ignorance and ill will, deliberately concealed the fact.

The chief propagandist for this new approach was again an apostate, Pablo Christiani by name. But he met a formidable adversary in the person of Moses ben Nahman, who is referred to in the non-Jewish documents dealing with this controversy as Bonastrug de Porta.[33] After a series of private conversations with the apostate, the venerable rabbi was finally compelled to engage in a public disputation with him. The disputation was held in Barcelona in 1263, in the presence of the king, the bishop, the leading Aragonese Dominicans, Raymond de Peñaforte and Raymond Martini, the Franciscan Peter de Janua, and members of the nobility and local citizenry. Shortly after the close of the disputation a Latin record of the proceedings was prepared. Its value, however, is vitiated by the obvious bias of the author and his inadequate understanding of the subject as a whole. Nahmanides also published his own account of the disputation about the same time. He too was not very careful with details, but in the main his work may be accepted as an authoritative account of the actual proceedings. The king had guaranteed the rabbi complete freedom of speech, and the latter, therefore, spoke with a frankness that was not without risk. The Christian disputant sought to prove from legends of the Talmud that the Messiah, who was human and yet divine, had already appeared, that he had died to atone for the sins of mankind, and that with his advent the commandments of Judaism had lost their validity. Nahmanides succeeded in proving that the literal meaning of the passages cited by the opposition admits of no christological interpretation. He further argued—against his own convictions—that belief in the Aggada is not obligatory, and that the basic quarrel between Judaism and Christianity was not over their respective messianic concepts. He then went over to the attack and assailed some of the Christian dogmas concerning the nature of the Divinity as absurd. He even gave veiled warning of the imminent collapse of Christian world power.

The disputation, which maintained a dignified and scholarly tone only with great difficulty, continued for four days, on the 20th, 27th, 30th, and 31st of July. It was never formally closed, but was interrupted for fear of disturbances by fanatical mobs. Members of the secular clergy, the nobility and the burghers, and even the head of the Franciscans, who were less aggressive in their missionary zeal than the Dominicans, urged the .discontinuance of this dangerous spectacle. According to the Latin report, the disputation came to a sudden end because Nahmanides fled from the city. The fact is, however, that Nahmanides remained in Barcelona for a whole week after the end of the disputation in order to attend the Christian sermon which was to be delivered in the synagogue on the Sabbath. According to Nahmanides' account, the king frequently joined in the discussions and at the end told the rabbi, "I have never seen a man defend a wrong cause so well." On the Sabbath the king accompanied the Dominicans to the synagogue and personally addressed the Jewish congregation—a thing unheard of during the Middle Ages. The rabbi was again permitted to reply to the king and the friars. The following day Nahmanides took his leave of the king, received from him a gift of three hundred *solidi,* and returned home safely.

In staging the disputation the friars hoped, no doubt, to score a sensational victory over the foremost rabbi of the day and obtain the conversion of masses of Jews. But the accounts show that they were inadequately prepared. For one thing, the disputation convinced Raymond Martini of the need to devise better methods of interpreting the talmudic *aggadot* in a christologic sense. The friars failed to make the desired impression either through their knowledge of the Midrash, their scholastic approach, or the weight of their personality. On the other hand, Nahmanides' presentation of his case revealed his greatness as a talmudist with a well-founded and integrated religious outlook. Yet the great spiritual qualities of the Jewish protagonist do not of themselves explain the sudden interruption of the disputation without reaching a decision. The complete freedom of speech accorded the rabbi is understandable only in the light of contemporary political conditions. The Christian zealots who launched this undertaking for the glory of their faith failed to assure themselves in advance of royal approval for their attempt to deal Judaism a deadly blow.

James I was certainly far from any such heretical leanings as were ascribed to his contemporary, Emperor Frederick II, the Hohenstaufen. Throughout his reign he cooperated with the papacy, vigorously persecuting the heretics in his kingdom. He fought the Moors with true crusading zeal, and even prepared to go on a crusade to the Holy Land, but was prevented from doing so by outside circumstances. His interest in the Disputation at Barcelona was not merely that of the statesman and warrior who wishes to pay the Church its due, but that of a pious Christian desirous of saving wayward souls. But the opportune time for imposing Christianity upon the Jews by force had not yet arrived. The Jewish courtiers still exercised considerable influence. The king's sympathy for Nahmanides personally is attested by the rabbi's own statement and by

154

the words of the document bestowing upon him a gift from the crown. One must not, however, lose sight of the official character and purpose of the great debate which brought together the leading personalities of both camps. On the soil of historic Spain approaching the end of the Reconquest, and in the part of the peninsula closest to the classic centers of the Inquisition and the persecution of the Catharist sectarians, an indication was given of the direction the war against the Jews was to take during the next two centuries.

After the Disputation of Barcelona the friars redoubled their efforts. The king, in his characteristic manner, supported the friars on some occasions and at other times took measures to protect the Jews.[34] On August 24, 1263, he granted one of the Jewish notables of Barcelona permission to establish a synagogue in his home. Yet during the same last days of August 1263, less than a month after the disputation, James I issued a series of rescripts designed to facilitate the missionary work of the friars. At the call of the Dominicans, the Jews were required to assemble in their synagogues or in other designated places in order to listen to the sermons of the friars and dispute their faith and Scripture with them. The Jews were required to bring their religious books along for that purpose. Another decree, dated August 29, 1263, ordered the Jews to erase from their books within three months all blasphemous references to Jesus and Mary which Pablo Christiani and the Dominicans would point out to them. Failure to do so was punishable by a heavy fine and the destruction by fire of the entire book containing the objectionable passages. In every aljama twenty or thirty of the leading members were to be selected and, under oath, made to assume responsibility for the execution of the order. A special decree dealt with the fourteenth book of Maimonides'·Code, the one entitled "The Book of Judges," which contains references to Jesus in the section dealing with the laws of kingship. The Jews were ordered to

155

surrender to the royal officials all copies of this book so that they might publicly be consigned to the flames.

Almost immediately new orders came from the royal chancellery, mitigating the severity of the above decrees and even countermanding some of their provisions. On August 30, 1263, James I ordered that no Jews should be compelled to go outside the judería to listen to the preachers. Even when the sermon was held in the Jewish quarter, the Jews were free to choose whether they wished to attend or not. Notwithstanding the recent privileges to the Dominican friars, the king ruled that Jewish attendance at the missionary sermons was at all times to be voluntary. Likewise, the decree ordering the expurgation of blasphemous references from the Jewish books was modified on March 27, 1264. The Jews were given a month's grace in which to appear before a specially appointed commission of censors and prove that the passages condemned by Pablo Christiani were not blasphemous. The commission included, besides three leading Dominicans—Raymond de Peñaforte, Raymond Martini and Arnold de Segarra—also the Franciscan Peter de Janua and the bishop of Barcelona, both of whom were more restrained in their zeal than the fanatical Dominicans. In February 1265, James I freed the Jews of Barcelona from the obligation to answer to the Dominicans regarding the contents of their books. A year and a half of intensive effort on part of the Jews, accompanied by pleas and arguments, finally bore fruit.

The aggressiveness of the friars is indicated by the following instance. A namesake of Nahmanides, Astrug de Porta of Villafranca del Panades, brother of the bailiff Benveniste de Porta, was sentenced to expulsion from the country on the charge of blaspheming Jesus in the course of a disputation. The king commuted the sentence to a fine of one-third of his capital. In order to enable him to raise the large fine, Astrug was given extra-legal privileges for the collection of his debts. The documents dealing with this case indicate quite clearly that the overwhelming influence of Benveniste de Porta had to be brought to bear in order to have the verdict set aside.[35] Disputations such as the one which involved Astrug de Porta in difficulties appear to have become frequent around this time.

The Dominicans could not forgive Rabbi Moses ben Nahman (Nahmanides) for his part in the disputation. On April 12, 1265, "Bonastrug de Porta, a Jewish teacher of Gerona," was haled before the royal tribunal in Barcelona.[36] Raymond de Peñaforte and his associates charged that Nahmanides had blasphemed the Catholic faith and even embodied these blasphemies in a book, a copy of which he had given to the bishop of Gerona. The book in question was probably Nahmanides' own Hebrew account of the disputation, or a similar work. Nahmanides pleaded in defense that he had made the statements in question in the course of his disputation with Pablo Christiani at the royal palace, after being promised complete freedom of speech by both the king and De Peñaforte. Moreover, he had written the book at the request of the bishop of Gerona. He could not therefore be brought to trial on these charges. Upon advice of his council, the king was ready to make a concession to the Dominicans and impose a sentence of banishment for two years upon Nahmanides and order his book burned. But the friars were not satisfied with so "mild" a sentence. James I, therefore, adjourned the trial with the ruling that the defendant was to be arraigned before the monarch personally. In reality, that meant indefinite postponement of the entire matter. The king's council included the bishop of Barcelona and a few other secular clerics as well as three jurists, all of whom, it seems, were inclined to clear the rabbi of Gerona.[36a]

At this very time the Inquisition was conducting an investigation into the private life of a financial broker of Gerona suspected of observing Jewish rites. The man was a born Christian, and there is no indication of his having been of Jewish descent. Nothing was found to substantiate the charges and the accused was cleared by the king. He was, however, required to vow to the Dominicans never to cross the threshold of a Jewish house in Gerona.[37] This is the first known instance in Spain of inquisitional preoccupation with Judaizing Christians. Late in 1266 the prominent bailiff Judah de la Cavalleria, his son-in-law Astrug Bonsenyor, royal secretary for Arabic correspondence, together with several other members of their family were accused of desecrating the crucifix; but James I dismissed the charge against them.[38] Judah de la Cavalleria was at this time at the height of his career, and Bonsenyor had conducted the negotiations with the Arabs after the fall of Murcia earlier that year. It was to be expected that the king would defend his valuable aides, particularly since no substantial evidence against them was available. The whole thing may have been pure libel. But it wasn't mere accident that made the leaders of the highest Jewish aristocracy the target of these charges. It may very well be that in intellectual Jewish circles religion often became the object of sport, and devoted Christians felt that the time had come to put an end to this. At any rate, the instances cited indicate in what direction the Inquisition sought to expand its drive against heresy. But many generations were yet to pass before similar accusations would again lead to formal trials, on the eve of the expulsion.

The Dominicans in Aragon soon realized that they could muster little local support for their activities, and they turned to Rome for assistance. They obtained from Pope Clement IV letters reaffirming the stand taken by Gregory IX against the Talmud. On July 15, 1267, the pope wrote to the archbishop of Tarragona ordering him to collect all the Jewish books throughout Aragon and turn them over to the Dominicans and Franciscans for examination, and he highly recommended Pablo Christiani as a valuable collaborator in the investigation.[39] Later that same month Clement IV issued the bull *Turbato Corde*—reissued several times by his successors—

which became the basic directive of the Inquisition for the prosecution of Judaizing heresies. It ordered the inquisitors to proceed against converts from Judaism who reverted to their old faith, against Christians who accepted Judaism, and against Jews who proselytized among Christians or converts. In a letter to James I—which bears no date, but must have been written about the same time as the others, possibly somewhat earlier—Clement IV demanded the punishment of the man who had "composed a tract full of falsehood concerning his disputation with Pablo Christiani in the presence of the king, and even circulated copies of the book in order to disseminate his erring faith." R. Moses ben Nahman departed for Palestine shortly thereafter, arriving in Jerusalem on the 9th of Elul, 5027 (1267), and, while this pilgrimage was the realization of the lifelong aspiration of this sage and mystic, one cannot escape the conclusion that his old enemies, the Dominicans, had made life unbearable for him in Catalonia.

The bulls of Clement IV strengthened the clerical agitation against the Jews. Again James I intervened on behalf of his Jewish subjects. In April 1268, he ordered the authorities at Jativa to take measures against a possible stoning attack upon the Jews on Good Friday.[40] In the fall of 1268, he issued new charters of privilege to the leading aljamas of Catalonia and those of Perpignan and Montpellier. The king reaffirmed his previous order that Jews were not to be compelled to attend missionary sermons delivered outside the Jewish quarter, where they would be exposed to abuse and injury. In order to prevent violence by the rabble, which usually accompanied the friars into the judería on their proselytizing missions, the preachers who entered the synagogues to deliver their sermons were enjoined from taking with them more than ten men, citizens of good repute. The Jews were not required to reply to the allegations that the Talmud contained hostile references to Christians, unless specific blasphemies of Jesus, Mary and the saints were pointed out. The Jewish apologists had apparently won their point that the talmudic laws concerning idolatry (*Aboda Zara; Abodat Kokhabim*) and the references to Gentiles (*Nokhrim; Goyim*) did not deal with Christianity and Christians at all. Further privileges permitted Jews to purchase foodstuffs from Christians and to sell to them ritually slaughtered meat. The king confirmed the full ownership rights of the aljamas to their synagogues and cemeteries. He excused the Jews from wearing the badge, and required them to wear only the round cape. The Jewish courtiers and officials were permitted to dispense with the cape as well. The interest rate was left at the previously established rate of twenty per cent.

These charters, which were issued at the time when religious fanaticism was mounting, were paid for in good coin, as both the state account books and the contemporary responsa of Rabbi Solomon ibn Adret (*Rashba*) indicate. The rabbi, a young man at the time, received a query regarding

> large expenditures made by the communities in the interests of public welfare and safety, namely, protection-money paid during the Christian festivals and like items, municipal improvements, expenses in connection with the king's order to wear a broad badge, and to return to the Christian debtors the interest collected above the legal rate and suffer forfeiture of the principal upon investigation by two Christians. The community made large expenditures to obtain mitigation of such measures. The size of the badge was reduced by half, and the badge is not required when one wears a cape. Also the excessive interest has to be returned but the principal is not forfeited.

On another occasion, Ibn Adret was asked

> regarding converts . . . who bring it about that the priests want to prevent Jews from eating meat slaughtered by them or drinking their wine or buying their bread, and expenditures have to be made to bribe them to muzzle their mouths and also the priests' and judges'. Likewise

there are expenditures made annually on the eve of a certain holiday of theirs for protection.

The problem dealt with in this responsum revolves around the relations between Jews and converts who continued to observe Judaism and maintained ties with their Jewish brethren. The rabbis permitted the use of meat slaughtered by them as well as their wine, and the clergy protested against such contact between converts and openly professing Jews.[41]

Ibn Adret took part, about this time, in an important trial in which he defended the rights of a Jewish orphan against some powerful state officials who sought to defraud the child.[42] As the child's guardian, Ibn Adret filed suit before the royal court against the heirs of the late bailiff, Benveniste de Porta, and the executor of his will, Judah de la Cavalleria. The decision favored the highly influential defendants. Sitting in the royal council at the time were the bishop of Barcelona, a number of knights and Churchmen, and the Dominicans De Peñaforte and De Segarra. In pronouncing judgment in favor of the Jewish financiers, whom they thoroughly disliked, the members of the council were guided by the interests of the royal treasury and not by the dictates of equity and justice championed by the rabbi who was later to appear as spokesman for the Jewish communities in political matters of far greater consequence.

The religious agitation appears to have subsided after 1268. Nevertheless, a growing feeling of insecurity overtook the Aragonese Jews during the last years of James the Conqueror's reign. State officials dealt in an arbitrary manner with Jewish communities and individuals. The plague of informing harassed the aljamas, both from within and without. In order to check the latter evil, James I provided, for the benefit of a number of aljamas, that trials resulting from denunciations against them be conducted in accordance with Roman Law and the procedures obtaining in the most advanced courts of Aragon. These called for a written record of the court proceedings, the right of defense counsel, liability of the accuser and the informer to retaliation (law of *talio*), written publication of testimony, limitation of torture, and the right of appeal to the king's tribunal. Letters addressed by the community of Perpignan to the aljama of Barcelona requesting the latter to intercede on its behalf with the bishop of Huesca, the royal chancellor, indicate that the law of *talio* was introduced to aid the Jews in their struggle against informers. The letters, which were probably written by the poet Abraham Bedersi, read in part as follows:

> You know the hardships which have overtaken us— your ears have heard of them and your eyes have seen them—when misfortune befell us and troubles multiplied because of tale-bearers. They continuously put our affairs to grief, dissipated our wealth so that the rich sank low, and they caused death wherever they had the power. You have witnessed strife and violence in the city. . . . But one day, God, who did not want us to perish but rather to thrive in our work, inspired our great and glorious lord, the king, our life's breath, to regard our affliction and take pity on us, and in the abundance of his grace to grant us the privilege of *talio*, whereon we hung our weapons, our bow and our sword. When the earth changed and the terrors passed, we called it the happiest day of our lives. The hoped-for day has arrived; we beheld that for which we had yearned. This will console us for our painful losses, this will create justice and right, for we may say to every enemy and conspirator against our life, "You are plotting your own death." This will shut the mouths of those who would incite against us. This privilege will prevail against all trouble, and every tale-bearer will no longer tread an easy path. This will cut off every glib lip; this will gouge out every spying eye.[43]

PEDRO III AND HIS JEWISH OFFICIALS

The short reign of Pedro III (1276-1285), the son and successor of James I, affords a good opportunity for a study of the political forces which shaped the lot of the Jews. The wealth of archival material which has survived from that period enables us to clarify the motives behind the various changes in this king's policy toward the Jews and their consequences.[44]

Early in his reign Pedro III ordered the review of all the privileges granted by his predecessor to Jewish communities and individuals.[45] The review was essentially a pretext to enable the king to exact a price for the confirmation of the privileges. He did confirm them for the most part, but added no new ones, except where changes were made necessary by internal developments within the aljamas. The period of growth and expansion for the Jewish communities had come to an end. The successors of James the Conqueror strove to preserve the status quo, yet as time went on they were compelled to make concessions to the anti-Jewish forces. A warrior-king like Pedro III could not dispense with the loyal service of Jewish officials. Their influence was great wherever and whenever the crown had need of servants of proven fidelity, who could also be discarded with ease whenever the situation called for it.

By the time Pedro III ascended the throne the important Jewish functionaries of James I had either died or retired from public service. New men, who had begun their public careers under the aegis of the Infante Pedro during his father's lifetime, were now advanced to positions of the highest authority. Judah de la Cavalleria continued as bailiff of Saragossa until the end of 1276 and died shortly thereafter.[46] Not for three generations was his family to regain the position of prominence attained by its brilliant ancestor, but under quite different conditions. Judah's place as bailiff of Sargossa was now filled by Moses Alconstantini, *alfaquim* of Pedro III, and son of Solomon Alconstantini, the distinguished interpreter of James I.[47] Moses, and others like him, such as Muça de Portella and Aaron ibn Yahia, held various offices in their native Aragon and extended their activities also to the areas under colonization in the kingdom of Valencia.

In Catalonia, the old center of culture and progress, Jewish influence was on the wane. In Barcelona, Jews no longer held any state office. But the family of Ravaya, natives of Gerona, attained a prominence reminiscent of the best days of the Reconquest. Back in the 1260s, Astrug Ravaya and his son Joseph had lent the Infante money, and as a result became farmers of royal revenues. From 1268 on, Joseph appears as bailiff of Besalu, near Gerona, and from 1271 also of Gerona and its district. Like most of the earlier Jewish bailiffs in Catalonia, both father and son served not only as bankers and tax-farmers of the crown, but also as administrative officers in a modern sense. We find their signatures and remarks, in Hebrew, on documents dealing with the sale of castles or the suspension of penalties imposed upon rebellious peasants. Moses, another son of Astrug Ravaya, joined the family enterprises at the beginning of Pedro's reign. In 1277, Astrug granted on behalf of the king certain privileges to the inhabitants of the village of Palamos in Catalonia. His two sons soon broke through the narrow confines of local administration. By the end of 1276, Joseph held an important post in the combined fiscal administration of Aragon and Catalonia. In 1279 he is mentioned as the king's *thesaurarius* (treasurer), a position to which he had been appointed earlier. He and his Jewish colleagues must be credited with the technical advances made in the central administration of Aragon. New procedures were introduced into the royal chancellery at this time. Royal decrees thenceforth required the signature of the responsible state official, and Joseph Ravaya was one of the first to sign royal orders in that capacity.[48]

In the kingdom of Valencia the Jews were assigned a special role. Pedro III found it necessary to continue his father's policies in this territory. In 1277 the Moslems in the southern part of the kingdom rose against their Christian conquerors and only with the capture of the fortress of Montesa, late that year, was the uprising put down. This revolt, and the policy of expropriation applied to the Moslems in the wake of it, further enhanced Jewish influence in that region. Moses Alconstantini was appointed bailiff in Valencia. He had been unable to retain his post in Saragossa, and he ran into difficulties also in Valencia. Occasionally, Jewish officials would take a hand in military operations. In 1277 Muça de Portella, royal bailiff and *merinus*, negotiated the surrender of the rebel contingent from the villages around Montesa. Samuel Alfaquim drew up—from 1279, at any rate—the terms of surrender and charters of privilege for the Moslems. He arranged for the sale of the Moslems taken captive in Montesa and collected the tribute from the vanquished. Samuel's brother, Judah ibn Manasseh, who was also an interpreter, held the bailiwick of Jativa in lease. Jews with a knowledge of Arabic were thus still very useful to the state.[49]

The wide range of functions performed by Jews in the colonization of the new territories and the extent of their authority are truly remarkable. Aaron ibn Yahia collected revenues from a number of villages which he owned. Solomon Vidal, bailiff of Villareal, was engaged, from 1276 to 1282, in the distribution of land to settlers in his district. Solomon Bafiel, bailiff of Murviedro, had houses, orchards, and pasture lands in the neighborhood of the city, which he leased to tenants. In Alcira, the Jewish bailiff allotted parcels of land to Moslem settlers during the years 1279-1282. This Jewish official replaced the Christian bailiff who had distributed the properties of the Moslems among Christians, a policy of which the king did not approve.[50] The last case affords a good illustration of the reason why Jews were preferred to Christians in certain positions. A Christian would be inclined to adopt a rigid anti-Moslem attitude, whereas political necessity made a policy of conciliation toward the peaceful Moslem population the wiser course. Jews were best equipped to carry out such a policy. It is difficult to define exactly the duties performed in Valencia by such men as Muça de Portella, Aaron ibn Yahia, and Joseph Ravaya, who were residents of Aragon and Catalonia. Joseph Ravaya, it seems, was sent to Valencia on special missions, as representative of central state administration. De Portella and Ibn Yahia remained in the kingdom of Valencia for longer periods, had a hand in the local administration, and even acquired property there. In the large and colorful body of officialdom that served Pedro III, the Jews were but a small minority, but it was a conspicuous minority charged with the implementation of a particular policy, a task for which the Christians were not well suited. The Jewish population in Valencia, however, reaped no lasting benefits from this policy, and no new communities were founded in the region during this period.

The Ravaya family and the other Jews who sat in the royal chancellery also influenced the affairs of their own communities. Their signatures appear not only on documents pertaining to the taxes of Jews, but also on those which deal with matters of law and communal administration.[51] One sometimes gets the impression that there existed in the chancellery of Pedro III a special section for Jewish affairs, presided over by Jews. However, it was too early as yet for such departmentalization. Whoever was connected with the royal chancellery and possessed sufficient ability, initiative and rank was able to expand the sphere of his activities. It stands to reason, therefore, that the Jewish officials were permitted to specialize, so to speak, in Jewish problems. But for all their remarkable success, the Jewish functionaries were not always able to bring relief to their people. The Jewish population bore a disproportionately large share of the costs of Pedro's military campaigns, and the tax collectors were hard and exacting.

Anti-Jewish agitation, which had calmed down considerably during the last years of James I, flared up anew under Pedro III. The presence of Jews in the state administration was exploited to the full by the opposition to the crown among the estates. Jewish life and property were again in danger. Pedro gave the Jews his protection, for they were a useful element of the population and indispensable to the crown. But in the end the king was forced to compromise with the mounting tide of antisemitism. During the Easter season of 1278, anti-Jewish disturbances broke out in Gerona, which already had a tradition of violence.[52] The priests of the episcopal church together with their servants hurled stones into the judería from the church steeple and adjoining rooftops and severely damaged Jewish gardens, vineyards and the cemetery. When the royal herald arrived and ordered the attackers to desist, he was met by catcalls and laughter. Pedro III, who was in Valencia at the time, learned of the event from his Jewish advisers and immediately dispatched two letters to Gerona, threatening to punish the bishop who had tacitly permitted the attack. The king cited a similar incident which occurred during his father's reign, when James I and members of his retinue moved, sword in hand, against a frenzied mob of clerics. This incident must have happened shortly after the Disputation at Barcelona. Now, as then, the excesses were symptomatic of deep and widespread unrest.

The revived anti-Jewish campaign was inspired from Rome. Nicholas III (1277-1280), one of the most energetic popes of the Middle Ages, had recently been elected to the throne of St. Peter. In a bull issued on August 4, 1278, he ordered that preachers be sent out to the Jews all over Europe, with a view to converting them.[53] In Aragon, the spiritual leader of this movement was the Dominican Raymond Martini. He had taken part in the disputation with Nahmanides and in the events which followed. He had published at that time his *Explanatio Symboli Apostolorum* to serve as a guide to Christianity for Jews and Moslems. He had now completed his larger work, *Pugio Fidei adversus Mauros et Judeos* (The Dagger of Faith, against the Moors and Jews), which became after a while the standard text for all those who wished to convince themselves and others that the fundamentals of Christianity were em-

167

bodied in the Talmud.[54] It is difficult to determine how wide a circulation the book attained at this time and what its immediate influence was, but its very appearance is a sign of increased religious fanaticism.

The events which followed the publication of Nicholas III's bull closely resemble those of the years 1263-1268. On April 19, 1279, Pedro III sent instructions to all his officials to compel the Jews to attend the sermons of the friars in the synagogues and to protect converts against abuse by their former coreligionists. The missionary activities of the friars, however, led to widespread disturbances. Riots would often break out during the sermons. In Huesca, a mob carried a simulated Torah scroll through the streets, to the accompaniment of derisive chants and mimicry, in a grotesque parody of Jewish rites. In Calatayud and several other places the populace actually stormed the walls of the judería and tore down the gates, while a sermon was being delivered inside. Eventually Pedro had to follow his father's example and regulate the activities of the preachers. He allowed only a few reputable citizens to accompany the friars into the synagogues. The Jews, he admonished, were to be persuaded by argument and not by force. At the same time he ordered the Jews to listen patiently to the friars and refrain from interrupting them with invective retorts.[55] To be sure, Pedro III, like his father, lacked a consistent policy on this question. But he was determined to suppress the disturbances which, if unchecked, were certain to engulf the Jewish communities in a tidal wave of violence and destruction. Also, the Jewish notables at court continued to stand guard over the interests of their people and interceded on their behalf on every occasion.

Contemporaneous with all this ferment, and perhaps in some way related to it, was a notorious case of informing which poignantly underscored the complexity of that problem and demonstrated Pedro's readiness to protect the Jewish communities. The culprit was a young man of aristocratic family,

Vidalon de Porta by name, a nephew of Benveniste de Porta. He had begun plotting against the Jewish communities during the lifetime of James I. After Pedro III succeeded to the throne "he bored more deeply, and in his arrogance he strove to corrupt everything, and, without mainstay, to become a judge and, without money, a lord; for his house was empty. He was a rich man's son who had become impoverished, and he intended to empty the land and lay it waste." So reads Ibn Adret's cryptic account. When the representatives of all the aljamas of the kingdom were one day summoned to appear before the king, Vidalon was on hand to betray them with his denunciations. The delegates of the communities, after consultation with royal finance ministers, the brothers Joseph and Moses Ravaya, lodged a complaint against him before the king. Pedro III ordered his arrest and directed the court judge to initiate an investigation in cooperation with the Jewish communal leaders. Later, acting upon a request from the aljamas, the king transferred the case to the two most respected rabbis of Catalonia, R. Solomon ibn Adret and R. Jonah Gerondi (the younger), namesake and cousin of the noted pietist who, together with R. Solomon of Montpellier, had led the battle against Maimonidean philosophy a generation earlier. Ibn Adret sought to compromise between the Jewish communities and the family of the accused, and so avoid the shedding of blood; but more influential persons prevailed upon the king to press the case. The king ordered the two rabbis to arrive at a verdict and forward it to the court judge for execution. Still the rabbis hesitated, striving for a compromise and trying to persuade the king to approve such a course. When a year went by and no decision was forthcoming, Pedro III lost all patience and threatened to have the rabbis brought before him in chains unless they pronounced sentence. The rabbis then found the informer guilty and advised the king "that he may proceed according to his law; that we have found him deserving of the death penalty, if he should wish to put him to death." Since the royal judge had died in the meantime, Pedro himself ordered that the accused be bled to death, and the sentence was carried out publicly in the square in front of the Jewish cemetery of Barcelona.[56]

In 1280 Pedro III was faced with a revolt of the Catalonian nobility.[57] It need hardly be added that the Jews were made to bear a huge share of the cost of suppressing it. While laying siege to Balaguer, where the rebellious barons had fortified themselves, Pedro III issued two decrees, one to aid the Jews in the collection of their debts, and another ordering an investigation of possible violations by them of the laws governing interest. The two apparently contradictory edicts had one and the same aim—the enrichment of the royal exchequer. On the one hand, the Jews had to be assisted in the collection of their debts so that they would be able to pay their taxes; on the other hand, here was a good opportunity to fill the royal coffers with the money from fines imposed for actual or alleged violations of the law, or to use the threat as a means of exacting further contributions from the Jewish communities.[58]

The great effort required to put down the rebellion necessitated the investment of the Jewish officials of the crown with such broad powers as they had not been given throughout the entire history of the Jews in Spain, either up to that time or thereafter.[59] Not only was the administration of taxes and finance concentrated almost entirely in the hands of the Ravaya brothers, but Joseph Ravaya and his associates placed their signatures—mostly in Latin, sometimes in Hebrew—upon documents dealing with the supply of arms and the outfitting of ships, or upon summonses sent to the king's vassals—among them the king of Majorca—to be ready for a military campaign, or for a session of the royal tribunal, or for the surrender of their strongholds to the king. They issued patents of appointment to judicial officers or orders for their dismissal. No political considerations or objections on the part of the Church or the third estate could interfere with their work. For a few years they exercised complete control over the country's entire economy and even over some branches of the military establishment. They founded new villages and negotiated the terms of settlement with the Christian settlers; they established new Moslem communities; they kept the fortresses in repair and appointed their commandants. Hebrew notes made by Jewish scribes are found on the backs of charters of solemn privileges, awarded to the highest dignitaries of the realm. Jews collected the taxes, farmed out state revenues and held the local officials to account. Joseph Ravaya also signed royal decrees regulating certain administrative and juridical matters of the aljamas and gave the latter whatever aid he could. The Jewish communities naturally derived certain benefits from the fact that some of their members occupied positions of great influence. In the summer of 1280 Pedro III granted to several of the aljamas, and to a number of private Jews, broad, and for him extraordinary, privileges, including specifically the right to collect compound interest.[60]

THE RELIGIOUS AND FEUDAL REACTION

In 1282 Pedro III launched his famous expedition against Sicily.[61] Already in January of that year he began extorting from the Jews subsidies for the equipment of his armada, and the burden of taxes and tribute grew progressively heavier during the next few years.[62] Several of the king's Jewish aides accompanied him to Sicily. Notable among them was his finance minister, Joseph Ravaya, who died on the island in December 1282.[63] His brother, Moses, was at the same time entrusted by Infante Alfonso, the king's deputy in Aragon, with broad fiscal powers and the authority to farm out the state revenues.[64]

But a reaction prejudicial to the Jews had already set in. The Christian estates—the clergy, the nobility, and the burghers—took advantage of the king's absence to make their

171

first successful attempts to break the influence of the Jews in the government. The Churchmen saw in the exercise of public office by Jews a clear violation of Canon Law. The nobility looked upon the Jewish favorites of the king as the instruments of their suppression. The merchants, lawyers and civil servants among the urban population cast covetous eyes on the high positions held by Jews. Together they formed an opposition which the young infante was compelled to heed. In February 1283 came a decree to compel the Jews, when swearing, to take the prescribed Jewish oath in full, omitting none of the curses and anathemas. A little later he ordered an investigation of the charges that Jews were having illicit relations with women of other faiths and were guilty of other offenses, and he approved in advance the findings of the court judge who was charged with the inquiry.[65] The king's subjects were especially insistent in their demands for the dismissal of the Jewish officials. Moses Alconstantini, the last Jew to serve as a bailiff in any of the principal cities of the realm, was removed from his post in Valencia even before Pedro's departure for Sicily. To be sure, his unscrupulous conduct had brought forth complaints not only from Christians but from Jews as well. It is significant, however, that the infante's mandate for the prosecution of the deposed bailiff ordered that he be given the punishment "a Jew deserves"—a formula never before used in any of the chancelleries of Spain.[66] After the death of Joseph Ravaya the family's properties were impounded by the crown, and early in 1283 Moses Ravaya lost his position.[67]

Upon his return from Sicily, Pedro III himself had to accede to some of the demands of the estates, including those affecting the status of the Jews.[68] Among the grievances aired at the Cortes of Tarazona, in September 1283, were complaints against the Jewish tax collectors, who were accused of arrogance and violence. On the strength of the famous *Privilegio General*, the instrument embodying the royal concessions, the king forbade Jews to hold such offices as gave them juridical or executive authority over Christians. In December 1283, the anti-Jewish legislation was extended to the kingdom of Valencia and its capital city. As in Aragon, Jews were forbidden to exercise jurisdiction over Christians. The laws governing loans and interest were confirmed. There was renewed insistence upon the application of the Jewish oath. Certain immunities which Jews had enjoyed, in the purchase of goods suspected of having been stolen, were withdrawn. Jews were no longer allowed to slaughter their animals in the Christian slaughterhouse and were required to wear the round cape like the Jews of Barcelona. At the Cortes of Barcelona, held during the same month, Pedro III confirmed the legislation enacted by James I in 1228.

In addition to being motivated by nationalist class interests, the anti-Jewish legislation of this period also bears definite marks of clerical intolerance, such as found expression in the agitation of the friars. In the laws for Valencia it is stated that

> on every Sabbath in the synagogues the Jewish rabbis pronounce the ban against any Jew who bears testimony in favor of a Christian against a Jew, and that in accordance with an enactment of their rabbis the Jews swear, on a certain holiday every year, that any oath which they might take during the forthcoming year in a compact with a Christian shall be null and void, and they shall not be held accountable for the breach thereof either before God or their faith.

Here is a libel, created for the persecution of the Talmud, which became embodied into law.

But the anti-Jewish forces did not yet triumph completely. The Jews immediately opened negotiations with the court, seeking the mitigation and, if possible, the abrogation of the above measures, and the king proved amenable to their pleas.

In 1284 Pedro III and Infante Alfonso were again surrounded by Jewish assistants whose services were needed in the war between Aragon and France.

The outstanding Jewish official at this time was Muça de Portella.[69] He, his brothers and their associates had charge not only of the royal revenues and other financial matters but also of such cares as the reenforcement and armament of the fortresses on the Castilian and Navarrese frontiers. At times they even administered the incomes of bishoprics and baronial manors. They were assisted by a staff of Jewish secretaries and subordinates. However, the king was now even less inclined than he had been in the days of Judah de la Cavalleria and the Ravayas to give clear and precise definition to the title and prerogatives of the Jewish official. His position rested on the king's personal confidence in him, and occasion alone determined the tasks he was to perform. Muça de Portella was primarily an official of the royal household, though for a time he also managed the finances of the province of Aragon. (In Catalonia no Jewish officials are to be found after 1283, and in Valencia a few isolated ones appear during 1284-1285, only to disappear thereafter.)

In 1286 Muça de Portella met death by assassination, under unknown circumstances. His entire fortune was confiscated by Alfonso III and earmarked for the expedition against the island of Minorca; but the family seems to have come to terms with the court and retained both its wealth and its prosperous position. They found it necessary, however, to move their residence from their native Tarazona to a hamlet near Borja. Ishmael, a brother of Muça, was also engaged for a time in the collection of revenues, and then served, until 1289, as *dispensator* (financial steward) to Infante Pedro, brother of Alfonso III. James II (1291-1327) sent him on a secret diplomatic mission and also appointed him crown rabbi over all the Jews in the province of Aragon. In the beginning of the fourteenth century the surviving members of the Portella family left Aragon and settled in Navarre. Thus ends the sad chapter of the elimination of the Jews from the service of the state. Most of the grants of land and other property which Jews had received in various parts of the country, particularly in Valencia, were cancelled. The important role which the Jews had played in the colonization program of the Reconquest thus came to an end.

From now on the Jews become primarily a sponge to be squeezed dry for taxes. Yet this policy required the preservation intact of the Jewish communal autonomy and the protection of the Jews from the dangers to which they were exposed in the midst of internal unrest and foreign war. Accordingly, in September 1284, Pedro III forbade the Dominicans to proceed with an inquisition of certain Jews of Barcelona accused of harboring converts from Judaism in their homes.[70] The Jews of Gerona—who suffered greatly during the occupation of the city by the French in 1285, and again when it was recaptured by the Aragonese forces, even though they helped defend the city against the French—received letters of protection from the king permitting them to emigrate to other localities or to return to their home city, as they wished. At the same time Pedro III instituted a new system of taxation which, even by the standards of that day, was nothing less than a predatory raid upon Jewish wealth.[71] Thoroughgoing investigations of the administrations of the aljamas were carried out for the sole purpose of finding the desired basis for tax assessment. The extortionate policy appears to underlie the decrees of January 1285 ordering a close surveillance of all localities situated near the Castilian border to prevent the escape of Jews from the country.[72] Representatives of the aljamas were summoned periodically to the royal court in order to give an accounting of their management of communal funds. They had to travel about from place to place, following the court's movements, and were persecuted if they took their leave too soon. On one occasion the king ordered twenty of the richest Jews of Saragossa arrested and brought before him. The community was required to put under the ban all those who took flight to escape the crushing taxes.[73] All the possessions which Navarrese Jews had in Aragon, consisting of land, merchandise and money, were confiscated. In the end, the communal deputies were compelled, under pressure from the royal officials, to enact a series of *takkanot* (communal statutes) to raise the required levies through a complicated system of poll and property taxes as well as a tax on the gross volume of business. Supplementary demands and regulations kept coming from the crown. During the later stages of these developments a decisive but questionable role was played by one of Pedro's favorites, David Mascaran, whose name suggests descent from a family of courtiers of Judah Halevi's day. He evidently incurred the hatred of his coreligionists and finally fell by the hand of one of them.[74] The spoliative fiscal policy of these two years brought the Aragonese aljamas to the brink of economic ruin, and nothing that Alfonso III could do was able to put them back on their feet again.[75] It was now too late to reverse the catastrophic trend which had begun during the reign of his father.

For the turn for the worse in the political and social status of the Jews had begun in 1283. The process of dislodging the Jews from the positions they had earned for themselves during the Reconquest was then set in motion, and it continued, sporadically, throughout the last two years of Pedro III and the short reign of Alfonso III (1285-1291). In 1286 and again in 1289 Alfonso III was confronted by demands from the estates, among them one calling for the removal of Jews from public office, and was compelled to confirm the promise made by Pedro III.[76] Actually, however, the die had been cast during Pedro's lifetime and all his successor did was to continue the liquidation of the Jewish gains, at the same time shielding the Jewish communities from the more drastic consequences of such a policy. The nine years of Pedro III's reign, more than any other period, were characterized by this oscillation between the two extremes in the treatment of the Jews. In spite of the luster which the phenomenal, but temporary, achievements of individual Jews shed upon this period, and the energetic action that the king sometimes took to protect the Jewish population, the final balance sheet shows that Pedro III pursued an opportunistic policy with regard to the Jews, adapting it to the needs of time and place. He favored the Jews when political necessity demanded it, and was ready to change his course and make concessions to the anti-Jewish forces whenever expediency dictated it. The close of the Reconquest brought to an end those political conditions which enabled qualified Jews to take part in the state administration and the resettlement of the devastated and depopulated territories. It was the inevitable result of general changes taking shape during this period, and was not at all dependent upon the personality of a particular king. There was really little difference in this respect between Castile and Aragon. Castile merely retained for a longer period the character of a state engaged in a war against Islam. Moreover, Arabic influences lingered there a few generations longer than in Aragon.

A Summary of the Period

During the thirteenth century the political structure of Spain underwent marked changes which in turn affected the wellbeing of its Jewish communities. At the beginning of the century the peninsula still bore a predominantly feudal character. The barons and the knights, preoccupied with the prosecution of the war against the infidel, maintained an attitude of tolerance or laxity toward Jews and Judaism. By the end of the century, however, most of the Iberian peninsula had been unified into several large states. In each of them, a uniform code of law for the entire country, or for each of its major divisions, was soon to go into effect. A professional bureaucracy was gradually being trained. In the economic sphere the Jews came up against the competition of the Christian burghers. The mendicant friars kept a watchful eye on the Jews. The war of Reconquest was virtually ended, and existing borders were being carefully guarded. The Spanish rulers now began to bring their treatment of the Jews in line with the prevailing nationalist and religious mood of Christian Europe. Castile, no less than Aragon, began the liquidation of the policy which had prevailed throughout the Reconquest. Aragon was in that respect a little ahead of its neighboring kingdom, where the decisive turn did not take place until a few generations later. Essentially, however, the Jewish policy of both kingdoms had the same purpose. It was directed, consciously or unconsciously, toward the assimilation and absorption of the Jews into the Christian society through conversion or, failing that, their expulsion from the land.

During this period the right of the Jews to their own existence was still recognized. Even after the close of the Reconquest the state still needed the Jews for the large revenues it derived from them in a variety of ways. It is difficult to estimate with any degree of exactness what percentage of the total budget of the state was covered by the Jewish taxes. In Castile at the end of the thirteenth century the fixed tax (*pecho*), which was paid in a lump sum (*en cabeza*) by all the aljamas collectively, amounted to two million gold *maravedis*, besides the surtaxes (*servicios*) and special levies. The obligations of the Christian citizenry were limited, during the thirteenth century and even thereafter, to military service and a land tax payable in fruit. Payment in grain was required also of the Moslem farmers. The revenues from the cities were not very large. The bishoprics and the large abbeys contributed heavily to the expenditures of the state both by outfitting military units and taking care of other military needs, and by covering the expenses of the court whenever the king, in his travels, availed himself of their hospitality. The income from other sources—like the port customs, the fees of the chancellery, fines of all sorts, the mintage and salt monopolies, to mention only a few—was irregular and uncertain, except when these sources of revenue were farmed as concessions to men of capital, mostly Jews, who were able to advance money to the crown on their account. A more accurate estimate of the Jewish share of the tax load in Aragon can be made on the basis of an extant tax-register of the year 1294. The fixed tax of the Jews at the time accounted for twenty-two per cent (22%) of the total of all the direct taxes paid by the Christians, Jews and Moslems. To that must be added the frequent special subsidies and forced loans exacted from the Jews for financing military campaigns, diplomatic missions, royal marriages, and like needs.[77]

The political, economic, and cultural importance of the Jews declined with the waning influence of their notables at court. In Castile, to be sure, the influence of the Jews in the conduct of the state and in its financial administration was still considerable, and in Aragon, too, the Jewish aristocracy regained some of its positions at court in the fourteenth century. But these small circles of men of culture and wealth could easily be either assimilated into the Christian society or expelled from it. Jewish society—whose social structure will be discussed in the chapter which follows—was based upon a petty bourgeoisie of shopkeepers and artisans. The Spanish rulers had already ceased to encourage and support the economic development of these groups and even sought to curtail their rights. But even during the period of stabilization which followed the cessation of the Reconquest, this petty bourgeoisie continued to play an important role in the economy of the cities and of the country as a whole.

The Christian municipality and the Jewish aljama remained, for the most part, separate political entities. The Jewish community maintained its own economic policy. The municipality sought to supervise Jewish trade and handicraft, but such control was possible only when Jews did their work or conducted their business outside the boundaries of the judería. There were localities, in Castile particularly, where the Jews assisted in the town's fiscal administration, contributing the experience which they acquired as tax-farmers. The Jewish physician, often an appointee of the municipality, was very popular with all elements of the population, including the poor classes and the monks. The class of educated burghers, which rose alongside the nobility, paid little attention to the principle of religious segregation and entered into friendly personal and professional relations with Jews. Jewish textile merchants employed Christian workingmen, and Jewish artisans had bishops, grandees and prominent citizens as their clients.

In the development of the economic life of the cities, the stewardship of their finances and the administration of justice, the various elements of the population were brought together, to the chagrin of the zealots in both camps. Christians would sometimes turn to a Jewish arbitrator to settle disputes among them, and Jews would carry their cases to the Christian notaries and judges, in violation of Jewish Law and custom. Christian officials began to exercise supervision over the Jewish communal administration and the Jewish courts, and to take an interest in Jewish customs. The Jew, whose business brought him into close association with Christians, had to become conversant with Spanish Law. The respected Jewish citizen, if he did not possess sufficient talmudic erudition to earn the title of "Rabbi," was addressed by the Christians as "Don" or in Catalonian, as "En." The bearing and demeanor of the Jewish courtier had all the dash and grace of the Christian knight. It is safe to assume that the Jewish inhabitants of the small Castilian towns dressed like their Christian neighbors, in spite of the legislation of Alfonso X prescribing an extremely modest garb for the Jews, though no distinguishing badge. Only in Catalonia, it seems, was the Jew made conspicuous by the long round cape topped by a hood, such as was worn by the monks. What distinguished the Jew even more than the particular cloak was the badge imposed upon him by James I. But even the badge could be easily covered. The highly-placed Jews were, of course, exempted from all identifying marks or clothes.[78]

The delicate threads of natural human relations formed a bond between Jews and Christians which was further cemented by a common allegiance to and reliance upon the ruler of the land. (The concept of patriotism as a consciousness of a common fatherland was still foreign to the thinking of those generations.) In spite of the religious difference and mutual distrust, the Jews saw in the king—even as the Christians did—a ruler by divine grace, the guardian of justice, right and security on earth. The Spanish kings fully recognized that their responsibilities to the Jews in this regard were the same as those owed to the other inhabitants. They proclaimed this principle on many occasions, and also abided by it—except when they allowed themselves to be swept along by the anti-Jewish currents, under the influence of religious agitation or their own wilfulness.

There is no doubt but that the status of the Jews of Spain in the thirteenth century was superior to that of their brethren in the rest of Europe, who were exposed to constant plunder and violence. Yet even in Spain they felt a sense of insecurity and a consciousness of a state of internal war. The Jews sat on the crater of a volcano seething with religious and nationalist tensions. It erupted from time to time, prompted by internal strife and foreign war and by the agitation of the Church. The Jews reacted cautiously yet energetically. They sought to prevent defections from their faith and to bring back the converts, willing or forced, into their fold. The Jews even gained a few proselytes. Those who owned Saracen or Tartar slaves—a thing possible only among the wealthy, during the happier periods—abided by the talmudic law concerning slaves: they circumcised them and gave them their freedom, conditional upon their observance of Judaism. When such occurrences became known, they were likely to lead to trouble. These acts of proselytization were deliberate assertions of religious superiority, and the Christians were quick to react to them. Both Jews and Christians were interested in the preeminence of their faith.[79]

Christian Spain stood out among the Christian states of Europe as at once a land of religious fanaticism and religious tolerance. Both were natural phenomena in a country where members of all three monotheistic faiths lived and worked side by side. In the everyday relations among the several communities there were frequent manifestations of genuine cordiality. The reader will find evidence of this throughout most of this book. We will cite here only one of the finest example. We referred earlier to the account by the Infante Don Juan Manuel of the passing of Sancho IV, attended during his last hours by his Jewish physicians, Isaac and Abraham ibn Wakar. The infante became celebrated later as a war hero and a leading exponent of chivalry in Castilian literature. In his *Libro de los Castigos* (The Book of Admonitions), written in his old age and dedicated to his son, the infante advises his son always to keep in his service a physician of Don Isaac's family, for he found no other physician as capable or as trustworthy. In his last will, drawn up in 1339, the infante wrote,

> Even though Don Solomon, my physician, is a Jew, and is therefore ineligible to serve as executor of my estate, yet, inasmuch as I have found him to be always indescribably faithful, I request that my sons retain him in their service and entrust their affairs to him. I am confident that they will profit thereby; for, were he a Christian, I would know what to entrust to him. I so charge my ex-

ecutors, for I am confident that he will show the same solicitude for my soul as he showed for my body.

The last statement refers to the execution of the terms of the will regarding the distribution of charity for the salvation of the soul of the departed. In a codicil to his will he again urges his son to include Don Solomon among his advisers, "For I know well that this will serve him (*i.e.*, the son) to greater advantage than anything else. Inasmuch as I, his father who loves him heart and soul, order him to do so, he need have no fear that he might be better served otherwise." It is worthy of note that the man whom Don Juan Manuel describes in one of his books as the one true and loyal friend he has found, is identified by a present-day Spanish scholar as the said Don Solomon, the infante's physician. This supposition is borne out by the poetry of Todros Halevi.[80]

In the theological literature of the day such a humane note was most unusual. The name of the great Catalonian mystic, Ramon Lull (died 1315), comes up in this connection. In his *Libre del Gentil e dels Tres Savis* (The Book of the Gentile and the Three Sages), he brings together the protagonists of the three faiths in a friendly disputation. The Jew, Christian and Moslem, in turn, expound their respective faiths before a pagan who has come to them in search of salvation. The sages do not interrupt one another's exposition, but the pagan sometimes interposes a question. After they have completed their discourses the three learned men, in an inspired mood, bid farewell to the grateful pagan and refuse to hear his decision as to the faith he has chosen, intending as they do to continue their discussion further on even terms. They obtain one another's permission to prolong their remarks at the next opportunity and beg each other's forgiveness for any possible slight inadvertently cast upon another's faith. The author strives to remain objective in his presentation of the arguments of each of the three religions. A distinguished Spanish scholar of a generation ago suggested that Judah Halevi's *Kusari* served as a prototype for Ramon Lull's polemic work. His knowledge of Judaism was probably derived, in part, from Maimonides' *Guide of the Perplexed.* He sought to learn all he could from the learned Jews and converts with whom he came in contact. This is the impression gained from his discussion of the doctrine of the unity of God and the diverse views on Resurrection and the Hereafter. His treatment of the messianic hope reveals understanding. Divine justice, he says, requires the fulfilment of his national aspirations as recompense for the trials and tribulations which the Jew could have escaped through apostasy. The power of humility in the heart of the Jew is greater than the power of arrogance in the hearts of the Christian and the Moslem. Lull combines perception with malice in dealing with the divergent concepts of resurrection among the Jews. They cannot arrive at unanimity in dealing with the problem of the Hereafter because all their thoughts are centered on the hope of redemption from their mundane woes and their heavy yoke of taxes. Another cause for their confusion is the fact that the Hebrew tongue is no longer in functional use among the Jews, to the point that they lack sufficient texts on philosophic questions. They limit themselves to the study of the Talmud, which is so involved as to leave no room for the problems of the Hereafter. This study leads them to concentrate instead upon legal matters so as to enable them to acquire the benefits of this world. Basically, Ramon Lull is unable to evaluate Judaism objectively. Skilful writer that he is, he artfully employs the exposition of the Jewish sage to develop the teachings of his own faith. The discerning reader will recognize readily that the author holds Christianity to be the true faith. At the end of the disputation, which closes presumably without a decision, there is an allusion to other works in which the same question is to be dealt with again. The book of this poet and mystic remains, nevertheless, a noble testimonial to the desire of the Christian to understand the Jewish soul. Except for a similar work by Peter Abelard, it is doubtful whether anything approaching it can be found in the Christian polemic literature of the Middle Ages. There is nothing like it, of course, in Jewish literature of the period. The struggle for survival, both physical and spiritual, demanded of them, first of all, a sound understanding of themselves rather than an overindulgence in tolerance and broad-mindedness. Even the tolerance of Ramon Lull was only literary. We know that he, who devoted a lifetime to the conversion of the Moslems, obtained from James II of Aragon permission to preach to the Jews. There is good reason to suppose that in his oral sermons he was far less gentle than in his written works.[81]

The other polemic works written in Spain had as their purpose the furtherance of the religious conflict in its cruder aspects. We mentioned earlier the *Pugio Fidei* of Raymond Martini. The book is clearly the result of the failure of the formal Disputation held in Barcelona in 1263. After the author learned from experience that the talmudic sayings, in their original form, cannot be adduced in support of Christian dogma, he went to the trouble of creating—on the basis of the authentic Midrash, and by means of abridgements, combinations and additions of all sorts—a collection of forgeries of obvious Christological content, thereby to mislead the susceptible.[82] Its appearance presaged havoc and destruction for the future. The instruments which brought masses of Jews to apostasy at a later period were prepared in the second half of the thirteenth century.

V

THE INNER LIFE OF SPANISH JEWRY
DURING THE THIRTEENTH CENTURY

THE CULTURAL PROBLEM

The historical process which transferred the Jews of Spain from the political jurisdiction of the Moslems to that of the Christians was virtually completed by the middle of the thirteenth century. All the lands south of the Pyrenees, with the exception of the kingdom of Granada, had now fallen under Christian rule and were incorporated into one or another of the three large Iberian states—Aragon, Castile, and Portugal. The first two, which were eventually to be united under one crown, were still independent of each other and pursued divergent domestic and foreign policies. The Jewish populations of these two kingdoms each had their individual characteristics, but the basic problems confronting all of Spanish Jewry were intrinsically the same. Sufficient documentary material for an adequate study of the history of the Jews in Portugal is still lacking. The life of the Jews of the small kingdom of Navarre, nestling in the Pyrenean slopes, will be treated in our subsequent discussions only to the extent to which it helps clarify the development of Spanish Jewry as a whole.

The events which altered the political face of the peninsula within a relatively brief historical epoch also wrought fundamental changes in the social and cultural life of the Jews. The modern historian who studies inner Jewish life during this period finds himself asking the following questions: Were those generations of Jews aware of the magnitude of the role fate had thrust upon them? How did they bear their destiny— did they make peace with it, or rise above it? In seeking an answer, one must realize that such crucial problems of history can be solved only when set against their proper background of the prevalent conditions of life and of the accepted concepts and viewpoints which leave their stamp upon the individual's consciousness, give it direction and guidance, yet also limit its sense of perception. For many centuries now, Jews had been restrained from bold political action by their hope of ultimate redemption which was beyond the power of man to accomplish but rested entirely in the hands of Providence. The general incapacity of medieval man for undertaking comprehensive solutions of great political problems helped perpetuate this state of mind. Judah Halevi's farsighted views were not shared by his contemporaries, many of whom preferred to seek careers in the courts of the Christian rulers. It is hard to tell to what extent the Jews of Spain, in the second half of the thirteenth century, still remained cognizant of the great changes which had taken place during the preceding two hundred years. Human beings in general— and this was especially true of medieval man—are inclined to regard conditions which arose in their own time and were crystallized before their very eyes as having existed, unmodified, from time immemorial. Nevertheless, the cultured Spanish Jew, who read the Hebrew poetry of the "Golden Age," could not help realizing that the earlier order had changed and the foundations upon which rested the well-being of his ancestors had crumbled. Deep in the heart of every Jew was the cherished memory of his nation's political independence on its ancestral soil. Yet even the humble Jew, not given to such grandiose political dreams, but abiding by the simple faith of the Middle Ages, could not fail to see that his generation was called upon to play an important role in the religious and social orientation of Spanish Jewry.

As in general European history so in Jewish history, and especially in the history of the Jews of Spain, the thirteenth century marks a cultural turning point. This period ranks in importance with the Golden Age of Judaeo-Arabic culture. During the latter period Jewish tradition, aided by Graeco-Arabic rationalism, had received its classic formulation. The centers of Jewish culture were at that time to be found in the courts of the autocratic Moslem princes. In the thirteenth century, this cultural heritage, nurtured and fostered by an enlightened aristocracy, was transplanted to a different social scene agitated by new conditions and currents. The Jews now had to adjust themselves to a Christian state and society, dominated by medieval feudalism. In the cities a democratic order was developing. The popular monastic movement, typified by the Dominicans and Franciscans, was attempting a new interpretation of Christian tradition.

As Jewish culture moved from the Moslem south to the Christian north, it left the princely courts and descended to widely scattered, even isolated, communities. The refined, pleasure-loving courtier and the high-handed, unscrupulous politician now met with the simple, sober townsman and the superstitious villager, as well as with the pious ascetic and the rapt mystic. No longer was the ideology of a small aristocratic upper stratum to dominate. The true national religious ideals, streaming originally from popular fonts, strained to return and fructify the soil of their origin and make the entire people the bearer of its inherited religious values. Positive steps were taken in that direction. Religious reformers bitterly critical of the existing situation, came forth to fashion new religious and social concepts. The movement which arose as a reaction against the culture of the aristocracy and its estrangement from the traditional values was popular in origin, ascetic in character, and steeped in the national mythos. The work of the Spanish reformers may be compared to that of the sages of the Mishna, who had sought to save their people from secularization and disintegration. A generation which witnessed so great an effort must still have possessed considerable vitality and could be led to appreciate the decisive role history had placed upon it. The historian's duty is to reconstruct the various spiritual currents, set them against their true background, and thereby reveal their actual direction.

LOCATION AND STATISTICS OF THE JEWISH SETTLEMENTS

Before beginning our consideration of the inner life of Spanish Jewry, it is necessary to determine insofar as possible the numerical strength of the Jewish population and its distribution according to provinces, cities and villages. The reader must bear in mind, however, that direct statistical information concerning either the Christian or the Jewish population of any medieval country, Spain included, is almost completely lacking. Only for a few cities do we have any reliable statistical data. Nevertheless, we are in a better position for a statistical study of the Jewish communities than we would be for that of the Christian population. As an "asset" of the royal treasury, the Jews were subject to special surveillance, and registers of their tax payments were compiled at frequent intervals. On the

189

basis of these tax rolls we can arrive at a cautious estimate of the number of taxable families. This information, supplemented by certain conclusions to be drawn from the available knowledge of the compass of the Jewish quarter and about some of its inhabitants, will give us a fairly clear statistical picture. To be sure, it will not be exact in every detail, but it will be closer to the facts than the many exaggerations which have come to be accepted in modern historical literature.

During the thirteenth century the Iberian peninsula was a sparsely populated territory, and it remained in that state to the end of the Middle Ages. The economy of the peninsula, and especially that of Castile, was predominantly agrarian. Only a few cities developed as centers of commerce and industry, and to these the Jews were mostly attracted. If we take the tax rolls of the Jews of Castile for the year 1290 as our basis, it follows from computations too detailed to be entered into here that the Jewish residents of all the lands under the Castilian crown totalled no more than 3,600 tax-paying families—a sizable number for the time.[1] England, by way of comparison, had at that date, the year of the expulsion, no more than 3,000 Jewish souls, according to considered estimates. We will now examine the several communities individually.

The Jewish community of Toledo, whose many distinguished members and spacious quarter made it the subject of legend, was already popularly credited with a fantastically large population early in the thirteenth century.[2] But the tax-rolls seem to me to indicate for Toledo and the villages within its orbit a Jewish population of not much above 350 families. Andalusia, in the south, which had been a constant battleground from the Almoravid invasion until its reconquest by the Christians, was virtually depopulated. We need not consider here the reports which credit the flourishing Andalusian cities at the height of Moslem power with hundreds of thousands and even millions of inhabitants. The fact is that at the time of their conquest by the Christians these cities and their Jewish quarters were empty and desolate.[3] In the beginning of the fourteenth century special inducements were needed to increase the size of the Jewish community of Seville. In 1290 it numbered about 200 families. The aljama of Cordova was smaller still, neither the city nor its Jewish community having retained much of their former splendor. Jerez de la Frontera is the only city for which we have precise data. According to the aforementioned *repartimiento* of 1266 the Jews owned some ninety houses in the city. The list is not complete, however, since Jewish homes outside the judería were not included. On the other hand, some of the houses listed therein were allotted to Jews of Toledo and other localities in the north, but we do not know to what extent the latter really augmented the size of the local community by taking up residence there. In 1294, the tax levy upon the community of Jerez was extremely small, no doubt because of financial straits. The rural Jewish communities of Andalusia began to grow numerically only in the fourteenth century. Of all the once illustrious aljamas of southern Spain, only that of Seville succeeded in attaining once again a high level of material and cultural prosperity.

Western Spain had a meager Jewish population. In Leon, in 1294, the tax-collector travelled "from place to place in search of Jews."[4] In Santiago de Compostela, an archiepiscopal seat and commercial center and a shrine to which pilgrims flocked to pray before the reputed sepulcher of the apostle James, a few Jewish families appear in the fifteenth century. In Portugal, likewise, the numerical and cultural growth of the Jewish population did not begin until the fifteenth century. In northern Spain, Burgos had the largest Jewish community, with about 120 to 150 families.[5] There were, in addition, several communities in both Old and New Castile—in Cuenca, Segovia, Avila, Medina del Campo, Valladolid, and Carrion—each with an estimated population of fifty to a hundred families. In Segovia, there were in 1390 fifty-five Jewish home owners, living on land belonging to the cathedral. It may be that this was "the community of sixty-five families" for whose welfare the cabalist R. Jacob Gikatilia, whose grave was reputed to be in Segovia, had uttered prayer more than a century earlier. The property book of the cathedral of Avila for the year 1303 shows some forty Jewish homes located on the cathedral's land. To these, ten more Jews are to be added whose names appear in other documents. About fifty Jewish families, according to my estimate, lived in the citadel of Soria. The rest of the city, inhabited entirely by Christians, had a population of only 700 souls. In several places the local church or monastery enjoyed the privilege of settling Jews on its lands, with the number of such families limited to forty in Palencia, thirty in Sahagun, and twenty in Villadiego. One must assume that these were the only Jewish residents in those localities. The sums paid in taxes by these communities in 1290 offer no grounds for the assumption that they had grown since their establishment. So distinguished a community as Guadalajara consisted of no more than twenty or thirty families. The Jewish population of Medinaceli was no larger, and that of Peñafiel was undoubtedly smaller. Peñafiel was reputedly the final resting place of the noted cabalist R. Joseph Gikatilia. Don Isaac ibn Wakar, physician to the local overlord, Infante Juan Manuel, had a home there. Yet the tax-collector could not find a single Jew there in 1294. But these small communities, made famous by their distinguished members, deserve mention. A great physician, or a mystic wrapped in his recondite lore, might take up residence in an isolated hamlet and find there a livelihood or patronage, and eternal rest.

In concluding our survey, we can say that during the thirteenth century there was only one large Jewish community in all Castile, the one in Toledo, distinguished for its scholars, intellectuals and financiers. Next in rank was the aljama of Burgos, in the north. The Andalusian communities showed no signs of recovery as yet. It was in the lesser communities, scattered throughout the area between these cities, that Jewish culture was preserved and fostered in Castile during the thirteenth century.

Tudela, the old and notable community of Navarre, had ninety Jewish taxpayers in 1391, but we do not know how many families it had in its prime. In Pamplona there were sixty-six Jewish home owners in the fourteenth century. Both the above communities were on the downgrade by this time. In Estella there were in 1265 twenty-nine houses occupied by Jews, for which they owed a rental and a land-tax to the royal treasury. But the rental for six of these houses was already omitted from the account books of the crown, either because they had been sold to Christians or were no longer leased to Jews. The above three aljamas were the largest in Navarre. In addition, a number of small Jewish settlements were scattered throughout the Pyrenees. But even during the best years there were no more than three or four hundred Jewish families in all Navarre.[6]

The leading Jewish community in Aragon was that of Saragossa. Its population is to be estimated, on the basis of documents from the fifteenth century, at approximately 200 families. There is no reason to suppose that the size of the community was any greater two centuries earlier. Between the middle of the thirteenth century and the middle of the fifteenth, the aljama of Saragossa experienced a period of prosperity followed by decline and ruin, and then revived once again. In the end the boundaries of the judería remained unchanged, allowing for no further expansion. At the highest point of its growth its size probably equaled that of the aljama of Huesca concerning which we have more exact figures. A *takkana* of the year 1340, governing taxation, reveals that Huesca had at the time 300 male Jews fifteen years of age and over. In Calatayud the situation was about the same. Eight other Aragonese communities had from thirty to fifty Jewish families each, and there were a number of even smaller size. In some villages the Jews did not even organize a communal administration of their own, nor did they attach themselves to one of the larger aljamas, but paid their taxes together with their Christian or Moslem neighbors.[7]

In Barcelona, the capital of Catalonia, the location of the Jewish quarter (*callum*) in the heart of the old city, in close proximity to the cathedral and the old castle of the count, allowed no room for expansion. During the fourteenth century some Jews settled on another street, called *Sanahuja*. There is no mention in the documents of any Jewish homes outside these limits. A royal rescript of the year 1377 calls attention to the small compass of the Jewish quarter of Barcelona. When the restoration of the community, following its destruction in 1391, was contemplated, the number of Jews expected to respond to the king's invitation to resettle in the city was estimated at 200 families, a figure approximating the size of the community prior to the catastrophe. A similar estimate for Lerida put the number at 100 families. The other noteworthy Catalonian communities were Gerona, famous for its great rabbis but with a population undoubtedly smaller than that of Barcelona, and Tarragona and Tortosa, whose growth appears to have fallen short of the expectations held out for them at the time of their reconquest. Of particular importance are the small rural communities in Catalonia, whose number increased throughout the fourteenth century. In nearby Perpignan there were from 200 to 250 resident Jewish families at the beginning of the fifteenth century, but no other community in the south of France ever approached that number.[8]

At the turn of the thirteenth century the city of Valencia had close to 250 Jewish taxpayers, all of them listed in an extant tax register. Unfortunately, we do not have an equally detailed document for the period immediately preceding the reconquest of the city, which would have made it possible to determine the changes which took place in the composition of the community during its transition from Moslem to Christian rule. It does appear certain that the Jewish courtiers, who settled in the kingdom of Valencia during the reigns of James I and Pedro III and grew rich there, disappeared from the province as soon as the treatment of the Jews took a turn for the worse. But the native Jews of Valencia who, like those of Toledo and Andalusia, largely spoke Arabic and bore partly Arabic names, were joined by immigrants from Catalonia and Aragon, without any Arabic background whatever. In the second half of the fourteenth century the increase in the Jewish population necessitated widening the boundaries of the judería. Hasdai Crescas' estimate of the size of the community at the time of its destruction as one thousand families cannot be relied on as fact.

Outside the capital, communities of about fifty families each existed in Jativa, Murviedro, and Castellon de la Plana. The government appears to have kept the taxes of the Jews at a low figure for a long time—as was also the case in Andalusia—in order to attract Jewish settlers to the territory, but to no avail. Throughout the Middle Ages the province of Valencia was settled principally by Moslem peasants in a status of partial serfdom. Denia, which had been the seat of an Arab prince and of a Jewish community, fell into virtual desolation, with only a handful of Jews remaining there. The strong efforts on part of the government, from 1238 to 1283, to encourage the settlement of Jews in these areas met with little success. The cause of this is to be sought not in political and economic restrictions but in the low cultural level of the territory.[9]

Finally, there was the community of Majorca, which reached its prime in the second half of the fourteenth century, when it was said to have had more than a thousand families—an unlikely number even if we are to include the Jews living in villages surrounding the capital.[10]

Totaling the estimated number of Jews in all the lands which came under the Aragonese crown by the end of James the Conqueror's reign, we arrive at a figure not much different from our total for Castile.

Our aim in the foregoing statistical survey was to present the reader with a realistic picture of the situation as it existed at the time, rather than to arrive at absolute accuracy in every detail. The variegated culture of the Middle Ages was supported by much smaller populations than those with which we are accustomed to deal today. Even the largest Jewish communities in Spain, which were undoubtedly also the largest in Europe, never consisted of more than 200 to 400 families. Hebrew culture blossomed even in the smaller centers—a fact very important for the understanding of the social and religious life of the time.

Of equal interest and importance are the general characteristics of Jewish dispersion and settlement on the Iberian peninsula. New settlements remained close to the old established centers; the Spanish Jew did not readily change his residence. Except for a certain type of indigent scholar or craftsman, the Spanish Jews were not accustomed to migrate from place to place, as their brethren in France and Germany were compelled to do by political and economic pressures. We encounter the same family names in the same localities from the beginning of the twelfth century, through the persecutions of 1391, and down to the final expulsion. This also explains why the Jews did not at first settle in any appreciable numbers in the western part of the peninsula. The expansion of the field of Jewish settlement was controlled, not by economic causes alone, but by political and cultural factors as well. The territories reconquered during the thirteenth century—Andalusia, Murcia, Valencia, and Majorca—held no attraction for Jewish settlers at first and played no significant role in Jewish cultural life during this period. The stage on which the dramatic internal religious conflict—to be discussed later—unfolded itself, embraced primarily Toledo, Barcelona and the many lesser communities scattered throughout Aragon, Catalonia and northern Castile, that is, those areas where Christian influence was already paramount.

THE SOCIAL-ECONOMIC STRUCTURE

The social-economic structure of the Jewish communities in Spain varied with time and place, and one must guard against pre-judgments ascribing to them a uniformity which did not in reality exist. Information on the subject is regrettably scant and is derived mainly from incidental accounts that have reached us. In Toledo the tenor of communal life was set by the scions of the old aristocratic families of Abulafia, Ibn Ezra, Alfakhar, Ibn Shoshan, Ibn Zadok, and others whose forebears had resided in Toledo under the Moslems or were brought up from Andalusia by the Christian rulers. Out of these circles came the aforementioned scholars and courtiers, as well as the tax-farmers and financiers whose far-flung operations were spread over all Castile. They were the owners of large estates in the south and the operators of textile shops in Toledo, Seville and Cordova. The rest of the community consisted of small shopkeepers and artisans. (There was a street known as Shoemakers' Lane in the judería of Toledo in the fourteenth century.) Additional data concerning the crafts practiced in the community are found in fifteenth-century documents. In the rabbinic responsa of Castile, mention is made of Jews engaging in "the production of clothing in a stall," meaning the manufacture and sale of cloth. This was the occupation pursued, no doubt, by the more prosperous of the lower middle class. Jews of Toledo cultivated their own vineyards outside the city. In the smaller communities within the capital's orbit, where civil and even criminal jurisdiction had to be entrusted to men who could barely read, there were not likely to be found men qualified to engage in monetary operations. Certain institutions of the aljama of Toledo also seem to indicate that influence in communal affairs was exerted not alone by the wealthy aristocracy, bred in the culture of the Arabs, but also by the simple Jews whose way of life had come to resemble that of their Spanish Christian neighbors. The economic life of the few other

197

large communities of Castile presented an equally diversified picture. In the small towns and hamlets, however, conditions varied widely according to time and place.[11]

The famous community of Avila, consisting of about fifty families, was made up principally of small shopkeepers and artisans, among them blacksmiths and dyers. One of the latter, "Rabbi Judah the dyer," appears to have been an ordained rabbi. The Jews of Avila also had land under cultivation and owned small herds of sheep and cattle. At times they would lend money on interest to Christians. The one distinguished personality in the entire community was Don Joseph de Avila, one of the leading tax-farmers during the reign of Sancho IV. The cabalist Moses de Leon also lived there for a while, at the time of the appearance of the "prophet" of Avila whose career will be discussed below. Among the fifty-five Jewish home owners in Segovia, listed in a document of the late fourteenth century, twenty-three were artisans—weavers, shoemakers, tailors, furriers, blacksmiths, saddlers, potters, and dyers. There were also a few merchants, one physician, and even one toreador. The social pattern of the lesser communities of New Castile remained unchanged until the expulsion. There were a few cultured, well-to-do families, a number of scholars supported from public funds, with the rest of the community belonging to the already familiar types of the lower middle class. In cities like Avila and Segovia the Jews resided in the center of the town, on Church land, in houses leased from the local cathedral. Their forebears had probably occupied the same ground at the time of the Reconquest and even earlier under the Arabs. No separate Jewish quarter existed, and the Jews lived among the other inhabitants of the city. Their homes were sometimes in a dangerous state of disrepair or imminent collapse. Evidence of wealth and economic progress are not commonly found. Yet they found the place spacious and comfortable. Cities such as these had grown but little since the days of the Reconquest.[12]

The material decline of the small community of Guadalajara, famous as the residence of Moses de Leon, author of the
Zohar, is reflected in two extant documents from the last decade
of the thirteenth century. These record the transfer of two
houses, a courtyard and a stall from Jewish ownership to the
possession of Franciscan convents enjoying the patronage of
Queen Maria and her daughter, Infanta Isabel. These houses
adjoined the homes of prominent Christians. The importance of
the transaction is attested to by the signatures on the instrument of sale, among them that of "the rabbi Don Joseph
Camanon, physician to the Infanta," a man of high social
standing, who was at the same time a distinguished member of
the group of cabalists which made Guadalajara famous as a
center of mystic lore. But a century later, the community, now
enjoying the protection of a celebrated branch of the Castilian
nobility, was on the road to recovery. It was completely wiped
out during the persecutions in 1414, yet revived successfully to
become once again the center of both Torah and secular learning. At the close of the thirteenth century, however, the community appears to have passed through a grave economic
crisis. In one of the aforementioned documents, reference is
made to a former synagogue which appears to have passed into
non-Jewish hands.

The cabalist R. Isaac b. Moses ben Sahula, who was intimately associated with this community, complained, shortly
after 1280,

> Fate in its treachery thwarted me, and laid its heavy
> hand upon me, and after taking me into its custody aban-
> doned me in another land. I dwell in forsaken cities,
> doomed to dispersion. I behold the inhabitants of the land,
> crestfallen and depressed, moving awe-struck through a
> vale of woe, hungry and thirsty . . . for words of wisdom.

Such was the plight of Castilian Jewry during the reign of
terror initiated by the aging Alfonso X. The communities were

on the brink of dispersion and their members disheartened. Worried and distraught, they could devote no time to serious learning and sought comfort in parables and anecdotes drawn from Arabic literature, the heritage of their ancestors, the founders of the community. Isaac ibn Sahula therefore composed for them his *Meshal ha-Kadmoni* (Parable of the Ancients), attractively couching his mystic and ascetic teachings in secular literary forms.[12a]

In Medinaceli, not far away, a Jew named Abraham entered, in 1280, into a contract with the archdeacon of the church of Siguenza regarding the exploitation of the local salt mines. Abraham obligated himself to put a certain number of salt mines into operation within a given time. He took an oath upon a Torah to do his work faithfully, to the satisfaction of reputable citizens, both Jews and Christians. After extracting the salt, he was to turn half of the yield over to the archdeacon and keep the other half himself. At the end of four years the mines together with all their installations were to revert to the church. Abraham received from the church a sum of money, an ass, a workingman to assist him, and a house near the mines to live in. Abraham's sons pledged themselves to carry out the terms of the contract in the event of their father's death. Other Jewish operators of salt mines are found in the thirteenth and early fourteenth centuries. But Christians had a larger part in the exploitation of the salt mines of that region than did the Jews, and eventually the latter were eliminated entirely.[13]

After the close of the Reconquest opportunities for Jewish economic expansion became limited. Landed estates were acquired only by wealthy royal favorites. In north Castile, as already mentioned, attempts were made to restrict the right of the Jews to acquire land; but the Christians never succeeded in gaining this objective. On the other hand, as late as the middle of the fifteenth century we find in a place called Haro, near the border of Navarre, Jews and Moslems conspiring not to sell land to Christians. The Christian municipality, in retaliation, forbade both the local inhabitants as well as those of the entire district to sell or lease to Jews or Moslems any land whatever, be it garden, field, or vineyard, declaring all such sales and leases null and void. The Christians had become impoverished as a result of the wars raging in that territory and feared their holdings would fall into the hands of strangers. According to a modern historian of the town, the Jews owned considerable acreage in what was termed the "Jewish precinct." The members of the community posted their own guards around it, and cultivated their grain fields and vineyards themselves or leased them to Christian or Moslem tenants. At the same time Jews had land under cultivation in the Christian precincts. At the time of the expulsion, Haro numbered forty-eight Jewish taxpayers, a number of them artisans—potters by trade. The Christian population at the same time consisted of seven priests, thirty-two knights, five paupers, and 263 regular taxpayers.[14]

The royal legislation, the deliberations of the Cortes, and the rabbinic responsa of the time tend to create the impression that the Castilian Jews were for the most part tax-farmers and moneylenders. Actually these occupations were limited to the small upper stratum which, to the outside eye, appeared representative of the entire Jewish population. The repeated complaints on the part of townsmen and villagers against "Jewish usury" actually arose out of everyday petty transactions, involving purchases of goods on credit. The type of small Jewish community, so common in Germany, where all or most of the members were professional moneylenders, was virtually non-existent in Spain. In the responsa of R. Asher b. Yehiel there is a case of Reuben,

> who is an artisan, a dyer or saddler, and has an annual expense in the form of gifts to the judges and officials, to keep them from trumping up charges against him—the usual contribution that handicraftsmen are required to make out of their handiwork. Now the community also

201

subsidizes the judges when resorting to their courts, and it demands of Reuben that he contribute his share. But Reuben replies, "What have I to do with you, that you have come to me when you're in trouble?"

It would appear from this responsum that only Reuben derived his livelihood from handicraft, whereas the remainder of the community dealt in finances. But we learn from another responsum of the same rabbi, this one dealing with the apportionment of taxes, that in a certain other Castilian community there were not many more than a hundred members with fortunes amounting to 120 silver *maravedis*. Only about ten had greater wealth and there were some who didn't even possess that much. A sum of 120 *maravedis* could, at this time, purchase a small wardrobe. The members of this community, then, barely eked out a livelihood, working, apparently, in the handicrafts. In Valdeolivas, in the district of Cuenca, there were twenty Jews in 1388, of whom there were six shoemakers, three tailors, one smith, one weaver, and one itinerant journeyman, the latter a rather common type among Spanish Jews. They were all either poor or of modest means, with fortunes ranging from 80 to 5,300 *maravedis*. Yet several of them were addressed as "Don" and one is called "Rabbi."[15]

In the thirteenth century the community of Talavera de la Reina was small and dependent upon the notables of Toledo. It enjoyed a steady growth, and in the quarter-century preceding the expulsion numbered 168 taxpayers. Thirteen of its more affluent constituents—six of them members of the same family —whose "fortunes" amounted to 30,000 *maravedis*, were engaged in basket-weaving. There were three silversmiths, two shopkeepers, and a few physicians and tax-farmers. But the artisan type—the blacksmith, the saddler, the tailor, the shoemaker, etc.—was the predominant one in the community. Altogether there were thirty-seven taxpayers worth between 10,000 and 30,000 *maravedis*—a modest sum, if we take into account the constant depreciation of the coinage through the years. There were seventy-one in the 1,000 to 10,000 *maravedis* class, while sixty owned no more than 100 to 500 *maravedis*.[16] The Castilian communities were similarly constituted also during the thirteenth century. As in ancient times during the Second Commonwealth and the talmudic period, and as in the countries of the Near and Middle East to this very day, so in medieval Spain, and especially in Castile, the handicrafts provided the economic basis for the communities of the simple, pious Jews who originally formed the greater part of the Jewish population.[17] Only in the provinces along the French border do we find any trace of that much maligned economic type, common among the Jews of northern Europe.

In Tudela, Navarre, in the early fourteenth century, the Jews still continued the aforementioned practice of annually leasing from the government the *alcaiceria*, the shops of the silversmiths and shoemakers, and buildings and land adjoining the commercial center. A similar arrangement appears to have been in force in Pamplona. The Jews still retained a measure of the economic position and influence which they had secured for themselves during the early days of the Reconquest, but a decline had evidently set in. There are instances of real property, which had been in Jewish hands for generations, passing out of their control. Shem Tob Falaquera, a member of one of the distinguished families of Tudela, writes plaintively in 1264 that

> The time is one of stress and danger . . . troubles aplenty beset us, and every man is poverty-stricken by the wrathful rod of fate and must wander through the land in search of sustenance; hardship closes in on every side and misfortune approaches from every direction. . . . There is no righteous man left in the land, and transgressors are legion.

In his didactic work, *Ha-Mebakesh* (The Seeker), a rich man is presented propounding this advice, "Choose to be a

tiller of the soil or a merchant, but if thou canst lend thy
money on interest, seize the opportunity, neglect it not."
"Divide thy money into thirds; invest one third in land, keep
one third in cash on hand, the remaining third into safekeeping
send." But poverty is becoming more and more widespread,
and no means of checking it is available. "Many a rich man
found his wealth a snare, and after climbing to the height of
opulence tumbled down into the abyss of penury." These re-
verses afflict even the Christian knighthood, and their effect
upon the Jews is ever so much more disastrous. "These plagues
and mishaps befall even the mighty grandees and their liege-
men. . . . How much more grievously hurt is the unhappy Jew
who all of a sudden is impoverished and reduced to suffering."
Among the representative social types appearing in this work,
all apparently drawn from contemporary society, there are,
besides the "money men," also the master craftsman, the physician and members of other professions, as well as the "warrior" who prefers the hazards of battle to a lowly, even if
longer life—all scoffed at by the seeker for the path of life
eternal.

The aforecited advice of the rich man, "If thou canst lend
thy money on interest, seize the opportunity, neglect it not," is
symptomatic of the times. In the thirteenth century Navarre
fell under the rule of the dukes of Champagne, who brought
with them the unsavory demeanor of the French nobility. At
the same time religious and economic intolerance on the part
of the Christian urban population became more pronounced.
The Jewish inhabitants of this small kingdom soon entered
upon a mode of life similar to that of their French brethren.
A number of extant tax-ledgers from the third decade of the
fourteenth century, written in Hebrew, contain an accounting
made of their property by Jews of the Pyrenean communities.
These list in detail the debts of money and grain which the
local peasants owe them, with the significant notation that the
legal instruments embodying them are worthless, "since all my

debtors have involved me in litigation over them." They complain of the heavy burden of taxation, "which imposed so great a yoke upon me that I can no longer support myself honestly." Besides the house or a small plot of ground remaining to the family, the only asset generally mentioned is the bed, the only permanent item, apparently, of all their property. There is no mention of profits derived from commerce or handicraft.[18]

In Aragon the social-economic structure of the Jewish communities still followed in the main the lines along which they had begun their economic development in the days when the Jews had laid the foundations of commerce and industry in the new or revived cities. In Saragossa, Huesca and Calatayud the Jews engaged in "the production of clothing in shops."[19] These Jewish *draperos* (cloth merchants) were among the founders of urban commerce. In their own community they enjoyed a high social standing, second only to that of the courtiers' circle. The Jewish community insisted upon concentrating the clothing industry within the walls of its own quarter, while the Christian municipality sought to compel the Jews to produce and sell their merchandise in shops and stalls located outside the judería's walls, where they would be subject to the direct supervision of the municipal authorities. The Jewish artisans—shoemakers, weavers, tailors—began to organize into mutual-aid societies which even maintained their own synagogues. Many of the merchants and artisans, in addition to engaging in business or handicrafts, devoted part of their time to the cultivation, by their own labor, of a field or vineyard they owned in the environs of the city. As late as the fifteenth century the Jews of Huesca are described as being "for the most part cultivators of fields and vineyards from whose produce they draw their livelihood"[20]—this despite the wide diversity of commercial and industrial pursuits characteristic of this community, as revealed by other documents. The annual grape harvest was an important event, engaging most of the Jewish population. In Aragon, as in parts of Castile, the Jewish community—like the Christian town—retained its semi-agrarian character until the expulsion. Many-sided as the Jewish economy in Aragon was, the period of its growth and expansion, nevertheless, did not extend beyond the thirteenth century. From the end of that century on we witness the limitation of the broad privileges granted earlier to the Jewish communities by the kings of Aragon to encourage them in the development of domestic and foreign commerce. The Jewish role in the economy of the country diminishes as competition from the Christian burghers increases and political restrictions multiply, with the overall situation aggravated by repeated economic crises which swept over all Europe toward the end of the Middle Ages.

In addition to a number of scattered documents, an important and still largely untapped source of official information regarding the social structure of the Aragonese communities is to be found in a variety of tax-schedules, covering both direct and indirect levies whose proceeds went to cover the expenses of the crown and the public administration. The method of combining revenues from various sources into a composite plan of taxation, characteristic of the financial administration of most European cities, was first imposed upon the aljamas of Aragon by Pedro III as part of the rapacious fiscal policy of the last days of his reign. In time, however, this system of taxation, unpopular though it was, became an integral part of the administrative machinery of the Jewish communities.

The tax statute of the aljama of Huesca of the year 1340[21] opens with a paragraph dealing with the poll-tax and exemptions from it. Among the groups exempted were members of the community whose wealth amounted to less than fifty *sueldos,* scholars "who study day and night, having no other occupation," the poor supported by charity, and servants. The communal leaders were authorized to exempt certain needy members from payment of this tax, provided the total sum involved in these exemptions would not exceed a certain specified figure. Then there followed a complex system of taxes of varying rates, levied upon both property and business transactions. A tax of one-half of one per cent ($\frac{1}{2}$%) was levied on the value of houses and gardens adjoining them; and another, of one per cent (1%) on fields, vineyards and gardens not adjoining the owner's house. There was a tax of one-and-one-half per cent ($1\frac{1}{2}$%) of the amounts of direct loans of money and of commercial credits (*commendae*) in kind—grain, oil, honey, textiles, etc.—extended to Christians and Moslems. The tax on loans to fellow Jews was much lower, only five-twelfths of one per cent ($\frac{5}{12}$%), since these bore no interest. Loans extended to aljamas, servants, students and the sums involved in betrothal and marriage contracts and in wills went untaxed. There were taxes on mortgaged real estate, on rented homes and stores, on the purchase and sale of land, textiles, grain, foodstuffs, gold and silver, furs and other merchandise, as well as on the purchase of clothes and various other necessities. Finally, the daily earnings of an artisan, if they were above a certain amount, were taxed. Teachers and the readers and sextons of the synagogues were exempted.

The social-economic pattern of one of the large Spanish communities is reflected in the above ordinance. This social stratification had been in existence half a century prior to the enactment of this statute, but the administrative setup founded upon it did not develop until the fourteenth century. The poor of the community were numerous. The others, fortunate enough not to have to resort to charity, derived their livelihood in a variety of ways; but men of means were few. The economic structure of the Jewish community was essentially the same as that of the Christian town. The only difference lay in the fact that interest-bearing loans, forbidden between Jew and Jew as well as between Christian and Christian, but permitted between members of different faiths, were more commonly contracted between a Jew in the role of creditor and a Christian as debtor. The communal statutes paid particular attention to profits derived from loans; and the government, in levying taxes upon the aljamas, took special interest in such transactions. But in general the small loans and commercial credits (*commendae*) yielded only a small side-profit to the Jew, whose principal income was derived from his store or craft, or from his field and vineyard.

Loans and *commendae* also figure prominently in a similar statute, dated 1327, of the aljama of Murviedro.[21a] However, the taxes levied here on such transactions were lower than those of Huesca, and commercial activities between Jews were not taxed at all. Though Murviedro lay near the Mediterranean coast, not far from the great port of Valencia, there appears to have existed no interest at all there in marine commerce. We know from other sources that this community counted as one of its members a man of greath wealth and prominence even among non-Jews. But the aforementioned statute gives no evidence of opulence. The minimum income for purposes of taxation was very low. Every paragraph of the statute testifies to the poverty of the community, the need of its members for all sorts of side incomes, and its leaders' resort to stratagem in an effort to exhaust every possible source of taxation. Every Jew in town, resident or visitor, was required to pay at the end of every month a poll-tax of one dinero. Only unmarried women and the poor were exempted, as well as widows and old people over sixty, supported by charity. As in other localities, so in Murviedro, a large portion of the revenue of the aljama was derived from a tax on the sale of meat and wine. Wine was an everyday drink for Jews as well as Christians, the latter drinking Jewish wine and cursing it at the same time. Every Jewish community had its taverns. The tax, however, was levied on the grape harvest as well. Land, as such, was not taxed in Murviedro. Artisans—specific mention is made of shoemakers and jewelers—paid a tax on their earnings, with those earning less than six dineros a day exempted.

Evidence of economic decline is to be found, by the end of the thirteenth century, also in Catalonia, especially in Barcelona, the largest community of the province. The Christian middle class, which had come to replace the Jews in the state administration, began crowding them out of other fields of endeavor as well. Up to this time well-to-do members of the Barcelona community owned large holdings of all sorts of land, but no evidence of this is found after this time, and there is reason to assume that they lost most such property as a result of a consistent policy of curtailing Jewish ownership of real estate. Modern research, based upon abundant documentary material, has shown that in the province of Roussillon, from the fourteenth century on, Jews acquired vineyards and fields only in mortgages for loans.[22] The situation was the same, apparently, also in parts of Catalonia, notably in the districts of Barcelona and Gerona. In these areas there is no longer any evidence of Jews cultivating the soil. Despite the diversity of Jewish occupations in Barcelona—as will be demonstrated in the next chapter, on the authority of late fourteenth-century documents —the Jews had no conspicuous share in the development of the textile industry, which had begun to flourish among the Christians; nor did they have any appreciable influence on the commerce of the city.

Their modest role in marine commerce was reduced even further, especially in the traffic between Barcelona and eastern Mediterranean ports. In the middle of the thirteenth century, members of the Ascandrani family emigrated from Alexandria, Egypt, to Barcelona, married into some of its wealthy families, and continued to maintain commercial relations with the land of their birth. Other Jewish merchants likewise were wont to travel to Alexandria, but in the first half of the fourteenth century political and religious obstacles began to stand in the way of such trips. Isaac Cap, a member of Barcelona's Jewish aristocracy, and related by marriage to the Ascandranis, spent a few years in Acre, and in 1280 absconded without returning to their owners the sums of money which local citizens, both Jews and Christians, had deposited with him for safekeeping. As a result, the commanders of the Knights Templar and the Knights Hospitaler, the consuls of Venice and Pisa, and the representative of the king of Cyprus at Acre impounded the merchandise of Aragonese Jews trafficking in the Mediterranean, and Pedro III had to defend the rights of his Jewish subjects against these officials. A few years later Isaac Cap resumed his place among the leaders and judges of the aljama of Barcelona. The capture of Acre by the Mamelukes in 1291 severed communications between the eastern and western basins of the Mediterranean and the adverse effects of this were especially felt by the Jews. Their trade was now diverted to northwest African ports, with the Jews of Valencia and Majorca figuring prominently, and those of Barcelona taking but small part in it.[23] Those families, whose ancestors once served the counts of Barcelona with distinction, now turned to banking on a greater or lesser scale, with most of the community deriving its livelihood from handicrafts or petty business—as the materials dating from the closing period of the history of this glorious community show.

At the same time the aljamas of smaller localities—such as Vich, Manresa, Fraga, Alcolea, Cervera, Santa Coloma de Queralt, and others—made considerable progress.[24] These communities, and others like them, were established in the late thirteenth or early fourteenth centuries, and some of them grew to thirty or forty families. Jews, unable to find a secure means of livelihood in the larger cities, would seek the protection of the feudal lords or of monasteries. These authorities granted the Jews privileges not obtainable in the cities of the crown, imposed only a light tax on them, and were lax as regards usury, often contrary to the laws of the land. Such liberal terms, which were included in the charters of settlement, were likely in the beginning to blind the eyes of the Jews to the dangers of exploitation and repression to which they were exposed later on in the "lords' domains." The small communities organized themselves along the pattern of the large aljamas. Sometimes they were even granted criminal jurisdiction in capital crimes and the right to take measures in self-defense against outside attack. In some cases the lord of the village utilized the services of a Jew as steward of his household and supervisor of local trade. The community was granted hunting and fishing rights and permission to cut down trees and pick herbs in the neighborhood of the village. A Jew resident in a village had the right to open a store or a shop or to practice medicine, serving both the local lord and the rest of the population. These small localities were not without learning, even though villagers were generally known to be men of little culture: we have lists of books possessed by some of the villagers. They also maintained contact with the large commercial centers. In Catalonia—as in the Florentine region of Italy—there were villages which maintained commercial relations with the provincial capital. Insofar as their dependence on local overlords permitted, the small settlements affiliated organizationally with the nearest large community, where their relatives lived and in whose synagogues they held pews and in whose cemetery they interred their dead. (In the course of time the small aljamas established their own synagogues and cemeteries.) Residence in a village was not only convenient for political and economic reasons, but was also highly recommended in the Hebrew moral literature of the day.

In our survey of the economic condition of the Jews in Spain we have dealt at length with the occupations of the lower strata of the population. In studying the external politics of the Jewish communities we have become acquainted with the Jewish courtiers, the men of wealth, the possessors of large estates, slaves and concubines. The antagonism between these two social classes formed the background for political and religious conflicts within the several aljamas and within Spanish Jewry as a whole. The external circumstances of Jewish existence were determined in the royal courts; but the lines of the inner development of the Jewish people were forged within the walls of the juderías.

INTERNAL ORGANIZATION AND CONFLICT

The organization of the Jewish communities offered a wide field for independent inner political activity. The national-religious character of the Jewish community in Spain, as well as the specific aspects of its economy, caused it to assume the functions of a virtually autonomous political body. It was charged with the regulation of the religious, social, juridical and economic life of its members. In matters of jurisprudence the laws of the Torah prevailed. The decisions of the Jewish judges were recognized, confirmed and executed by the Christian kings and their officials. The aljamas had at their disposal effective means for the enforcement of their ordinances and the maintenance of religious law and order within their confines.

We do not know very much about Jewish communal administration in Castile in the thirteenth century.[25] At the head of the communal organization (Heb. *kahal*) stood the elders (*viejos*) or councilmen (Sp. *adelantados,* Heb. *mukademin*) and the judges (Heb. *dayyanim*). The *Rab* appointed by the crown over aljamas and provinces also appears to have exercised primarily judicial functions. The *bedin* (also called *al-bedinus, alvedi, vedi*), found in northern Castile and in Aragon, was both public prosecutor and police chief. Originally this office enjoyed high social standing, but its status declined in the fourteenth century. The administrative machinery of the community was still imperfect. In the aljamas, as in the Christian municipalities, certain traditions of the Arabic period still prevailed, as is attested both by the names and the functions of the various offices. The *dayyan* (judge) wielded the same decisive authority in the aljama as the *alcalde* did in the municipality. It was not necessary for him to be a great talmudic scholar, but he was required to consult the local rabbinic authorities before passing judgment. It appears, however, that this precaution was often neglected. The rabbis were also authorized when necessary to take drastic measures to maintain religious discipline. The council of elders, composed of representatives of the aristocratic families, directed the affairs of the community, including the administration of taxes and the law, with no clear demarcation existing between their authority and the prerogatives of the *dayyanim*. However, whereas the elders held their seats on the council by virtue of their lineage, the *dayyanim* were appointed for an indefinite term. Only toward the end of the thirteenth century did the practice of appointing new *dayyanim* annually come into vogue, an innovation which elicited, upon its introduction in Cordova, the following satirical remark from the poet Todros ben Judah Halevi, "They appoint judges and officers annually, like cowherds." Complaints against the conduct of the *dayyanim* and the official "rabbis" came from cabalist circles, and the high-handedness of the Castilian *dayyanim* is revealed in other sources as well. Power in the community fluctuated and men of secular and worldly pursuits as well as rabbinic scholars and pietists are found as communal leaders, depending upon which influences were in control at the time. We do not know whether at this time assemblies of the entire community were ever held. The poorer classes sometimes grumbled bitterly at the power of the rich, but in Castile we hear of no serious efforts on the part of the lower estates to obtain a voice in the government. We discussed earlier the authority of the *dayyanim* and their relation to the king and his court. The aljamas of a whole province or of the entire realm were sometimes placed under the supervision of a *rab,* or head elder, appointed by the crown.

We shall yet have occasion to deal with the conferences of representatives of the aljamas of Castile. In the fourteenth and especially in the fifteenth centuries these conferences became a regular instrument for the settlement of the common problems

of Castilian Jewry in matters of taxation, law and a variety
of religious and political questions. In the thirteenth century,
however, there is no evidence of such meetings. Only in a
document of the year 1290, dealing with the apportionment of
taxes, is mention made of delegates of the several communities
negotiating at the royal court about the size of the levy. Jewish notables from a few districts were appointed to apportion
the tax among the several aljamas, and Don David Abudar-
ham, elder of the aljama of Toledo, was designated to arbitrate
all disputes that might arise. Apparently, no need was felt as
yet for regular conferences.

Most of the Jewish communities were not qualified to administer their affairs independently. The elders of the aljama
of Toledo were authorized by Alfonso X to appoint the "elders"
in the towns about the capital. These "elders" were to be
chosen from among the local inhabitants and invested with
judicial authority to try both civil and criminal cases, even
though "there wasn't anyone in those places able to read a
single letter." The appointments were actually made and were
approved by R. Solomon ibn Adret as an emergency measure.
In the thirteenth century, a royal rescript directed the rabbis
of Burgos to appoint the *mukademin* (councilmen) of the
aljama of Sahagun in the kingdom of Leon, a day's journey
from Burgos, and the rabbinical tribunal of Burgos was to
serve as a court of appeals for the Jews of Sahagun—a most
surprising arrangement, since the Jews of Sahagun had long
ago been assigned to that monastery, on whose land they were
living, and were thus removed from royal jurisdiction. The
abbot retained only the right to receive an oath of loyalty
from the *mukademin* and to appoint over them a Jewish
albedin to collect the fines for the abbot. These meager bits
of information that we have concerning the internal organization of the Castilian aljamas bring to mind the complaints of
the poet Moses ibn Ezra about the "savages" of the north. The
primitive life of the lower strata stands in sharp contrast to

the richly colorful life of the upper classes, glowingly described in the Hebrew literature of that period.

The development of communal organization in Aragon, Navarre and Catalonia may be followed more clearly. In these regions every aljama of any size enjoyed complete autonomy. A permanent central organization of all the aljamas under the Aragonese crown did not exist. Only toward the end of the reign of James I and during that of his successor, Pedro III, would representatives of all the aljamas of the realm sometimes be summoned to the court to be informed of new tax levies. These representatives might take advantage of such an occasion to work out, in conjunction with royal officials, new statutes binding upon all the aljamas in the land, but occasionally these were limited to matters of taxation.[26] When, after the death of Pedro III, the government's fiscal policy resumed its stable and placid course, even these attempts at the creation of a central organ were abandoned.

The existence of such an institution was, apparently, not regarded as vital to the internal interests of the Jewish population. On the other hand, certain politically influential individuals were from time to time invested by the crown with a kind of supervisory authority over all the aljamas. We cited earlier the case of a member of the Alconstantini family whose claim to the office of chief *rab* and *dayyan* over all the aljamas of Aragon and Valencia encountered the opposition of R. Moses ben Nahman and Don Judah de la Cavalleria. In 1294 the queen of Castile wrote to James II of Aragon, bespeaking the confirmation of Solomon Alconstantini, her financial steward, as *Rab* and chief justice of all the Jews of Aragon. James denied the request, pointing out that the privileges upon which Alconstantini based his claim had been allowed to lapse during the reigns of his predecessors Pedro III and Alfonso III, "because the Jews of our land suffered great damage and destruction," and, furthermore, it was unfair to ask "that for the sake of one Jew we lose all the others." But only ten years later

215

Don Ishmael de Portella, brother of Don Muça, serving as a diplomatic agent of the king, also appears as *Rab* and judge over all the Jews of Aragon.[27] In similar fashion James I decreed in 1270 that a certain Jew by the name of Nasi Hasdai should act as the *rab* and *dayyan* of the Jews of Lerida, adjudging disputes among them according to Jewish Law, with the proviso that prior to rendering his decisions he must seek "sound legal advice" from two well-learned men within the community. These scholars were ordered to heed his summons at any time, and failure to do so without good and sufficient reason, rendered them liable to a sizable fine.[28] This man was apparently one of those "illiterate crown rabbis" of whom R. Solomon ibn Adret wrote that anyone who insults them is not liable to the fine of one pound of gold, the penalty prescribed by Talmudic Law for abusing a scholar. Such "rabbis" were more common in Castile. In Aragon, the aljamas would not long have suffered the exercise of authority by men unqualified for the position.

The smaller Jewish communities attached themselves to one of the large aljamas for the purposes of taxation and other matters of joint interest. Even a community like Tarragona, whose long history and importance entitled it, it would seem, to full autonomy, was at the end of the thirteenth century dependent upon Barcelona. The ties existing between the head aljama and its dependencies is described by Ibn Adret in the following words:

> Be advised that we (that is, the *kahal* of Barcelona), the *kahal* of Villafranca del Panadés, the *kahal* of Tarragona, and the *kahal* of Montblanch, maintain a common chest and a common purse for the payment of taxes and imposts levied upon us by the crown. Whenever they wish to pass new regulations governing the assessment of taxes either by the tax-assessors or by the submission of memoranda or by individual declaration, to meet the requirements of the king, we do not impose our will upon them, even

though we are in the majority and the city is supreme in all matters. If we should take action without their counsel, they would not heed us. Sometimes we send our men to them, and at other times their representatives come to us with their resolutions. Only if they fail to do either of these things at our request do we compel them by the arm of the government to come to us or to adopt in their communities the measures that are in force in ours. In other places however the head community decrees for its dependencies and subjects them to its will.[29]

In the course of the fourteenth century we find some communities detaching themselves from their head aljama, while new ones, recently organized, attach themselves to it. The larger communities thus spread their authority over a number of lesser ones, even as the cities extended their rule over the small towns in their geographic orbit. This administrative unit, the *Collecta* (so called, apparently, because of its preoccupation with the collection of taxes), remained the only permanent organizational tie uniting various communities of Aragon.

The attainment of local autonomy and the full development of their communal institutions stand out as the principal goals of the Aragonese aljamas. In no other Jewish settlement of the Diaspora is the influence of contemporary political concepts so manifest as in the administration of these aljamas, whose broad outlines as well as many of the details were patterned after the municipal governments of their neighbors. Early in the thirteenth century they began the practice of electing annually a definite number of communal officers. In Catalonia these were called *neëmanim* in Hebrew—a term corresponding to the *fideles* of several European cities—and in the Latin documents they were titled *secretarii*. In Aragon and Navarre they were designated as *mukademin* (*adelantados*)—the same as in Castile—or *jurados,* a Spanish title in use in those provinces. One of the earliest documents on Jewish com-

munal organization in Spain, dated 1229, is a charter granted
by James I to the aljama of Calatayud, authorizing it to elect
four of its notables (*probi homines*) as *mukademin* (*adenantati*), and defining their functions. The rabbi's (*arrab*) participation in the election was mandatory. No one elected to office
could refuse to serve. The community, however, could replace
the incumbent officials with others whenever it saw fit to do so.
The *mukademin* were empowered to prosecute malefactors, put
them under arrest, impose due punishment upon them, including the penalty of death. They were charged with the administration of communal affairs and could proclaim the ban
(*herem*) with the consent of the *kahal*. Every decision of the
mukademin which had the approval of the *kahal* or of a
majority of its notables (*proborum hominum*) was fully validated by the king. The same royal rescript contained a special
provision concerning two Jews, Acecri aben Cresp and his son-in-law Abraham, found guilty of giving false testimony. The
king ordered their banishment from the city and district of
Calatayud. Should they return to Calatayud, the *mukademin*
were empowered to apprehend them and sentence them to a
fine, corporal punishment, and even death.[30] The prerogatives
allowed the *mukademin* of this aljama exceeded, to be sure,
the limits of communal autonomy generally prescribed for the
aljamas of Aragon.

The full panorama of Jewish communal organization in Aragon unfolds itself before us only in the second half of the
thirteenth century. In a manner paralleling the development of
constitutional law among the Christians there were evolved
and adopted in the Aragonese aljamas, not without internal
contests, the juridical concepts of representative government
and obedience to the will of the majority. At first the communal authorities were, to be sure, chosen from among the
aristocratic families. R. Solomon ibn Adret wrote in 1264 to
the *kahal* of Saragossa:

No uniform practice exists in these matters. In some places the affairs of the community are conducted by its elders and councillors (בעלי=עצתם); there are others in which the majority is unable to do anything without the consent of the entire community; there are still other places where the members of the community choose certain men as administrators for a limited period and are guided by their decisions in all communal affairs. I see that you have adopted the last procedure, since you choose officials called *mukademin*. Wherever this practice is followed, the others are ruled out.

The patterns of communal administration were, in fact, far from stereotyped, but rather in a fluid state. The aljamas followed the political development of the Christian municipality, but their progress was slower because of the circumscribed character of their life and the stronger influence of religion on everyday life. In a responsum addressed to the small community of Murviedro, commenting upon a local controversy over the appointment of the synagogue reader, R. Solomon ibn Adret concludes that:

> In most places now communal affairs are managed by a council of the community's notables, since it is impossible for women, minors and the feeble-minded to have a voice in the management of affairs, and these few councilmen are assumed to be their guardians, taking care of their interests. Nevertheless, if some members of the community, other than the councilmen, protest, their objection is a valid one, since they have not been formally appointed.

R. Solomon's decision was once sought in the case of a community in which one of the three *neëmanim* chosen to superintend taxation was illiterate. He ruled that the choice was valid,

> since the third man, who is illiterate, is just as competent in matters of tax-collection, loans and payments as his learned colleagues are, if not more so. Very often, or per-

haps most of the time, a community will have a large number of *neëmanim* only because all the families in the city regard it as a matter of prestige to have one of their members elected to that office, be he learned or not.[31]

The communal statutes of Tudela, dated 1305, show all power concentrated in the hands of the aristocratic families.[32] "No enactment of the *kahal*," the statutes read, "shall become valid until the eight men—representing eight families—who regularly participate in the meetings of the *kahal* and the *mukademin* holding office at the time have affixed their signatures thereto. The families referred to are the following: Falaquera, Abbassi, Pesat, Shaib, Daud, Menir, Camis, and Orabuena." "No statute, already existing or to be enacted in the future, shall be invoked except as interpreted by eleven of the notables of the *kahal*." "The twenty notables of the *kahal* or a majority of them" shall determine the punishment of recalcitrants and informers. The names of most of the above eight families are familiar to the student of Hispano-Jewish culture. R. Joseph ben R. Shem Tob ibn Falaquera, one of the communal leaders named in the statutes, was probably a kinsman of the fâmed scholar R. Shem Tob Falaquera. These families were, at any rate, the bearers of the talmudic-philosophic culture of their time.

Characteristic of their position toward the religious problems of the day is the fact that in the month of Sivan (May/June) 1305, a few weeks before the proclamation of the well-known ban against those who read the philosophical works of Maimonides (see p. 301), they ordained that in all but two matters—the sabbatical cancellation of debts and the reduction of a debt in consideration for income derived by the creditor from houses of the debtor, held as security for the loan—"all judicial decisions rendered in this city shall be based upon the code of R. Moses (Maimonides), of blessed memory," and "that no resident of the city shall presume publicly in the synagogue to expound and decide the law in any way which contradicts the decisions of R. Moses b. Maimon in questions of ritual law." These prescriptions are recorded in the communal *pinkas* (record book) among a set of statutes governing mainly the maintenance of public order. The statutes reveal the high-handedness with which the aristocratic oligarchy ruled the community. A number of persons are denounced as rebels against authority (*becerros*) and warned that "anyone of them who dares to malign or slander the notables of the *kahal* or members of their families shall pay a fine of twenty *sueldos sanchetes* to the crown." For acts of assault against the same people a scale of fines, graduated according to the gravity of the blow, is provided. "Whoever refuses to pay the fine for slander shall suffer the lash publicly and be absolved, and whoever refuses to pay the fines for physical assault shall publicly suffer the lash and be placed under the ban (*niddui*) for a month's time." A heavy fine was imposed upon those who would conspire against the communal authority. The *bedin* was empowered to initiate an investigation into such a conspiracy even without receiving a formal complaint. Thus, the forms of social struggle, well known throughout southern Europe during the Middle Ages, are manifest here too. Through them the cultured oligarchy hoped to realize the social-religious objectives of the *kahal*.

The administrative machinery of the *kahal* was not developed to an advanced degree. Beside the *bedin,* whose functions are not very clear, there existed commissions of twenty and of eleven notables, representing the leading families; but the authority of these bodies is not defined. Only cases of *malshinut* (informing) were referred for a decision to a board of three men—Joseph b. Shem Tob Falaquera, Samuel b. Joseph Abbassi, and Hayyim b. Shem Tob Menir—all qualified for their task, no doubt, not only by their social rank but also by wisdom and piety. We know nothing of the manner of election or appointment of the three *mukademin*. At a later date (1348) we find them judging cases involving marital law in the surrounding villages, in conjunction with the local scholars. In 1305 the *mukademin* seem to have been mainly concerned with obtaining observance of communal statutes by issuing warnings to would-be transgressors, and were assisted in this duty by some of the notables. They also supervised the disposition of inheritances. They appear in general to have served as the executive arm of the "notables of the *kahal.*" Actual direction of communal affairs was vested in the council of "twenty notables and leaders of the *kahal,*" the counterpart of the twenty *meliores homines* of the Aragonese municipality of the early twelfth century, who became the twenty *jurados* heading the governments of Aragonese cities when the latter achieved corporate autonomy at the beginning of the next century.

In Saragossa, the counter-ban of 1232 against the anti-Maimunists was signed by eleven men, headed by Bahye b. Moses Alconstantini. The signatories were all, no doubt, representatives of the aristocratic families and included in their number a member of the Lavi family and one of the Benvenistes. The lust for power on the part of the Alconstantinis, however, met with considerable opposition, especially from a man like Judah ibn Lavi de la Cavalleria. The first expressions of intra-communal tension, based, like the contemporary social struggle within the Christian city, upon class interests, rose to the surface in 1264, at the very time when anti-Jewish religious agitation reached its height.[33] An organized group (*Hebrah, Haburah*) within the community challenged the "large taxpayers," and demanded that the amount of the individual's taxes be computed on the basis of voluntary declaration under oath (*per solidum et libram*). The rich, on the other hand, favored assessment by appointed tax-assessors. Both sides appealed to James I. The king, or his minister, at first favored the opposition group, but in the end rendered a decision in favor of the method of assessment, for fear that the method of self-declaration opened the way to possible perjury and evasion.

He compromised, however, with the demands of the poorer classes and ordered that the first group of assessors be chosen from their midst. Yet, at the same time, the prominent family of Ibn Baruch secured a private privilege whereby its taxes were to be determined by a special board of three assessors.

The nature of the opposition within the *kahal* can be better understood if we observe the class struggle going on in the Christian community of Saragossa at the same time. The principals in the conflict there were the Confraternity of the Holy Ghost, which was the guild of the farmers, and the artisans' guild, bearing the name of St. Francis. Both sides found support among the upper classes, the nobility and the knighthood. So within the judería, the opposing groups represented specific social economic strata, the *mukademin* naturally being members of the wealthy class.

In the midst of this controversy over taxation, Judah de la Cavalleria, the royal bailiff, appointed, with the consent of the *kahal*, four members of distinguished families as *mukademin*, among them one from the Ibn Baruch family and one from the Almeredi. (A Joseph Almeredi was the physician of James I.) Again, in 1271, the *kahal*, under the leadership of De la Cavalleria, appointed three *berurim*, one each from the families of Almeredi and Ibn Baruch, and the third, as a sop to the family's insatiable pride, was Solomon Alfaquim Alconstantini. But the Alconstantinis were not easily satisfied. They took their complaint to James I, basing their claim to greater authority upon the broad privileges received by their forebears. But the influence of Judah de la Cavalleria proved too powerful for them. Only the intercession of Infante Pedro and of the queen of Castile, the daughter of James I, saved Moses Alconstantini from drastic punishment.

Judah de la Cavalleria passed out of the picture quickly, following the death of James I. His place was taken by the bailiff and *alfaquim* of Pedro III, Moses Alconstantini, a man hated by his community. We hear complaints now, for the first time,

223

against the exemption from taxes enjoyed, on the basis of old privileges, by certain families, such as Ibn Daud, Eleazar, and the descendants of R. Asher. In April 1280 the communal council, consisting of the twenty-five *mukademin*, was empowered by the crown to appoint three *berurim*—here functioning as judges—for a period of five years. The royal decree is signed by Joseph Ravaya. But in August of the same year a new and seemingly contradictory decree from the crown called for the election of three "upright men" (*probi homines*) to administer the affairs of the *kahal*, and the royal bailiff was to compel the elected to assume the functions of their office. The community was torn with strife whose issues included not only the elections, but also the expenditures of the *kahal* and the apportionment of taxes which steadily grew more burdensome during the reign of Pedro III. Personal animosities sharpened the conflict. Contention between the *kahal* and one Joseph ibn Baruch over some buildings belonging to the eleemosynary establishment of the community caused the king to refer the matter to the two foremost rabbinical authorities in the realm, R. Solomon ibn Adret and R. Aaron Halevi de na Clara. A young scholar, R. Yom-Tob Asbili, was severely beaten by Moses Alconstantini and a member of the Eleazar family for having assisted the bailiff of Saragossa, at the latter's request, with a legal opinion in connection with the local family feuds.

In 1282 the *mukademin* excommunicated Abraham ibn Azfora, himself a member of the aristocracy, for berating them. The latter turned for help to the Infante, who ordered one of his agents to investigate the matter and lift the ban. The assassination in the spring of 1284 of the judge Solomon ibn Baruch, a royal appointee, moved the king to order an intensive investigation. Several Jews, suspected of the murder, were apprehended. One of the suspects escaped and was pursued beyond the Castilian frontier. After prolonged investigations over a period of months, the king applied to Solomon ibn Adret for an opinion on the case. The entire case was finally dropped without a decision. It appears that some influential Christians were interested in protecting the murderers. As a result of the troubled situation in Saragossa, Pedro III late in 1284 requested Rabbi Aaron de na Clara to assume the rabbinate of the city in order to restore peace to the community. The rabbi, however, did not remain there very long and soon returned to his home in Barcelona. After Pedro's death in 1285, things quieted down considerably in Saragossa. The entire conflict was quite characteristic of the times. When members of the community rose to positions of prominence and authority in the non-Jewish world, they sought to make their power felt in the petty affairs of the judería as well. The political upheaval of the eighties at once removed these domineering figures from the general as well as the Jewish scene. The social conflict was not renewed until three generations later, and then under somewhat different circumstances.

In Barcelona, the local Jewish artistocracy was represented by a board of neëmanim (secretarii). In 1241 the king authorized the election of two or three probi homines to seek out and punish, by fine, excommunication, or expulsion from the judería or the city, offenders guilty of abusing and slandering the kahal leaders. In 1272 this authority was broadened further. The aljama was permitted to choose two, three or more probi homines, "to exert themselves, investigate and discover all obnoxious persons who, by day or night, within the judería or without, speak or act maliciously against men of good repute; to correct through proper punishment and eliminate malfeasance and impropriety and all else that is contrary to Jewish law and proper custom; and generally to take measures to promote the welfare and prestige of the community." These officials were empowered to apply the penalties of expulsion, excommunication, and the lash (malkuth). In these documents there is laid down the basis for the authority of the berurei 'averot (sin or vice magistrates) who became an integral part of the administration of the Catalonian—and, at a later date, of the Turkish communities. Their function was to punish, often by extraordinary means, breaches of religion and morals. Alongside the *berurei 'averot* there existed also *berurei tevi'ot* (civil magistrates) to deal with monetary cases.[34]

The conflict of class interests led, in the late thirteenth and early fourteenth centuries, in Barcelona and elsewhere in Catalonia, to the creation of the *'Etza* (council). This institution served to increase the number of participants in the *kahal* administration without altering its essential character. The same families who had dominated it theretofore were able to control its composition thereafter as well. By way of illustration we quote from a *takkana* embodying the new change, in translation from the original Hebrew.

> We saw fit to enact and establish *takkanot* and practices in order to promote justice and peace, and have agreed as follows:
>
> The *berurim* shall not appoint anyone disqualified from giving testimony; the *berurim* shall consult with no one in choosing their successors.
>
> The *berurim* chosen at the beginning of the year may do nothing without the advice of the *yo'atzim* (councillors).
>
> The *yo'atzim* shall elect their successors annually.
>
> When the time arrives for the *berurim* and *yo'atzim* to choose their successors they shall retire into closed conclave outside the city, taking their own food. They shall remain so until their choice is made.
>
> The names of the elected shall be announced in the synagogue by the public reader during religious services.
>
> The election of *berurim* and *yo'atzim* need not be by majority vote, for if each of the *berurim* and *yo'atzim* chooses to appoint his own successor he may do so, even if his colleagues do not concur in his choice.[35]

The *takkana* thus sanctions the medieval practice of elections in secret conclave. Since each councillor chose his own successor, the same families were able to perpetuate themselves in authority while rotating the honors among their members.

The earliest reference to the *'Etza* is found in the documents bearing upon the communal dissension in Saragossa in 1264. A number of years later, in the eighties, this aljama had a permanent council of twenty-five *yo'atzim* or *mukademin*, with no clear differentiation between these two terms indicated. In most aljamas, the process of their constitutional development reached its culmination during the late thirteenth and early fourteenth centuries. Political direction and criminal jurisdiction remained in the hands of the heads of the *kahal*, the *neëmanim* or *mukademin*. The normal judicial functions were delegated to specially designated judges, the *berurim*. Other officials, temporary or permanent, took charge of taxation. In the well-organized aljamas, it was the practice even at that time to keep a written record of the transactions of the *kahal*. The minutes of the meetings of the *kahal* and of the courts were entered in special *pinkasim* (record books). The *kahal* scribes, copying the practice of the Christian notaries, made a record also of private contracts. All the *kahal* functionaries discharged their duties as deputies of the larger body, the *'Etza.*

At the beginning of the fourteenth century we find in the aljama of Barcelona, in addition to the seven *neëmanim, a* larger body of thirty men which finally crystallized into the Council of Thirty (עצת השלשים), patterned after the city of Barcelona's Council of One Hundred (*concejo de ciento*). Its composition and prerogatives were defined in the aljama's famous constitution of 1327 (see chapter VIII). Among the seven *neëmanim* who headed the community during the lifetime of R. Solomon ibn Adret, we find year after year members of the wealthy and cultured merchant families—Gracian (Hen), Perfet (Sheshet), Benveniste, Cap, and others—as well as R. Solomon himself and his sons. These were, for the most part, men grounded in the talmudic tradition, who deferred to the authority of their rabbi. R. Solomon himself was exceedingly active in the leadership of his own and neighboring communities and defended energetically the rights of his constituents. It may well have been due to his efforts that the aljama of Barcelona enjoyed a stabler and more efficient administration than any other community in Spain. Other famous scholars were prominent as leaders of the *kahal*. One of them was the cabalist R. Isaac b. Todros. Another, R. Judah Solomon, the teacher of the celebrated mystic Abraham Abulafia, served beside Ibn Adret, as judge. Control of the community was vested in the aristocracy of merchants, financiers and scholars, to the exclusion of the physicians and other intellectuals of suspect ideologies as well as of the numerous tradesmen and artisans. The constitution of 1327 sought to perpetuate power in the hands of the above class by entrusting to the Council of Thirty the appointment of *neëmanim* and judges, and designating the judges and *neëmanim*, in turn, as electors of the Thirty. Similar customs prevailed in most Aragonese aljamas, though in some places election procedures were not quite as primitive as those quoted from the Hebrew *takkana* above.

The influence of the middle and lower classes first made itself felt in the sphere of taxation. In the middle of the thirteenth century a fixed budget and a definite procedure of tax collection were as yet unknown. The annual tax due the crown and the other imposts, as well as the sums required by the *kahal* for charity, the maintenance of the synagogue and similar needs were apportioned among the members of the *kahal* in accordance with their wealth. The measure of the burden to be borne by each taxpayer was determined in one of two ways. It was either fixed by *kahal*-appointed assessors (*posekim*) who estimated each man's capacity to pay according to their own judgment, or computed the tax on the basis of the exact valuation of the individual's assets (*per solidum et libram*) as declared by him under oath and on pain of excommunication. The contest between the protagonists of each method was a prolonged one. We mentioned earlier the first conflict over this issue which broke into the open in Saragossa in 1264. The rich, who favored assessment, argued that in self-declaration under pain of *herem* lurked the risk of divine retribution (because of possible perjury). The middle and poor classes, on the other hand, felt wronged by the arbitrariness of the assessors, the agents of the wealthy. The means of most of the members of the community were small indeed as compared with the fortunes amassed by the highly-placed courtiers. Yet the famous royal bailiff, Muça de Portella, insisted on the privilege whereby he and his family were to bear no more than one-fifth of the tax burden of his aljama, Tarazona, even though this man was obviously well able to shoulder alone the entire budget of this small community. Some of the other bailiffs of the time shirked their communal responsibilities completely. Every community had quite a few indigent people. In one place a dispute broke out between the "magnates," who insisted that the poor go begging for their daily bread, and the "middle classes," who argued that this would be unreasonable. "Let them stay at home and not go begging, for they are our brothers, our own flesh. Let the community be responsible for their maintenance and let us all contribute according to our means." The very nature of the tax problem made it the focal point of the incipient class struggle within the Jewish quarter. It came, as well, within the scope of the lofty religio-ethnic ideology of the singular, and homeless, people. The well-known contemporary moralist, Bahye ben Asher, who appears to have been at this time a resident of Saragossa, vents his indignation at the current abuses, in his ethical work *Kad ha-Kemah* (The Jar of Flour):

> He who does not take meticulous care to contribute his share of the taxes along with his fellow members in the community robs the public and betrays his want of faith and his lack of trust in Reward and Punishment, denies the existence of a personal Providence and seeks to deceive the Lord as did Cain, the villain, who said that there was no

law and no judge and no after-life, but that all the affairs
of the universe depended on mere chance. So thinks he
whose hands are tainted with tax evasion. . . . How multi-
fold are the transgressions of one guilty of this sin! Why,
he undermines the foundations of the Torah and the very
roots of faith whereon all commandments of the Law de-
depend. How many homes of the rich and secure have
perished in consequence thereof; how many fortunes, how
many treasures have been forfeited and lost in its wake!
This is a sin grave above all others . . . many pains are
implicit in it. There is robbery of the public, which alone
is a criminal offense, and the public also contains the poor,
the orphaned and the widowed. . . . It includes yet another
sore—blasphemy of the Lord. It involves perjury, for whoever swears to pay the tax faithfully and fails to do so is
guilty of sin and lèse-majesté. . . . One also incurs the
maledictions of the public, including the poor, the orphaned
and the widowed. Mere common sense ought to teach a
man to beware of their curse, even the curse of a single
individual, not to speak of the curses of many . . . and
especially of the poor, orphaned and widowed. How many
impecunious persons are there of insecure livelihood and
heavy obligations, who shed their life-blood and pay taxes
with their marrow and blood . . . and here comes the
wicked and villainous rich man who says in his heart,
"There is no God," and wants to fill his chambers "out of
the oppression of the poor and the sighing of the needy"
in order to make his own burden lighter and the yoke of the
indigent, the orphaned and the widowed heavier. Why, he
flagrantly blasphemes the Lord. Woe unto them who grow
rich out of the cries of the poor, "for their worm shall not
die nor shall their fire be quenched," and he who sins in
this way testifies that he does not acknowledge his
Creator.[36]

The fight over taxation also brought about the first significant change in the composition of the *kahal* government. From
the aljama of Valencia complaints reached James II charging

the rich with shifting the burden of taxation onto the shoulders of the middle and the lower classes. The king accordingly decreed, in 1300, that all taxes, both royal and communal, shall thereafter be apportioned *per solidum et libram*, by the method of self-declaration. Every taxpayer shall take the required oath in the presence of three Jews, representing each of the three estates (*manus*). These three are in turn to be chosen by a board of twelve men, composed of four representatives from each estate. This Board of Twelve was also required to audit the tax accounts of recent years and to assist the *mukademin* in the election of their successors. The *kahal* thus followed the path of constitutional development in force in the municipality of Valencia as early as the eighties of the thirteenth century. Similar trends were at work also in other communities. Another step toward democratization was the introduction into a number of aljamas of the *Cisa* scheme of taxation, combining direct and indirect levies, which was then in vogue throughout Europe. We will have occasion in the next chapter to discuss the continuation of this social struggle in Jewish society in the fourteenth century.[36a]

The Judicial and Executive Powers of the Kahal

The duties of the *kahal* authorities encompassed a wider range of communal activities than would fall within their purview in a modern city. Theirs was the responsibility for obtaining strict observance of the laws and commandments considered vital to the preservation of the nation and the faith. They were charged with supervision over morals and religion, the prosecution of malefactors and the defense of the community against informers (*malshinim*). In Catalonia, Valencia and Majorca jurisdiction over criminal offenses and breaches of religion was in the hands of the *berurei 'averot* (sin magistrates), whereas in Aragon proper it was the concern of the *mukademin* or "elders" and, to the extent of their influence, also of the leading rabbinical authorities. Time-honored Hebrew tradition no doubt lay at the root of this institutional system, which was not peculiar to Spanish Jewry alone.[37] But the criminal jurisdiction exercised by Spanish Jews was much wider in scope than anything similar enjoyed by their coreligionists in other countries. Already the Moslem rulers in Spain had granted Jewish judges authority to impose the sentence of death, in contravention of both the legal theory of Islam and its application in the East. That the Jewish judges actually made use of this authority is attested by Maimonides, who states in his Code that "it is an everyday occurrence in the cities of the West to execute the informers who by their informing are known to have caused loss of Jewish property, and to hand such informers over to the non-Jews for execution, beating, or imprisonment for their crime" (*Hilkhot Hovel u-Mazik* [Laws of Assault and Injury] VIII, 11; cf. *Hilkhot Sanhedrin* XXIV, 4-8). The practice was apparently carried northward from Andalusia into Castile and Aragon, and later into Catalonia. In those provinces where the influence of the Christian Church was powerful, privileges of this nature were not granted as freely by the Aragonese kings as they were in central Spain.

Beginning with the thirteenth century there are extant charters of privilege covering capital jurisdiction; we also know some details of the application of the latter privilege. Criminal jurisdiction, as exercised by the Jews in Spain, served two distinct purposes—the maintenance of religious and moral discipline and the defense of the Jewish social and political position against the ravages of informers. Both these aims called for a broadening of the authority of the Jewish judges beyond anything they had known in any other country or any other period. The large measure of Jewish participation in the public life and culture of their country and the perennial state of war among the three nations and faiths living, as it were, under one roof, awakened passions and ambitions normally suppressed in the Diaspora atmosphere. The uncouth and unlettered Jews scattered in villages and small towns needed a disciplining hand, and the men whose duty it was to supply this discipline and guidance were themselves not free from the crude and foreign concepts of which, one would think, the Jewish people had purged itself long ago. Due process of law, as known in Spain, could find little support in talmudic Halakha. It was influenced rather by the inquisitorial procedures of Roman and Canon Law as adapted for use in the courtrooms of Christian Europe in the thirteenth century. The expansion of the prerogatives of the aljamas into the field of criminal jurisdiction paralleled the growth of the juridical authority of the cities. The secret trials of informers and denunciators frequently recall the methods whereby the party come to power in a medieval town got rid of the opposition.

The king lent his assistance to the prosecution of informers even when the acts of the latter could have served the interests of the state and the Christian population. Yet to deal with this problem there existed no uniform legal process to be followed by all the aljamas of the same kingdom. Some of the smaller communities had, in fact, the broader and more detailed privileges. Authorities in the Halakha, in expounding the effective law, sought a basis for it in talmudic jurisprudence. Scholarly personalities whom we are wont to regard as leading a life of piety and erudition, far removed from the affairs of the world, found it in their hearts to wield this cruel weapon against delators. The execution of the sentence was left to officers of the crown, but depended in the last instance upon the political powers of the place and the influence of the particular individuals involved in the affair. The aljamas were generally required to pay a sum of money to the crown as wergild for the life of the executed, a fact which in itself impugns the legality of such trials. Detailed information of Jewish criminal jurisdiction in general and its application to informers in particular has come down to us only from the fourteenth century. The jurisdiction, however, was already fully in existence by the middle of the thirteenth century and was even open to abuse by the masses who were inclined to counter any civil suit against them by throwing the charge of informing in the face of the plaintiff.

The *kahal* authorities maintained strict religious discipline within the community. A good example in Castile can be seen in the Toledan reformation of 1281, which will be discussed below. For Aragon, the responsa of R. Solomon ibn Adret contain a number of illuminating incidents. In Jaca the *berurei 'averot* wanted to fine a member of the community because his children's wet-nurse, a Jewess, went to bathe in the river on the last day of Passover. In another aljama the heads of the *kahal* excommunicated a wealthy Jew because he allowed work to be done on Saturday on a house which was being built for him by a Christian contractor. The Catalonian responsa of the fourteenth century are even richer in accounts of similar action taken by the *berurei 'averot*. Additional light on the period we are now discussing is thrown by the account books recording fines paid into the royal treasury by Jews. In the middle of the thirteenth century a Christian jurist prepared a private compilation of the laws of his native Old Castile and included therein a number of legal practices currently in force among the Jews, principally in the aljama of Burgos. This record lists a graduated scale of fines for various degrees of assault and vilification. Similar penalties are incurred for the desecration of the Sabbath or holidays by drawing another's blood by a blow, or forcing him to testify in a non-Jewish court, or by bearing arms, sitting on the wall of a house with one's feet dangling, or leading an animal to water by a chain. Anyone riding on an animal on the Sabbath was punished by fine and the animal was impounded by the *bedin* for the crown. Clothes left hanging outside the house over the Sabbath were confiscated for the crown by the *bedin*. There were other fines for transgression of a ban proclaimed by the *kahal*, for perjury, and for other offenses. Likewise the crown officers of Aragon and Navarre kept accounts of fines (*caloñas*) exacted from Jews for breaches of religion and custom—for theft, blasphemy of Christianity, transgression of communal bans and statutes, selling meat without a license from the *kahal*, taking interest from a fellow Jew. One Jew was fined "for wearing his hat on the Sabbath without a string." In one instance charges were brought before the bailiff-general of Aragon against a "rabbi" of Daroca for failing to inspect his ritual-slaughterer's knife, as required. According to a local *takkana* he automatically fell under the ban. In view of his poverty, he settled with the bailiff for a small fine. But a number of local Jews found themselves facing charges for permitting the said "rabbi," while still under the ban, to join them in a religious service. This gave the bailiff a "legal" excuse for mulcting the aljama. In the final settlement the aljama succeeded in scaling down somewhat the bailiff's exhorbitant demand.[38]

The *kahal's* interest in the religious and moral life of the community expressed itself in the formulation of political and economic policies as well. The *kahal* supervised the economic life of the Jewish quarter and the activities of its marketplace, controlling prices and excluding imports of meat and wine. The pattern of indirect taxation, introduced in the fourteenth century, could be manipulated to effect desired economic aims. It could be used to encourage certain branches of commerce and industry and to discourage others, and as an instrument in meeting Christian competition. Communal statutes sometimes forbade, and at other times permitted, the opening of new textile shops; they regulated the construction of houses within the Jewish quarter; they forbade travel to certain localities or temporary sojourn in specific villages. Limitations were imposed upon luxuries and laws prohibited gambling. These enactments sometimes encroached on the privileges and accustomed manner of living of the Jewish courtiers. The *kahal* of Jativa, for example, in 1283 forbade the wearing of jewelry and gaudy apparel. Infante Alfonso thereupon asked the aljama to exempt from the operation of these statutes a relative of Samuel Alfaquim, the king's Arabic interpreter. More examples of the same will come to light when we discuss the Toledan statutes of 1281.[39]

The *kahal* also gave some measure of attention to the wants of the poor and to education, but both these needs were still far from satisfactorily met. The talmudical academies, presided over by distinguished scholars, were of course not intended to provide a broad popular education. We hear very little during this period of the appointment of teachers for all the children of a community. The children of the upper classes received their broad and versatile education at the hands of private tutors, and the more refined families of the middle class also had to provide out of their own means for the private tuition of their children, which was, for the most part, undoubtedly limited to elementary subjects. It may be assumed with good reason that talmudic training in Spain did not at this time attain the high standards existing in Germany. There were many Jews of the middle and lower estates who did not know how to read or write. Among all classes laxity in religious observance was prevalent, both out of neglect and ignorance as well as out of deliberate heresy. The spiritual leadership of the day centered a great deal of attention upon the maintenance of sound family life; but beyond the many *takkanot* regulating the legal aspects of marriage, no uniformity of marital law and custom had as yet been achieved. There is reason to believe that monogamy was the rule of most Jewish families in Spain; but in those circles which were still under the influence of the social concepts of Moslem culture, there were to be found Jews who had two wives or kept concubines. Only gradually and slowly did the *Herem* of Rabbenu Gershom, enforcing monogamy, gain universal adherence also in Spain.[40]

CULTURAL CONFLICTS WITHIN THE COMMUNITY

We have thus far pointed out the economic and social tensions existing within the Jewish communities in Spain, and the undue influence that outside political factors exercised on their internal affairs. Overlying these tensions were differences in religious and moral outlook which sharpened the conflicts and kept the atmosphere of the aljamas charged with religious and factional strife. In most of the aljamas there functioned a few men who either were heir to high station in the world outside or had attained such position through their own talents. These men sought to impose their own religious ideology and their private interests on the entire community. Political conditions throughout the twelfth and thirteenth centuries favored the ambitions of these people by allowing them to manifest and develop their capabilities. A community which provided no field of action for such an individual remained culturally stagnant. At the end of the thirteenth century intellectual life in the Spanish communities began to show such signs of stagnation. It contrasted with the social ferment of the middle of that century, kept seething by the flames of political ambition and sensual passion, which inspired internal conflict as well as new contributions to literature and to religious zeal.

The poetry of Todros ben Judah Halevi (1247-ca. 1306) faithfully mirrors the life and the interests of the Jewish courtier class.[41] The poet moved in a circle whose members, though nurtured in the Judaeo-Arabic cultural tradition, readily assimilated the mores of the Christian knighthood as well. In Toledo, as in the provinces of Valencia and Andalusia, Arabic was still a current tongue among the Jews, and even among Christians, as late as the thirteenth and fourteenth centuries. The municipal notaries would execute official documents not only in Latin and Spanish, but also in Arabic. The education of a young man of the Jewish upper classes still included, as it had during the Arab period, instruction in Talmud, the secular sciences and prosody. These young aristocrats turned out verses in all three languages, but principally in Hebrew. It is to this practice that we owe the existence of a goodly quantity of poetry from the pen of Todros Halevi. His *Diwan* is, in effect, a compilation in verse of the poet's personal memoirs and his observations on his times and contemporaries. It becomes, therefore, a historical source of inestimable value, compensating in some measure for the lack of contemporary prose memoirs and factual histories—works of a genre foreign to the tradition and temper of the medieval Jew.

Todros Halevi's poetry is permeated by levity and hedonism and by an unbridled sensualism which seeks its objects even among the fair of the other faiths. Interspersed here and there are a few strains of a more refined erotic sentiment, reminiscent of the Italian *dolce stil nuovo*. The poet looked both to the Hebrew poetry of the Moslem period and to the songs of the Galician and Provençal troubadours for his models. We have seen earlier how the Jewish grandees would imitate the ways of the Christian knights. On their travels they would be accompanied by a retinue of young Jews, and also Christians, whom they pampered with gifts of delicacies and finery. The retainers would repay their patron for his bounty with lavish encomia, but spared no words of reproach and warning as well whenever he incurred their displeasure. Political rivals among the Jews would heap abuse upon one another in verse, even as the Christian cavaliers did. The laxity of morals in Toledo is attested not only by the poetry of Todros Halevi but also by a responsum of R. Solomon ibn Adret.[42] The dissolute behavior of the fast set of which the poet was a member drew vehement censure from contemporary moralists, among them the renowned cabalist Don Todros Halevi Abulafia, whose son Joseph also moved in this merry company. This disregard of sexual ethics was itself a by-product of freethinking in religion, which was but a step removed from apostasy. Todros the poet himself, during his brief interlude of repentance, described his erstwhile companions in the following words:

> Unbounded havoc time hath wrought.
> Our faith's Testament retreats before another,
> As comely skin before a scald.
> Sinners abound, miscreant rebels—

Jews so-called, who cherish Christian lore—
Who walk in darkness, from Moses' Law estranged;
Who transgress the sages' precepts,
Too blind to esteem the Hebrew faith.
Exceeding rare is the night in Talmud study spent.
"*Aleph-Bet* will suffice us," they say, "with a bit of
    script.
Hebrew we need not know; Castilian is our tongue, or
    Arabic...."
Reprobates are they! Assuredly, their forebears
Ne'er at Sinai stood nor the Covenant assumed.[43]

Such a Jew, once he became lax in the observance of the commandments of the Law, came to be regarded with suspicion by his coreligionists as one capable of informing against his brethren to his powerful Christian friends, thereby endangering the existence of an entire community or even of all the Jews of the realm.

The truth of the matter is that the poetry of Todros Halevi reflects the manner of life of only a limited circle within the Jewish community of Toledo. But this circle set the social tone for the Jewish aristocracy throughout Castile. The moral level of the Aragonese communities was no higher. Jewish courtesans established themselves in the judería of Saragossa, as they had done in Toledo. At the request of the bailiff Don Muça de Portella, Infante Alfonso ordered their expulsion from the city in 1283.[44] Documents from the Aragonese archives reveal a number of cases of carnal relations between Jews and Moslem or Christian women. Some of the Jewish officials of the Aragonese crown, like the high-handed bailiffs mentioned in the responsa of Ibn Adret, were, undoubtedly, indistinguishable from their Castilian counterparts. We recall also Nahmanides' references to the "Ishmaelites" of Saragossa and the "arrogant" of Barcelona.

There were, to be sure, among the Jewish courtiers men who stood ready to aid their brethren in time of stress. Some were even noted for their scholarship and were authors of works in Halakha, ethics, and even Cabala. Even a bon vivant like Todros Halevi turned repentant after the catastrophic events of 1280. He moved to Barcelona where he became the disciple of the distinguished Rabbis Solomon ibn Adret and Aaron Halevi de na Clara. Upon his return to Toledo he kept aloof for a time from his erstwhile companions among the aristocrats of the court and immersed himself in sacred studies. His poetry of this period is devoutly penitent and suppliant. But he could not withstand the lure of the court for very long and was soon back in the whirl of its political intrigue.

We do not know how the more scrupulous among the Jewish courtiers justified their role in their own minds, and how they resolved the inevitable conflict between the demands of their religion and the requirements of their office and chosen way of life. A minority of them indeed were completely apathetic to faith and tradition, retaining only social ties with their people. Justification for such a course—for those who felt the need to justify their position ideologically—stemmed from a rationalism inspired by the philosophies of Maimonides and Averroes. The Averroistic outlook, in fact, exercised a marked influence in several areas of the social and religious life of the Jews in Spain, and proved decisive in the fateful hours of their history. The descendants of these highly cultured aristocrats were to betray both their faith and their people during the period of great trial which lasted from 1391 through 1415. The scions of these apostates, in turn, would yet be haled before the tribunals of the Inquisition, charged with professing no positive faith whatever, and averring only that man is born and is destined to die, and that all betwixt is vain and meaningless.

Many attempts were made, from the thirteenth century on, to reconcile religious tradition with philosophy. Learned men produced works interpreting the tales and precepts of the Bible and the later Aggada allegorically. Their authors thus resolved their own intellectual conflicts and brought soothing balm to

240

minds similarly perplexed by assuaging their scientific conscience without impugning tradition. Some felt that, once they
had discovered the philosophic kernel hidden in the Torah and
tradition, they were free to discard the shell. Others satisfied
themselves with the oft-made distinction between two types of
truth: the one revealed by religion, the other arrived at through
philosophic speculation. The men who dared propagate these
ideas, by word of mouth and in writing, were, for the most part,
scholars and scientists—physicians, astronomers, and the like—
who had made research and study their life work. They were
mostly natives of southern France. Intra-communal differences
had been more or less satisfactorily settled there, and since the
Albigensian Crusade Jews no longer figured prominently in
public life. A different situation prevailed in Spain. The highly
polished Jewish courtier artistocracy of Spain was cut of a
different cloth. They are justly berated in a contemporary
moralist work,[45]

> They look upon the commandments as mere customs or
> hygienic measures, theorizing that the health of the body
> is therapeutic to the soul. The commandments become a
> subject for philosophic speculation, and philosophy itself a
> rationalization of their indulgence in sensual pleasure. . . .
> Hence they are ever in pursuit of iniquity; they are quick
> to shed blood and eager to fornicate, and ready to violate
> all the precepts of the Torah.

Such a diatribe was not directed at authors and scholars,
physicians and astronomers—who, incidentally, ranked higher
socially in Spain than their counterparts did in southern France
—but was intended to expose the religious and moral nihilism
which was gnawing away at the conscience of the courtier
group, the practical men of the world. These Jews who, utilizing
the opportunities opened up to them during the twelfth and
thirteenth centuries, attained political power and high office in
the administration of the reconquered territories, resorted to
the type of political ruthlessness which had become prevalent

in the cities and states of southern Europe. Casting all restraint to the winds they did not wince at violence, plunder and even murder. Having succumbed—in thought—to convictions so completely antithetical to the faith and traditions of their people, they did not hesitate to trample upon the vital interests of their coreligionists. Not without good reason did the Jewish community rise up to challenge the domineering Alconstantini family in its pretensions to authority over Aragonese Jewry. There was cause, too, behind the assassination of David Mascaran, who had had a hand in the formulation of the oppressive tax measures of 1285.[45a]

VI

MYSTICISM AND SOCIAL REFORM

THE MYSTICAL VIEW OF ISRAEL

The same thirteenth century, marked by social tension, also witnessed the growth of interest in mysticism. The cabalistic movement contributed decisively to the shaping of Jewish history. It is worthwhile for the historian, therefore, to trace the roots of this movement in its native soil in terms of the conditions prevailing at the time of its emergence. For the cabalists were not absorbed solely in mystical thought; they also opened a vigorous attack against the dominant courtier class and participated actively in the efforts to raise the level of religious and moral life. Considerable influence on this reform movement was exercised by recent arrivals from northern France, scholars schooled in the talmudic tradition of *Tossafists*, and by immigrants from Germany, disciples of R. Judah he-Hasid and R. Eleazar ha-Rokeah. In Spain such men were looked upon either as benighted and credulous fools or as paragons of the purest pietism. Their preaching quite likely gained the sympathetic attention of the petty shopkeepers and artisans and the poorer classes residing in the towns and hamlets inside Spain. The pietists were joined in their efforts by Spanish cabalists.

Castile was the birthplace of the Cabala in the form which subsequent generations accepted as authoritative. Among the foremost masters of the Cabala were men of distinguished family, such as *el rab* Don Todros b. Joseph Halevi Abulafia of Toledo and Rabbi Don Moses b. Simon of Burgos, as well as others of lesser social station, as R. Jacob ha-Cohen, R. Joseph Gikatilia, R. Isaac b. Solomon ibn Sahula, and R. Moses ben Shem Tob de Leon, all residents of the small towns of New Castile, north of Toledo—Segovia, Avila, Guadalajara and others. The canon of the Cabala, the *Zohar*, including the portions known as the "Ra'aya Mehemna" and the "Tikkunim," was composed in Castile, and these works abound in allusions which can be satisfactorily explained by referring them to the reigns of Alfonso X and Sancho IV.

The critical study of Jewish mysticism in its historical setting was greatly furthered in our time by the researches of Gershom G. Scholem.[1] Without intending to repeat any of Professor Scholem's conclusions, we will attempt in the following pages to relate this great metaphysical movement to its physical background.

The whole current of mysticism, along with its individual eddies, had a single goal. The mystics—like the rabbis of the tannaitic period when faced with Hellenistic rationalism—sought to remove Judaism from mundane entanglements to the sheltered precincts of Halakha and Aggada and guide it toward a way of life, mytho-mystic in outlook and ascetic in practice.

The attack against rationalism in the name of faith is typical of all the cabalistic works produced during this period. It is most pronounced in Nahmanides' commentary to the Pentateuch. His vigorous opposition to the allegorical interpretation of the Torah is expressed on every page of this work, the most popular of Nahmanides' writings. His avowed aim was "to silence the mouths of the men of little faith and meager wisdom who scoff at the words of our sages," and to refute the opinions of Abraham ibn Ezra and Maimonides, on whom the rationalists leaned for support. He denies categorically that the universe operates according to fixed laws and that the wise man with insight into these laws can base his course of action upon them. All creation is a miracle. Divine providence guides the world. From the overt miracles man learns of the existence of the covert ones, immanent in the operation of the universe. "One cannot be said to profess the faith of Moses unless he believes that all the phenomena to which we are subject are miracles every one, not caused by any natural law."[2] This is the ideology of Judah Halevi, carried to greater extremes.

The Jewish mystics accomplished what the apologists could not. The extensive material of the Halakha and Aggada was presented to the Jewish intellectuals, illuminated by a new light and made to appeal to their hearts and to those of the simple masses as well. The divine Law and the unique fate of the Jew were represented as emanations from the world above. What is more, they serve as channels whereby the individual may exert an influence upon the higher spheres. The precepts of the Torah and the heavy burden they imposed, even the terrible *Galut* in all its cruelty, glowed in a new and enchanting light which dispelled the doubts in the minds of the rationalists and brightened the world of the simple believers, who remained steadfast in their faith in the face of the mounting tide of tribulation. The obvious antitheses between monotheism and polytheistic idolatry were formulated as manifestations of the struggle of Satan against God. Ordinary political rivalries take on cosmic significance; clear and simple differences in belief and conceptions of history are projected into an atmosphere dazzling in its brilliance. The people singled out for suffering on this earth and for ultimate redemption became, in a metaphysical sense, the preferred seed, "the holy root, the truth-bearing stock," thus creating a new, mystically clothed, ethnic concept. The quarrel between Israel and Edom is conceived of as a struggle between the world of light and the realm of Satan. To veer from the faith, to act against the people's interest, to compromise with the outlook of the non-Jewish world or with rationalist philosophy, even to accept service in the princely courts, and—worst of all—to enter into intimacy with Gentile women, is to surrender to Satan. These are the problems dealt with throughout this entire literature, beginning with the commentaries and homilies of Nahmanides, down to the latest portions of the *Zohar*.

The literature embodying this outlook was created principally on the soil of Christian Spain; hence its special bitterness against "Edom," the classical symbol for Rome and the term which in medieval Hebrew literature designated the Christian world. Statements originating in the tannaitic and amoraic Aggada were given a new and often strange connotation. "By thy sword shalt thou live" (Gen. 27. 40) is Esau's (Edom's) assigned lot; he must wage war and shed blood.

> "Fear not, thou worm Jacob, and ye men of Israel; I help thee, saith the Lord, thy Redeemer, the Holy One of Israel" (Isaiah 41.14). Behold, over all the idolatrous nations of the world the Holy one, blessed be He, has appointed known rulers . . . and they all serve their gods . . . and they all shed blood and wage war; they rob and despoil and fornicate and participate in all sorts of iniquitous deeds and wax stronger in their power to do evil. Israel's strength and power of victory is in his mouth (*i.e.*, prayer), like the worm, whose strength and power are

246

only in its mouth, yet with its mouth it breaks down everything. Therefore is Israel called a worm.

Alas, daily we cry and moan and weep—"Remember, O
Lord, against the children of Edom" (Psalms 137. 7)—and
He heeds us not.

No people degrades Israel and spits in their faces as much
as the sons of Edom do.[3]

We can understand such anguished protests coming from
pious Jews who spent their lives among a knighthood that was
ever fighting, either in the reconquest of their land or in rebellion against their lords. The situation was poignantly summarized by the venerable Nahmanides at the Disputation of
Barcelona, when he rose to explain to the king the messianic
concept of universal peace propounded by the Prophets. In the
course of his argument he said,

From the time of Jesus down to our own day the world has
been full of violence and rapine, and the Christians shed
more blood than the other peoples and are lewd in their
morals as well. Oh, how difficult things would be for your
Majesty and your knights if they were no longer to train
for war![4]

The *Galut* (Dispersion) too is conceived not alone in its
physical and historical aspects, that is, as a political condition
and a religious mission to disseminate the precepts of the Torah,
but also in a metaphysical sense, as a cosmic development, as
an earthly symbol for a phenomenon of a higher order. The
sages of the Mishna, in teaching that the Divine Presence is in
exile along with Israel, manifested their pious belief that God
was with his people in their adversity. The cabalists taught
that one of the emanations of the Divinity is actually in exile.[4a]
Galut is a process within the Divinity itself. Intrinsic in *Galut*
are ascetic virtues of a high order. This is how Nahmanides put
it to the king during the disputation,

Our Law and Truth and Justice are not dependent upon a
Messiah. Indeed, you are more important to me than Mes-

siah. You are a king and he is a king. You are a Gentile
sovereign and he is a king of Israel. The Messiah is but a
king of flesh and blood like yourself. When I serve my
Creator under your jurisdiction, in exile, torment and sub-
jection, exposed constantly to universal contempt, I merit
great reward; for I offer of my own flesh a sacrifice to God,
and my reward in afterlife will be ever so much greater.

In his eschatological work, *Sefer ha-Ge'ula* (The Book of
Redemption), Nahmanides wrote,

Even if we were convinced in our hearts that our own
transgressions and the sins of our fathers deprived us of
all consolation and that the *Galut* will be prolonged without end, and even if we thought that it is the will and purpose of God to afflict us with political enslavement on this
earth, this would in no way weaken our adherence to the
precepts of the Torah, for the sole rewards which we antici-
pate are those of the world-to-come—the beatitude of the
soul which, having escaped Hell's torments, enjoys the
bliss of Paradise. We do, however, hold fast to the promise
of redemption, since it is affirmed by the Torah and the
Prophets. In the face of our adversaries—Spain, Rome and
the adherents of the various faiths—we profess our belief
in it, substantiating it with valid proof, and we draw comfort from the words which tell thereof.[5]

This ascetic approach does not seek to supplant in the mind
of the believing Jew the ethnic sentiments which his faith naturally generates. Jewish pietism, with its overtones of mysticism,
deepened the sense of "foreignness" imbedded in the consciousness of a people living in exile in strange lands which are dedicated to foreign forms of worship. The talmudic saying that "He
who resides outside of *Eretz Yisrael* is likened unto one who has
no God (*Ketubot* 110b)," was interpreted to mean that the
fullest observance of the commandments was possible only in
Eretz Yisrael, for the Law of the Lord is mystically wedded to
the Estate of the Lord.[6] The longings for Zion's restoration

grew keener, the messianic strivings became livelier, under a new motivation superimposed upon the old. Nahmanides revived the Judaeo-Christian belief that the six days of Creation symbolized six millennia of human history. The sixth day of Creation was symbolic of the sixth millennium in the history of man, "at whose inception the beasts—the kingdoms who know not the Lord—would be the rulers."[7] The trials of the Patriarchs presaged the tribulations of their descendants. Israel's travail in Egypt was a foreboding of its latter-day bondage to "Edom." The prophecy of Moses, unfulfilled during the era of the Second Temple, referred to the ultimate redemption. This reasoning was meant to counter the arguments of the contemporary Christian polemists. Nahmanides, more than any of his predecessors, reaffirmed the traditional concept of the Messiah. Just as he rejected the wholly spiritual interpretation of messianism developed by the Christians, so was he unable to accept the rationalist view of Maimonides, who conceived of the Messianic Age in purely political terms (cf. *Mishneh Torah,* Book XIV, chaps. 11, 12). He was inclined to accept literally the glories of the Messianic Era envisioned by rabbinic legend. The Messiah will restore Nature, blighted by Adam's sin, to its primordial perfection and beauty, and will banish death and the impulse to evil from the earth. Yet the Messiah has no divine properties. He abides at present in the Garden of Eden, the home of Adam before his fall. He goes into exile at times, suffering penance for the transgressions of his people. He appears in Rome periodically, and will continue to appear there until he accomplishes its destruction.[8]

Messianic prophecies form an integral part of the *Zohar.* Some of these are built around late midrashic material. Others contain allusions to the later crusades and to the collapse of the palaces of Rome, similar to those encountered in contemporary Christian apocalyptic literature. Even the detailed eschatological computations in the *Zohar* correspond closely to those found in Christian works. The treatment of this aspect of the subject at the hands of both rationalist and mystic calls for further investigation. Here too the reaction against the rationalists' concept of the Messianic Age is apparent. The cabalists believed in the imminence of revolutionary changes in the entire order of nature, physical as well as spiritual. By reviving the messianic eschatology they bolstered the popular faith in the supernatural.

THE AIMS OF ETHICAL-SOCIAL REFORM: R. JONAH GERONDI

A marked affinity existed between the ideologies of the ascetics and mystics and the aims of the practical reformers bent upon achieving a higher standard of social morality. One of the staunchest defenders of the faith against the inroad of rationalism was R. Jonah Gerondi, whose last years—he died in 1263—were spent in Toledo. His two treatises on practical ethics, *Sefer Sha'arei Teshuba* (The Book of the Gates of Repentance) and *Sefer ha-Yir'a* (The Book of Piety), introduced a new note into Jewish literature in Spain. Though R. Jonah was conversant with German-Jewish pietism, his own ethical teachings followed the accepted aggadic tradition. They contained, however, overt allusions to certain social ills specific to Spain, with counsel for their amelioration. He singled out for censure those who were lax in the observance of the commandments of *tefillin, mezuza, sukka,* and the ritual washing of the hands, those who partook of cheese and other foods prepared by non-Jews, those who removed their beards, and those who carried their litigation with fellow Jews into non-Jewish courts. He enjoined his coreligionists not to conceal their Jewishness from non-Jews, not to fawn upon the latter, and not to be impressed by their manners. He denounced current immorality, insisting that concubinage without formal marriage was forbidden, as was cohabitation with an unmarried woman or with a slave woman. Especially interesting, from the social-economic point of view, is his warning not to perpetrate injustice by depriving our fellow man of his field, vineyard, or any other possession, even if we pay their price. We are enjoined not to harbor this wicked design, nor plan it in our thoughts, for it is written, "Thou shalt not covet!" And if a man desires that his fellow sell to him a field or vineyard or any one of his belongings, and the latter does not want to do so, and if the man knows that if he were to importune his fellow with incessant entreaties the latter would be ashamed to deny the request, he must not entreat him for that would be a form of coercion.[9]

We know of instances where Jewish owners of large estates succeeded in annexing the small holdings of their neighbors through persuasion and coercion. Like R. Asher ben Yehiel, who, some forty years after the death of R. Jonah, fled from Germany and became the rabbi of Toledo, so R. Jonah called for "zealous efforts to castigate those who in some places lord it over our people and confine a debtor in chains even when he is unable to pay."[10]

A sense of mutual responsibility animating the entire community was, in the eyes of R. Jonah, the keystone of social salvation. Every individual is duty-bound to seek the well-being of his society and the correction of its aberrations, and the community as a whole is responsible for the welfare of every single member in it. The effort to arouse this type of idealism in the hearts of his coreligionists distinguished the preachings of R. Jonah Gerondi.

Let everyone pray daily, in his most felicitous style, that those of the holy people who are sick be restored to health, and that those who are healthy be spared illness and injury, and that the Holy One, blessed be He, save His people Israel from the hands of hostile nations, from an evil spirit, from the pinch of poverty, and from all forms of adversity, and that He set free those of His people who are in captivity, that He ease the pains of women in labor, and that He restore to His true faith those who turned from it under duress.

"Thou mayest not hide thyself . . ." (Deut. 20. 3)—we are herein admonished not to be lax in saving our fellow man's property, real or movable. . . . It is highly desirable that there be in every city a group of high-minded men ready to come to the assistance of any Jew or Jewess who find themselves in distress. . . .

"Thou shalt reprove thy fellow and not bear sin because of him" (Lev. 19. 17)—we are herein admonished not to assume part of our fellow's sin by failing to reprove him. If an individual sins, and his sin becomes manifest, the entire community suffer punishment because of him, if they fail to reprove and reprimand him. . . . In order to escape this punishment the community should appoint honest and stout-hearted men as supervisors in every street and square of its quarter, to keep an eye on their neighbors, reprove them for their trespasses, and eliminate wrongdoing.[11]

The same religiously motivated concern for the common welfare underlies his condemnation of the anti-social elements in Jewish society who will be denied salvation in the world to come. Among them are "those who ravage the Lord's vineyard" —the informers and the sinners who beguile others into sin. Then there are "those who cast a spell of fear upon the land of the living" (Ezek. 32. 24, 26), that is, domineering individuals, dreaded by the community. For their crimes against the public welfare, these bear a threefold guilt,

> for the pain caused the community by their terrorization . . . for the many misfortunes resulting from such terrorization . . . and for the repression of members of the holy people, worshippers of the Blessed Name . . . who may be subjected to the will of other men only in order to make them serve God, for it is written, "For unto Me the children of Israel are slaves" (Lev. 25. 55), and not slaves unto slaves.

252

The same punishment awaits those who consider themselves beyond the jurisdiction of the organized community.

> When the leaders of the people and the holy communities assemble to serve God and enact statutes which set forth divine precepts, they thereby sanctify His Holy Name . . . and the man who exempts himself from communal jurisdiction rebels against the resolve to serve God and withdraws from the community of those who sanctify the Holy Name and manifests his reluctance to sit in their council and be inscribed in their roster.

These words were directed against the Jewish grandees who exerted much-resented pressure upon the communities. It is the duty of the moral reformer to wage a relentless campaign against them.

> He who does not actively join in opposing those who pursue an impious course and promote iniquity shares in their guilt and transgresses the commandment "Thou shall not bear sin because of him" (Lev. 19. 17) . . . and it behooves every man who is God-fearing and pure of heart to turn zealot when he observes the highly placed behaving treacherously.[11a]

The author had the specific ills of the communal life of Spanish Jewry in mind when he offered these warnings and admonitions. Nor did they go entirely unheeded. Reform was already under way. A responsum of R. Solomon ibn Adret records the case of a man "who sought to eliminate corruption in his locality and bring the culprits to account, and who had established contacts at the royal court with a view to obtaining royal authorization for his plans." The notables of his community warned him, under pain of excommunication, not to seek such authorization. Ibn Adret ruled that their objections were without validity, since the thing they really objected to was the rule of law and decency.[12] The influence of R. Jonah's teachings was felt long after his death, in the social and religious ferment of the following generation.

The social reformers were doubly zealous in their efforts to heal the breaches of family morality which appeared in certain segments of Jewish society in Spain. German-Jewish pietism lent inspiration to these endeavors. The centuries-old ban against polygamy, associated with the name of Rabbenu Gershom of Mayence, was gradually achieving acceptance also in Spain. Two interesting responsa from the pen of Rabbi Solomon ibn Adret throw light on the subject. A scholar of Castellon de Ampurias in Catalonia inquired whether

> the enactment of Rabbenu Gershom, of blessed memory, forbidding bigamy and also divorce without the woman's consent, was intended to apply even if the wife has remained childless after ten years of marriage, in which case the (divine) commandment enjoins the husband either to divorce her or to marry another in addition to her, and whether the aforesaid prohibition extended to all countries or was meant to apply only to Germany and France, having become necessary there because of specific conditions prevailing at the time of its enactment.

In the course of his reply Ibn Adret stated,

> What the full intention of Rabbenu Gershom was I do not know, but it would seem to me that he did not intend to make his ban universal . . . and in the case of a wife who remained childless for ten years after marriage, where the husband is required (by divine precept) to marry a second wife in order to beget progeny, I do not believe that Rabbenu Gershom meant to forbid him to do so. In any case, whatever its author's intention was, this enactment was not accepted in our realm nor have we heard of its acceptance in Provence which borders on France. In fact, there are a number of men in our community, among them scholars and communal leaders, who married a second wife while wedded to the first, and no one has ever questioned the propriety therof.

As he grew older, Ibn Adret began to take a different view of the matter. At a later date he received the following inquiry:

> Reuben had married a woman of good family and she bore him a daughter. Later on, the man, succumbing to passionate impulse, acquired a slave woman and she soon conceived of him, without formal wedlock. He converted her to Judaism before she bore the child, and after the child's birth he continued his relations with her. He did not mend his evil way, but persisting in his sin, he caused her to become pregnant a second time. He has now rejected his lawful wife, though she had done no wrong, and he had come to hate not only her but their daughter as well. Please advise us whether the leaders of the community are in duty bound to compel this man to set aside the slave woman even if he had married her. Let us know also whether, in any community within your jurisdiction, custom and ordinance governing similar situations forbid the marrying of another wife in addition to the first. Advise us what the law is and how the communal authorities are to act in this matter.

Ibn Adret's answer was clear and emphatic. The man's behavior, he said, was vile. To the request for guidance he made this reply:

> With reference to your question whether there is in force in our community an enactment forbidding bigamous marriage, which would cover a case such as this, let me state that—God forbid it further—it has never happened in our midst that a man, even the most wanton, should commit such an offense—to cohabit openly with his slave woman, then convert her to Judaism and marry her, and worse yet, to cast aside, in favor of the slave, the wife of his bosom. The altar of God sheds tears over such a tragedy. Already in olden times Rabbenu Gershom of blessed memory, the Light of the Diaspora, pronounced the ban against anyone who would, while wedded to his wife, marry another woman, even one of equal rank with his wife, how much

255

more so a woman of this type. There were but two or three instances in these parts of men marrying a second wife while still wedded to the first, and in each case only because the first wife bore her husband no children. Even then, the husband did so only after taking great care to assuage his wife's feelings. And with all that, I haven't yet seen even one such marriage turn out happily. Your illustrious community, whose fame is far-flung, must not allow its young men to practice iniquity and create a precedent of inconsiderate treatment of the daughters of Abraham. It behooves a community of such pious, learned and wise men as yourselves to compel this man to take his first wife back and thereby stem the evil.[13]

Concubinage, too, now incurred the disapprobation of the rabbis. The first to forbid the practice was R. Jonah Gerondi. In his *Gates of Repentance,* he wrote:

"Degrade not thy daughter by making a harlot of her, lest the land fall into harlotry, and the land become full of lewdness" (Lev. 19. 29). The rabbis explain (*Sanhedrin* 76a) that herein one is warned not to permit his daughter to enter into sexual relations not sanctioned by wedlock . . . for concubinage, without formal wedlock, was permitted only to the king, whose authority effectively restrained others from having converse with his concubine, so that the king's relation to her was tantamount to marriage. Beyond this royal privilege the rabbis decreed that relations even with one's bride are forbidden until the marriage benedictions have been pronounced. Intercourse with a slave woman is a capital sin . . . for the sinner defiled the holiness of God by loving and possessing "the daughter of an alien god" (Malachi 2.11). His alien offspring will be a snare to him and a reminder of his sin. The father shall bear guilt because of the son; he betrayed the Lord by begetting alien children. The heavens will proclaim his guilt and the earth will rise up against him; his sin will diligently press for his downfall and he will end by hanging from a tree.[14]

R. Jonah was supported in his campaign by Nahmanides. In the admonitory epistles which he sent from Palestine to his sons in Spain, where they quickly gained wide circulation, Nahmanides urged upon them moral chastity and continence in the pursuit of sensual pleasure. To his younger son, who was an official of the Castilian court, Nahmanides wrote,

> He who has lewd converse with Gentile women defiles the covenant of our patriarch Abraham . . . and is called a transgressor against God . . . a sinner . . . a traitor and an abomination, a defiler of the divinely cherished sanctities, and he renders himself odious to heaven; for it is written (Malachi 2. 11), "Judah acted treacherously, an abomination was committed in Israel and in Jerusalem, for Judah has defiled the holiness of God which he loved, and espoused the daughter of an alien god."[15]

THE REFORMS IN TOLEDO IN 1281

Another pietist personality who exercised a reformatory influence upon his community was the venerable sage and mystic, Todros b. Joseph Abulafia of Toledo. The poetry of his young namesake, Todros b. Judah Abulafia, reveals the low state of morals which characterized the Jewish courtier society in the Castilian capital in the third quarter of the thirteenth century. The repeated remonstrances of Don Todros the elder went, for a long time, unheeded. Then came the disastrous events of 1280-1281. By command of Alfonso X a number of the prominent courtiers were put to death. The most influential of them, Don Çag de la Maleha, was publicly hanged. Jewish communities together with their leaders were arrested and languished in prison for a long time. It seemed as if the Jewish notables were made to atone for the waywardness of their people. The hearts, contrite and repentant, were now amenable to reform in the pietist spirit. Like Ezra the Scribe in his day, Don Todros rose and expelled the alien women from the Jewish quarter. There is extant the sermon which the old rabbi delivered to his congre-

gation at the time, seeking to implement the teachings of R.
Jonah Gerondi, whose writings served as the authoritative
guide and program for the reformers of that day. Taking as his
text the words of the Prophet Hosea, "Come, let us return to
our Lord, for He has torn and He will heal us, He has smitten
and He will bind up" (Hosea 6. 1), he declared, "This verse
means to assert that the punishments which we suffer daily,
and the ever-increasing burden of exile, come upon us by design
and not by accident or the imperative of natural law." In
a lengthy argument he challenged the belief in astrology, which
was then an essential part of the creed of the rationalists. Clam-
oring for both religious and social reform, he demanded stricter
observance of the Sabbath and greater attention to prayer at
the appointed times; and he denounced usury and perjury. In
common with the author of the *Gates of Repentance,* who had
recommended the appointment of "supervisors in every street
and square of the quarter to keep an eye on their neighbors,
reprove them for their trespasses and eliminate wrongdoing,"
Don Todros demanded of his congregation the elimination of
imprecations from oaths and he urged as a highly desirable
measure that

> men be appointed in both the business districts and the
> residential neighborhoods to take to task whomever swears
> or curses, and have him fined by a court for the first and
> second offenses, and if he does not desist have the court
> inflict corporal punishment upon him as the judges see fit.

He demanded also other reforms:

> In transactions where weights and measures are involved,
> a short measure is sometimes dealt out or the thing to be
> weighed is thrown onto the scale so that excess weight is
> registered. . . . It is therefore necessary to appoint as in-
> spectors of weights and measures two respectable men of
> rank who would show no preference or deference to any-
> one, for in this sort of pilferage no restitution is possible.
> If a single witness should come and testify under oath that

he saw someone steal from a non-Jew, the accused is to be punished, provided the witness is not a personal enemy of the accused. If the accusation is made by two witnesses, his punishment is prescribed by the law. Anyone who sees a theft committed is to be compelled, under pain of excommunication, to report it to the court immediately, so that the name of the Lord may not be publicly defamed.

If anyone protests the decision of a judge on the ground that the judge passed judgment by himself without consulting with another scholar, the said judge is to be required to consult with another scholar, or perhaps with two scholars—with one at least—so that the law may thus be clarified and true judgment rendered.

The burden of the sermon was the improvement of morals. Slave girls should be modestly dressed, so that men would not covet them. Pressure is to be put upon Jewish slave-owners to compel them to liberate or sell their Moslem slave girls who had become objects of immoral advances. If the owners claim that they cannot afford to do this, then the least that the community can do is to invoke the dreaded weapon of excommunication and in solemn ceremony declare that any Jew who is found to have had relations with a Moslem woman shall feel the full weight of the *herem* and *niddui* of the *kahal* of Toledo. Anyone having knowledge of such offenses is duty-bound to report them to the judicial authorities. Our sages, said R. Todros, took a grimly serious view of this type of transgression, and every man in Israel must make a zealous effort to eliminate the vice.

The words of Rabbi Todros made a deep impression which translated itself into effective action. "The entire congregation scrutinized their past behavior with contrite heart, proclaimed a fast, called an assembly, pledged themselves to observe every commandment, without distinction, and in solemn council concurred that he who keeps a mistress shall not be included in the quorum of ten worshippers for communal prayer." Every Jew who owned a Moslem slave girl or employed a Jewish girl

259

as a servant in his home was ordered, under pain of the most severe forms of excommunication, either to remove her from his household or else marry her formally. An investigation was started with the aim of ferreting out thieves and other felons.

Among those who undertook to implement the stern advice of Rabbi Todros was a scholar of Toledo by the name of R. Jacob ibn Crisp. He wrote to Rabbi Solomon ibn Adret, as the foremost rabbinic authority of the day, for guidance in "the administration of the city and the punishment of miscreants." Ibn Adret's responsum is highly revealing, both in the insight which it gives us into the character of its author as well as in the information which it yields concerning the situation in Toledo and the legal weapons which the Jewish communal authorities in Castile were able to employ in order to enforce internal discipline and order.

Know that "a soft tongue breaketh the bone" (Prov. 25. 15). Whoever would level and clear a way before the people by removing the stumbling blocks must proceed gradually from the lesser to the greater. . . . Know, too, that you cannot deal in the same manner with all people. . . . There is a time for everything, and there are times when overlooking a transgression is a beneficence, all depending upon the particular situation. . . . It seems to me that it is vital that the new reforms (instituted during the emergency) should first become well-established, beyond controversy. . . . Until the arms of those who exercise authority grow strong, looking the other way would be a great *mitzva*, and he who observes this *mitzva* actually lends support to the reform and fortifies it as with a wall. That accomplished, let your hands be strong and you shall proceed in the direction desired. . . . It is my advice that you begin with a soft tongue, trying once and twice, making more and more friends, the right hand embracing even as the left repels. Perhaps they will repent their evil way, and there will be no more sinners. But if they hearken not and continue to transgress, "they shall perish by the sword";

tear and pull, "take a cane and strike them on the skull."
. . . But in this there is need of moderation, consultation
and deliberation, so that the punishment that many may
suffer is inflicted for the sake of heaven. For the sterner
the measures taken and the stronger the hand applying
them, the greater is the need for caution against being
carried away by wrath. The judge should always be appre-
hensive lest the flame of righteous indignation burning
within him hide from him the true and proper course.
Therefore, when the zeal for punishment rises within him,
let him not "swallow it while it is still in his hand," lest he
eat it unripened, but he should allow it to ripen and mellow
in the council of elders, righteous of heart. If there are any
notorious criminals whom you have sought to mollify but
who nevertheless persist in their malevolence, you may, in
concurrence with the elders, punish them by the lash, by
cutting off an arm or a leg, and even by death.[16]

THE SOCIAL BACKGROUND AND THE RELIGIOUS AIMS
OF THE ZOHAR

The reformers, for all their zeal, failed nevertheless to effect
any lasting improvement of the morals of the courtier aristocracy. We are led to this conclusion by the pronouncements
on the subject in the basic and most authoritative work of
the Cabala, *Sefer ha-Zohar* (The Book of Splendor), which
was composed, according to an eminent authority in the field,
between the years 1280-1286.[17] Its author, Rabbi Moses de
Leon, was unquestionably deeply concerned over the social ills
which afflicted Jewish society and earnestly strove for their
correction. Not the least of his concerns was the moral laxity
prevalent among the higher classes, as the following admonitions from the *Zohar* indicate:

> Fortunate indeed are the people of Israel that the Holy
> One blessed be He, has chosen them from among all peo-
> ples and has entrusted to them the sign of His covenant.
> For, whoever bears this mark upon his person, descends not

into Gehenna, if he guards it properly and does not let it stray into alien precincts so as not to betray the name of the King. For he who betrays this trust, betrays the name of the Holy One, blessed be He; for it is written, "They have betrayed the Lord by begetting alien offspring" (Hosea 5. 7).

They who respect not this sacred covenant cause a rift between Israel and their Father in heaven, as is written, "And you shall stray and worship other gods and do homage to them; and the Lord shall be wroth with you and shut up the skies and there shall be no rain" (Deut. 11. 16, 17). For he who betrays this sacred covenant is likened to one who does homage to an alien god.[18]

The *Zohar* also inveighs against other lewd practices which were apparently common among the urbane aristocracy of its day.

Three there are who drive the Divine Presence from the world and bring it about that the abode of the Holy One, blessed be He, is removed from the world, and the cry of human beings remains unheard. They are the following: He who lies with a woman in menstruation. . . . He who lies with a Gentile woman. . . . Of this it is written, "And the people began to have illicit relations with the daughters of Moab . . . and the anger of the Lord blazed against Israel" (Num. 25. 1, 3). The heads of the people who knew what was going on and made no effort to stop it were the first to be punished, as is written, "Take all the chiefs of the people and hang them, for the Lord's sake, in broad daylight" (Num. 25. 4). . . . In every generation the heads of the people are held accountable for this vice, if they are aware of it but do not make a determined effort to eradicate it, for it is their duty to become zealous for the Lord's sake when they see His covenant defiled. He who lets this mark of holiness enter alien precincts transgresses the commandment, "Thou shalt have no other gods before Me" (Exodus 20. 3). . . . The third is he who causes

262

the child by him begotten, the one with which his wife is pregnant, to be killed while in its mother's womb.[19]

In a number of places in the *Zohar* the author addresses himself to the contemporary religious leaders, charging them with being derelict in their duty to chastise and reform the wayward of their communities. He paints for them a horrifying picture of a man, ridden by pain and disease visited upon him by God as punishment for his failure to reprove his neighbors for their sins, exemplifying in his person the observation of Eccl. (7. 15), "There is the righteous man who perishes in his [own] righteousness."[20]

Manifest in the *Zohar* is the author's hatred of the wealthy, incontinent aristocracy, which held the destinies of Spanish Jewry in its hands. The Averroistic outlook of this group drew particularly severe and contemptuous criticism from the pen of the cabalist.

> Fools who know not and discern not wisdom say that the universe operates through mere chance without divine guidance. "The fate of man and the fate of beast is the same; as the one dies so dies the other—the same breath is in all of them" (Eccl. 3. 19). And when Solomon observed these fools saying these things he called them "beasts," for they degrade themselves to the level of beasts by uttering such nonsense. . . . May they perish! They are indeed beasts. They are fools. They lack faith. Woe unto them, woe unto their souls! 'Twere better had they never come into the world.[21]

The author of the *Zohar* was conscious of the social conflicts which flared up during this period within the Jewish communities, and his heart was with the poor and lowly.

> R. Eleazar asked R. Simeon, his father: "We've been taught that there are three sins which cause famine to be visited upon the earth, and all three are to be found among the rich, because of their arrogance, and are not found among the poor. Why is it then that God lets the poor

perish and preserves the rich? They will only multiply their sins against Him!"

R. Simeon replied: "You have asked a good question. . . . Observe, now! Of all the inhabitants of the earth none are as close to the Supreme King as those who serve as His 'vessels.' And who are they? 'A broken and contrite heart' (Ps. 51. 19) and 'he who is of a contrite and humble spirit' (Isa. 57. 15), these are the vessels of the King. And when famine strikes the world and hunger and privation bear down upon the poor, they weep and cry before the King; and the Holy One, blessed be He, feels closer to them than to anyone else, as is written, 'For He has not despised nor loathed the affliction of the poor man, nor has He hidden His face from him, but whenever he cried to Him, He listened' (Ps. 22. 25). And then the Holy One, blessed be He, takes note of that which causes famine to descend upon the earth. Woe unto the wicked, who are the cause of it all, when God is moved to scrutinize the world upon hearing the cries of the poor! God save us from ever offending them, for it is written, 'I will be certain to hear his cry' (Ex. 22. 22). . . . Woe unto the rich when there is famine in the world, and the voice of the poor reaches to God. The poor man's offering, you see, comes closest to God, for his heart is contrite."

When the Holy One, blessed be He, visits judgment upon the world . . . it is for the sin of the heads of the people. . . the sin of subverting justice and of distorting it. Do not wonder why God allows the lowly to expire through the failure of the mighty to do justice, for the poor are God's vessels and are close to him and when famine comes they cry to Him and He listens to them . . . and He calls before the bar of justice those who brought this suffering upon the poor . . . as is written, "And when he will cry to me I will listen, for I am kind" (Ex. 22. 26).

"A prayer of the poor man, when he grows faint and pours out his complaint before the Lord" (Psalms, 102. 1). . . . The prayer of the poor man is received by God ahead of all other prayers.

"Happy is he who is considerate of the poor" (Ps. 41. 2).
. . . How great is the reward that the poor merit of the
Lord . . . for they are closest to God, as is written, "A
broken and contrite heart, O God, Thou wilt not despise"
(Ps. 51. 19).
The poor man is closer to God than anyone else, as is
written, "And when he will cry to Me, I will listen" . . .
for God abides in these broken vessels, as is written, "I
dwell on high, amid holiness, but also with the contrite and
humble in spirit" (Isa. 57. 15). . . . Therefore, we have
been taught that he who reviles the indigent scoffs at the
Divinity. . . . And it is also written, "Do not rob the poor
because he is poor, or crush the needy at the gate; for the
Lord will defend their cause and despoil of life those who
despoil them" (Prov. 12. 22, 23). Their Guardian is mighty
and He holds sway over all. He requires no witnesses and
no associate judge, nor does He take a bond as do other
judges.
He who looks after the welfare of the poor man, God sees
to his welfare and prolongs his life even when his day comes
to depart this world. "The wages of a hired man shall not
remain with thee overnight" (Lev. 19. 13). He who with-
holds the poor man's hire from him, in effect deprives him
and his family of their life. Just as he reduces their vitality, God reduces his days and shortens his life in this
world. . . . Even if long life and many good things had
been decreed for that man, they are all withdrawn from
him. What is more, his soul does not rise aloft.
Happy is he who encounters a poor man, for this poor man
is a gift sent to him by God.[22]

The cabalist preacher urges his money-mad contemporaries
to eschew wealth and espouse the Torah. He tells the story of
a young man who came to the academy of a distinguished sage
to study Torah, in the hope that he would ultimately be com-
pensated for his study with material wealth.

One day he approached his teacher and said to him,
"Master, where is the wealth?" "It is obvious," reasoned

the teacher, "that he is not motivated in the pursuit of learning by any lofty ideal," so he retired to his chamber. There he heard a voice saying to him, "Do not frown upon the young man, for he shall yet be great." The master went back to the student and said to him, "Sit down, my son; sit, and I will give you riches." Presently, a very rich man came along and gave the student some of his wealth, and the love of Torah waxed stronger in the young man's heart. One day the teacher found the young man sitting and weeping; whereupon he asked him, "Why do you weep?" The student replied, "Will I forfeit my share of the world-to-come because of this wealth? I seek only the spiritual rewards for good deeds." Thought the master, "It is evident that his study is now heaven-intentioned." He summoned the rich man and said to him, "Take your wealth and distribute it to the poor and the orphaned."[23]

The Torah teaches mankind that God is closest to the poor, the humble and the contrite of heart. A measure of this valuable lesson seems to have escaped the members of the wealthy Jewish aristocracy of Spain, who had directed the internal affairs of their communities during the flourishing period of Judaeo-Arabic culture. The social problem engendered by this partial blindness cropped up again in Jewish life at a later date. The scene was now Christian Spain, where Jewish society molded itself along the patterns of medieval urban life. The appearance of the *Zohar* on Spanish soil, as well as the composition of the *Sefer Hasidim* (Book of the Pious) in Germany, testify to the recrudescence of pietist and mystic movements in Jewry. There were certain qualities common to both the Jewish mystic preacher and the Christian mendicant friar who summoned the members of his faith to repentance and extolled the virtues of poverty. There were, to be sure, fundamental differences between the Jew and the Christian in matters of faith and dogma, in political fortune and in social structure; but comparable developments within the camps of the two religions point not to mutal influences but rather to certain

fundamental laws of history common to all humanity. A comparative study of the two can, however, give us a better understanding of the new type of religious and social reformer, whose
personality is revealed in extant literary sources, scant as they
are.

The author of the *Zohar* did not write the book for limited
circulation among fellow cabalists only. The work he composed
was, it would appear, intended by him to serve as a guide for religious conduct among a much wider public. Through the mystic haze shrouding it, a real-life setting is clearly discernible.[24]
The tales told in the *Zohar* are not figments of the imagination,
invented to provide a frame for the discussions and teachings
of the ancient sages. They are, without doubt, as much a part
of the contemporary scene and events as are the stories concerning St. Francis of Assisi and his companions. While the
author of the *Zohar* put his teachings into the mouths of sages
of the Mishna and the Talmud, he made no effort to conceal the
true social setting of his work. These teachers, who both embody and propound the author's ideology, were meant to stand
in sharp contrast to the communal leaders, rabbis and other
notables so well known to us. Both the social environment and
the way of life of these mystics were different from those of the
sages of Mishna. The cabalist initiates of the *Zohar* wander from
place to place. They sit down to hold discourse in the shade of
a tree in the fields, or in a cave where they seek refuge at night
from highwaymen who waylay Jews in order to rob or kill
them. They encounter tradesmen and toilers on the road and
engage them in conversation. They sometimes obtain a night's
lodging in an inn, like travelling merchants or wandering jour-
neymen. At other times they receive the hospitality of a private
home. Wherever they may spend the night they make certain
to rise at midnight. In one place two scholars inquire of their
host before retiring whether there is a cock in the village to
awaken them precisely at midnight. The latter surprises them
with a description of a water-clock, constructed on scientific

principles, which he himself had devised and so designed that it strikes the hour of midnight. In fact, he tells them, this clock had already struck that hour for an old man who stayed with him, and who had risen, awakened by the clock, to engage in study at midnight. That night, to be sure, the two men are awakened at midnight by this unusual alarm clock. Now, such an incident, as related in the *Zohar*, could not have occurred in a Galilean village in tannaitic times. But it is not pure fiction either. Just as the water-clock was a reality in medieval Spain, such a clock having indeed been devised by a Jewish scientist at the behest of Alfonso X, so were these mystics and the manner of life and deeds ascribed to them, part of a real Jewish experience in Spain.

Another story tells of a scholar coming to a village which was being ravaged by an epidemic. When the villagers learn that a very pious man is stopping at the local inn, they go to him and implore him to save them from the plague. The visiting sage asks them to select forty of the worthiest men among them. He then divides them into groups of ten and stations one group in each of the four corners of the village. He leads them in prayer, penitence and the recitation of biblical verses, and he succeeds thereby in saving the village from disaster. In much the same way the friars were wont to exorcise devils and plagues out of a house or a town. Like the friars, too, the Jewish mystics are in a perpetual state of war with the realm of Satan. Of one of their number it is told that he once entered a house and was greeted by a call to arms: "Come, gather hither! Here comes one of our adversaries; let's assault him before he leaves this house!"

The mystics of the *Zohar*, like St. Francis and his companions, have a singular affinity for nature and for all living creatures. They spend their time in the fields and sit down to rest in "a verdant meadow through which a stream flows." As they sit and study "the field emits a multi-scented fragrance." On occasion "birds gather and spread their wings over them, some arriving and some departing." In one place "three trees spread their branches in three directions in order to shade them, and a fountain of water wells up before them. . . . They sit under the tree and drink of the water and find it refreshing." They praise the beauty of the place, "What roses! What fragrant herbs all about! How superior this fountain is to all other fountains!" They remonstrate with the birds, and sometimes send them on errands. "Birds of the sky, you are not respectful of your master. . . ." "Proceed, ye birds, and tell the one in charge of you. . . ." "O good dove, ever trustworthy messenger that thou art, go thou and tell him. . . ." Finally they leave them alone, saying, "These fowl have undergone much toil of yore, and we do not want to trouble living creatures, for it is written, 'And His mercy is over all His works' (Ps. 145. 9)."

St. Francis and his companions felt that their mission was to go about the earth singing the Lord's praises, playing the role of "the Lord's Minstrels" (*ioculatores Domini*). The same designation, "the King's Minstrel" (בדיחא דמלכא), is applied by the author of the *Zohar* to King David. "The craftsman's speech bespeaks his craft. David was the King's Minstrel, and even though he was in grief he resumed his customary joviality in the presence of the King in order to entertain the King." The eschatological passages of the *Zohar* predict messianic manifestations for the early part of the fourteenth century, the period which figured so significantly in the apocalytic prophecies of contemporary visionaries among the Franciscan Spirituals. The author of the *Zohar* disputes the accepted belief that the gift of prophecy is vouchsafed only to one who possesses the combined qualities of wisdom, strength and wealth (See *Guide of the Perplexed*, II, 32; cf. Abravanel's commentary *ad loc.*). In these near-messianic times, even muleteers may have wondrous mysteries revealed to them.

The Holy One, blessed be He, will reveal deep secrets of the Torah in the age of the Messiah, "for the earth shall be full of the knowledge of the Lord as the waters cover the sea" (Isa. 11. 9) ; and the Scriptures also tell us, "And men shall no longer teach their fellows and brothers, saying, 'Know the Lord', for they shall all know me, from the least to the greatest" (Jer. 31. 33).

At times prophecy falls into the mouths of children and they foretell even more than a prophet. One child remarked, "Is it so strange that children have the gift of prophecy? Does not Scripture say, 'And all thy children shall be taught of the Lord' (Isa. 54. 13)? They are certainly taught of the Lord and prophecy issues from them."

PIETISM AS EXEMPLIFIED IN THE RA'AYA MEHEMNA

Near the close of the thirteenth century an anonymous çabalist composed the *Ra'aya Mehemna* (The Faithful Shepherd) and the *Tikkunim* as a kind of sequel to the *Zohar* and a commentary on it. An analysis of these works provides us with an insight into the personality of their author. He typified the popular moralist preacher whose social mission brought him into ideological kinship with the contemporary Spiritual Franciscan friar.[25] Within the Franciscan Order, the Spirituals constituted a movement whose adherents insisted upon the strictest observance of the Rule of St. Francis, with emphasis on absolute poverty. In their preaching they blended the teachings of their founder with the apocalyptic speculations of the twelfth century south-Italian mystic, Abbot Joachim of Fiore. Abbot Joachim prophesied the imminent dawn of a new age, an age devoted entirely to spiritual pursuits and aspirations, destined to witness the revelation of an "Eternal Gospel," to be preached to the world by a new, contemplative Order, consisting of spiritual men (*viri spirituales*), endowed with spiritual intelligence (*spiritualis intelligentia*). This new age, which he termed the Era of the Holy Spirit, would be the third in the history of mankind, following upon the Era of the Son or Age of the New Testament, which was drawing to a close and which had in turn been preceded by the Era of the Father, or the Age of the Old Testament. In this third and final age, the Era of the Holy Spirit and the Eternal Gospel, mankind will live by the grace of the Spirit in peace and justice and happiness. The prophecies of Abbot Joachim had been composed for the most part during the last decade of the twelfth century, and had been motivated by the political events of the day, whose focus was the strained relationship between the Empire and the Papacy. They embody a critique of existing political, social and religious conditions. The more sharply outspoken Franciscan Joachimites of the following century developed this censure into a systematic attack upon the worldliness of the Church. They bitterly opposed the Church's feudalism, scholasticism and jurisprudence, and all the secular sciences which the official clergy cultivated. To the Spiritual friars all this represented a subversion of the true Gospel. And whereas Joachim spoke in subdued and veiled generalities, purporting only to reveal, through his method of exegesis, the hidden meanings of Scriptural passages, his zealous followers preached boldly and clearly the advent of the Church Spiritual (*ecclesia spiritualis*), to be founded upon the letter and the spirit of the Rule of St. Francis of Assisi.

The author of the *Ra'aya Mehemna* fulminated in a similar vein against the Jewish communal leaders in whom he presumed to recognize a latter-day incarnation of the primeval rebels against divine authority. To him "they are the kin of those who said, 'Come, let us build a city and a tower with its top in heaven, and let us make us a name' (Gen. 11. 4)." Likewise, "they erect synagogues . . . not for the glory of God but rather to make a name for themselves." They despoil the poor, "and when they see Israel in straits, they shirk their obligations and refuse to come to the aid of their people, even though they have the power to help. They neglect the Torah and those who devote themselves to Torah, and prefer to bestow their favors

271

upon members of other faiths." They "neglect the Torah themselves and show no consideration for men of learning and piety who wander from city to city uncomforted, and they even evade their full share of the tax burden." Pleading the burden of heavy taxation, they allot to the scholars only a paltry stipend, which they pay in base coin, while in their own coffers they store "the 'blank' silver coin minted at the time."[25a] "They, the spurious throng (*'ereb rab*), are wealthy and live in peace and contentment, without any sorrow or grief whatever, these robbers and bribe-seekers." "They are a brood of miscreants . . . treacherous as the vipers and scorpions, for they contravene the precepts of the sages and pervert justice." The officially appointed rabbis and judges also draw heavy censure from the author's vitriolic pen and are charged with contributing to the degeneration of morals in their communities.

Sharply contrasted with the wealthy, who are "resplendent in their outer attire but are rotten within," are those poor who are "beautiful within though their dress is shabby." They are the erudite, but indigent, mystic and pietist preachers, reduced to veritable mendicancy and dependent for their sustenance upon the bounties of the rich.

> And they, the wicked lot, regard us as they would the putrid carcass of a dog, for the wisdom of the scholars has a foul reputation among them, in every city and every place where Israel is scattered among the nations. And this spurious breed (*'ereb rab*) become the shepherds of Israel, the Lord's flock. . . . No good can come to the scholars from them, and righteous and God-fearing men are compelled to wander from city to city, knowing no comfort and smarting under the ban.

The powers that be in the Jewish communities persecute the poor cabalists with the weapon of excommunication, on the pretext of heresy or other offenses. "In many places they are allotted a pittance . . . so that the learned, righteous, and God-fearing live in want and grief, leading a dog's life . . . unable to find a resting place."

A perennial struggle rages between the dominant estate of the Jewish community and the school of mendicant preachers. Evil spirits, the brood of Lilith, and all the forces of corruption rise and surge across the earth like the primordial Flood and threaten to shatter the Ark of Noah which bears the company of the spiritually elect, by poverty ennobled. But in the end, in the approaching Messianic Age, the Ark will reach dry land, and then the new spiritual era will begin. The bitter waters of the Halakha will be sweetened by the revealed arcana of the Cabala. The Tree of Knowledge will be supplanted by the Tree of Life. The rule of the arrogant rich will fade away and their place will be inherited by the humble cabalists, the true Israel, bearing out the prophecy, "And I shall leave in the midst of you a people humble and poor, and they shall take refuge in the name of the Lord" (Zeph. 3. 12). Pursuing this allegory the cabalist writes cryptically,

> "And they who are wise shall shine as the splendor of the firmament" (Daniel 12.3)—this refers to those who immerse themselves in that splendor which is called 'The Book of Splendor' (*Sefer ha-Zohar*). It is like the Ark of Noah into which are assembled two out of a city and seven out of a country, and at times only "one out of a city and two out of a family," for they suffer the fate described by the verse, "Every son that is born shall be cast into the river" (Ex. 1. 22). This is the light of this book—and all due to you. And who caused it? The Raven. You will at that time fulfil the mission of the Dove (Hebrew, *Yonah*). For another messenger, your namesake, acted like the raven who was sent out of Noah's Ark first, and did not achieve his mission. He became involved with the ignorant and contemptible, because of their money, and did not pursue his mission to call the righteous to repentance, and he can therefore be said to have failed his master. But in you, the mystic purpose of the mission of Jonah (Hebrew,

Yonah) will be realized. Just as Jonah descended to the depths of the sea, so will you fathom the depths of the Torah. This is the meaning of the verse, "For Thou didst cast me into the deep, into the heart of the seas" (Jonah 2. 4).[25b]

There is an allusion here, not clearly expressed, to two movements in Jewry, one of which failed to execute its mission fully, so that it was left to the other to complete the redemptive process. It is noteworthy that Joachim of Fiore and the head Franciscan Spirituals, in their homilies, likewise used the symbolism of the Raven and the Dove to denote different tendencies in the Benedictine Order and, later on, the Dominican and Franciscan Orders, respectively. In the view of the Christian Spirituals the Dominicans became the pillars of the established hierarchy, were patronized by the wealthy, and became keen students of Aristotelian philosophy. The Franciscans clung, by and large, to their revolutionary ideas concerning absolute poverty, hated science as breeding arrogance and heresy, and never forgot that their founder wanted to create a broad popular movement rather than an exclusive sect or order.

The author presents his principal thesis in a series of allegoristic homilies.

Misfortune befell the people of Israel when they became so engulfed by a "mixed multitude" (cf. Ex. 12. 38) that "it could not be known that they entered into them" (Gen. 41. 21). . . . "Her oppressors" (Lam. 1. 5)—they are certainly of that "mixed multitude" of whom it can be said "Your rulers are unruly and associates of thieves; every one of them loves a bribe" (Isa. 1. 23). "Her enemies are at ease" (Lam. 1. 5)—these are Esau and Ishmael and the seventy sovereign nations, all of whom live in ease and wealth, while Israel suffers in straits and want. Woe unto the world because of this!

As the ship of Israel is tossed upon the tempestuous sea in the final stage of its tribulations, the captain approaches Jonah.

And what did he say to him? "Arise, call upon your God!" (Jonah 1. 6), for trials are coming upon you and your descendants. Creditors are gathering and surrounding your ship, ill winds . . .

"Arise, call upon your God!". . . . Behold, the wicked maid-servant is mistress over you. . . .

"And the men rowed hard to bring the ship back to land"— through repentance—"but they could not" (Jonah 1. 13). . . .

"And the Lord appointed a great fish to swallow Jonah" (Jonah 2. 1)—this is an allusion to the very first exile . . . concerning which the Lord said, "I will go down with you into Egypt" (Gen. 46. 4), meaning—in the interpretation of the Rabbis—that "wherever the people of Israel went as exiles, the Divine Presence accompanied them" (Bab. Talmud. *Megillah* 29a). . . .

"And the Lord appointed a great fish to swallow Jonah". . . and also the faithful shepherd through whom the Torah would be given to Israel. . . . And this is the big fish which is also called "the great crocodile" (Ezek. 29. 3), namely Egypt. . . .

"And the Lord appointed a great fish to swallow"—this is the scourge of poverty. . . . "And Jonah prayed to the Lord his God from the belly of the fish" (Jonah 2. 2)—from hunger due to poverty, which touches the belly of Israel. Then "the Lord commanded the fish and it spewed Jonah out upon the dry land" (Jonah 2. 11)—by dint of worry brought on by poverty they will attain redemption from exile, as is written, "And the impoverished people Thou wilt save" (II Sam. 22. 28). This is the prophecy of Jonah who prophesied that Israel will be redeemed from exile through hunger and poverty, for the righteous Eternal One is poor. . . . Now this Jonah (*Yonah*) is the Dove (*Yonah*) of the Ark of Noah.[25c]

These homilies, embellished with the symbolism of Noah's ark and its dove and of the Prophet Jonah, convey the author's conception of the process of universal history and his eschatological message. The congregation of the select, now engulfed by the powers of evil, will ultimately be redeemed; and the spiritual Truth, now submerged beneath the materialistic forces of history, will rise to the surface and stand revealed in the end of days. The Tree of Life will in the end supersede the Tree of Knowledge. The Cabala will replace talmudic dialectics and hair-splitting argument over questions of ritual. The spiritual Torah will emerge from its tomb, the Mishna. The Messiah will then break out of the prison in which he is confined by the powers of evil which dominate the *Galut* socially and politically. This Messiah is the mendicant cabalist idealized. He is a suffering Messiah, pained by his people's transgressions, "pounded in the mortar of poverty," pursued and persecuted unremittingly. He undergoes exacting penance in order to expiate his people's sins. Dressed in the threadbare garb of the mendicant mystic preacher, he wanders, astride his donkey, from city to city, suffering everywhere the abuse of the rich. However, the glory of the Messianic Age which he will usher in lies not in the political and social liberation which it will bring, but in its spiritual triumphs. The messianic redemption will make the spiritual sense of the Law of Moses preeminent; it will plant the Tree of Life in place of the Tree of Knowledge and will mark the victory of the brotherhood of mendicant cabalists over the existing ruling caste. Only the "learned" cabalist initiates will share in this redemption, and of the masses of the people only those who will be ready to accept their leadership.

In the final exodus from the *Galut* under the learned they will be like the slave who walks alongside his master's horse. Just as He said to them when they stood at the foot of Mount Sinai: "If you accept my Torah, well and good; and if not, your burial place will be right there" (Bab. Talmud. *Sabbath* 88a; *Aboda Zara* 2b), so at the exodus in the final redemption He will say: "If in the exodus from the *Galut* you are willing to accept the learned over you in the relation of a man on horseback to the slave who serves as his groom, well and good; if not, you will remain in the *Galut* to the day of your burial." As for the "mixed multitude," just as it was said of them, "And the people saw it, and trembled, and stood afar off" (Ex. 20. 15), so will they be far removed from redemption. They will see the learned and the holy congregation in all their glory, but will remain afar off.

Our cabalist author lists poverty as one of the characteristics of messianic times. It is not, as the Talmud sees it, one of the final tribulations of messianic travail, but rather a religious end in itself. Poverty is a means of sanctification voluntarily assumed. It is a becoming trait, not only of the people to-be-redeemed and of its redeemer, but of the Divinity itself. Here is a case of a tradition turning dogma. It is an indication both of the nature of the current social conflicts as well as of Christian influences which succeeded in coloring the Jewish outlook in spite of the stubborn opposition of the rabbis and religious teachers.

The historical outlook of the *Ra'aya Mehemna* and its revolutionary eschatology were unique in the Hebrew literature of its day. Nevertheless, its homilies reveal the existence of certain latent forces in Spanish Jewish life which for some reason lacked sufficient drive to break through to the surface and translate themselves into decisive action. The social criticism they contain draws an accurate picture of existing social conditions and is corroborated by evidence from other sources. It adds to the information of the historian who labors to reconstruct the period from fragmentary documentary evidence. At the very least the work bears witness to the existence of religious and social ferment seeking various means of concrete expression.

The Messianic Movement of 1295

This social and religious agitation continued throughout the reigns of Alfonso X (1252-1284) and Sancho IV (1284-1295) and reached its climax in the messianic fervor which swept the Jewish communities in the year 1295, a short while after the death of Sancho IV. Our knowledge of what actually took place at the time is meager. Rabbi Solomon ibn Adret deals, rather cautiously, with the matter in his famous responsum, "Concerning the Prophet of Avila."[26] According to both oral and written reports which reached Ibn Adret from the communities directly involved, this "prophet," who was ignorant and illiterate, had seen visions both during his waking and his sleeping hours, in which an angel had revealed himself to him and had spoken to him. With this angel as his mentor and at the latter's dictation the "prophet" wrote a verbose treatise which he called *The Book of Wondrous Wisdom,* and then proceeded to compose a long and detailed commentary on it. One correspondent even forwarded to Ibn Adret a synopsis of fifty chapters of the work.

Nothing remains of any of these writings, but their general nature can be readily surmised. The thirteenth and fourteenth centuries abounded in Christian mystical works purporting to reveal the future. Some of these apocalyptic writings alluded to contemporary political events. For the most part they propounded the teachings of the Franciscan Spirituals. Those of the fourteenth century came down to us especially well-preserved, and like the writings of the "prophet" of Avila they consist of "prophecies" accompanied by long and detailed commentaries. The extant texts contain, along with the apocalyptic tracts, also the analyses and criticisms of them by the orthodox theologians, couched in the familiar terms of scholastic argument. The theologians would carefully weigh the contents of these works to determine whether they are to be approved by the Church or proscribed as heretical. They were most circumspect, even hesitant, in arriving at a decision.

The phenomenal authorship of one such apocalyptic work is described—in the year 1300—by Arnaldo de Villanova, a celebrated physician with Spiritualist sympathies. He relates that "a man, almost wholly illiterate . . . saw a vision of the future and wrote it down in eloquent Latin and polished style." The author himself did not understand his own writings and asked a monk to interpret them for him. Contained in these writings were prophecies concerning the liberation of Palestine and wars in southern Europe. In this same year of momentous messianic expectations, the year 1295, the Franciscan Spiritualist friar, Pierre Jean Olivi, venerated by his admirers after his death as a saint and a prophet, dispatched a letter from Narbonne to the sons of King Charles II of Naples and Sicily. The young princes were at the time held as political hostages in Catalonia and had asked Olivi to visit them. In this epistle, replete with apocalyptic speculation couched in mystical symbolism, the friar sends his royal disciples a message of encouragement.

"The time of pruning has come and the voice of the turtledove is heard in our land," sighing and breaking out in a groan instead of a song. . . . Just as in the six-hundredth year of the life of Noah "the fountains of the great abyss gushed forth and the windows of the heavens were opened," so that no one could have escaped except in the ark built by God's command, so ought dissolute Babylon sink into the deep sea. . . . The ark, having weathered the flood, came to rest upon the tallest mountains. Then the dove, sent forth, brings back an olive branch in its beak, meaning that it will preach evangelical peace to the entire world.

The writings of the "prophet" of Avila must have belonged to this genre of popular eschatological literature. Ibn Adret's responsum on the subject likewise resembles the opinions rendered by the Christian theologians in similar cases. Rabbi Solomon concludes his careful discussion with the following words:

The people of Israel, heirs to the true faith, the true seed of Jacob the man of truth, would rather bear the yoke of *Galut* and its vicissitudes than believe in anything without proper and prolonged investigation in order to separate the dross from the sterling truth, even when that which is told to them appears to be substantiated by signs and portents and reliable testimony; for the people of the God of Abraham love the way of truth.

Of the events themselves which in 1295 shook the Castilian Jewish communities to their very foundations, the following account was given by the apostate Abner-Alfonso of Burgos (see below, pp. 328 ff.) after his conversion. There appeared, he tells, two prophets, one in Avila and the other in the village of Ayllon. (We know nothing concerning the Jewish community in the latter locality.) Both men foretold great and wondrous happenings and soon came to be regarded by the Jews in their vicinities as saints and prophets. They announced that in the year 5055 A.M. (1295 C.E.), on the last day of the month of Tammuz (June/July), a blast of the Messiah's horn would summon the Jews out of exile. The Jews, most of whom believed wholeheartedly in this prophecy, were filled with awe and anticipation. They prepared themselves for the great day through fasting, charity and prayer. On the momentous day they rose early and, robed in white as on the Day of Atonement, assembled in the synagogues for prayer. Suddenly crosses appeared on all their garments, not only the clothes on their backs, but even those which they had left at home, in chests. This portent frightened the Jews. Some saw in it the work of Satan; others hesitated to pass any judgment; while still others interpreted it as an omen from the Christian Savior and declared themselves ready to embrace Christianity. Abner, who at that time enjoyed a high reputation as a practicing physician in Burgos, relates that some who became emotionally upset by these events turned to him for professional advice, for their parents regarded their experience as a symptom of mental illness. Abner himself was deeply stirred by the events and they had a decisive influence upon his future career. Another convert, who had only hearsay knowledge of the event, reported that the rabbis discussed the matter in their sermons and said that it was nothing but a prank of the devil. This is all that is known of those disturbing events. Meager too is our own account of the ideological currents and popular movements which were critical of the way of life and thinking of the dominant Jewish aristocracy. We do, however, have a much fuller and clearer picture of the personality of the great spiritual leader who guided the Jewish communities of Spain through these troubled times with firmness and discretion and served as a moderating influence between the two conflicting tendencies—Rabbi Solomon ibn Adret.

Ibn Adret's Communal and Religious Authority

Rabbi Solomon ben Abraham ibn Adret (c. 1233-1310), a member of one of the aristocratic Jewish families of Barcelona, served for nearly half a century as rabbi of this influential community, adding distinction of service to distinction of birth.[27] Privately, he engaged in financial operations, extending loans to non-Jews, including the royal treasury.

Still a comparatively young man, he was asked to make important decisions in matters affecting the administration of the Jewish communities. His advice was solicited more and more with the advancing years, and his extant responsa number in the thousands. He was resident in Barcelona during the great Disputation of 1263, at which Nahmanides ably championed the cause of Judaism. Ibn Adret himself had occasion to dispute matters of faith with Christians and to counter, both orally and in writing, the arguments of Raymond Martini, the learned Dominican friar, and others like him. These Christian theologians and polemicists relied, it appears, to a large extent upon the anti-Jewish writings of the eleventh century Mohammedan scholar Ibn Hazm, who had in his day crossed literary swords with Samuel ha-Nagid. Ibn Adret therefore devoted a special work to a refutation of Ibn Hazm's strictures upon Judaism. The Disputation of Barcelona fired the mendicant Orders with renewed missionary zeal and the Jewish communities were compelled to take defensive measures against the agitation and incursions of the friars. Though Nahmanides had not yet left Spain for the Holy Land, the communities turned to Ibn Adret for aid and advice in the equitable distribution of the expenditures entailed by these measures. The kings of Aragon held the rabbi of Barcelona in high esteem and frequently referred to him, for an opinion or decision, complicated matters in litigation. One of his extant responsa is, in fact, addressed to a royal official who turned to him for advice.[28]

He participated actively in the leadership of his community, and his name as well as those of his sons appear several times among the *neëmanim* of Barcelona. Ibn Adret stood guard vigilantly over the interests, not only of his own and neighboring communities, but of the rest of the Jews of the realm as well. As late as 1306, in his already declining years, he helped the community of Montblanch rid itself of a particularly irksome burden resulting from the ill-advised generosity of James II, who had assigned to a Jewish convert to Christianity certain income from the Jewish slaughterhouse of the city. When justice demanded it he did not hesitate to defend the rights of the individual against the powers that be. Early in his rabbinic career he took up the cudgels on behalf of an orphan in his community and defended his interests against some of the high and mighty of Barcelona, namely, the heirs of Benveniste de Porta, supported by Judah de la Cavalleria and the officials of the crown. Ibn Adret's preeminence in rabbinic matters was recognized beyond the borders of Aragon. During the critical days which the community of Toledo experienced in 1281, its leaders turned to him for guidance in dealing with the grievous problems confronting them.

Ibn Adret's greatest contributions were in the areas of Jewish law and public administration. Thousands of his responsa, dealing with problems in these fields, are extant, all of them written in a vivid and precise Hebrew style. His knowledge of Latin enabled him to familiarize himself also with the

Roman Law and the local Spanish legislation. He was thus eminently qualified to take the leading part which he did in the formulation of the constitutional principles underlying the body of public law by which the Jewish communities—whose corporate nature resembled that of the Christian municipalities —were governed. He strove in every way to strengthen the authority of the *kahal,* and he vigorously opposed the efforts of some of the Jewish grandees to dominate Jewish communal life. Those among them, however, who, like the Ravaya family, were the mainstay of their communities in time of need, readily received his cooperation and support. On one occasion he threw the full weight of his erudition behind Don Muça de Portella who sustained his *kahal* in its attempt to compel one of its members to grant his wife a divorce. This celebrated courtier appears from this incident to have been himself a staunch defender of the Law and as such probably enjoyed the friendship of the distinguished rabbi.[29]

The responsa indicate that Ibn Adret favored an aristocratic form of communal government, that is, one in which the highest officials of a community would be chosen from among its old families which combined wealth with talmudic learning, piety and civic responsibility.[30] Such, in fact, was the case in Barcelona. It is not clear whether Rabbi Solomon, who seems to have been one of the chief supporters of such a regime for the *kahal* of his native city, was aware of its inherent shortcomings. He was frequently called upon to arbitrate intra-communal disputes, and there were times when his decision, based upon the merits of the case, favored the lower classes. Wherever possible he sought to eliminate the sources of contention "in order that love, brotherliness and peace might be restored."[31] While his correspondence of the last stage of the Maimonidean controversy does reveal the influence of the cabalists' point of view, he never made their social ideology his guide to communal administration. Truth and justice were his only goals and the formal Halakha his only guide.

Ibn Adret combined strict construction in the interpretation of the Halakha with extreme caution in its application. He was reluctant to sit in judgment over cases with political overtones or those of a criminal nature which might end in a mandatory sentence of death. In advising others, however, he wrote, "He who seeks the public welfare cannot decide strictly on the basis of the law of the Torah, but must act according to the needs of the hour."[32] Whenever he felt that religious discipline and public morality were at stake, he called for the application of the law in all its severity in order to effect reform. Characteristic of this reformatory zeal is the letter which he wrote in 1281 to Rabbi Jacob ibn Crisp of Toledo, in which he urges him to proceed from gentle to severe measures, to begin with soft speech; but, should that not avail, to end by "tearing, pulling, and by clubbing the skull." (See page 260 above.) Similar utterances can be found also in his later responsa, even those written in his old age. Yet we also find him offering the more mellow advice that "everything has its proper time, and there are times when it is even commendable to overlook a transgression, all according to the needs of the hour." Remarkably enough, this quotation appears in a responsum addressed to Castile, where the Jews enjoyed greater autonomy with broader jurisdictional powers than they had in Aragon. In a responsum in which he discussed the case of a Jew who in resentment against the communal authorities shouted in the streets, in the presence of Christians, that Jews exact a higher rate of interest than is allowed them by royal ordinance, Ibn Adret concluded that the man was to be considered an informer, deserving the penalty of death, and that such a sentence would be quite in order, "had we the same powers here as in Castile."[33]

When actually confronted with a case of informing, Ibn Adret was not at all eager to pronounce judgment. When King Pedro III demanded that he pass the death sentence upon one of the most dangerous informers of that day, he kept postponing the decision and sought to find a compromise that would avoid bloodshed, and not even royal pressure could overcome his hesitancy. During the reign of James II, around 1300, he received from the Jewish community of Valencia the transcript of a trial of an alleged informer with the request that he decide the case. Ibn Adret replied that he would adjudicate the matter only upon a written order from the king and a royal promise to underwrite his decision.[34] Ibn Adret opposed the prevalent tendency to broaden unduly the concept of *malshinut* (informing). He wrote to one of the Aragonese communities,

> I have examined the text of the *takkana* (ordinance) and I find that its purpose is essentially to curb the lawless and the informers, as is, in fact, stated in the preamble . . . and it is evident from its content and wording that its principal intention is the elimination of malfeasance and *malshinut*, a purpose truly worthy of such distinguished men, men of discretion and counsel, as you are. Would that all the communities had their heart in this matter, always! There is no evidence, however, that there was any intent to prohibit that which is permissible, worthy and proper; for, if such were the case, this would not be a constructive measure, but rather a destructive and disruptive one. For if you were to provide by communal enactment that no one may enter a monetary claim except in his own interest, you would thereby be abolishing the institution of guardianship, for the guardian does not act in his own interest . . .

In another case, where one Jew obtained a warrant from a secular court to arrest another Jew against whom he had a monetary claim, and actually had him arrested with the help of an official of the court, Ibn Adret was asked whether the claimant and his agent who assisted in the arrest were to be prosecuted as informers. Rabbi Solomon replied,

If the claimant had sufficient cause against the defendant
to detain him so that he would not both default payment
and escape legal action, he is not to be treated as an informer. It happens every day that men against whom legal
action is pending are taken into custody in order to prevent them from absconding with other people's money
and escaping abroad. Indeed, but for the fear imposed by
the authority of the state, men might despoil and consume
one another's substance with impunity, and he whose arm
is strongest would prevail. The world, however, rests upon
justice.[35]

The relation of the Law of the state to the Jew resident therein
and to his Law was a matter of concern to Jewish legal authorities since the early centuries of the Diaspora. Out of this concern evolved the halakhic principle which, in the formulation
which it received in the Talmud, states that "the law of the
realm is law [unto us]" (*dina de-malkhutha dina*). Between
the Jewish Halakha, however, and the jurisprudence of the
medieval Christian state lay a wide gulf of ideological differences, making it necessary for the rabbis frequently to examine
and clarify the implications of the above principle in the light
of existing political and juridical conditions. The rabbis of
Catalonia were inclined to place limitations on the scope of
this principle in line with the promptings of their own ethical
conscience. They were no doubt encouraged in this by the
political order then evolving in southern Europe, where feudal
autarchy was being replaced by government based, in theory,
upon the principles of justice drawn from Roman Law. Rabbi
Moses ben Nahman (Nahmanides), known for his gallant
defense of Judaism at the Disputation of Barcelona, was the
first to show his daring also in this matter. Disagreeing with
some of his predecessors who ruled that *dina de-malkhutha dina*
applied only to the private interests of the crown, he wrote,

It appears to me that when we say that "the law of the
realm is law," we mean the royal legislation in effect

throughout the realm which the king or his royal predecessors have enacted and which are inscribed in the chronicles and legal codes of the kingdom; but any temporary
measure or new law for which there is no precedent and
which is instituted for the purpose of mulcting the people
is but royal robbery, and we cannot regard that as law.[36]

Ibn Adret, in his responsa, takes the same position. But an
occasion could arise where even this position, essentially one
of compromise, became untenable. Where the Jewish and non-
Jewish law were in direct conflict, it became necessary to take
an even stronger stand. There was a case in Perpignan where
a father demanded that the dowry of his deceased married
daughter be returned to him, as provided by the king's law and
by local custom. The case was referred to Ibn Adret by the
beth-din of Perpignan. Ibn Adret replied that if the parties
involved did, before the marriage, enter into a contract stip-
ulating the return of the dowry in such an eventuality, this
stipulation must be kept.

> However [he continued], to adopt this as a practice simply
> because the Gentile law so provides, seems to me to be
> forbidden beyond doubt, for it means imitating the Gen-
> tiles. And the Torah admonishes against this. "Before
> them" (Ex. 21. 1), it is written, "but not before a court
> of Gentiles" (Bab. Talmud. *Gittin* 88b). . . . Our people,
> which is the estate of the Lord, is prohibited by the Torah
> from showing a preference for the law of the Gentiles
> and their ordinances. What is more, it is forbidden to
> carry litigation into their courts even in matters in which
> their law is identical with the Jewish law. We here are,
> therefore, amazed how the seat of justice in your city, en-
> dowed as it is with learning and perspicacity, could be a
> party to actions which our Torah forbids.[37]

Ibn Adret interested himself also in philosophy and was
familiar with the current schools of thought, but he himself
contributed nothing original to the philosophy of Judaism.

He found the teachings of his master, Nahmanides, with their mystical underlining, acceptable to him. He placed himself in the forefront of the movement to restore the Halakha and Aggada, in their literal simplicity, to the luminous position they had previously occupied in Jewish life and culture. While not opposed in principle to the attempts to reconcile Jewish tradition with philosophy, he could not countenance the allegorical interpretation of the Scriptures, and he had no patience with those who cited scientific evidence to contradict the Halakha. Of the latter he wrote,

> And if one should persist in his error and say, "I love these foreign ideas which have come to my notice and I shall pursue them," we will say to him, "The words of the sages cannot be discredited—that is impossible; let him who would cite evidence against them, and a thousand others like him, be set at naught, for they cannot invalidate even a tittle of that which the sainted sages of Israel have validated."[38]

Ibn Adret, accordingly, assisted with his counsel the movement for the moral rehabilitation of the Toledo community in 1281. The pietist teachings, which were then penetrating Spain from the Jewish communities to the north, received his encouragement, and he worked all his life to strengthen their influence among the Spanish Jews. However, he dissociated himself completely from the extreme mystical currents, suspecting them of heresy. He persecuted Abraham Abulafia and was wary of popular "prophets," like the one of Avila. Sometime after 1280 he rose to the defense of the reputation of Maimonides and his works, when certain Ashkenazic rabbis, in Europe and in Palestine, sought to revive the ban of R. Solomon of Montpellier against the writings of Maimonides. In this matter Ibn Adret identified himself with the position taken by Nahmanides at the time of the original controversy over this subject in 1232. Nahmanides at the time had written several letters defending Maimonides and protesting against the ban. In one of the letters Nahmanides had offered a constructive program for ordering the intellectual life of Spanish Jewry. As things turned out, Ibn Adret found it necessary, in the closing years of his life, to take up the cudgels on behalf of this program and its implementation in Spanish Jewish society. He was moved to this action by the process of deterioration of religious and social values which he himself had witnessed over a period of two generations. The immediate stimulus was provided by a spark from abroad, from the fires of controversy kindled once again by a resident of Montpellier, R. Abba Mari ben Moses ben Joseph, known as Astruc of Lunel.

This second stage of the Maimonidean controversy has, like the first, been the subject of much discussion in the literature of modern Jewish scholarship.[39] While one may differ with some of the conclusions arrived at in these discussions, this is not the proper place to deal critically with them. My purpose here is to focus upon this controversy the light of certain realities of Jewish life in Spain, without a knowledge of which the full gravity of the issues involved in this conflict cannot be apprehended. The cities of Languedoc—Montpellier, Narbonne, Perpignan—were the home of a number of versatile Jewish intellectuals, among them the well-known translators of Arabic works into Hebrew. Some religious zealots, also resident in these communities, began to suspect that the vines of philosophic rationalism, cultivated by these intellectual circles, had produced some very dangerous fruit. The rationalists, in their writings and oral preachings, at times adopted a radical approach to the Sacred Writings. They interpreted the biblical miracles allegorically and assigned a symbolic function to the commandments of the Torah. It was also reported that they denied personal immortality and stripped the messianic ideal of its traditionally assigned concrete forms. To the fundamentalists such ideas were, naturally, naked heresy and outright blasphemy. Here was Averroism of a most daring and dangerous kind! The situation became the subject of a rather extensive exchange of letters between members of the communities of southern France and the leaders of the *kahal* of Barcelona. These highly interesting documents were collected by R. Abba Mari himself, who entitled his compilation, *Minhath Kenaoth* (An Offering of Zeal).[40]

Modern Jewish scholarship, in dealing with this correspondence, did not always see it in its true historical setting. The locale of the heresies described in these letters is southern France, but any historian who fails to notice the organic connection between the contents of these documents and the situation in Spain is likely to arrive at the wrong conclusion regarding the seriousness of this vital problem. It may be that in their ivory towers the Provençal intellectuals on occasion tossed about heretical ideas. But there is no doubt that, in Spain, Averroism was much more common and its practical results more grave and more evident in daily life than was the case in Languedoc. Little of that is reflected in the *Minhath Kenaoth*, either because R. Abba Mari omitted from his compilation much of the material dealing with Spain, since he was not primarily interested in the situation there, or perhaps because the Spanish leaders concerned in this matter deliberately kept silent regarding the deviations in their own country and preferred to use the situation in Provence as an example and a warning to Spanish Jewry. Then again, in Barcelona, though the community did not lack rationalist sceptics, they were awed into silence by the authority of Rabbi Solomon ibn Adret. One is likely to come away from a superficial reading of the documents with the impression that Ibn Adret was forced into action by outside pressure; but a thorough examination of all the details makes it clear that R. Solomon was the one who gave direction to this entire campaign.

In 1303, R. Abba Mari wrote a letter to R. Solomon decrying the conditions in southern France.

Today there are many who tear down the fences, who despise instruction and scoff at admonition, who relinquish the fundamentals of faith and hold to hollow superstitions, who, embracing foreign teachings, would dissolve the covenant and dissipate the wealth of the Torah. These men preach homilies full of blasphemy, and even compose books in science and in philosophy, drawn from Averroes and based upon Aristotle.

Of Ibn Adret, whom he addresses as the "foremost leader of his generation," he makes the following request:

Give us counsel how we may erect a fence that the foxes will not breach. Dispatch your saber-like words to the wise men of this land and your letters to its notables. I know for certain that when your word arrives it will be honored, and all will be in league with you.[41]

Ibn Adret replied in terms indicating that he well appreciated the gravity of the situation and that he was disturbed to find foreign philosophy, the handmaiden, seeking to supplant its mistress, the Torah. He was fully in accord with Abba Mari's purpose, but preferred for the latter to take the initiative in stemming this tide of heresy. He felt that his own intervention would be ineffective, for it would be said of him, "Who has dared to come into our very own house to chastise us and to point out the way of wisdom to us?"[42]

There is reason to assume that Ibn Adret had a studied purpose in assuming this tone of conventional humility in his reply to the French zealot. R. Abba Mari countered with a letter calling upon R. Solomon to follow the example of the illustrious Rabbenu Gershom of Germany, who met the crises of his day with vigorous action. He urged the Catalonian rabbi, "the lustrous crown of our generation," to extirpate this dangerous heresy by placing its adherents under the ban.[43] In his reply Ibn Adret again expressed agreement with R. Abba Mari and then launched into a severe critique and denunciation of the rationalists, in language more vehement than that employed by R. Abba Mari himself.[44] However, since Ibn Adret even now indicated no readiness to take positive action, R. Abba Mari gathered the impression that the rabbi of Barcelona had no wish to become personally involved in this entire controversy.

Action, however, did come out of Barcelona, through another channel. A certain Crescas Vidal, a native of Barcelona and a scion of one of its distinguished families, at this time resided in Perpignan. Ibn Adret wrote to him, asking him for authentic information regarding certain heretical writings which were rumored to be circulating in southern France. He likewise urged him to exert every effort to stem and suppress heresy wherever it existed. Accompanying this letter was another from Crescas' brother, Bonafos Vidal, a venerable gentleman, prominent in Barcelona, who had served for many years as a member of the board of *neëmanim* of the *kahal*. Don Bonafos too urged his brother, "Rise ye princes, defenders of the land; seal the breaches, ye builders of fences; build ye fortifications, a wall and gates and bars, round the Torah!"[45]

It appears from Don Crescas' reply that what prompted the inquiries and exhortations from Barcelona were the writings of R. Levi b. Abraham b. Hayyim. R. Levi was the author of a work entitled *Livyat Hen* (A Garland of Grace), an anthology of all sorts of scientific and metaphysical knowledge. There is hardly anything in this book which can be construed as heretical. The author himself was at this time living in Narbonne, in the home and under the patronage of Samuel de Scaleta (Heb. *ha-Sulami*), a wealthy man with training in philosophy, who was at the same time a pious Jew, a practicing ascetic and a loyal admirer of R. Solomon ibn Adret.[46] Crescas Vidal urged R. Solomon to forbid, under pain of excommunication, the study of philosophy and science by young men, and proposed the text of a *herem* (edict of excommunication) which the rabbi did later adopt. It is difficult to believe that Don Crescas composed the text on his own initiative. The text reads:

No young man under thirty years of age shall study any "Greek or Chaldean books" (*i.e.*, works of philosophy or science) other than medical works; and teachers of the same shall likewise fall under this ban and excommunication.[47]

Don Bonafos replied to his brother that his recommendation to ban the premature study of philosophy was well received in Barcelona. However, it was decided, with the concurrence of R. Solomon, to write first to Montpellier and urge that community to investigate the charges of heresy emanating from there.[48] Ibn Adret, in his own reply to Don Crescas, now clearly stated his position and revealed his intentions. In a letter full of denunciatory blasts against the rationalists he wrote:[49]

"Did a nation ever exchange its gods, which are not God" (Jer. 2. 11)? But these people exchanged their glory for foreign follies and pursue them. Before our very eyes they exchanged their honor for disgrace and substituted alternate lore for our perfect Torah, and in the columns of smoke which they raise they see true signs. It behooves us, therefore, to don the mantle of zealotry, for we should feel ashamed ourselves if we haven't wit enough to put the sinners to shame. . . . May they vanish and a thousand like them, but not a tittle of the Torah. . . . I have cast lots, one for God and one for the devil, and I drew the lot for God. What am I and what is my life that I should fear their sullying my honor? Let them curse me; God will bless me. Before Him I kneel and bend the knee, for I know that my time is in His hand. If He desire my death, I shall die; if He preserve me in life, I will live in His presence in the manner of my forefathers. That land, I know, has holiness, for dwelling therein are men saintly, wise, and scholarly, who, even if they seem small in their own eyes, are the leaders of Israel. Why, then, this modesty which prevents them from baring their arms against the ravagers before their very eyes? . . . Now this plague which threatened to destroy our home and ravage our heritage, we have expelled it from our land, empty, scorned and despised. It left the halls of Castile and Aragon, where formerly they had sought to ensconce it. It has now been driven out completely; not a one is left of the hellish throng of them. We beheld this and rejoiced and thought, "Now our Lord will bestow his affection upon us and shed his refreshing dew upon us so that we may live in His presence in our house, in beauty and holiness." But now two or three have arisen to give us alarm . . .

This is how Ibn Adret saw the situation in Spain itself; yet it is difficult to reconcile his description with the facts. Did they really believe that in Spain everything was in order, but that it was these "destructive little foxes" of southern France who now arose to stir up trouble?

Of R. Levi ben Abraham, Ibn Adret wrote in the same letter,

He is worse than the Gentiles who differ with us in their interpretation of a few verses. His colleagues do not spare even a letter of the Torah. The Gentiles do leave most parts of the Torah intact, but he and his colleagues distort everything. Is there a Gentile who overturns all of Scripture and says that Abraham and Sarah stand for matter and form?

One must combat them without fear, as the psalmist says (Ps. 139. 21), "Do I not hate, O Lord, those who hate Thee? Do I not strive with those who rise up against Thee?" "For these people," he goes on to say, "are opposed to all religion and to the scriptures of all nations; and if this were to become known abroad, all their silver and gold would not save them from prosecution," alluding, of course, to the Inquisition.

Yet, for all his zeal and his desire to see punitive measures taken against the allegorists in France, Ibn Adret still wished to maintain the appearance of one reluctant to interfere in the affairs of other communities. He tells Don Crescas, "As regards your proposal to ban and excommunicate anyone who would study Greek philosophy before he has become well versed in Torah and saturated with the knowledge of its precepts, it would be preferable if the communities within which the deviations exist were to take the lead in such an action." And this Ibn Adret persisted in urging. A letter to this effect, signed by R. Solomon and other leaders of the *kahal* of Barcelona, arrived soon thereafter in Montpellier. In ringing tones of fiery zeal the message exhorted the *kahal* to action, proposed the steps to be taken, and promised active support.[50] It concludes on a prosaic but practical note,

> We have been alarmed by reports from your holy community as well as from other sources to the effect that dangerous heretics have arisen in the land. This is bad news, for their number may increase if we do not bar the door in their faces. It is obvious that these men, having completely lost faith, sin and lead others into sin. We do not know what they rely on for support. Observe how the Gentiles punish their heretics, even for a single one of such heresies as these men expressed in their books. Why, if anyone would dare say that Abraham and Sarah represent matter and form, they would wrap him up in twigs and burn him into cinders. All the nations trace their lineage to them; and these say that they are nothing but symbols! Their books and sermons are but thorns in our sides. If you were to see fit, as we hope, to ban and excommunicate anyone who would study Greek philosophy before he has reached the age of thirty and has acquired a deep knowledge of the divine Torah received by our forefathers through the hand of Moses, and put the teachers as well under the curse, we would affix our hand thereto in the name of God and be your allies in the cause of the Lord. Then your land would regain its former tranquility, for the enemies of the Torah will have been put to shame. Who is better qualified than you are to rush to the defense of our divine Torah, and who of all of God's people is worthy of preceding you? If you will form the

vanguard we will follow you, and we will not withdraw until your children and ours will have taken possession of our ancestral heritage, bequeathed to our forefathers by Moses and the prophets. Know ye that your injunction will penetrate as deeply in our land as in yours, and whatever folly there lodges in a man's heart will be expelled by your censure.

Upon receipt of this letter the *kahal* of Montpellier began to consider, in the late summer of 1304, the advisability of publishing a *herem* against the premature study of philosophy. However, the action was effectively blocked by the strong opposition of the Ibn Tibbon family, headed by R. Jacob ben Makhir. This learned physician, in a strongly worded letter addressed to Ibn Adret, argued that the allegorism of the rationalists is no less legitimate than the symbolism of the cabalists. Secular studies were not only permitted but highly desirable, for they raise the prestige of the Jew in the eyes of his Gentile neighbors.

We would do well [he said] to learn from the example of the most civilized nations who translate learned works from other languages into their own, and who revere learning and the learned without inquiring into their religion, even when they write critically of their own faith. Has any nation changed its religion because of this, or did their faith falter? How much less likely is that to happen to us who possess a rational Torah which we follow?[51]

This opposition forced the zealots to retreat. Abba Mari again suggested that the *kahal* of Barcelona proclaim the ban. But Ibn Adret appears now to have regretted his involvement in this matter, and sought to mollify all those whom he had previously antagonized. He and his associates assured the *kahal* of Montpellier that they had no intention of interfering in their internal affairs. At the same time they rejected the suggestion of Abba Mari to proclaim the ban in Barcelona, there being no necessity for it, since heresy, they felt, was not a problem there.[52] It is difficult to accept this assertion at face value. The rabbi and the notables of Barcelona were either very reluctant to cast aspersions on their own community or they were not yet certain whether they could count on the support of the community in so drastic a step.

Things, however, did not remain quiet very long. Early in 1305 one of the zealots of Montpellier made the rounds of the Provençal communities in an effort to line up support for his cause. Letters continued to be received by Ibn Adret urging him to vigorous action. New outcroppings of heresy among the rationalists were being reported. Abba Mari once more pressed Ibn Adret for a *herem* to be issued from Barcelona, motivating his insistence by the fact that his own *kahal* lacked the power to enact a *herem* without royal consent, a situation of which everyone must have been aware all along.[53]

The zealots placed their principal hopes upon "the meeting of the two great luminaries," R. Solomon ibn Adret and Rabbi Asher ben Yehiel (born in Cologne *ca.* 1250, died in Toledo *ca.* 1328). Rabbi Asher had been forced to leave his native Germany and, after making his way through France, arrived in Montpellier. From there he had proceeded to Barcelona and finally to Toledo, whose community chose him for their rabbi. While travelling through Provence he had seen, according to his own report, that the Jews there were "highly cultured, polished, and sagacious"; but upon closer scrutiny had found that only a few, here and there, "had their hearts firmly planted in the Torah." "And I said to these few," he tells us, " 'Why don't you take courage and step into the breach to prevent Truth from being cast to the ground?' And they said to me that they would not be able to accomplish anything without the cooperation of the notables of the land." In Montpellier itself, where he was received with high honor, he had found the situation equally disappointing. "It is a great city in Israel, from which Torah emanates to all who seek it; but 'her princes

are like harts' (Lament. 1. 6); they hide their faces and fail
to remove the stumbling blocks. Every man, therefore, does
as he pleases with none to tell him, 'What is it that you are
doing?' Such license is the fault of the men in authority, and
the Lord will call the elders and princes of his people to
account, for it is clear that they have the power to prevent
this."[54]

From Barcelona, R. Asher addressed a letter to Abba Mari
to give him encouragement and to strengthen his hand, but
his words echo a note of despair.

> My heart tells me [he writes] that words of admonition
> will not correct them, for they are deeply rooted in sin and
> heresy, and it is difficult for them to rid themselves of it.
> Nor is it a problem involving only one or two individuals,
> for the "root bearing gall and wormwood" has spread to
> every city. Even those who revere God's word, nevertheless
> shield their relatives. Those who now carry on their activ-
> ity secretly will soon dare come out into the open and
> will brazenly declare, "We have the upper hand; who
> dares to come and lord it over the disciples of Aristotle
> in their own homes?" Israel will split into sects even as
> the kingdom of the house of David did in ancient times.

R. Asher recommended that a general conference be called of
representatives of all the communities concerned with this
problem, that they might take counsel together and arrive at
a joint decision.

> Let a date be fixed for a gathering of all the leaders of the
> people in one of the large cities, and Rabbi Solomon will
> also delegate to it some of the notables of this land; and
> with the help of his pleasing words and mellow counsel a
> godly plan may be devised for turning the hearts of all
> Israel as one to the Law of Moses without neglecting,
> at certain times, the other sciences.[55]

Now, this recommendation regards this whole matter not as a
local problem, but as one which transcends regional and politi-

cal boundaries. Its tolerant approach to secular learning is not at all characteristic of Rabbi Asher, and he himself admitted later on that he espoused it against his own better judgment. It follows, therefore, that this recommendation too was formulated by the same people who were the leading spokesmen in this controversy right along.

R. Abba Mari had to wait a long time for Ibn Adret's answer. When it did come—after a lapse of eight months, according to Abba Mari—it contained an apology for the delay which, R. Solomon explained, was due to his prolonged illness and the many burdens of his office. The letter itself was similar in tone and in content to the earlier ones. Ibn Adret severely criticized the Jewish leadership in southern France for winking at the excesses of the rationalists. The latter appear to have become emboldened of late, as manifested by overt acts of impiety. He demanded that the Provençal authorities resolve, at long last, to resort to effective punitive measures, presumably the proclamation of a *herem*; and he, for his part offered to obtain widespread endorsement of their action. "Let them begin," he writes, "to punish and to correct as they see fit, and I will marshal a goodly number of communities ready to counter-sign their action."[56] There was a sound foundation for this promise, for Ibn Adret had not been completely idle during these eight months. Sometime late in 1304 or early in 1305 one of his favored disciples, R. Samson ben Meir, a native of Toledo, had gone at R. Solomon's behest to the Castilian capital and carried with him the entire correspondence that had been exchanged so far in this affair and brought it to the notice of the local authorities. This is how R. Samson reported on his mission to Abba Mari.

> I gathered up all the letters dealing with this matter, both those written by individuals and those sent by the *kahals* of your country, and I brought this whole collection down to the city of my birth, Toledo—for I now make Barcelona my home—and I read this correspondence to the communal

leaders and the scholars there. They were astounded, and they said to me, "Tell the Rabbi that we are ready to ban by *herem* anything which, according to his decision, should be banned." I reported this to the Rabbi and he said, "I shall act accordingly." He is writing to you as well as to the honored dignitary (*i.e.*, the *nasi*) of Narbonne. You two need not obtain anyone else's consent to this. Merely forward a copy of the text you will have agreed upon, even an unsigned copy. The Rabbi has entrusted me with this pious mission because he has been like a father to me ever since I came to this city to study under him. . . . Over fifty communities will add their signatures thereto and I myself will bring the documents and signatures to Montpellier.[57]

When R. Samson visited Toledo, Rabbi Asher was in all likelihood already established there as rabbi and was able to influence local public opinion. His trip, it may be safely assumed, was part of a plan carefully worked out in Barcelona. The interested parties there wanted the *herem* countersigned by all the *kahals* of Spain and southern France.

Upon receipt of these communications Abba Mari sent to Ibn Adret, over his own signature and that of the *nasi* of Narbonne, the requested text of the *herem* for publication in Barcelona. He also addressed a laudatory epistle to R. Samson, paying tribute to the success of his mission to date and urging him to carry it to its successful conclusion. He wrote:

Behold how fortunate you are. We have toiled for years, we have thrust our arm up to the elbow into the thorn bushes, and we garnered only spines, whereas you have succeeded in picking the roses. Therefore, carry on your work with circumspection and be our guide, for yours is a dedicated mission. Proceed—under the direction and with the blessing of the Rabbi, and with your own characteristic wisdom and diligence—to circulate this enactment throughout the land in order to obtain the signatures of the notables of every city. When you arrive in the far-famed community of Toledo, the seat of R. Asher ben Yehiel, and he himself sees it, he will rejoice and obtain the signatures of all the scholars and dignitaries of that city.[58]

At long last, after all these protracted negotiations and careful preparations, a twofold *herem* was promulgated in Barcelona in midsummer of 1305, on the Sabbath preceding the Fast of the Ninth of Ab. The first of the two bans, opening with the familiar plaint from the sixth chapter of the Ethics of the Fathers, "Woe unto human beings for their disregard of Torah," decrees:

> From this day on and for the next fifty years, no member of our community shall study the "Greek" works on science and metaphysics, either in the original (*i.e.*, in Arabic) or in translation, before he will have reached the age of twenty-five; nor may any member of our community teach the aforesaid disciplines to anyone under the age of twenty-five, lest these studies draw the student away from the Torah of Israel which is superior to this other learning. . . . We have exempted from our decree the study of medicine, although it is a natural science, for the Torah has given the physician permission to practice the art of healing.

The text of this *herem* has been preserved for us in the editions of the collected responsa of Rabbi Solomon ibn Adret. However, this "received" version—which is the same as the one circulated by the opponents of the ban—appears to have passed through the hands of an unscrupulous editor who expurgated the text to suit his own ends. For the original text of the *herem* exempted also the study of astronomy and the philosophy of Maimonides. Our authority for that is Ibn Adret himself, who pointed out in a letter,

> We have expressly exempted from the scope of the enactment the science of astronomy and all the works of

301

Maimonides, the *Guide* and all his other books which are more precious than gold, both those written in Hebrew and those written in Arabic.

The reformers appear to us to have acted with circumspection and with relative tolerance. In setting the age of twenty-five as the proper time to begin the study of metaphysics they actually conformed to the academic practice then in effect among the Jews as well as among the Christians. Students did not, for the most part, enter upon the study of philosophy until the age of twenty-five or thirty.[59]

The second *herem*, which begins with the words of the Prophet Jeremiah (2. 3), "Israel is the Lord's hallowed portion," denounces and outlaws the allegorists and their teachings:

> They preach blasphemous homilies and scoff at the words of the sages. . . . They say that the scriptural account from Genesis to the divine revelation on Mount Sinai is all allegory. Abraham and Sarah stand for matter and form; the twelve sons of Jacob are the twelve constellations; the four kings who did battle against the five represent the four elements and the five senses. We have heard that they impugn the biblical commandments. The *Urim* and *Tumim*, they say, are the instrument called the astrolabe. They make light of the phylacteries and the prayers. They even have the temerity to speak critically of Moses and to claim that the Torah is not of divine origin, but that its precepts are merely customs and ordinances established by Moses. . . . These are mortal sins, and all Israel are duty-bound to ban and excommunicate these sinners. They will receive no atonement for their sin until they die and are consumed by the flames of Gehenna. . . .
>
> Therefore, by authority of the Court on High and of the court on earth, we excommunicate these transgressors, and place them under a curse and under the ban. They will continue to sink lower and lower until they return

and repent fully and sin no more, and never again malign the words of the Torah and of the sages of the Talmud. We declare the books which they have composed to be works of heresy and the possessors of them heretics, and like them subject to this decree of excommunication, until they burn these books. . . .[60]

In order that they might not be accused of disrespect toward Maimonides the authors of the *herem* introduced into the text the following quotation from the *Guide of the Perplexed* (Part III, Chapter 41), in support of their action:

I take this position also in the case of any sin the commission of which manifests rejection of the Torah or opposition to it. Even when a Jew eats meat with milk, or wears garments of wool interwoven with linen, or in cutting his hair rounds the corners of his head, committing these acts in such a way as to make it clear that he scoffs at the Torah and does not believe in its truth, I apply to him the words, "he blasphemeth the Lord" (Num. 15. 30), and I hold him to be deserving of the penalty of death, in punishment, not for the particular sin, but for heresy. . . . His property is to be destroyed by fire and not given to his heirs, as is the case with others condemned to die by the courts. I hold also that any Jewish community which has presumptuously and openly transgressed any precept of the Law deserves the penalty of death. This is proven by the case of the tribes of Gad and Reuben, against whom all Israel was ready to go to war (cf. Joshua 22). As was explained to them later on in the warning which they received, they, by agreeing to commit the particular sin, committed heresy and rejected the entire Torah. They were rebuked for "turning away from the Lord," and they, in their defense, replied, "not in rebellion nor in treachery."

To the texts of the double *herem* a circular letter was appended, explaining the reasons for the ban and inviting the various communities to countersign it.[60a] The styles of all three documents reveals the hand of Ibn Adret. These documents

303

bear, in addition to the rabbi's signature, the signatures of the seven *neëmanim* of the *kahal* of Barcelona along with those of some thirty other men, apparently the members of that body which later came to be called the "Council of Thirty." Ibn Adret made a point of stressing in a letter to R. Abba Mari and the *nasi* of Narbonne that "all of the notables signed, not a man abstained."[61] All of the signatories belonged to the upper class of the Jewish community of Barcelona. These were the scholars and the merchants who were the pillars of the aristocratic regime, whose nature was described earlier. A group so homogeneous found it possible, in the end, to agree upon a course of action. The voices of the members of the liberal professions—the physicians and the translators—remained unheard.

The sponsors of the *herem* thus took an important step which, to the eyes of a contemporary, appeared as a great achievement. A uniform order of study was established, aimed at guiding all Israel, by way of the traditional paths of learning, back into the sphere of the Halakha and the Aggada. Actually, however, this apparent achievement left no mark whatever upon subsequent cultural history. In southern France the opposition was so strong as to cause the zealots to retreat. Among the opponents of the *herem* were not only members of the liberal professions, like Jacob ben Makhir, but also so eminent a rabbinic authority as R. Menahem Meiri, whose outlook upon learning, however, differed from that of R. Solomon ibn Adret. The contest was already decided in their favor by the time Philip IV ordered the expulsion of all the Jews from his realm, in the summer of 1306. As for Spain, we know only of the concurrence of the "elders" of Toledo in the *herem.*[62] Thereafter, we find no traces of the *herem* or of its effects either in Barcelona or in Toledo, or anywhere else, as if the thing had never happened at all. The attempt to profit from the experiences of three generations involved in cultural conflict, and to devise effective means of strengthening religious and national allegiance, ended in complete failure.

Yet this program of reform, which kept within the recommendations made by Nahmanides in the early stages of this conflict, was not very ambitious and represented only modestly the real aims of the pietists. For the mystically oriented pietist movement, which had been active in Spain since the second quarter of the thirteenth century, aspired, consciously and by implication, to a thoroughgoing reform of all aspects of Jewish social and religious life. Similar forces were operating also in the Christian Church during the thirteenth century. Students of medieval Christianity point out quite correctly that the thirteenth century was fraught with potentialities for a social and religious reform more genuine and more pervasive than that effected in the sixteenth century by the Protestant Reformation. Jewish history did not parallel the history of the Christian Church in every respect, but the historians' evaluation of thirteenth century Christianity can be applied with equal truth to contemporary Judaism. Reformist tendencies were very much in evidence. Efforts in that direction were made, but were not carried through. The Jewish leadership of that day was also charged with a great responsibility. They could not achieve the political salvation of their people, but they were capable of revitalizing its social and religious life by realizing in everyday activity the ideals of the sages of the Mishna. The political structure of the Jewish communal autonomy made that possible, and the current religious awakening, stimulated by the new mysticism, created the necessary atmosphere for it. But the perfect confluence of all the currents striving in that direction was never achieved, and the beacon that might have illuminated the path of subsequent generations was never kindled.

VII

THE ERA OF DECLINE IN CASTILE

The period of the Reconquest had imposed large tasks upon the Jews of Spain, and a number of the leaders, fully aware of the situation, had striven to be worthy of their mission. It had been necessary at that time to create a basis of existence for Spanish Jewry under political conditions that had become radically changed; to develop the communal institutions in line with the new organizational needs and ideas; to infuse, in the light of the decline in religion and morals, a new spirit into the religious tradition. The leaders had succeeded in their efforts, outwardly at least. Undoubtedly they had accomplished a great deal; their achievements had been, in a sense, creative.

But even in their own days it had been obvious that their political successes were illusory and fleeting, and that their high aspirations for introducing religious and moral reforms were not materializing.

In the generation following the death of Ibn Adret, Spanish Jewry produced no outstanding leaders able to cope with the complicated spiritual and social tasks. Nor did great preachers arise in their midst to evoke a creative religious movement. The energies of the Spanish Jews were dissipated in internal social conflicts which lacked any significance or purpose, in political intrigues, and in polemics with detractors of Judaism, in which the defenders showed themselves inept in religious controversy. This absence of inner aim and purpose makes the task of the historian difficult, especially since only fragments of books and documents have come down to us; yet it is from such inadequate material that the history of those times must be reconstructed.

In Castile the end of the thirteenth century did not, as in Aragon, witness a radical change in the Jewish policy of the government. Nor were there any marked differences in the social structure of the kingdom, whose population was still one of peasants and warriors. A center of international commerce had been developed only in Seville, and even that city was largely concerned with warring upon its southern Arab neighbors. The commercial importance of the cities of the interior, like Toledo and Burgos, was no greater than before. The spirit of the Reconquest continued to prevail in Castile down to the time when civil war caused an upheaval in the country and until, at the close of the fourteenth century, the kingdom was drawn into the general currents of European politics. The political and administrative organization of the state of Castile, moreover, was as yet inferior to the efficient governmental apparatus developed in Aragon. The absence of a permanent body of public officials and the dominance of the king's favorites still determined the rise and fall of Jewish grandees at the royal

307

court. It is to the credit of the Jewish courtiers that, under the conditions prevailing in those years, they had a part in the development of an efficient system of administration for the state. The Jews not only took part in the farming of the taxes, but held posts in other departments of the chancelleries of the kings and the infantes, as well as in the accounting department and the secretariat. The prosperity or adversity of the Jewish communities still depended, as before, upon the influence of the Jewish favorites.

This period, however, did not hand down to us lovely poems such as those of the age of Todros ben Judah Halevi, in which the conditions of the times were more fully portrayed. Anti-Jewish feeling was on the increase. The forces arrayed against the Jews in Castile did not, indeed, include the Inquisition, which persecuted the Jews of Aragon so relentlessly; but the fomenters of the religious agitation made common cause with the estates, the knights and the municipalities, and all, as one man, demanded the removal of the Jews from the service of the state. They occasionally achieved their objective but only until the renewal of the war against the Arabs compelled the kings to reinstate the Jews in public office.

It appears that during the reign of Ferdinand IV (1295-1312), while the king was still a minor and his mother, Doña Maria de Molina, acted as regent, the anti-Jewish demands of the estates were complied with. But when, in 1302, Ferdinand himself took over the reins of government, he lost no time in informing the Cortes that, in view of the financial situation and of the unfavorable reports from the front, it would not be advisable to discontinue farming out the taxes or to forgo the services of the Jews.[1] The old rivalries between the Christian and Jewish courtiers thereupon flared up anew. Don Samuel, a Jewish *almoxarife*, who was a native of Andalusia, sided with the nobles who wanted to bring about a break between the king and his mother. According to a Christian chronicler, Don Samuel was deep in the king's confidence and exercised much influence in his entire household. He conducted the diplomatic negotiations with Portugal, Aragon and Granada until his death in 1306, which occurred while he was on his way home from a diplomatic mission to Aragon, "to the distress of the king and the joy of the country."[2] But the Moslem war made it imperative to continue Jews in the service of the state. Don Judah Abravanel of Seville underwrote loans of money, cloth and rusks bought from Genoese merchants for the siege of Algeciras. The aged Abraham ibn Shoshan and his associates were granted wide powers for the collection of taxes throughout the country. In the year 1307 we still find the Mohammedan population of the kingdom of Murcia subject to the jurisdiction of a Jewish *almoxarife* by the name of Don Isaac ibn Ya'ish. This is the last known instance of a Jew in such a post.[3]

The opposition to the Jews was greatly strengthened at that time by renewed agitation against the payment of interest on loans. Already in the thirteenth century certain trends of Christian opinion in Europe, and especially in France and England, had favored enlarging the scope of the ban on interest and including the Jews under this ban, even though the latter enjoyed special privileges in this respect which had originally met with the approval of the Christian public. Clement V (1305-1314) was the first pope who sought to compel the Jews of Europe, by means of an economic boycott imposed by the Church, to forgo all transactions involving interest. When instructions to that effect reached Toledo, the local Church tried to compel the Jews to refund interest already paid them and to cancel undertakings to pay interest given by their Christian debtors when signing the promissory notes. Ferdinand IV thereupon took a hand in the matter and addressed angry letters to the priests of Toledo in which he declared that such matters did not come within the competence of the Church, but of the state alone. "All the Jews," he wrote, "and all their possessions are mine. If the Church carries out its intention, the Jews will be ruined and thus be unable to pay taxes." The king proclaimed that those who gave effect to the Pope's decree would be deemed guilty of treason. A Toledan knight threatened, in the name of the king, to take very severe measures against the priests if they maintained their anti-Jewish ban or brought Jews to trial before an ecclesiastical court. This same knight even put several of those who had published the papal bulls under arrest; the priests were then forced to yield.[4] The Church seems nonetheless to have continued its agitation against interest for several years thereafter, and the king himself condoned it under certain conditions. Jewish moneylenders in Toledo, who could not escape to hiding places beyond the reach of the priests, were haled before Christian judges and imprisoned for several years.

The death of Ferdinand IV, in 1312 (leaving a minor as heir to the throne), and the rule of the infantes who formed the regency, again prepared the ground for a resurgence of the anti-Jewish activity. A factor favoring the opposition was the stand taken by the great reforming Council of Vienne (1311) and the Spanish ecclesiastical council held at Zamora in 1313. The Zamora synod demanded that effect be given to the regulations of the Church concerning Jewish testimony, the dismissal of Jews from public office, their complete segregation from the Christians, and other regulations with regard to badges to be worn by Jews on their clothing, payment of Church tithes, erection of synagogues, observance of the Christian holidays, interest, and the like. The Cortes which met in 1313 adopted similar resolutions, and in addition demanded, for example, the abolition of the privilege which the Jews enjoyed of judging capital cases involving Jews and Christians. In the following years they demanded the dismissal of the Jewish *almoxarifes,* accountants, secretaries, scribes and other court officials; and they also complained of alleged harshness on the part of Jewish tax collectors.[5] Despite all these demands,

310

the protocols of the Cortes contain a reference to a certain "Rab Don Mosse" who collaborated with a Christian official in auditing the government accounts, and to the employment by the infantes-regents of Jewish officials in their own households. In the service of Don Juan Manuel, whose kind and enlightened treatment of his Jewish physicians has been described elsewhere in this book, we find Don Judah ibn Wakar, who was probably the son of the physician Don Isaac. Don Judah was of a more practical turn than his father and obtained from his royal masters (in instances which will be discussed below) the authority to act as judge in capital cases, which thus afforded him an opportunity to enhance the prestige of the Jewish Law in the eyes of the Christians.[6]

The Development of the Jewish Community

Within the Jewish community the contrast between the rich aristocrats, on the one hand, and the small shopkeepers and artisans on the other was as marked as in earlier generations. Toledo was still the center of the Jewish capitalists, but there were also Jews who engaged in government finances in Burgos, Seville, Cordova and other cities, and, in the course of the fourteenth century, they extended their operations to all the other cities of the kingdom. The economic status of the Jews in general was bound to deteriorate as opportunities for settlement in newly conquered areas decreased. The Jews sought to settle in small towns and villages: the increase in the number of Jewish communities in the Andalusian villages can be explained only by the presence of an agricultural Jewish population.

Only in large and growing cities like Toledo and Seville could the Jews attain any considerable degree of prosperity. In Seville the Jews, like the Christians, succeeded only in the course of the fourteenth century in populating the large area allotted to them after the expulsion of the Moslems. The Jewish quarter of Seville, which was close to the cathedral,

311

was unquestionably very large, so that it was not easy for the Jews to occupy its entire area. At the end of the fourteenth century there were twenty-three synagogues in Seville, not all of which could have been merely *minyanim*. The Jewish upper classes of Seville had at that time a very considerable share in the farming of the municipal revenues, which were collected within the city walls and in the adjacent district under the municipal administration. The methods of taxation developed by the central government of Castile were adopted in the fourteenth century by the large municipalities, which took advantage of the experience of Jews who had been in the service of the state. Had the local Christian merchants possessed either the requisite ability or experience, the municipality of Seville would not have let Jews take any part in its administrative affairs. This is proved by the example of Barcelona and the other cities of Catalonia and of Aragon, which allowed the Jews no part in their municipal administrations. Yet the influence of the Jews in the conduct of the municipality of Seville increased during the civil war, precisely when the anti-Jewish fever was running high. So strong a center of Jewish influence as Seville was bound to become a center of anti-Jewishness and the starting-point for the persecution of the Jews in general in the year 1391.

References have been found to Jewish physicians who occupied municipal posts in Seville in the fourteenth century, something for which there was no counterpart at that time in Toledo nor in the large cities of Aragon. The Jewish municipal physicians of Seville belonged to the Zemerro family, who probably had come from Toledo originally and engaged in moneylending as well as in medicine. The economic activities of the wealthy Jews seem to have been confined in the main to tax-farming and moneylending; but they also had shops where textiles were sold. (The shops were leased from the municipality at a fixed rental.) There is little to indicate that the Jews of Seville engaged in maritime pursuits; but the lack of information on this point may be due to the scantiness of the documentary material now extant. There is reason to assume that most of the Jews of Seville were artisans. Andalusia was virtually the only province in Spain where wealthy Jews were still permitted to buy sizable landed estates in the fourteenth century. In the localities within the economic radius of Seville there were Jewish tax-farmers, shopkeepers and artisans, and doubtless also landowners who gathered the crops from their fields, vineyards and olive groves with their own hands. It was typical of the cultural and social relationships prevailing in Seville that Jewish and Moslem women were engaged as professional wailers by Christians as well as by their own coreligionists. (It was customary for the Spanish Jews to have women wailers at funerals.) There were also cases of Jewish women kept by Christians as *barraganas*, that is to say, concubines who enjoyed certain rights defined by prevailing custom.[7]

Jewish capitalists who controlled the credit and the tax-farming of the state were even more conspicuous in Toledo. Jews served the Church in Toledo in similar capacities. But they were firmly excluded from any part in the fiscal administration of the city. Though Toledo was still "a mother city in Israel," it had already lost its hegemony over the other Castilian communities. The economic decline of the Jews, as described by a contemporary Jewish scholar, may be paraphrased somewhat as follows: In olden days the Jews of Toledo had been wealthy and few in numbers; many houses had then been concentrated in the ownership of a single individual who would by no means consent to part with any of them; but now they were eager to lease their houses in order to derive an income from them. From this it also follows that the Jewish quarter was now more densely populated than previously. Jews also rented houses and shops in the Christian commercial quarter. Handicrafts were very much in evidence in the Jewish quarter, as mentioned above. Toledo was one of the few Spanish cities in which, as late as the fourteenth century, cases of Jewish ownership of Moslem slaves still came up for decision. Jewish surnames borne by some Christians of Toledo suggest the possibility of Jewish descent.[8]

In the meantime, the aljamas of Castile were developing along the same lines as the municipal institutions of the Christians. In the aljamas, as in the municipalities, the loose and undefined leadership of the aristocratic families was superseded by the hard and fast system of the closed council (*concejo cerrado*), as in the well-known example of the city of Venice, to which no parvenus were admitted. Alfonso XI encouraged this development, regarding a stable municipal oligarchy as a counterpoise to the influence of the powerful nobles. It was thus that the "elders," whose number was not fixed, lost their primacy in the aljamas, and that the leadership was taken over by a specified number of overseers (Heb. *me'ayenim*; Sp. *veedores*), with whom were associated judges appointed annually to deal solely with legal matters. Also in farming out its revenues the aljama followed the complicated procedure customary in the municipalities. The aljama farmed out the *almahona*, a combination of direct and indirect taxes levied chiefly on wine and meat, to a wealthy member of the community, or to a group of such men, under a contract known as *alancel*, in which the terms were defined and the various types of taxes described in detail. This method of collecting taxes was not in the interest of the poorer classes. At a session of the Cortes held in 1312 representatives of the estates complained of a decline in the revenues from the Jewish population, only one-fifth of the taxes having been actually paid by them. The estates declared that over five thousand rich Jews were exempt from taxes. Jewish tax payments were derived, so they said, from the *alcabala* (indirect taxes), which were levied only upon the poor and upon non-resident Jews who came to collect their outstanding loans.[9]

Whereas in Aragon Jewish communal affairs were administered solely by the local *kahal*, the aljamas of Castile were federated on a countrywide basis, as is indicated by the *haskama* (statute) of 1432, the entire text of which has been preserved (see below ch. XI). This model organization was developed during the fourteenth century, but only a few scattered data are available on the subject. As in the thirteenth century, so in the fourteenth it was customary for the king, queen or one of the infantes to appoint a Jewish courtier as the *rab* of a certain district from time to time. After the middle of the fourteenth century appointments of a *rab de la corte* (court rabbi, who was the counterpart of the Christian *alcalde de la corte*) were made on a more permanent basis. This court rabbi served the whole Jewish population of Castile, supervising the administration of its laws, finances and taxes. He presided at the conferences of the representatives of the local aljamas who were convened, like the Cortes, as occasion required, and as far as possible, also at stated intervals in various localities, probably wherever the royal court happened to be in residence at the time. At these conferences the sum total of the taxes levied upon the whole Jewish population was divided among the local communities according to their financial capacity, and general *haskamoth* were adopted as binding upon all the aljamas in regard to taxation, administration of justice, election of *me'ayenim* and judges, Jewish education, laws pertaining to domestic relations, and other matters relating to religion and morals. These *haskamoth* were based on the Talmudic Law, but the influence of general law—Roman and that of the *fueros* (local laws)—was more marked in Castile than in any other country.

This statement applies in particular to procedural and criminal law. The powers of criminal jurisdiction vested in the Jews of Castile seem to have reached their widest extent in the fourteenth century and exceeded those granted Jews in any other country. They were impowered to impose a sentence of death, not only on informers, but on murderers and adulterers as well. The permissible sentences included the severing of limbs

315

(hands, feet, etc.) according to a system of graduated punishments depending upon the gravity of the crime. In imposing such penalties the Jews emulated the severity of Christian practices hoping thereby to demonstrate the strictness of their moral code before the Christian world. Cases of this sort go to show how primitive were the religious and moral ideas of the age, ideas which were shared even by scholars and pietists.[10]

In the administration of the aljamas the jurisdiction exercised by Jews and Christians overlapped in curious fashion. "Powerful men" (*omes poderosos*) interfered in the affairs of the municipalities and the aljamas, laid down the law as to how the wine-tax should be farmed out, and even forced Jews to contract marriages according to their whims. Within the Jewish communities themselves there emerged this specifically Castilian type of bully who terrorized the people and imposed his will upon the judges and other members of the aljamas. In the fourteenth century there were numerous instances of plots and attacks upon the lives of communal judges, such as had been known in Aragon only in the thirteenth century and had long since ceased to occur there. Even among the judges themselves men of violence were to be found who did not shrink from bloodshed. There was the case of a certain judge who "conducted himself presumptuously in the synagogue and in the presence of the notables of the community, spoke wickedly, and declared that he had ordered the deed to be done and so it would be done"—meaning that he had given orders for a certain Jew to be beaten unmercifully.[11]

Rabbi Asher's Communal Leadership

Early in the fourteenth century (approximately 1305-28), the incumbent of the rabbinate of Toledo, the leading Jewish community of Castile, was Rabbi Asher ben Yehiel,[12] a member of an important family of Cologne, Germany, who was poor when he came to Spain and who died there in poverty. R. Asher and his sons (R. Jacob and R. Judah) maintained themselves on the meager salary attached to their office and by occasional moneylending. In Germany, R. Asher had witnessed the arrest of his teacher, R. Meir of Rothenburg, and the destruction of the Jewish communities in the massacres of 1298. R. Asher had worked selflessly and indefatigably for the political and religious rehabilitation of the ruined German communities. He had been born and bred among the simple and modest pietists of Germany (who so often died the death of martyrs), with their *yeshivoth*, their simple communal institutions, and their ethical wills (such as R. Asher and his sons themselves left behind when they died). It is difficult to determine whether R. Asher accepted the social and mystical doctrine of Rabbi Judah the Hasid in its entirety, but he was undoubtedly influenced by him. The cultural pattern of the Spanish Jews and their arrogant and undisciplined ways were certainly alien to his spirit. Nevertheless, he succeeded from the very start in establishing his authority as a talmudist and as an ethical personality.

He had been invited to come to Toledo by the pietists of Castile, who realized that their country needed a teacher and leader of his stature. R. Asher brought with him Ibn Adret's ban on secular learning and on those who treated the teachings of the sages with levity. Utterly different though he was from the Spanish Jews, R. Asher soon made himself at home in Castile, and within a short time was recognized not only formally but in fact as the leading religious authority of the entire country. The judges and aljamas brought their difficult cases to him, and Queen Maria de Molina commanded him to decide matters too difficult for the authorities.[13] The entry of this man, whose whole life was dedicated to learning and piety, into the oligarchy of court grandees who dominated the Jewish community seems to have been a novel phenomenon in Castile; yet on the whole he had their support. In flagrant cases submitted to him, R. Asher's responsa were couched not in the style of a quiet pietist and retiring student, but resembled

317

rather the decisions and commands given by the supreme political and judicial authority of the country. This German pietist unhesitatingly accepted the harsh code of Spanish justice. He was on good terms with the aristocrats and intellectuals when they acknowledged his authority, and at other times fought them without waiting, as Ibn Adret had done, for an opportune occasion.

In his later years, R. Asher entered into a sharp conflict with R. Israel b. Joseph Israeli, the communal secretary. This R. Israel was an intellectual of aristocratic lineage and was well versed in Moslem philosophy. In most matters R. Israel saw eye to eye with R. Asher. The question at issue was whether, under the *takkana* of Toledo in regard to a husband's inheritance of his wife's property and the rights of a wife in her husband's estate, there was room for special contracts granting husbands and wives equal rights in each other's estates, as was the Christian custom. R. Israel took an affirmative stand, which rested on current custom and on the decisions of a communal elder and judge, the physician R. Abraham b. Shoshan and of the latter's deceased son, R. David, whom R. Asher had known and esteemed. But R. Asher rejected R. David's decision: "Who dared question what he did? He gave decisions under the royal authority!" R. Israel, however, was unwilling to yield to the talmudist in this instance. He considered himself competent to interpret the *takkana* by virtue of his mastery of the language (Arabic) in which it was written, and defined the difference between its philological-common-sense meaning and its halakhic interpretation.

> For words contain whatever meaning Reason assigns to them; then the religionist comes along, interprets them and derives from them whatever he desires. For example, Reason argues that if a man takes a wife for the purpose of having children, whether he be Jew or Gentile, she should be called his wife. Subsequently the religionist appears and nullifies the Gentile's marriageability, saying that a Gen-

tile has no status in marriage. . . . The wife of a pagan is thus his wife according to Reason but not according to religion. Similarly, if the ritually unclean woman washed her body thoroughly in any bathhouse in clean water, Reason would declare her clean; but according to religious law she is not clean until she dips herself in a *mikva* (ritual bath) of forty measures of water, even if such water is full of mud.

One hears in these words the echo of the legal criticism which was wide-spread in those days. Rabbi Asher, however, stood his ground and refused to countenance the interpretation of Jewish Law according to Israel Israeli's method. "Although I know nothing of their secular wisdom," Rabbi Asher said of those who held rationalistic views, "blessed be the Merciful God who spared me from it. For examples and evidences come along for the purpose of diverting man from the fear of God and His Torah."[14]

Rabbi Asher was not disposed to admit the claims to special privilege of "the great who walk in the court of the king." He was asked whether such men may be compared, in the matter of property rights (*hazakah*), to those who belonged to the house of the Babylonian exilarchs. He replied:

It appears to me that no such comparison can be drawn. For the exilarchs were of royal (Davidic) seed and, as it were, ruled over Israel by permission of the king and bequeathed their rule to their children. . . . They, therefore, enjoyed the reverence due to royalty; if they confiscated a person's land, the owner had no right to enjoin them from it. In these generations, however, if an Israelite finds favor with the king, the nature of his authority is not such as to prevent a landowner from enjoining him, and he can do so in front of two witnesses. The reverence due such a person is not as obligatory upon people, for the man's power will not last forever. . . .

Similarly, I took issue, when I first came to this country,

in the case of the daughter of one of the (Jewish) grandees who (widowed or divorced) gave her son to a wetnurse, by virtue of a decision by one of the great men of this land who thereupon permitted her to remarry within the twenty-four months' period. (He decided this) on the example of Rav Nahman who gave such permission in the case of a member of the exilarch's house. But I forbade it.

Rabbi Asher was also asked whether there was any support for the view that a man might bequeath his property to his eldest son and the latter to his eldest son and so on, in accordance with the custom of royalty and the laws of primogeniture practiced by the nobility, thereby excluding the other heirs. He replied:

No son of the Covenant must even consider such an act . . . and whatever scholar has anything to do with it and gives him (the maker of the bequest) support is in the position of aiding transgressors.

In like manner he, following the teaching of Jonah Gerondi,[15] fought throughout his life against the custom of the Spanish Jews to put their debtors in chains. He also opposed the custom among the Spanish Jews to compel a husband to divorce his wife upon her declaration, "I do not want him." The Spanish Jews relied for their custom on Maimonides, while R. Asher relied on the tradition of his French teachers.

. . . in the multitude of our sins, the daughters of Israel in this generation are shameless, so that there is reason to suspect that she cast her eyes upon another. [And again:] The daughters of Israel in this generation being bold, if a woman were able to extricate herself from her husband's authority by a declaration that she does not like him, Father Abraham would not have a single daughter dwelling with her husband; they will cast their eyes upon another man and rebel against their husbands.

Nevertheless, he turned down the invitation of the rabbinic leaders of the Andalusian communities (Cordova, Seville, etc.) to countersign their ban dealing with compulsory divorce. He replied, "I have never assumed authority to pronounce a ban without the consent of the majority." He added, "I shall submit a document to the community and shall try to get the communities of Cordova and of Seville, and of whatever towns join them, to sign that they will not compel the granting of a divorce except as the sages, of blessed memory, prescribed."[16]

There were occasions when Rabbi Asher wrote after the manner of a man conscious of his strength and of his ability to make his will effective. It came to his notice, for example, that certain Jews would make a legal assignment of their property to others, Jews or Christians, and then borrow money. When the creditor would demand repayment, the lender would produce the document proving that his property was in the hands of others. Rabbi Asher minced no words in describing this breach of law and ethics and concluded by saying:

> All such documents of subterfuge and underhandedness which have been made to this day should be voided and torn up by the court into whose hands they fall. A law must be promulgated in Toledo prohibiting scribes and witnesses from writing and signing deeds of gift in which scheming and slyness are apparent. They are obligated to bring such matters to the attention of those who stand at the head of the community according to whose orders such scribes must act. If they disobey, they are to be removed.[17]

In another instance he took a firm stand against Rabbi Jacob ben Moses of Palencia. Involved was a law of the Sabbath whereby, under certain circumstances (*'erub haserot*), carrying objects from place to place was permitted. Rabbi Asher had refuted Rabbi Jacob's arguments and had asked him to order his community at Paredes to follow their previously established custom. Rabbi Jacob had not done so, and Rabbi Asher now wrote:

> . . . I have been told that you remain obdurate in your rebelliousness. . . . I therefore command you that, after this letter has been handed you in the presence of witnesses, you repair the open alleys. . . . And if you do not repair them in accordance with my letter, I shall impose a ban upon you. If you had lived in the days of the Sanhedrin, you would have been put to death, since you are uprooting the teaching set forth for us by Rav Ashi and are taking issue with all the great men who have lived to this day. . . . Therefore, return, and do not stray from the Torah of Moses our Teacher, peace be upon him. . . .

At the same time he addressed himself to one of the scholars of that community urging the imposition of the ban (*niddui*) upon "this crazy Rabbi Jacob ben Moses," so as to prevent any fool and ignoramus from nullifying the Torah of Moses. If Rabbi Jacob persists, so Rabbi Asher continued to his correspondent,

> I command you regarding him by the authority of His Majesty the king, that he (Rabbi Jacob) pay a fine of a thousand *zuz* to the governor of the city. . . . And I command that you show this letter to the governor so that he may collect the above-mentioned fine. If all this is of no avail, I further command you that you keep me informed of everything. For it is our duty to impose a ban upon him in all the communities of Spain and he must be condemned to death according to the law of a rebellious elder. It is our obligation to give our lives for the law of God and to destroy the evil from the midst of us.[18]

In criminal cases R. Asher confirmed the verdicts of the Jewish authorities and sanctioned the unusual penalties customary in Spain. In 1320 he was asked by the courtier Don Judah b. Isaac ibn Wakar to suggest the punishment to be meted out to a Jewish woman who had had carnal relations with a

Christian in the city of Coca. The matter had been brought by the Christians to the attention of the infante Don Juan Manuel, who at that time began his rule as regent of the kingdom (after the deaths of the infantes Don Pedro and Don Juan). Don Juan, who was then visiting Coca in the company of the Jewish courtier, decided that "the case did not come under his jurisdiction because the woman was a Jewess, and commanded that we judge her according to the laws of our Torah." In those days the Jews felt in duty bound to demonstrate zeal for their own laws. Don Judah suggested that the woman's nose be cut off. R. Asher concurred.

Don Judah then accompanied Don Juan Manuel to Cordova, where they were told about a Jew who had blasphemed against God. By invoking the aid of the goverment, Don Judah helped the elders to seize the blasphemer, who was a hard man and had powerful knights on his side, and to gather evidence in the case. Don Judah obtained the infante's consent to have the man tried under Jewish law and in accordance with R. Asher's judgment. Rabbi Asher wrote:

> You have asked me a difficult question, involving a capital crime. In all the countries I have ever heard of capital matters are not judged [by Jews] except here in Spain. I was greatly puzzled when I first came here, how it was possible to judge capital matters with the Sanhedrin not in existence. I was told that this was due to the royal will, and, what is more, the [Jewish] community judges with a view to saving life; a great deal more blood would be shed if such cases were judged by the Gentiles. I have therefore let the custom stand, though I have never agreed with them (the Jews of Spain) on the subject of the taking of life. Indeed, I note that all of you agree on the elimination of this evil from your midst. There can be no doubt that this man blasphemed openly and the matter is already known among the Gentiles. The latter being very strict with those who blaspheme against their law and faith, the

blasphemy would assume greater proportions if in this case punishment were not meted out.

The rabbi concluded: "If I were taking counsel with you, I should be inclined to recommend that his tongue be drawn out of his mouth and partly cut off." He wrote separately to Don Judah ibn Wakar:

> I note that all your actions are for the sake of Heaven, in order to uproot the evil from our midst. I have also been told in another place things have turned out for the best as a result of your aid, to the benefit of the entire community.

The incident is typical of the religious views prevalent in the Christian environment of the day, where sins of that nature were involved. It is known that Louis IX of France was a zealot and on many occasions ordered the cutting out of the tongue of a man guilty of blasphemy. No wonder that Jews did the like.[19] The laws against informers were more in consonance with the practices of the German Jews. In most cases of this nature R. Asher merely confirmed, by virtue of his rabbinic authority, the penalties imposed by the Jewish notables. In 1312, at the very time when the infante Don Pedro visited Seville, the case of a Jewish informer attracted much attention. It was found that

> He carries information to the Gentiles about the Jews and and about the Jewish community. . . . The Jewish community is very much afraid of this man, who can be found every night in the court of one of the most powerful men among the Gentiles. Now the Jews have been granted authority by the crown to try him in secret and, if found guilty, to execute him.

Rabbi Asher agreed with the sentence of the judges of the *kahal* of Seville. He wrote, "They did well in sentencing him to hang."[20]

In another instance R. Asher, burning with indignation, attempted to stir the communal leaders to vigorous action against the plague of informing.

> Know ye, all who see this letter, that for some time now astounding cries, complaints and accusations have reached me against this man, Abraham. . . . It is charged that he has several times caused the forfeiture of Jewish money, public as well as private, to Gentiles; that he played a treacherous role in the cancellation of debts; that he constantly threatens Jews with confiscations and the desecration of their synagogues; that he mocks the words of our sages in the princely courts and seeks to disparage our faith in the eyes of the populace. . . . The communal leaders have already consulted me about him several times. . . . And now the distinguished R. Joseph Halevi, whose spirit the Lord has stirred with zeal, has taken action in the matter. Let all the notables who wield authority take to heart what I have written.[21]

THE JEWISH COURTIERS OF ALFONSO XI

Jewish influence at court increased after Alfonso XI, at the age of 14, took over the reins of government in the year 1322. Following the advice of the infante Don Felipe, the king appointed as his *almoxarife mayor* Joseph Halevi b. Ephraim b. Isaac aben Shabat, who was known as Don Yuçaf de Ecija, after his Andalusian birthplace.[22] The king gave Don Yuçaf a seat in his privy council beside two of his Christian favorites. According to a Hebrew tale of those days,

> The Lord prompted him to go to the royal court, to collect taxes and render other services to the king. He was a true Joseph—steadfast in his piety, wise, skilled in music, very good looking, and the Lord was with him. And when the king found him to be trustworthy and efficient, he appointed him over all his kingdom. There was no one greater than he in the kingdom of Castile. He was next to the king and great among the Jews. Joseph had princes in his service, dining at his table. He provided himself with a car-

riage and horses, and fifty footmen ran before him (cf. II Samuel 15.1).

This Jewish courtier's social position and his fondness for music are manifest from a letter addressed to him by Alfonso IV of Aragon in 1329. Therein the king informs Don Yuçaf of his recovery from an illness, and asks him to send to Aragon for his diversion the Castilian musicians who had performed for him at their last meeting.

Don Yuçaf was loyal to his people and to his religion. He built a synagogue in Seville and presented the Jewish community of his birthplace Ecija (the Hebrew deed of gift has been preserved in a Spanish translation) with certain lands "for the service of God," namely, the maintenance of a *yeshiva*, the dean and his pupils, and for the purchase of prayer books for the donor's synagogue. Better times seemed to have dawned for the Jews, as in the early years of the reign of Alfonso X.

But the old rivalries between the Jewish and the Christian courtiers also revived. The appointment of Don Felipe's Jewish favorite to a post at court angered the other infantes, who had been ousted. Of the two Christian grandees who had sat with Don Yuçaf in the privy council, one was murdered by a mob, and the other was later executed by order of the king. There were plots against Don Yuçaf's life as well. In 1326 Alfonso sent him with a retinue of knights to Valladolid to escort his sister, Doña Leonor, who was to assist at the reception of his betrothed, a daughter of the king of Portugal. While Yuçaf was in Valladolid, his rivals stirred up the local rabble against him on a charge of political conspiracy. Doña Leonor saved his life by taking him under her own protection. When the privy council was reconstituted two new Christian members were appointed, but Don Yuçaf retained his seat. In 1328, however, he too was dismissed from the council upon the demand of the Cortes, which had been summoned to vote a special tax for the prosecution of the war against the Moslems. Don Yuçaf appears again, nevertheless, in 1329 and 1330 as the *almoxarife mayor* negotiating with the king of Aragon.

Among Don Yuçaf's rivals was a Jewish physician and astronomer, Don Samuel ibn Wakar of Toledo, who in 1331 obtained the concession to the mint, which had previously been held by men in the confidence of the estates. The concession had been granted Don Samuel with the object of increasing the royal revenues, but the Christian populace held him responsible for a rise in the cost of living, which he was supposed to have caused by debasing the currency. Don Samuel and his associates were also accused of buying up all the commodities in the kingdom at high prices for export, so as to be able to import supplies of silver for the mint. Moreover, it was said that Don Samuel had undertaken to farm the taxes of La Frontera (the southern frontier province) but that Don Yuçaf had outbid him by offering the king a larger sum. In order to injure his rival, Don Samuel persuaded the king to forbid the export of any goods from Castile to Granada. The result was a considerable decrease in the income of La Frontera. This measure constituted a violation of a commercial treaty between Castile and Granada and, according to a Christian source, eventually led to bad relations between the two countries.

A third Jewish grandee at the court of Castile was R. Moses Abzaradiel, the king's scribe, whose signature in Latin characters appears in the thirties on royal documents dealing with finances and taxes, such as privileges granted to bishops, monasteries, nobles and municipalities, tax exemptions, gifts from the royal revenues, port dues, salt mines and knights' salaries. Moses Abzaradiel was learned in the Torah, and at one time served as a judge in Toledo.[23]

ABNER OF BURGOS AND HIS CAMPAIGN AGAINST THE JEWS

The very great influence exercised by the Jewish courtiers could have no effect on the major trends of the king's policies. Alfonso XI was the hero of the renewed Reconquest and, in internal affairs, sought to enhance the power of the crown and to institute religious reforms in the spirit of Christian kings like Louis IX of France and Edward I of England. Such an attitude was propitious for a recrudescence of the religious agitation against the Jews. One of the most powerful protagonists of that agitation was the best known apostate ever to arise in medieval Jewry.

In mid-summer of 1295, late in the month of Tammuz, while the Jews of Castile waited for a sign of redemption, a hail of crosses—so runs the Christian tradition—suddenly fell down upon them from the skies. There lived at that time in the city of Burgos a Jewish physician by the name of R. Abner, to whom those who had seen such visions (see p. 280, above) came for advice and medical treatment.[24] This young man had himself long been tormented by doubts and misgivings; then, after many years, he was privileged, as he thought, to have the truth of Christianity revealed to him (probably in the twenties of the fourteenth century). Abner himself described this "revelation" in the following terms:[25]

> I saw the poverty of the Jews, my people, from whom I am descended, who have been oppressed and broken and heavily burdened by taxes throughout their long captivity —this people that has lost its former honor and glory; and there is none to help or sustain them. One day when I had meditated much on the matter, I went to the synagogue weeping sorely and sad at heart. And I prayed unto the Lord, saying, "I beseech Thee, O Lord God, for compassion, that Thou mayest take note of these afflictions which beset us. Wherefore art Thou so wroth with Thy people these many days, Thy people and the sheep of Thy pasture? Why should the Gentiles say, 'Where is their God?' And now, oh Lord, hearken unto my prayer and my supplication and cause the light to shine upon Thy desolate sanctuary and have mercy upon Thy people Israel." After the great anxieties of my heart and all the toil I had taken upon myself, I rested and fell asleep. . . . And in a dream,

I saw the figure of a tall man who said to me, "Why dost thou slumber? Hearken unto these words that I say unto thee and prepare thyself against the appointed season; for I say unto thee, that the Jews have remained so long in captivity for their folly and wickedness and because they have no teacher of righteousness through whom they may recognize the truth."

On awaking, Abner did not at first attribute any particular significance to his dream, but resolved to study and to examine the fundamental principles of Judaism in the books of the Torah and the prophets and the sages and the commentators and the philosophers. Nevertheless, he was greatly troubled in spirit, until he finally resolved to put the whole matter out of his thoughts and to cling to the religion into which he had been born, whether good or bad, as his fathers had done, for he was no better than they. But after much fasting and self-castigation, Abner again saw in a dream the man who had appeared to him three years earlier. The man rebuked him sternly: "How long, O sluggard, wilt thou slumber? When wilt thou arise from thy sleep? Upon thy back rest all the sins of the Jews and their sons throughout their generations." Suddenly Abner saw that his robe was covered with crosses, "like the seal of Jesus of Nazareth." Now the man spoke comfortingly to Abner, saying: "The seal of God is truth. I have blotted out, as a thick cloud, thy transgressions, and as a cloud thy sins. Return unto me, for I have redeemed thee" (Isa. 44. 22).

Thus Abner wrestled in spirit for some twenty-five years, until (shortly before the year 1321) he announced his profession of the Christian faith in a book in Hebrew entitled "The Wars of the Lord." (The work has not been preserved except for some passages quoted in later literature.) Abner translated the "Wars of the Lord" into Spanish at the request of the infanta Doña Blanca, mother superior of the convent Las Huelgas near Burgos (d. 1331). He was baptized and was thereafter known, after the city in which he spent his later years, as

Maestre Alfonso de Valladolid. In the 1320s and 1330s Abner wrote many books and pamphlets in which he assailed both the religion of his fathers and his Jewish brethren. His magnum opus was called *Moreh Zedek* (Teacher of Righteousness), which is extant in a Spanish translation (*Mostrador de Justicia*). Other and smaller works of Abner included *Minhath Kenaoth* (An Offering of Zeal), *Sod ha-Gemul* (The Secret of Retribution) and *Migdal Oz* (A Tower of Strength), some of which have been preserved in the Hebrew originals. Abner did not confine himself to literary polemics, but proceeded to launch a very menacing assault upon the Jews themselves.

The personality of Abner of Burgos, with its many interesting facets, is far more sharply and clearly defined for us than that of any other medieval Jewish apostate. It was Abner who fathered that ideology of apostasy which was destined, about two generations after his death, to bring wrack and ruin upon Spanish Jewry. It is therefore necessary to deal with his personality at length. His religious motivations are known to us only from his post-conversion teachings. During his lifetime his apostasy was attributed to a variety of motives. At all events, his motives must be sought within the wide scope of the internal and external quarrels and troubles that were the portion of Spanish Jewry in those days. It is obvious from Abner's own words (as quoted above from his *Moreh Zedek*) that the foundations of his belief in the religion of his fathers had been undermined by the tribulations of his people and by the non-fulfilment or misinterpretation of its messianic prophecies. It was only after his inner struggle was at an end that he sought theoretical confirmation for his new views in Hebrew literature. In a sense, his spiritual stresses marked the conclusion and the finale of the upheavals that rocked Spanish Jewry during the thirteenth century. In the course of his twenty-five-year struggle Abner doubtless pursued various theological and philosophical studies, the details of which can only be inferred from his writings. Here and there he makes reference to mystical doctrines, and those references may have been intentionally brief: it is not likely that, living in Burgos as he did, he should have had no contact with the mystics whose teachings were then widely current in northern Castile in particular. Certain crucial parts of his ideology are, in fact, based on the teachings of the cabalists of the earlier period. He was also versed in Jewish and Moslem philosophy. He read Christian theological works—the only explicit reference is to Augustine—and took over the Christological method of interpreting the Midrash from Raymond Martini's *Pugio Fidei* (Dagger of the Faith), making very clever, careful and imaginative use of the forged midrashim of the famous Dominican.

In the Jewish intellectual circles in which Abner moved during the critical years of his ideological development Maimonides was regarded as the authoritative interpreter of the Jewish tradition. In these circles philosophic questions on which the various schools took different positions were discussed and argued over as if they were cardinal principles of faith. From the same circles also came Abner's sharpest adversary, his former friend and disciple, R. Isaac Policar (or Pollegar), the latter a member of a wealthy family resident in Burgos and other north Castilian cities. Castigating his erstwhile friend turned apostate, R. Isaac writes,[26] ironically,

> Let me tell you what I think will happen to you: Now that your sinful conduct has led you to take this step, you have no right to attempt either to ease your own conscience openly, or to convince the ignorant of the wisdom of your act, by any means other than the language and reasoning of the faith that you have adopted. Even to me and to others like me you cannot speak otherwise, lest you do yourself harm. The displeasure of the Lord, however, is not with your foolish thoughts, but must be directed against us who are to blame for your fall, for we did not act to restrain you and to threaten you with disgrace when, in your arrogance, you publicly preached that the primal sub-

stance was formed matter, that the void exists, that angels are corporeal, and all the other heresies and mockeries which you propounded in your foul book which you entitled, "The New Philosophy." ... And when you saw that we paid no attention to your activities and did not refute or respond to your mockery—Truth lost all value in your eyes. Then, since you did not find it worth your while to attack only a few of the true beliefs, you renounced most of them, ending in total heresy. Do not, however, expect to fulfil your desire to rise to a high position—the motive for your action—for the high office which you are pursuing is eluding you; for you were, apparently, not born under the Star of Plenty.

Similar testimony is given by the philosopher Moses Narboni,[27]

There was a scholar, an older contemporary of mine, one of the singular men of his time, who composed a treatise on Determinism, in which he stated that "the possible" does not exist, but only "the inevitable," since everything is predestined. ... Now this man, called Abner, possessed great knowledge, so that I do not believe that he was himself in error, but that his intent was to mislead others. For he had come upon hard times, and he realized that he could expect no assistance, only opposition, from his coreligionists, who, being strangers to philosophy themselves, hated those who cultivated it—so he turned aspostate. ... For he was not one of those pious men whose faith remains unimpaired even by extreme material want. ... Later, when he saw that what he had done was wrong even according to philosophy—for even a philosopher should not discard the Torah in which he was nurtured—he tried to absolve himself of guilt by preaching an all-embracing determinism, claiming that everything was preordained.

Abner did, in fact, compose after his conversion, and perhaps even before it, several works dealing with the subject of determinism. One of them survives in a Spanish translation still in manuscript. In this work Abner presented a theory of absolute determinism which is a curious blend of the Pauline and Augustinian doctrines of predestination, with Moslem fatalism and the lore of astrology. According to this view, all is in the hands of Heaven, including the fear of Heaven. The human being has no choice, not even in matters of faith. In Abner's inner struggle with his doubts concerning Divine recompense, raised by the enigmatic phenomenon of "the suffering saint and the prosperous sinner," the question of human freedom was a pivotal one, and the determinist position on this question appears to have given him the inner peace which he sought. As to the alleged economic motives for his conversion, Policar himself testified that he was never blessed with opulence. As Maestre Alfonso he held only the minor office of sacristan in the church of Valladolid. The Christians befriended him only to the extent to which he proved useful to them.

In his *Moreh Zedek*,[28] Abner deals at length with the reasons which prevented Jews from taking the path to Christian "repentence," namely: 1) Most people are naturally disinclined to change their customary and conventional way of life; 2) slander and enmity are the lot of converts; 3) conversion brings shame upon a man's family; 4) the convert finds himself in alien surroundings where he has no relatives or friends; 5) his wife and children do not go with him; 6) he loses his status in the Jewish community; 7) he is doomed to poverty because he must leave his possessions with strangers and may no longer lend money at interest; 8) public baptism is an embarrassing experience; 9) a man's pride causes him to refrain from repentence; 10) the leniency of the Christian rulers encourages the Jews in their recalcitrancy; 11) a wise and good man would be inclined to change his religion when he discovers doubts and defects in it which are avoided and remedied in another religion. But it is exceedingly difficult for such a person to study the other religion because its tenets are profound and it is not easy to find a teacher capable of interpreting them, the other religion being still young. Sometimes the difficulty is that the seeker for truth lives in a distant country, as was the case with Maimonides; or that the teachers themselves err and cause their pupils to err, like Elisha ben Abuya; 12) God himself does not desire the sinners to repent—a reference to Abner's doctrine of predestination. Replying to those who held that it was forbidden to forsake the faith of one's fathers (a traditional problem in the Moslem philosophy and one then widely discussed among Jews as well), Abner asserted that reverence for one's forebears did not deter the seeker of truth. When a man reaches maturity he should not adhere to the faith of his fathers merely because he was born and bred among them and is accustomed to their ways, but only if he is convinced of its truth by long study and much disputation with the scholars of the age. Abner held up the example of Abraham who, though he apprehended his Creator at the age of three, did not proclaim his faith until he was fifty-two years old, after he had resolved all his doubts. "And then he disregarded the honor due his father and his mother and the love of his kin and neighbors and the honor due his teachers, all for the honor of the Creator, blessed be His name." Abner declared this to have been his own course of action when he adopted Christianity.

Abner's friends spoke truthfully when they said that he remained a Jew at heart. Holding the views that he did, Abner did not belong in the fold of orthodox Catholicism; he was merely a typical *mumar,* a heretic within the Jewish camp. His books (mostly written in Hebrew and later translated under his own supervision) were addressed to his old Jewish associates, with whom he continued to wrangle to the end of his life. His Hebrew style, his fluency in composition, and his way of skipping from one topic to another put him in a class with the aggadists or eschatological writers like R. Abraham b. Hiyya and the contemporary mystics rather than with the Christian and Jewish schoolmen.

Abner, following Raymond Martini, attempted to find in talmudic literature support for the basic teachings of Christianity, namely, the doctrine of the Incarnation, the Trinity, and salvation through the Messiah. He sought testimonials for his adopted faith in the writings also of the philosophers, who, he felt, occasionally alluded to Christian tenets without consciously recognizing their truth. According to Abner, the philosophic and theological writings of all peoples, the Jews included, contain direct or implied references to the doctrines of the Trinity and the Incarnation, which to him were the key to his own and his people's salvation. The Cabala was particularly helpful to him in his search. There can be no doubt that the streams of mystical thought then meandering through Spanish Jewry had a decisive influence upon Abner's thinking in the course of the intellectual crisis which he resolved by his conversion to Christianity. Abner began with a critique of the rationalist interpretation of Judaism, cultivated by the Jewish intellectuals who were his friends—and for this he found ample support in cabalistic doctrine—and moved ultimately to a position of complete identification with the Christian ideology.

The course of Abner's ideological development can be traced through his polemic with the friend of his youth, Isaac Policar. A short time after his conversion Abner sent Policar a tract that he had written, explaining his messianic doctrine. Policar replied in a Hebrew pamphlet, dubbed by Abner "The Epistle of Blasphemies" (*Iggereth ha-Harafoth*), which contained the personal attacks upon the apostate quoted earlier. Policar's main purpose, however, was to oppose to Abner's Christian faith his own rationalist credo. Taking as his authority the political theory of Aristotle, he seeks to prove that

> law and convention are absolutely necessary for orderly human behavior. . . . Because we are endowed with a rational soul, we are obliged to accept those tenets whose truth had been logically established. However, the human being, in his youth—and, indeed, in the case of most people, throughout life—has neither the leisure nor the disposition to learn these tenets through the study of their sources,

namely, the exact sciences. Therefore, the founder of the
divinely revealed faith found it necessary to incorporate
into it all those fundamental truths without which the
human being cannot achieve perfection and to make them
part of Tradition, so that a man would not remain throughout his entire lifetime, until he dies, ignorant of them.

Only the Torah of Moses fulfils these conditions, both in its
ideology and in its law. The people of Israel were distinguished
from all other nations and consecrated to keep this Torah.
Those who observe the commandments of the Torah, suppressing their base instincts, merit eternal life. Following this brief
exposition of the fundamentals of his rationalist doctrine Policar set forth his belief in the Messiah who is destined to redeem
his people. "No thinker would believe that our faith is contingent upon the coming of the Messiah. . . . Yet we must believe that his coming is presaged in the Torah." Policar then
cites biblical verses to show that the order of nature will not
change in the Messianic Age, and that contrary to Christian
belief the Messiah has not yet come and the messianic prophecies were not fulfilled in the days of the Second Temple.[29]

Isaac Policar circulated the *Epistle of Blasphemies* throughout Spain. Abner replied to it with a tract which he called,
"Refutation of the Blasphemer" (*Teshuboth la-Meharef*), but
not until some ten years after the appearance of the *Epistle*,
claiming that it had only recently come to his attention.
It is more likely, however, that Abner let Policar's pamphlet lie for several years and then picked it up again and
penned a reply to it during the anti-Jewish campaign of the
1330s, when he felt that an audience receptive to his ideas
would be found within the Jewish camp. In the intervening
period he had kept his polemic with Policar alive by producing
a work on "Divine Providence and Predestination" which he
called *Minhath Kenaoth* (An Offering of Zeal). Abner now
charged that Policar wrote his pamplet in order to improve his
own reputation within the Jewish community where, as a

336

result of opinions previously expressed, he was considered a heretic, lacking reverence for the teachings of the Sages. But it was not the Lord's desire that he should succeed therein.

> For he made known your presumptuousness and your folly through my *Minhath Kenaoth* without any intention on my part. God knows that my heart is pure and that I had no desire to enhance my reputation at the expense of yours. . . . I meant only to glorify God and to stem dissension in Israel. I had been expecting a reply from you to my *Minhath Kenaoth* for a long time. But while you announced all over that you were writing a refutation of my work, time passed and none appeared. You talked much but did nothing. I realize now that it is a stratagem on your part whereby you try to present yourself to them as a wise man, while withholding your writing from me. This I regard as powerful evidence of the weakness of your words and the words of your colleagues who are akin to you. You are afraid to show me your arguments lest I expose your errors.

In the body of the work Maestre Alfonso advances, against the position of the religious rationalists, two telling arguments which had already been used by the cabalists of the preceding century in their war against rationalism. He writes:

> Your statement in the first chapter that, "because we are endowed with a rational soul, we are obliged to accept those tenets whose truth has been logically established, and since the [average] human being has neither the leisure nor the disposition to learn these tenets through the study of their sources, namely, the exact sciences, the founder of the faith found it necessary to incorporate into it all those fundamental truths without which the human being cannot achieve perfection and to make them part of Tradition, so that a man would not remain throughout his entire lifetime, until he die, ignorant of them," is full of serious error. Precisely because man possesses a rational soul he does not have to accept any traditional belief; for that

337

which one learns from tradition, whatever the reason for it, can be called knowledge only in a homonymous sense, and in accepting it he is not functioning as an active thinker. Yet according to you it is for the exercise of that function that man needs those tenets, as you put it: "Because we are endowed with a rational soul etc. . . . a man should not remain throughout life ignorant of them." Furthermore, the human being, as a rational being, should know all the sciences in the world, for a knowledge of *all* of them is necessary for his achievement of perfection as a rational being, not merely a knowledge of a few of them, as you specify when you say, *"those* without which the human being cannot achieve perfection." Now, if the perfection of the human being cannot, because he is a rational being, be achieved by his derivation of even all existing knowledge and creed from tradition, how can it be achieved by his acquisition of only a part thereof, two or three doctrines perhaps, from the same source?

The fact is that a human being is ready to accept authoritative tradition not in his capacity as a rational being, as you claim, but as a master of some specialized branch of knowledge which takes some or all of its basic premises from the established traditions of a higher and more comprehensive science. The specialized lore, whose premises are the tenets you mentioned, is the Torah, which you extol. But a man acquires his knowledge of its basic tenets not because he is a generally rational being, but as one versed specifically in the Torah. . . . From your statement, "so that a man would not remain throughout his entire lifetime, until he die, ignorant of them," it appears that you regard these tenets not as premises on which the Torah is based but as the Torah itself or as parts of the Torah, and that one's purpose in learning them is not the performance of any commandment (*mitzva*) but merely the attainment of knowledge as an end in itself. . . . But this does not accord with the teachings of the Torah or the Prophets or the Sages. For if those tenets were part of the Torah itself, then Scripture would not have imparted them in veiled references but in clear and explicit statements, like the other commandments; for it is written, "It is not hidden from you nor is it far away . . . but the thing is very near to you" (Deut. 30. 11-14). Certainly they would not have been stated in metaphors which, if taken literally, indicate the opposite of their real meaning, for example, "the mouth of God," "the hand of God," "the eyes of God," "the feet of God," and like phrases which, in their literal meaning, imply the corporeality of God; or expressions such as "God regretted," "He was grieved at heart," "God savored the pleasing odor," and others like them, which, taken literally, would imply that God undergoes change and assumes accidents; or references to God in the plural (i.e., Elohim, and adjectives and verbs in grammatical agreement with it), which, in the literal sense, deny the unity of God. Then there is the verse "In the beginning God created" and others of similar meaning which literally aver creatio ex nihilo, a tenet denied by some philosophers, and the biblical accounts of the miracles, likewise discredited by the same philosophers, and you say that "the perfection of man is unattainable without a knowledge of those philosophies."

Likewise, your statement—which you base on the words of Maimonides (Guide of the Perplexed, III, 54)—that the verse, "Therein shall man glory, understanding and knowing Me" (Jer. 9. 23), means that a man must know and understand the philosophic theories which explain the existence of God, His unity and all His other attributes, is nonsense. The same verse explains forthwith what is meant by "understanding and knowing Me" when it continues, "that I am the Lord who practices kindness, justice and righteousness on earth," meaning that man must know and understand that the Holy One, blessed be He, exercises His Providence over the earth and practices in it kindness, justice and righteousness. This interpretation is borne out by the cantillation of the verse, in which the caesura (ethnahta) comes not at Me but at earth. The Massoretes obviously had the same interpretation. This thought is re-

peated in another verse of the same prophet (Jer. 22. 16),
"He judged the cause of the poor and destitute, then it was
well; for is not this knowing Me, sayeth the Lord?"

The sages also held the same view, as we read in the Midrash (Exodus Rabbah, XXX, 19), "Rabbi Eleazar said,
'The entire Torah rests upon justice.' " The Talmud (*Sab-
bath*, 31a) tells this tale: "A Gentile came to Shammai
and said to him, 'If you can teach me the entire Torah
while I stand on one foot I will become a proselyte.'
Shammai rebuffed him. The same man then came to Hillel.
Hillel converted him to Judaism and said to him, 'What is
hateful to you do not do to others!—this is the entire
Torah; the rest is commentary thereof, go and study it.' "
It follows from the foregoing there isn't in the entire
Torah a principle of faith which is pure faith and nothing
else. Not even the belief that God is One and Eternal, and
that reverence and love are due Him, falls into that category. The tenets of faith are all motivations for the performance of the commandments, of which the [ethical]
laws are the most important, and which are all encompassed by the commandment, "Love thy neighbor as thyself," of which Rabbi Akiba said, "This is a fundamental
principle of the Torah" (*Sifra* to Leviticus 19. 18). We
read also in *Midrash Tanhuma* (ed. Solomon Buber,
Deuteronomy, p. 32), "Six hundred and thirteen precepts
were communicated to Moses at Sinai. Came King David
and reduced them to eleven [principles], as is written
(Psalm 15): 'O Lord, who shall sojourn in Thy tent; who
shall dwell on Thy holy mountain? He who walks blame-
lessly etc. . . . He who does these things shall never falter.'
Then came the prophet Isaiah and reduced them to six
principles (Isaiah 33. 15): 'He who walks in righteousness
and speaks uprightly etc.' Then came Micah and reduced
them to three principles (Micah 6. 8): 'He has told thee, O
man, what is good; what does the Lord require of thee but
to do justice, to love kindness, and to walk humbly with
thy God?' Then came Amos and reduced them to two
(Amos 5. 4, 5): 'For thus said the Lord to the house of

Israel, "Seek Me and live, but seek not Bethel." ' Then came Habakkuk and reduced them to a single principle (Habakkuk 2. 4): 'The righteous man shall live by his faithfulness.' "

All of the eleven principles enumerated by King David, or the six offered by Isaiah, or the three of Micah, are not abstract tenets that call for no action. The purpose of all the precepts and the tenets of faith underlying them is the practice of all that is implied in the commandment, "Love thy neighbor as thyself." The sages take the same position in the Talmud (*Berakhoth*, 17a) when they say, "The goal of wisdom is repentance and good deeds." They further state (*ibid.*), "The Psalmist said 'The fear of the Lord is the beginning of wisdom; all those who practice it have good understanding' (Psalms 110. 10). The Psalmist did not say, 'those who study it,' but 'those who practice it.' " Likewise King David, when he enjoined his son (I Chronicles 28. 9), "And thou, Solomon my son, know the God of thy father and serve Him," put the knowledge of God before the service of God, by which is meant the performance of the commandments, which sustain all creation and of which the ethical laws (*dinim*) are the most important. For therewith alone can human beings serve their Creator, by acting to their fullest capacity as the agents of His will to make creation endure. This is what is meant by the statement of the Talmud (*Sabbath*, 10a), "The judge who renders a just decision in law, the Holy Writ regards him as though he had become a partner of The Holy One, blessed be He, in the act of Creation."

This is also why the sages said in tractate *Kiddushin* (fol. 40b), "It is not study but deeds that are the more important." Even those who held the view that study was more important gave as their reason the fact that study leads to deeds. The study and interpretation of the Torah, they taught, provide the motivation for the performance of the commandments and are not ends in themselves. They said that study is important because it serves as the efficient cause for many good deeds, and that good deeds are important because they are the ultimate reasons for study. Since study creates the inclination and disposition to do many good deeds, it is better for man than the observance of those few commandments which may aid in the acquisition of knowledge, especially if it is knowledge of philosophy, which consists mostly of doubts and controversial opinions, denies the miracles and divine wonders, *creatio ex nihilo*, resurrection, divine providence, and retribution. Knowledge should, on the contrary, promote the performance of the commandments and the love of God and his worship, which is the collective term for all the commandments, as is written in Deuteronomy (30. 16), "That which I command thee this day, to love the Lord thy God by walking in His ways," and further on (30. 20), "To love the Lord thy God by obeying Him, and to cleave to Him." It follows therefrom that man's love of God is not identical with his comprehension of the secret of all creation and his reflection upon it with his intelligence, as Maimonides asserted (*Guide*, III, 51), but those intellectual pursuits have as their purpose the love of God which is identical with obeying Him and walking in His ways. . . . From this standpoint the study of the various branches of knowledge has as its purpose the performance of the commandments, and the love enjoined by the Torah is one which is "not hidden from you nor is it far away." It is not a love which is contingent upon the comprehension of the secret of all creation, which is very far away and beyond the capacity of the human being to grasp. The other view appears to suffer from a contradiction, for most of those who pursue that knowledge are free-thinkers who make light of the Torah and of the commandments to a greater extent than other people.

The love of God enjoined by the Torah stems from the acceptance of principles of faith, confirmed by tradition and implied in biblical verses, sometimes in terms whose literal sense contradicts their true meaning, so that they might serve as authoritative and useful premises for the commandments for every class of people at its level, for

the intellectuals at the level of their intelligence and for
the masses according to their needs and their limited ra-
tionality. . . . He, however, who takes the first position
which we described above, that the value of the commandments is in their contribution toward an understanding of
philosophy, does not believe in the Torah of Moses, its
Prophets and its Sages, but in the faith of the philosophers
who love the [speculative] sciences more than anything
else, for all their divergent opinions and controversial
theories.
This, R. Isaac, is the lore which you extol in your *Epistle
of Blasphemies* and in all your writings that I have seen
or heard of. If you should have the good fortune to change
your outlook before you die, as Maimonides did in his last
years when he said that all the sciences were ancillary to
the Torah,[29a] it would do you good. But I know that the arrogance of your heart and your desire to prevail in controversy will prevent you from doing so. I thought I would
accord you the honor of learning and understanding, but
the Lord has withheld honor from you.[30]

After this general introduction Abner set out to derive the
basic tenets of Christianity from Jewish tradition itself. He
attempts to furnish proof of the trinitarian doctrine from talmudic and midrashic sources, as well as from the writings of
the philosophers. He quotes, for example, this comment of R.
Simlai (*Midrash Tehillim* to Psalm 50): " 'The Mighty One,
God, the Lord (*El Elohim YHWH*) spoke and called the
earth' (Psalms 50. 1). Why are three names of God given in
this verse? It is to teach us that God created the universe
under these three names to correspond to the three virtues
(*middoth*) through which the universe was created, namely
wisdom, understanding, and knowledge (*hokhma, tebuna,
da'ath*)," Abner's identification of the virtues of *hokhma, tebuna,* and *da'ath* with the three aspects of the Trinity is based,
no doubt, upon the cabalistic theory of Sefiroth.[31] He sought
allusions also to the doctrine of the Incarnation in the dicta of

343

the Jewish sages and in the writings of the pagan philosophers.
According to Abner, they were aware of the existence of some
form of universal incarnation, of a divine immanence in all
things.

> The sages of the Talmud tell us (*Baba Bathra* 25a) that
> the Divine Presence is everywhere, and that there is no
> place in the Universe without it. . . . Avicenna, Themistius,
> and Alexander (of Aphrodisias) aver that the active Intel-
> lect is present in all bodies. . . . This, it seems to me, is the
> reason why in ancient times people worshipped idols. . . .
> Many wise men, even King Solomon in his old age, were so
> misled. . . . Rabbi Abraham ibn Ezra wrote (commentary
> to Exodus 33. 21) that the exalted Name (of God) is com-
> posed of three distinct consonants to connote a Body of
> three dimensions. Now this application of the term "Body"
> to God has wondrously mystic meaning, and renders in-
> telligible the use of such words as the Presence (Heb.
> *Shekhina*), the Dweller (Heb. *Shokhen, Yoshev*), and the
> Dwelling (Heb. *Makom, Ma'on*) to denote the Divinity.
> He goes on to say that the mystic term *Shi'ur Koma* is
> likewise to be understood in this sense (*i.e.*, the measure-
> ment of the Body), as is evident from the statement of
> Rabbi Ishmael, "Whoever knows the measurement of the
> Creator is certain of his share in the world to come," to
> which Rabbi Akiba added, "I am guarantor thereof."[31a] It
> seems, then, that Rabbi Akiba, who had deep theosophic
> insight, shared with Rabbi Ishmael the knowledge that
> God is incarnate in physical bodies and is measured rela-
> tive to them. These sages herein revealed that the salva-
> tion of mankind is to be achieved through an awareness of
> the incarnation of the Divinity. . . .
> Then there is the theory of Divine incarnation in the
> human race as a whole in the form of the Active Intellect
> which is in all human beings. This is the sense of Hillel's
> utterance (*Sukka*, 53a), "If I am here, all are here. . . ."
> The belief in this kind of incarnation also gave rise in
> antiquity to a form of idolatry, namely the deification of

certain human beings. Among those who are said to have proclaimed themselves divinities were Nebuchadnezzar, king of Babylon, Hiram, king of Tyre, Tiberius Caesar and Gaius Caesar, as well as some philosophers. . . . As one of the latter said, "I am the Active Intellect . . ."

I want to make it clear, however, that neither one of the two doctrines of universal incarnation discussed above supports the precepts of the Torah and the belief in rewards and punishments in afterlife. They, rather, undermine allegiance to the Torah. . . . The doctrine of incarnation which could encourage observance of the Torah and the belief in rewards and punishments in afterlife is the one which teaches that there is an incarnation of the Divinity in the *individual* human being, whereby every human soul remains a distinct and separate entity, distinguished and separated from every other soul over an extended period of time, so that each and every soul may, individually, receive its own merited recompense, according to its deeds during its sojourn on earth. . . . However, since this concept of incarnation in the individual may, like the other two described earlier, also misguide people into idolatry and polytheism, the Torah of Moses, whose purpose is to eradicate idolatry, could not reveal it, even though it would have encouraged observance of its precepts and sustained the hope for afterlife. This knowledge had to remain concealed until monotheism would be firmly established by means of continued admonition by a succession of prophets and by recurrent punishment for lapses from it.

This is the reason why the Torah of Moses makes no mention of recompense in afterlife and no references to the triune nature of the Godhead, limiting itself only to covert allusions to them, in order to save the masses from the error of polytheism, as already indicated. For in the early days, when the wise men referred to God by the name *Elohim*, which is plural in form, to denote His many attributes, the masses assumed the existence of many gods whom they identified with natural forces. Then came the patriarchs, Abraham, Isaac, and Jacob, and began to use the name *El Shaddai,* signifying a sole and self-sufficient Power. For although God is immanent in the physical world, He has existence apart from it and is independent of it. . . . However, since the masses would not even then give up their idolatrous polytheism, the patriarchs used also the name YHWH, which emphasizes God's oneness and His non-dependence upon the physical world. . . . But the patriarchs did not publicize the name YHWH to the extent to which Moses did, who found the Hebrews in Egypt eagerly pursuing idolatry. . . . In the course of time, when they observed that in everyday life righteous men often suffer the misfortunes due sinners whereas sinners reap the rewards due the righteous, they, being unaware of the rewards and punishments which come in afterlife, since the Torah does not speak of them, rebelled against the Torah. This is why Malachi, the last of the prophets, chastised them in the following words, "You have wearied the Lord with your words, yet you say, 'Wherein have we wearied him?' In that you say, 'Every one that doeth evil is good in the sight of the Lord, and He delighteth in them, or where is the God of justice?' (Malachi 2. 17)." And he continues, "You have said, 'It is vain to serve God; what has it profited us to have kept His charge and to have walked mournfully before the Lord of Hosts?' (3. 14)." Then the prophet prophesied to them that the Messiah, scion of David, would appear and resolve the doubts which they harbor concerning the promises of recompense to be found in the Torah, as is written, "Behold, I send my messenger, and he shall clear the way before Me, and the Lord whom you seek will suddenly come to His temple; and the messenger of the covenant in whom you delight cometh, saith the Lord" (3. 1). The commentators who interpret this verse explain that the "messenger of the covenant" refers to the Messiah, scion of David, who will teach them a covenant and a law for which they yearn, which will help them understand the enigma of the suffering saint and the prosperous sinner here on earth. This is the salvation which the Messiah was to bring, namely, an understanding of the triune nature of the Divinity and the fact of individual incarnation which holds forth the promise of rewards in the world to come.[32]

After their return from the Babylonian captivity, Abner continued, the Jews were ready to accept the true doctrine, but Zadok and Boethus arose who denied the survival of the soul and restrained the people from repenting. When Jesus of Nazareth and his disciples appeared to reveal the doctrines of the Incarnation and the Trinity, people did not understand the true meaning of their teachings and fell into the error which the prophets and sages had escaped. They lapsed into polytheism by regarding the three aspects of the Godhead as three separate divinities. This is one of the principal reasons why the Jews generally remained steadfast in their faith and rejected Christianity, regarding it as idolatrous. The possibility of this kind of misunderstanding prompted the Jewish sages to continue to conceal the truth. This is the reason why God had the Jews remain over such a long period of time in the state of exile which had been ordained for them. Among those who failed to comprehend the doctrine of the Trinity, Abner names, along with Mani and Arius, also Elisha ben Abuya. It is related of him in the Talmud that he turned heretic. His heresy, according to Abner, was his denial of the trinal nature of God and his acceptance of two deities.[33]

This doctrine of Abner's, whose main features were presented above, helps us understand how a Jewish intellectual of that day, conversant with contemporary religious trends, both mystical and rationalistic, might embark upon an ideological quest which would eventually lead to his acceptance of Christianity. His experience is also typical of that of other men who, generations later, learned from him how to cast off the spell of their own philosophic rationalism and to seek peace of mind in the Christian mysteries. This, in fact, was the principal purpose of this highly gifted apostate's propaganda. In it he laid the foundation of a philosophy of history and religion which was further developed later on by certain Christian thinkers of the Renaissance.

At the end of his *Refutation of the Blasphemer* Abner charged that Isaac Policar, though he ended his *Epistle* with the signature "a Jew," is not a Jew at all, but a sectarian and a heretic. To Policar's charge that he, Abner, quoted exempla (*aggadot*) of the Talmud and misinterpreted them to suit his purpose, Abner replied:

> You are greatly in error. We do not mean to deny or contradict a thing in the Torah of Moses, God forbid. But we do deny and contradict the interpretation which you and your colleagues put upon the Torah of Moses and we bolster our critique with the words of the great sages who are accepted by you as the bearers of your tradition and the ones who received the Torah from the Prophets (cf. *Aboth,* chap. I).

Abner's rule for the treatment of Rabbinic teachings is this:

> It is worthwhile to pay heed to whatever seems reasonable in their teachings, whether they concern a precept or a tenet of faith upon which the precepts rest. For we are bound to heed the sages in a matter of precept and divine worship more than we are in a matter that does not involve a precept or an act of worship. Also, in case of the precepts, it is more appropriate to heed their words whenever their teachings are acceptable to reason than when reason rebels against them. This is the difference between the faith of the Jews—of whom you are not one—and the faith of the Christians. Whereas the Jews accept the Rabbinic interpretation of the biblical precepts even when it is not logically tenable, as in the case of the dietary laws, some of the laws of injury and damage, and others, the Christians grant only that much of their interpretation of the precepts and the tenets underlying them as they find to be logical after minute analysis. Then there is a sect in-be-

tween, consisting of those who accept out of the teachings of the sages that which seems logical to them according to their own superficial view, not after a minute analysis such as the Christians make, since they are incapable of it. Unlike the Jews, they reject that which their superficial analysis finds logically untenable, for the accepted Jewish ideology no longer binds them. To this middle sect belong the heterodox and the heretics of every generation, who have risen above simple belief but have not attained perfect faith. If anyone were to analyze your words he would find that you fit into this middle sect, for you have resigned from all religion, and particularly from the Jewish religion.[34]

Abner displays a hatred not only for the rationalists among the Jews but for Judaism in all its aspects. Nor can we say, after an analysis of his works, differentiating their several strata, that his active hatred of the Jews represents a late stage in his ideological development. It would not be possible to find a Christian theologian of the Middle Ages who produced so comprehensive and methodical, and so venomous, a denunciation of the Talmud as did this apostate. In the last chapter of his *Teacher of Righteousness*[35] Abner reviews all the books of Maimonides' Code (*Mishneh Torah*) in an attempt to prove that Christian morality and custom are superior to talmudic law and ethics, and that it is the Christians, therefore, who merit the name "saintly Israelites," whereas the Jews do not deserve to be called "Israel" at all. In place of the Jewish festivals which commemorate the exodus of the Jews from Egypt and God's providence over them, the Christians established holy days celebrating the Messiah and the redemption of the soul. The Sabbath is of pagan origin; the Christians restored Sunday as the day of rest, as it was originally observed by the fathers of mankind. Abner treats the development of the other Jewish holidays similarly, and he stoops to casuistry and distortion in his sharp attack upon the Jewish chronology generally. The sacrifices, according to Abner, were intended as a means of arousing prophetic fervor. Since the ministry of Jesus, however, there is no longer any need for prophets. The treatment of leprosy is a matter for medicine, not for religion. Christian family law is superior to that of the Jews. Jewish business law is inferior to the Christian law, which is based on the researches of expert jurisconsults. Abner includes, of course, the usual libels about the hostility of the Talmud toward non-Jews. He includes in his attack upon the Talmud some of the stock arguments of the Karaites, already drawn upon earlier by men like the apostate Nicholas Donin. He also made use of arguments current in contemporary Jewish rationalist circles. He was—to the best of my knowledge—the first to contrast Talmudic Law with European jurisprudence. Abner demands that the Christians refrain from eating and drinking with Jews, just as the Jews abstain from the food of non-Jews. He warns the Christians against using the services of Jewish physicians.

The Jewish religious leaders especially became the targets of Abner's invective.

> R. Simlai said (*Sanhedrin*, 98a): "The Son of David (*i.e.*, the Messiah) will not come until all judges and officers disappear from Israel." By that he meant their rabbis and communal leaders who prolong their exile by keeping alive their foolish faith and vain hope. R. Hama b. Hanina said (*ibid.*): "The son of David will not come until even petty authority ceases in Israel," that is, until the Jews possess no authority, not even such petty authority as is exercised over them by their rabbis and communal wardens, those coarse creatures who lord it over the people like kings. They hold out vain promises to them in order to keep them under their constant control. Only with the elimination of these dignitaries and judges and officers will salvation come to the masses.[36]

In his discussion of the doctrine of salvation through the Messiah, Abner returns to the eschatological passages of the

Bible from which Jewish scholars were wont to prove that the messianic prophecies had not yet come to pass. Here too Abner either adopted a new approach or enriched the old ones with innovations of his own. Using, apparently, the interpretations of Porphyry the neo-Platonist (*ca.* 232 - *ca.* 305), quoted by St. Jerome, Abner sought to prove—contrary to the Christian tradition—that the fourth kingdom of the book of Daniel refers to Greece and not to Rome.[37] This argument, along with most of the other arguments advanced by Abner, were taken up in later Hebrew polemic literature. The Jewish polemists, instead of debating theoretical problems of biblical hermeneutics, sometimes asked the practical question, "Where is the universal peace prophesied by Isaiah (2. 1-4)?" To that Abner gave the answer already offered by the early Christians, that "this prophecy points to the great measure of peace that will prevail among the nations who agree to walk in the ways of the Lord, not to a universal peace." The words of the prophecy are to be taken in a spiritual sense and refer to an indefinite time after the advent of the spiritual Messiah, "when many nations will gather to hear and accept his new doctrine . . . and, since they will all be of one faith, peace will prevail among them. . . . Therefore Jesus commanded (Matthew 6. 9, 12) that his followers pray daily, at every opportunity, in the following words, 'Forgive us our debts as we forgive our debtors,' and this, a person's forgiving those who have wronged him, will lead to peace."[38] This is how Abner justifies—as Christianity has always done—the existing order.

But the Jews raised another question: "If God has rejected us, how is it that we still survive among the nations, in spite of the mounting hatred of us?" The various peoples favor Jewish physicians, state officials, and artisans, and even prefer their services to those of Christians and Moslems? What is more— by ascribing this argument to his Jewish adversary Abner betrays his own vicious intent—the Jews don't have to go to

351

war and do not have to till the soil. "We are at ease. We exact
usury from the peasants and from the other elements of the
Gentile population who toil for us. . . . The fact that we pay
taxes to the kings of the Gentiles is not as great a hardship as
you think, for you too pay taxes, even as we do, and even if
we had a Jewish king we would still have had to pay them.
Now we have it better, for we lend money on interest and exact
from you, Christians, much more than we pay in taxes, which
we would not be able to do in our own land under a Jewish
king. What is more, we are free from the burden of sacrifices
and the other commandments, whose observance is obligatory
only in the Promised Land."

Abner counters these arguments, which he ascribes to his
Jewish adversaries, by saying that the preservation of the Jews
in the Diaspora is evidence of God's compassion for all his
creatures.

> Furthermore, the grace which you enjoy you pay for with
> degradation and oppression, for many of you are killed
> in every generation, and many are expelled from their
> countries. Often you are treated the way a master treats
> his bonded slaves and your property is confiscated. From
> time to time they despoil you, then they wait until you
> earn some more, and they strip you again,

just as kine and fowl are bred for their milk and eggs and
finally slaughtered. Then again, not all the Jews are moneylenders or physicians. Also, the Jews are not pressed too hard
because excessive pressure strengthens their allegiance to their
faith.

> That is why many discerning Jews curse the Pope and
> the Christian monarchs, in word and in thought, for not
> enacting repressive legislation against them and for not
> oppressing them to the point of causing them to repent and
> adhere more firmly to their Law, whereby—so these Jews
> think—they would merit redemption.[39]

Maestre Alfonso leaves no doubt as to his own solution to the Jewish problem. Bloody persecutions are the only means of redeeming them.

A blow of the rod is a means of directing a boy toward study and good behavior, as Scripture advises (Proverbs 29. 15, 19), "Rod and reproof impart wisdom," and "By mere words a slave is not disciplined, for though he understands he heeds not." The book of Ben Sira expresses it this way, "A wink to the wise, a fist for the fool." Now, R. Yohanan said (Sanhedrin, 98a): "When you see a generation steadily dwindling, await him (i.e., the Messiah)." R. Yohanan called attention there to what we see happening time and again, that when many Jewish communities are massacred and the particular generation of Jews is thereby reduced in numbers, some Jews immediately convert to the dominant Christian faith out of fear, and in that way a handful are saved. . . . Were it not for this course of events R. Yohanan would despair of salvation for the Jews. . . . Also the statement that the Messiah will not come "until the informers are on the increase" (ibid., 97a), calls attention to the fact that when there are many informers who report the evil habits of the Jews to the government . . . and there is no one to offer them aid and succor, they immediately turn to the right path out of fear and are saved in this way quite by accident. This is the situation envisioned by R. Eliezer, when he said (ibid., 97b): "The Holy One, blessed be He, will set up over them a king whose decrees will be as harsh as Haman's and in that way will he return them to the right path." This "right path," however, is not the path of repentance and good deeds as they understand them. . . . For in various periods they suffered very severe persecutions, as under Titus and Hadrian and Constantine and others, and they returned to the right path of repentance and good deeds as they understand them, but deliverance did not come to them. . . . But when great persecutions cause a particular generation to dwindle, then this experience brings salvation to subsequent generations, that is, to the descendants of those members of the suffering generation who turned to the right path. . . . R. Nehemiah spoke in a similar vein (*ibid.*, 97a): "In the generation of the Messiah's coming shamelessness will increase and prices will rise, etc.," meaning that high prices will cause impoverishment . . . and the pain of impoverishment will lead to an increase of shamelessness among them, that is, they will no longer be ashamed to profess the truth openly and convert to Christianity. . . . They will no longer be inhibited by shame from revealing matters of faith which they previously kept secret, that is to say, they will dare to deviate from the interpretations of the Bible accepted among them hitherto, as they say (*Sanhedrin*, 38a), "Wine's in, secret's out." Those who do so will be regarded as heretics by the masses who will not know the secret, that is, the salvation that awaits any Jew who seeks it.[40]

In such malice-filled homilies did the apostate portray his personal vision of the latter days, the condition of the poor and oppressed Jews of his time, the character of the forced converts of his day whose descendants were to be the "true" Christians of a later day, the nature of the cruel king whom God would set up to rule over Israel, and finally, the spectacle of the hoped-for massacre of large numbers of Jews. He revealed also his own character, that of a malicious informer. The plan which the enemies of Israel were to carry out in its entirety in the year 1391 is outlined here for the first time. The aging fanatical apostate who wrote these diatribes launched his "holy war" himself, not only in words but also in deeds.

Gonzalo Martinez and Plan to Annihilate the Jews

The anti-Jewish agitation seems to have drawn sustenance also from the difficulties inherent in the foreign policy of Castile.[41] By introducing the economic policy mentioned above (page 327), Don Samuel ibn Wakar laid himself open to the charge of having brought on the war with the king of Granada and with the king of Morocco who hastened to his aid. The Moroccans laid siege to Gibraltar, and in 1332 their king, Abu al-Hassan (Albohacen), went up in person to continental Spain with the object of conquering Alfonso's kingdom.

At that time a Christian courtier, who had risen high in the king's service under the wing of Don Yuçaf de Ecija, came out as an overt enemy of the Jews.[41a] In 1336 the king rewarded Gonzalo Martinez de Oviedo, his *dispensero de la casa del rey* (major-domo), for his faithful services by appointing him head of the Order of Alcantara. According to a Hebrew tale of those days, as recounted in the chronicle *Shebet Yehuda*, Gonzalo was jealous of his master Don Yuçaf, and said: " 'Shall a Jew rule over us?' And he devised evil to destroy him."

Then he counselled the king, saying: "Sell me ten Jews of thy kingdom, and I shall weigh eight ingots of silver and deliver them to the king's treasury." And the king said: And who are they?" And Gonzalo said: "The first is thy functionary Joseph, who hath destroyed thy treasures and the substance of thy people, and Samuel ibn Wakar the physician, whom thou hast appointed as thy counsellor, and eight other rich Jews of thy kingdom. Sell them to me with their sons and their little ones." And the king said: "So be it." . . . And he wrote as the enemy dictated. This is how the king sold Joseph and Samuel the physician and eight rich men and their sons and all their lands and possessions to Gonzalo Martinez. (Examples of such "sales" of courtiers who fell into disfavor with the king— sales of their persons and their property—are to be found in contemporary documents.) And Joseph and Samuel were seized on one day, and Joseph died in prison . . . and at the king's command they carried him with honors to the city of Cordova, and chariots and horsemen (an escort of knights) went up with him . . . and the king released his wife and his sons from all claims and from any accounting for moneys collected by him.

Don Samuel died in prison under torture, and was accorded Jewish burial only a year later.

Gonzalo also plotted the ruin of the other Jewish notables, above all, of R. Moses Abzaradiel. "And he said to them: The king demands great sums from you, far more than you can furnish. And he feigned to mediate between them, but in his heart he was resolved to destroy them root and branch." The Jews, however, managed to come to terms with the king. "And the man Moses returned to the king's gate. He was the king's chief scribe. And he rose to great power in the kingdom of Castile."

In the spring of 1339 Abu-l-Malik (Abomelique), son of the king of Morocco, landed in Spain, and Alfonso XI went down to the southern frontier to oppose him. Thereupon Gonzalo advised the king to adopt a tried and tested method of raising funds for the war.

> If it seem good to the king [he said], let him decree that the money be taken from all the Jews in all the cities of his kingdom; and out of what will be found with them I will give 4,000,000 *maravedis;* and when the king expels all the Jews from his kingdom, I will have the people of these lands give him another 4,000,000 *maravedis* in lieu of the taxes and services (*pechos y servicios*) received by the king from the Jews year after year.

Gonzalo intended the king to deal with the Jews of Castile after the manner of the kings of France and England, and as Alfonso X had attempted to deal with them in 1281. The amount to be extorted in this way was estimated, as in 1281, at twice the sum total of all the annual taxes paid by the Jews of Castile. In order to raise such a sum it was hardly worth while expelling the Jews from Castile, especially since there seems to have been no prospect of receiving a like sum from the Christian population. According to our Hebrew source, Gonzalo gave theological reasons for his proposal to expel the

Jews, and then added: "My lord the king goes out to make war against his foes while they sit at home eating and drinking"—a well-worn argument, which had also been employed by Abner of Burgos. Among the nobles opposing the plan to banish the Jews was "Don Gil" (Aegidius Albornoz), who had been appointed Archbishop of Toledo a short time previously. Don Gil, an ardent advocate of the Reconquest, later rose to the rank of cardinal and won high praise for his reorganization of the Papal State in Italy. Now he pointed to the benefits that accrued to the king from "his treasure," the Jews, and urged that the traditional Jewish policy of Spain should continue to be followed. Nevertheless, the king ordered the Jews to be imprisoned, and arrests were actually carried out in some cities.

The contemporary poet, Samuel ibn Sason, left us a poignant account of the plight of Castilian Jewry at this time. He describes the pall of gloom which settled upon the aljamas, smarting under the burden of heavy and extortionate taxation. He alludes also to restrictions upon the religious worship of the Jews. This is a reference, no doubt, to the revival of the libel against the "prayer against heretics" (*birkath ha-minim*) by the apostate Abner of Burgos, and the consequences thereof. This prayer, which is the twelfth benediction of the weekday *'Amida*, had long ago become a subject of dispute between the Jews and the Christians, the latter charging that the prayer was actually a curse levelled against the Christians, and the Jews denying that it referred to Christians at all. In 1336 Abner, armed with an order of Alfonso XI, summoned the Jews of Valladolid, where he was the sacristan of the local church, to a public disputation over the meaning of the prayer. Abner was declared the winner, and the king thereupon ordered the deletion of the benediction from the prayer books of the Jews.[42]

In the meantime Jewish scholars were making rejoinders to the acrimonious publications of the apostate Abner. R. Isaac Policar assembled his polemical writings against Abner in a more comprehensive work which he called *Ezer ha-Dath*. Though the book was a piece of occasional writing, the author tried to mask its topical character by making only oblique references to his opponent. The poet-rabbi R. Shem Tob Ardutiel (el rab Don Santob de Carrion), who wrote in Hebrew and Spanish, appears to have been one of Abner's opponents. His *Proverbios Morales*, with which only historians of Spanish literature are now familiar, were read in Hebrew by his contemporaries and were current in Spanish Jewry until the Expulsion.⁴³ In these verses R. Shemtov discusses the afflictions that befall the righteous, the same problem that so troubled Abner of Burgos and, seemingly, that whole generation. R. Shem Tob warned men not to aim too high, but to be content with their destiny and with the station which it had pleased Heaven to assign to them. He wrote his verses during the reign of Alfonso XI ("the good king, Don Alfonso"), and dedicated them to the king's son, Don Pedro, who succeeded his father on the throne. Among the other scholars who engaged in disputations with Abner were some of R. Asher's disciples. But none of them was a match for that ardent and satanic apostate.

All hopes of rescue were now centered on the Jewish courtiers. "And the man Moses (Abzaradiel) hearkened and was afraid and sent letters to all the Jews; and they assembled in their cities and fasted and wept and cried unto the God of their fathers: 'O Lord, let us not be destroyed by the hand of the adversary ...' " (*Shebet Yehuda*). The king was preoccupied at the time with the conduct of the war. Up to September 1339 he fought at the front. Then he returned to Madrid and turned over the command of the army to Gonzalo Martinez, who defeated the Moroccans. Abu-l-Malik was killed in battle. But Gonzalo was suddenly brought low, at the very climax of his career, by the intervention of the king's mistress, Doña Leonor de Guzman, with whose brother he was on bad terms. Gonzalo was charged with high treason, imprisoned and executed by order of the king. "And the Lord saved his people in the twelfth month, that is the first Adar" (*Shebet Yehuda*). The king revoked his decree for the imprisonment of the Jews.

> And the king decreed, and they sold all the possessions of the adversary and all the possessions of his brethren to the Jews who sit in the king's gate; and the king took the ring he had taken away from the adversary and gave it to Moses. And the man Moses went forth joyously, and all the Jews in the kingdom of Castile rejoiced and were glad because of the goodness the Lord had shown to Israel.

This contemporary author wrote in the style of the Book of Esther, which was entirely appropriate to the conditions then obtaining in the court of Castile. For here, too, the fate of the Jewish community was tied to the influence of the Jewish courtiers and to the vicissitudes of their fortunes in the intrigue-ridden royal court.

After Gonzalo's downfall the Jews regained their former status.[43a] Don Moses Abzaradiel, whose signature does not appear on the royal edicts after 1339, was replaced in the king's chancellery by other Jews. Jewish influence waxed in the administration of the taxes, both central and provincial. In 1342 the king sent a personal message to Pope Clement VI asking permission for the Jews of Seville to pray in the synagogue built in that city by Don Yuçaf de Ecija. In making the request, the king explained that the Jews had been invited to settle in Seville after the capture of the city from the Moslems because very few people were left there at the time, and because their presence was necessary and beneficial, for "they contribute to the welfare of the city, and at times even join the Christians in fighting the Moslems, and do not fear to risk their lives."[44]

Toward the end of his life the king was attended by a Jewish physician. When the mystic R. Shmarya of Negroponte, who had had religious disputations with Christian visionaries in southern France, came to Alfonso's court, the king valued his

359

services as a physician and astronomer. Alvarus Pelagius of
Portugal, a critic of European Christian society in general and
of Castilian society in particular, complained that the Jews
were too influential at Alfonso's court. Christian courtiers, he
charged, appointed unbelievers as guardians, kept Jewish and
Moslem women as mistresses, and sometimes even married
them, and proclaimed that all upright persons could be saved
through their own religions. Pelagius also asserted that there
were converted Jews at Alfonso's court who continued to practice the rites of their former religion. His criticism further
reveals the Averroist views held in that society and the aims
of fanatical critics in both the Jewish and Christian communities.

THE REFORM OF ALCALÁ DE HENARES (1348)

All his life Alfonso XI wavered between a policy favoring
the Jews and overt antisemitism. In the great reform laws enacted by the king at Alcalá de Henares in February 1348, there
was one section that had revolutionary bearing upon the status
of the Jews.[45] It was the king's intention to forbid the Jews to
lend money at interest. The propaganda of the Church had
borne its fruits. As his model Alfonso took one of the reforms
introduced in England shortly before the Jews were expelled
from that country. This goes to show that the Jewish problem
was international in the Middle Ages. The new Castilian law
enjoined the Jews and the Moslems from lending money at interest, abolished all the privileges previously enjoyed by the
Jews in that respect, forbade government officials to collect
debts owing to Jews, and called upon the Church to assist in the
enforcement of the law through its power to excommunicate.
The body of the law includes a declaration of the king's desire
that "the Jews remain in our kingdom, as the Holy Church hath
commanded, for they will one day accept our faith for their salvation, according to the words of the prophets." For this reason,
and as compensation to the Jews for the loss of an important

source of livelihood, the law permitted all Jews and Moslems to acquire, in addition to the houses and land they already possessed, land south of the Duero River, up to the value of 30,000 *maravedis,* and north of the Duero up to the value of 20,000 *maravedis.* When these figures are compared with deeds of contemporary land sales, it is seen that, judged by the standards of those days, the tracts were not inconsiderable in size. Nevertheless, in the southern part of the kingdom—within the confines of Andalusia—Jews had more numerous opportunities to settle on the land.

In Spain this reform was not so utopian as its English counterpart of an earlier period because most of the Spanish Jews did not depend upon moneylending for their livelihood. Permission to acquire land was not prompted by any specific desire to turn the Jews into farmers, or to grant them any rights they had not previously enjoyed, but to widen the foundations of their economic status. Had the influential Jews and Christians really desired to carry out these reforms, they could have done so. In any event, the majority of the Jews earned their livelihood by petty trade, handicrafts and the sale of produce from their fields and vineyards. The law was revolutionary only in that it would affect, first and foremost, a small group of Jewish financiers who were not accustomed to earning their bread by the sweat of their brow and who controlled the national credit and the farming of the taxes. The modest returns they could have derived from agricultural pursuits would, of course, have been far smaller than their income from transactions with the state. If that law had been enforced, the social and economic ruin of that group of Jews would have entailed grave consequences both for the state and for Spanish Jewry in general. A ban on moneylending at interest would have prevented the Jews from acting as tax-farmers and from exerting any influence at court on behalf of the Jewish community that depended upon their leadership and their sense of duty. The Jewish population would have been exposed to extortion on the part of those in power, both of high rank and of low. The religious agitation of the Church and the economic competition of the Christian merchants and artisans would have deprived the Jews of their livelihood in the course of time. Without some additional earnings the small Jewish tradesmen could not have paid their taxes, which were higher than those levied on their Christian fellows; yet nothing in the laws was designed in any way to ameliorate the tax burdens of the Jews. The whole Jewish population of Castile would have sunk to the lowest depths, to the status of a religious and economic pariah. This was the desire of the ascetic Christians and the Jewish fanatics alike. But there were only a few of these in either camp. Three years later, in 1351, the Cortes itself asked that the law be revoked, and it is not known whether any attempt was ever made to enforce it.[46]

KING PEDRO THE CRUEL AND DON SAMUEL HALEVI

Alfonso XI died in 1350 of the Great Plague that had ravaged Europe, Spain included, since 1348.[47] In 1354 an attack was made in Seville upon the Jews, who were accused of having desecrated the host. This disturbance may be attributed to the general religious and social unrest which had spread throughout Europe as a result of the plague. To the leaders of Aragonese Jewry, the occurrences in Seville portended greater dangers threatening all the Jews of Spain.[47a] And indeed it was in the same Seville, some thirty years later, that the violent agitation began which fanned the flames of intolerance that produced that great conflagration, the persecutions of 1391.

In the reign of King Pedro the Cruel (1350-69) the Jews again played an intimate role in Spanish history. The most prominent of the Jewish courtiers was Don Samuel Halevi of Toledo, the king's chief treasurer (*tesorero mayor del rey*), who was, apparently, versed in Jewish lore, and in any case felt bound to observe Jewish rites.[48] In 1357 Don Samuel built the magnificent synagogue in Toledo, which stands to this day and retains some traces of its former splendor. An engraved inscription in the synagogue, which bears witness to the high standing of the great courtier, reads as follows:

> Since the day of Ariel's exile, none like unto him has arisen in Israel . . . he appears before kings to stand in the breach. . . . Unto him people come from the ends of the earth . . . the king exalted him and set him on high, above all his princes . . . into his hands he entrusted all that he had . . . and since the day of our Exile no son of Israel has attained to such exalted estate.

Don Samuel's functions were not limited to financial matters. In 1358 he was sent to Portugal to negotiate a political treaty. In domestic politics he was involved in the many intrigues that were linked with the life-story of the king. Though few details are available concerning Don Samuel's activities, it is possible to discern a certain trend in his internal policy, which was to strengthen the royal house over against the mutinous nobles. The great historian of that period, Pedro Lopez de Ayala, who later betrayed Don Pedro, relates that in 1355 Samuel Halevi made a comprehensive inquiry into the activities of the tax-farmers and required them to pay over all moneys which they still owed. Furthermore, he asked the king for two fortresses, which he placed in charge of trustworthy officers, and within a short time accumulated a considerable treasure there for the crown. Royal administrative documents of the period which have been preserved confirm the literary data. These documents bear Samuel's signature and seal (a fort, the emblem of Castile), and a Hebrew inscription. Don Samuel confiscated the estates of rebellious nobles, employing Jewish officials for the purpose; and where these officials could not function adequately, he sent Christian knights. He signed all royal instructions relating directly or indirectly to the public revenues. He was associated with a Christian judge in the king's court and reviewed the obligation of the bishop of Cordova to pay taxes. His relatives and other Jews served under him as administrative officials. Neverthless, on a certain day in 1360 or 1361, he and all his kinsmen throughout Castile were suddenly arrested for reasons unknown to us. He was taken from Toledo to Seville; and, after an attempt had been made to extort a large sum of money from him, he died in prison under torture, like other Jews before him. His estate is said to have comprised great quantities of gold and silver, large tracts of land near Toledo and Seville, and eighty Moslem slaves. Don Samuel's tragic fate was not in any way connected with a design to debar Jews from the service of the state. Other Jews came in his stead. Most prominent among them were members of the Halevi and Benveniste families of Burgos.[49]

THE FATE OF THE JEWS IN THE CIVIL WAR

At that very time, the king's stepbrother, Henry of Trastamara, rebelled against him. This civil war brought devastation and ruin to the Jewish community of Castile. Already in 1355 the Jewish quarters of Toledo and Cuenca had been attacked by Christians and Moslems.[50] In 1366 the decisive struggle between the two brothers began. Each called to his aid foreign troops, both English and French, who had already ravaged France and now continued their outrages in Spain. The slogan of Henry's party was the liberation of the country and the overthrow of the "tyrannical" king. One of the demands of this revolt was, as usual in such cases, the dismissal of all foreign advisers—in this instance, the Jews.[51] Pedro was then generally called the "king of the Jews," though actually his conduct toward them was no different from that of his predecessors. All his harsh and evil deeds were attributed to his Jewish advisers. Henry's French knights, in whose country the Jews were not so influential as in Spain, exaggerated the importance and the role of the Jews in the civil war in their polemical verses. Henry used the anti-Jewish class bias as it served his purposes. The Jews suffered equally from the depredations of the soldiery of both parties. In the spring of 1366 the whole Jewish community of Briviesca, numbering about two hundred families, was massacred by Henry's troops and those of Bertrand du Guesclin, the famed commander of the French mercenaries.

Later, in April 1366, when Henry took the city of Burgos, he demanded an immense sum of money—about 1,000,000 *maravedis*—from the local Jews; and those who could not pay their share were sold into slavery.[52] One of Henry's first acts on ascending the throne was to declare a general moratorium on Jewish loans. This prompted the Christians of Segovia and Avila to attack their Jewish neighbors and to seize the promissory notes and pledges they had given them. When the new king entered Toledo early in May, he demanded, as in Burgos, a sum of 1,000,000 *maravedis* from the Jews, which was to be paid within a fortnight, for his French mercenaries.

The real reasons behind Henry's policy were, however, disclosed at the first session of the Cortes, which was held in February 1367, at Burgos. The estates then demanded that part of the Jewish loans should be cancelled and the term of payment for the remainder extended. The new king agreed to this proposal in principle, but rejected the other demands of the Cortes. They had urged that the fortresses in the Jewish quarters, which were intended solely to assure the safety of the Jews during the civil war and which had served both sides as a citadel, should either be demolished or placed under the command of Christian officers. The king evaded giving a definite reply by pointing out the perils to which the Jewish community was exposed. He flatly denied the allegations of the estates that the Jewish courtiers and favorites had no aim other than to harm the Christians and that they were to blame for all the country's misfortunes during the preceding years.

The Cortes, furthermore, demanded that no Jewish officials or physicians should be employed in the households of the king, queen or princes. The king replied, untruthfully, that such a demand had never before been made in Castile. While it was true, he said, that there were Jews at his court, he pointed out that no Jews were serving on his privy council and promised not to entrust them with a measure of authority that could prove harmful to the country. He also dismissed the complaints against the new powers granted to the Jewish tax-farmers, and declared himself ready to farm the taxes for a smaller sum to Christians provided that Christians could be found who were willing to undertake such functions. As a matter of fact, there already were influential Jews in the king's service at the time, among them the well-known Don Joseph Picho, Don Samuel Abravanel and others.

Meanwhile, the Black Prince (of Wales) came to Pedro's help. The English soldiery wiped out the Jewish communities of Villadiego and Aguilar de Campóo. With the aid of the English, Pedro defeated his rival at Najera in 1367. Like his predecessors, Pedro did not hesitate to avail himself of Jewish money and the advice of Jewish financiers. Henry went to France for reinforcements and when he returned the Jews again suffered from the political vicissitudes. When Valladolid went over to Henry, the Jews of the city were again endangered, and eight of their synagogues were destroyed. Other Jewish communities in that area had similar experiences. As Henry was approaching Burgos, he was informed—according to the contemporary Spanish historian Ayala—that the Jews in the fortress and their Christian commander were loyal to Pedro. When Henry entered the city, he was shot at from the Jewish quarter and from the fortress, which did not surrender until it was mined. The Jews of Burgos again had to pay a ransom of 1,000,000 *maravedis*. The Jews of Palencia also had to pay a heavy ransom. King Pedro, for his part, permitted the Moslems of Granada, whom he summoned to his aid, to seize the Jews of Jaen, who are said to have numbered some three hundred families, and to sell them into slavery. For months on end—from the latter part of 1368 till the early part of 1369—the battle for Toledo was waged furiously, until Pedro was killed in battle near Montiel in March 1369, and Henry II became the sole, acknowledged king. About 8,000 Jews are said to have been killed in the siege of Toledo. In June 1369, the king commanded that all the Jews of Toledo and their property be sold so as to provide him with approximately another million *maravedis*. With that order the misfortunes of the Castilian Jews reached their climax.[52a]

THE REIGN OF HENRY II

When peace was finally restored in the country, Henry II also adopted the well-tried traditional Jewish policy, taking the Jews under his protection and confirming their privileges. In his reign, as in the days of his fourteenth-century predecessors, the Jews had a large share in organizing the government finances on an efficient basis. Very influential indeed was Don Joseph Picho who, it seems, was not over-scrupulous.[53] Don Joseph was appointed to the post of *contador mayor*, which had been created in the middle of the fourteenth century. The functions of this official included farming out the taxes of the kingdom, making decisions in all that pertained to the allocation of the taxes, receiving financial reports from government officers, paying salaries and other fees. In this connection Don Joseph was given wide judicial and administrative powers in various spheres of public life. Though other Jews had preceded Picho in performing these functions, the appointment of a Jew to the post, which had been revived in the form defined above, was of great importance. Thereafter pains were taken not to appoint Jews as accountants—but Christians, the sons of Christians or converts. In the reign of Henry II a Jew by the name of Don Joseph ibn Wakar, who was the king's physician, was sent on a diplomatic mission to Granada. A scholar, he prepared a compendium on the history of the Spanish kings and gave it to a learned Moslem of Granada to be used as source material for the latter's work on the history of Spain. In contemporary documents the names of many Jews are mentioned as having served in the royal court and the provincial administration.

In general, the civil war wrought ruin and demoralization in the Jewish communities of Castile, and intensified antisemitism. While the Christian publicists undoubtedly exaggerated the part played by Jews in the civil war, there is reason to believe that they were not merely passive sufferers. Some of them joined the warring factions, serving either in a military or political capacity.[54]

Several Jewish communities in northern Castile were exterminated. On the mounds of the ruins "weeds of apostasy" sprang up: In publicistic Christian writings a trend toward secular anti-Jewishness appeared which had hardly been manifest in the Middle Ages before that time. Samuel Halevi, who was executed by his master several years before the civil war, was still held up after the war as the typical Jew, the minion of tyrants, who brings disaster upon the Christians. The Jews were blamed for all the country's misfortunes. The historian Ayala refers in several places to the Jews, without any show of open hostility; but in the didactic social poetry which he composed during the great ecclesiastical schism (after 1378), he fulminates against the officials who oppress the Christian population, and naturally includes Jews among these evildoers. When the taxes are allocated at the royal court, says Ayala, Jews come "who are ready to drink the blood of the poor Christians, flaunting the contracts made with them and promising gifts and jewels to the king's favorites." The bishops need money and themselves urge the king to farm the taxes out to the Jews as those most capable of increasing the royal revenues. The Jews promise to augment the income of the royal treasury by three millions more than were collected in the previous year, and the king approves, for "the poor man does not realize that all this blood comes out of his own side." Then come Don Samuel and **Don Abraham** uttering their "sweet words." Both Ibn Verga and Ibn Caci are mentioned as typical tax-farmers well known in their day.[55]

The secular manifestations of the anti-Jewish movement did not deflect it by so much as a hair's breadth from its theological aims. Apostates of the school of Abner of Burgos continued to preach the Christological sermons of their master, and compelled the Jews, with the aid of the authorities, to engage in public disputations. In 1378, Archdeacon Fernando Martinez began to preach inciting sermons in Seville that finally gave the signal for a wholesale massacre of the Jews of Spain. Such propaganda, as could have been foreseen, was bound to lead to the complete extermination of the Jews.

This mounting danger, threatening Jewish survival from without, was accompanied by increasing social unrest within the Jewish community. This inner ferment found its most poignant expression in two works, *Sefer ha-Kanah* and *Sefer ha-Peliah*, which, internal evidence indicates, were written by a contemporary cabalist whose identity remains unknown.[56] The social criticism of this anonymous cabalist is very similar to that of an earlier mystic reformer, the author of the *Ra'aya Mehemna* and the *Tikkunei ha-Zohar*, and is even sharper in tone. This latter-day cabalist, however, lacked the historical perspective of his predecessors, as well as their practical reformatory objectives and their faith in the resurgence of a spiritually reconstructed community of Israel. The social stratum against which the author of *Ha-Kanah* and *Ha-Peliah* directed the barbs of his criticism was similar in structure to the circles of the financiers and intellectuals chastised by the zealous mystics of the thirteenth century. In the course of time, however, the power of the Jewish aristocracy waned, but its moral depravity increased. Typical of the author's criticism of contemporary society are the following two tales—already quoted in modern historical literature—from the *Sefer ha-Kanah*, in which he draws a most uncomplimentary portrait

369

of the Jewish notables and the rabbis, the leaders of their community.

> On a certain day I came upon an old man, very venerable and handsome, and I turned aside and inquired, "Who is this man?" And I was told: "He is our great lord. . . ." And I saw that his mien was very angry and that he pulled at his beard. . . . And I said to him: "My lord, let us go to thy house of study that I may hear words of Torah from thy lips. . . ." And he answered me, saying: "I see that thou'rt a proud man. . . ." Thereupon he took me by the hand and led me to his home and there I saw Gentile women and concubines and female slaves and casks filled with wine . . . and then . . . he said to me . . . that the Holy One, blessed be He, had created man and given him eyes to behold all good things and to covet them and enjoy them. . . . "And now, my son, hearken unto my counsel. Let us eat and drink wine and gratify all our members. . . ." Hearing his vile words, I entreated the Lord and the house fell down upon them and killed them, and I led the city to repent.
>
> Once I went to a certain place and saw a splendid synagogue of exceeding beauty, and there were two chairs, one on the right hand and the other on the left, and two venerable elders . . . they addressed me in the vernacular . . . and I said: "These be the calves set up by Jeroboam ben Nebat to lead Israel astray." And I said: "Arise and sit in another place. . . . Wherefore should ye destroy yourselves and all this congregation?" Then both began to curse and revile. . . . And the whole congregation held their peace, for they were men who had not stood at Sinai. . . . And two serpents came out from the wall and stung them. . . . Thereafter there came others that were lesser and worse men than they. . . . And shortly thereafter they suffered persecution, and were uprooted and scattered.[57]

It may be that the two tales contain certain exaggerations of detail. However, these strictures of the *Sefer ha-Kanah*, like the homilies of the *Ra'aya Mehemna*, point up the sharp contrast between the mendicant, ascetic mystics, whose continuous wandering and constant mourning exemplify Israel's *Galut* (dispersion), and the complacent aristocracy which dominates Jewish society:

> Woe unto those who build themselves large homes and dwell in comfort in the land, for strangers will consume their means. How can they rest in comfort, they who have been driven from their Father's board and whose mother was divorced because of their sins. Why do they not study Torah, in order to ward off the [Divine] wrath. Woe unto those who devote themselves to the accumulation of wealth which is tainted and taints its possessor . . . Why not acquire knowledge and understanding? . . . Why should a man forfeit his soul and commit robbery, larceny and perjury in the accumulation of wealth which strangers will consume? . . . Woe unto those who joyfully and pridefully flaunt their colorful garments, forgetting that they are exiles among the nations, far away from their homeland. They should wear black, and groan and weep, and not beautiful clothes which they may have to doff in disgrace tomorrow. Even if they should be buried in this finery, they would only tempt the Gentiles to disinter them and then throw them to the dogs and birds of prey . . .
> Woe unto the fathers who allow their sons to indulge in food and wine, in dancing (*i.e.*, with women) and merriment, unaware of the dire fate in store for them, be it natural death, or violent death . . . or exile.[58]

Our cabalist opposes the collection of interest for a loan, even from Gentiles. "You will observe," he writes, "that those who, in the *Galut*, lend money on interest do not fare well."[59] Therein he is in accord with the Christian zealots who sought to dislodge the Jewish tax-farmers from government service. He must have been aware of their agitation and its aims. He makes many allusions in his works to the events of his own day and to what the future held in store, as he unfolds his dire prophecies of ruin, apostasy, pillage, disinterment of the dead, forced flight, wandering and expulsion.

The *Sefer ha-Kanah* and *Sefer ha-Peliah* contain, as did the *Ra'aya Mehemna* and the *Tikkunei Zohar*, criticism of current talmudic learning and current practice in the application of Talmudic Law. Our author's critique, however, is more concrete than that of his predecessors and more directly pertinent to the moot problems of his day. He does not hesitate to take a definite stand and to express an opinion on controversial questions of Halakha. Thus, on the question of levirate marriage he identifies himself with the position taken by the rabbis of France and Germany—which was contrary to the view of many Spanish rabbis—and he opposes this practice, though it was prescribed in the Bible, because, he argues, most men do not enter into such a marriage as an act of piety. He demands that the rabbinical courts use all the means at their disposal to compel the levir to give his brother's childless widow a release (*halitza*), instead of marrying her. He is not, however, opposed to bigamy, which is permitted by talmudic law and was still practiced in Spain in his day, even among the pious. But he stresses that bigamous marriage is permissible only if it is "heaven-intentioned," that is, if its purpose is the fulfilment of the biblical commandment of procreation, but not otherwise.[60]

Strict ascetic that he was, our author could not approve the practices of rabbis and teachers "who sell the Torah," that is, receive fees for teaching and for the performance of rabbinic functions. Here too, he argues against an old established custom of the Jews of Spain, where it had long been the practice to assign rabbis and teachers fixed salaries.[61]

The author of *Ha-Kanah* and *Ha-Peliah* is close ideologically to the foremost masters of the Halakha in his day, such as R. Asher b. Yehiel and his sons, R. Isaac b. Sheshet Perfet, and others. In line with their common ideology he is sharply critical of the rationalist rabbis who based their decisions in matters of Halakha upon their personal judgment or upon a superficial grasp of the biblical precepts, without reference to the Talmud and the later Codes. To him the Written Law and the Oral Law complemented each other and were inseparable.[62] The Cabala fully supports the Halakha as formulated by the great medieval codifiers of the Law. Characteristic of this point of view is the fact that in *Sefer ha-Kanah* the author lays down as the basis for his homilies the *Sefer Mitzvoth Gadol* (Great Book of Precepts), the famous Code compiled by the thirteenth century French scholar, R. Moses of Coucy. Yet the works of this cabalist abound in statements sharply critical of both the Halakha and the Aggada and of the current methods of talmudic study generally. His intention, to be sure, was to clear away all that he found objectionable in order to clear the ground for the resurgence of the true talmudic tradition as conceived by the cabalists. But there is more in his critique of the Talmud than is implicit in the ideology of the Cabala. His criticism includes, curiously enough, arguments against the Talmud which could be heard also in Jewish rationalist circles or could be found in the writings of anti-Jewish polemicists, both old Christians and apostates from Judaism. This critique of the Talmud was formulated and committed to writing by a loyal and devoted Jew. It stood there, in his works, for his contemporaries to read, and in the hour of decision, which was approaching, it was liable to corrode the very foundations of the faith. What is more, it appears that certain expressions and fragments of ideas found in the Christological polemics of the school of Abner of Burgos crept into the *Sefer ha-Kanah* and *Sefer ha-Peliah*, suggesting a certain catalytic Christian influence.

During this same period, the 1360s and 1370s, when grave dangers lurked without, hardy and devoted souls within the Jewish community continued their literary and educational endeavors. Traditionally oriented works were produced by both philosophic rationalists and mystics such as Moses Narboni, Samuel Çarça, and Samuel Matut, and by the moralist and student of Halakha, R. Menahem b. Zerah, and others of this type.

373

The disciples of R. Asher b. Yehiel, and of his sons, R. Jacob and R. Judah, furthered the study of the Halakha in the spirit of their masters. To the latter school belonged R. Israel b. Joseph al-Nakawa (Annacava), author of the *Menorath ha-Maor* (Lamp of Illumination), a work which presented to its readers gems of ethical teachings, drawn from the talmudic Aggada and from later rabbinic literature, as well as from the *Zohar*.[63] In the hour of trial these books helped sustain and strengthen the simple, wholesome faith of the true believers. They did not, however, provide a satisfactory answer to the doubts of those whose faith had begun to falter—those "who had advanced beyond simplicity but had not arrived at wholesomeness."

In *Ezer ha-Emunah,* a polemical work written by R. Moses Hacohen of Tordesillas in 1375, we find various references to the political tension of the period. Replying to the libels of the antisemites, the writer points out that the talmudic sages exhorted the Jews to pray for the welfare of the realm,

> for our lives and welfare depend upon the wellbeing of the state under whose government we live. What more convincing example could there be than that which you have seen with your own eyes, for when one king departed and another seized his throne, many communities were banished and many Jews were put to death by torture and were deprived of all their possessions and were like lost sheep. . . . Far be it from us to curse our kings, for they are a shield and a buckler and a refuge unto us and protect us against all disasters. For if we were subject to the multitude and did not fear the kings, there would be no security for us whatsoever. And you yourself say that the kings have given us charters for protection. He who beats a Jew pays a fine many times larger than he who beats a Christian. Moreover, if a Christian be found killed, the murderer is executed if he is found; and if he is not found, the people of the city nearest to the place where he was found pay no fine. But if a Jew be found murdered, on the ground

or any other place, we have letters from the late king and from His Majesty, the reigning king, providing that the people of the city nearest to where a slain Jew was found shall pay 10,000 *maravedis* or deliver up the murderer. . . . How can such a regime be called evil and not a regime of mercy and compassion?[64]

THE REIGN OF JOHN I

At the session of the Cortes which was held at Burgos in 1377 the enemies of the Jews saw their propaganda bearing fruit. The Cortes then forbade Jews and Moslems to accept notes of obligation of any kind from a Christian for fear that they might be a means of circumventing the law against usury. This law, which was confirmed as late as the fifteenth century, was not enforceable because the legislators intended that Christians should not buy goods from Jews on credit unless the Jews would take their word as their bond. The same Cortes revoked the law which imposed collective fines for the murder of a Jew. This was the law to which R. Moses Hacohen had referred so proudly only two years earlier. Now the lives of the Jews were at any man's mercy.[65]

The worst effects of these inimical laws were felt by the Jews only after the death of Henry II (in 1379), during the reign of his son John I (1379-90).[66] In 1380 the Cortes, which then assembled in the city of Soria, passed new anti-Jewish laws. First and foremost, the Jews were ordered to delete the benediction concerning heretics from their prayer book, and severe penalties were prescribed for anyone who recited that benediction. Alfonso XI's temporary decree was thus raised to the status of an official law. The libel about the benediction relating to heretics, which had stirred up various controversies ever since the days of Abner of Burgos, now had the seal of official approval.

Secondly, the Cortes deprived the Jews of jurisdiction in criminal cases. According to the historian Ayala, this action was due to a unique incident. Joseph Picho, the chief accountant of Henry II, was convicted as an informer and secretly executed by his Jewish enemies, with the help of government officials, on the strength of a writ issued in blank for the purpose to the Jewish judges. This incident occurred in 1379 at Burgos, during the coronation of young King John. No account of this matter is available other than that offered by the Christian historian. There is no reference whatever to it in the body of the law passed by the Cortes; only general theological reasons are given there; the Cortes declaring that "it has been customary for the Jews to appoint their own rabbis and judges and they have been permitted to try all their own cases, both civil and criminal. It is a grievous sin to approve this and to sanction the matter, for the Prophets have said that with the advent of our Lord Jesus Christ they shall be deprived of all authority and freedom." Such a prophecy had never been heard of until Raymond Martini and his disciples taught that "The sceptre shall not depart from Judah" (Gen., 49. 10) signified only that the Sanhedrin was not allowed to try criminal cases ". . . until the coming of Shiloh, that is, the Messiah." Here we have the theological source of the law in question. The king approved the proposal and decreed that thereafter rabbis, elders and *adelantados* would not be allowed to try criminal cases involving penalties of death, severance of limbs, and exile. Such trials and Jewish communal ordinances would have no legal validity whatever. The Jews were allowed to try only their civil cases, involving financial claims, and had to choose a local Christian judge to try their criminal cases. They had the right, however, to appeal from the verdicts of such Christian judges to the king's court.

Thirdly, the Jews were forbidden to circumcise their Moslem and Tartar slaves. This reform was in line with the spirit of the legislation of that age in general; a similar law had previously been enacted by King Pedro IV of Aragon.[67]

In addition to the discriminatory legislation, a change for

the worse occurred in the administrative sphere as well (so far as can be determined from the limited volume of documentary material examined by the author). In the reign of John I, royal documents no longer bore the signatures of Jewish officials, though these were numerous in the days of Alfonso XI and to some extent were still found in the reign of Henry II. This does not, however, signify that there were no longer any Jews at the royal court. When John I went to Portugal in 1383 in an attempt to seize the throne on dynastic grounds, he communicated with David Negro (ben Gedalya ben Yahya), one of the Portuguese notables who had joined the Castilian faction. During the campaign David carried out diplomatic missions in Portugal itself and also in Castile on behalf of John I, and also served the king in the administration of his finances. David was in the king's retinue in the campaign in which he suffered defeat. After that John took him to Castile, appointed him *rab* of all the Jews of the kingdom and gave him a seat in the privy council (until Negro's death in 1385).[68] In the latter years of his reign John I had in his service as a physician Don Meir Alguadex (who seems also to have been in charge of certain financial matters). This Don Meir translated Aristotle's *Ethics* into Hebrew, and in his introduction to the book refers to the hardships of his journeys with the court. Don Meir was appointed *rab* of all the Jews of the kingdom, and served as a protector of his people during the disturbances of 1391.[69] He was one of the leading members of a circle of Jewish intellectuals in Castile who were connected with a similar circle of intellectuals in Aragon. Since the information available about the Aragonese circle is fuller, it will be dealt with in detail in later chapters. To the Castilian circle belonged Don Solomon Halevi of Burgos who was known after his conversion as Paulus de Santa Maria. Another member of that circle was Samuel Matut, a writer on philosophy and the Cabala, who was a friend of R. Isaac b. Sheshet Perfet and a member of a celebrated family of Guadalajara. Samuel had commercial and perhaps also cultural relations with the aristocratic Mendoza family, who were very prominent in Castilian politics and literature. In Seville lived Don Samuel Abravanel, to whom R. Menahem b. Zerah dedicated his book *Zeda la-Derekh* because he had helped him during the civil war and because he was "an intelligent man who was fond of scholars" and "desired to study." This man who was so "fond of scholars" turned apostate shortly before the persecutions of 1391. Despite the suspicions of the Jew-haters he was appointed chief accountant after his conversion because he was "expert at figures and familiar with the royal revenues in the reigns of Henry II and John I."

Taken as a whole that period, which bore within it the seeds of disaster, is veiled in obscurity. The fuller information available about the Jews of Aragon can only partially fill in the details of the picture of Castilian Jewry because only in Castile did the ancient Spanish way of life remain unaltered by external influences.

ABBREVIATIONS

Adret ....*She'eloth u-Teshuboth ha-RaShBA* (Responsa of R. Solomon b. Abraham ibn Adret), vols. I-VIII[1]
Anuari ....Anuari del Institut d'Estudis Catalans
Anuario ....Anuario de Historia del Derecho Español
Asher ....*She'eloth u-Teshuboth ha-RASh* (Responsa of R. Asher b. Yehiel), Venice, 1607
BABL ....Boletin de la Academia de Buenas Letras, Barcelona
BAE ....Biblioteca de Autores Españoles
BAER ....Fritz (Yitzhak) Baer, *Die Juden im christlichen Spanien: Urkunden und Regesten.* Vol. I—Aragonien und Navarra; Vol. II—Kastilien/Inquisitionsakten
BAER, *Aragonien* .Fritz Baer, *Studien zur Geschichte der Juden im Königreich Aragonien während des 13. und 14. Jahrhunderts*
BAH ....Boletin de la Academia de la Historia, Madrid
CDIA ....Colección de documentos inéditos del archivo general de la Corona de Aragon
EUC ....Estudis Universitaris Catalans, Barcelona
Graetz ....Heinrich Graetz, *Geschichte der Juden*. Dritte verbesserte Auflage, 11 volumes
JQR ....Jewish Quarterly Review (New Series, unless otherwise indicated)
MGWJ ....Monatsschrift für Geschichte und Wissenschaft des Judentums
MHE ....Memorial Historico Español
RABM ....Revista de Archivos, Bibliotecas y Museos, Madrid
Régné ....Jean Régné, "Catalogue des actes de Jaime I, Pedro III et Alfonso III, rois d'Aragon, concernant les Juifs (1213-1291) . . . et sous le regne de Jaime II (1291-1327)," in REJ, vols. 60-70, 73, 75-78.
REJ ....Revue des Etudes Juives
RIBaSh ....*She'eloth u-Teshuboth ha-RIBaSh* (Responsa of R. Isaac b. Sheshet Perfet)
Sefarad ....Sefarad: Revista de la Escuela de Estudios Hebraicos (Instituto Arias Montano). Madrid 1941-
Tarbiz ....Tarbiz: A Quarterly for Jewish Studies (Hebrew). The Hebrew University, Jerusalem, 1929/30-
Zion ....Zion: A Quarterly for Research in Jewish History (Hebrew). New Series, Jerusalem, 1935/36-

---

1. Volume VIII is entitled *She'eloth u-Teshuboth ha-RaShBA hameyuhasoth le-ha-RaMBaN* (Responsa of R. Solomon ibn Adret ascribed to Nachmanides).

NOTES

NOTES TO INTRODUCTION

1. For my recent views on the general theme see my little Hebrew book, *Yisrael ba-'Amim* (Israel among the Nations), Jerusalem, 1955, and my articles in *Zion*, vols. XV, XVII, XVIII, and XXIII-XXIV. Additional support for the views there expressed will appear elsewhere.

1a. F. Martinez Marina, "Antiguedades Hispano-Hebreas . . . Discurso histórico—critico sobre lo primo venido de los judios a España," in *Memorias de la Real Academia de la Historia,* III (Madrid, 1799), pp. 317–468; Fritz (Yitzhak) Baer, *Untersuchungen ueber Quellen und Komposition des Schebet Jehuda* (Berlin, 1923), p. 58 f.; Ramón Menéndez Pidal, *Crónicas generales de España,* 3rd ed. (Madrid, 1918).

2. The source for this account is in a letter written by the bishop Severus, reporting the conversion of the Jews of Minorca (Migne, *Patrologia Latina,* vol. XX, 731 ff.; vol. XLI, 822 ff.). A monograph on this letter was published by Gabriel Segui Vidal, *La carta enciclica del obispo Severo, estudio critico de su autenticidad e integridad con un bosquejo histórico del cristianismo Balear anterior al siglo VIII* (Palma de Mal-

lorca, 1937). See also B. Blumenkranz, "Les auteurs chrétiens latins du moyen âge sur les Juifs et le Judaisme," in *REJ*, n.s., vol. XI [CXI] (Paris, 1951–52), p. 24 f., and the same author's *Juifs et Chrétiens dans le monde occidental, 430–1096* (Paris, 1960), p. 76, note 34, p. 283–284. According to Blumenkranz the above tract was composed in Spain in the seventh century. He bases his opinion upon purely literary considerations. However, the historical account which forms the content of the work and the political institutions mentioned therein belong to the end of the Roman Empire and could not have been invented in the seventh century as a pure literary fiction. Cf. Jean Juster, *Les Juifs dans l'empire romain* (Paris, 1914), vol. I, p. 464; vol. II, pp. 200, 250, 261–262.

3. The condition of the Jews under the Visigoths in Spain has been treated in a number of works. The following among the latest books are worthy of mention: Z. Garcia Villada, *Historia eclesiástica de España*, II (Madrid, 1933); S. Katz, *The Jews in the Visigothic and Frankish kingdoms of Spain and Gaul* (Cambridge, Mass., 1937).

4. For the history of the Jews in Moslem Spain see, in addition to Graetz's great work, R. Dozy, *Histoire des Musulmans d'Espagne (711–1110)*, nouv. ed. par E. Lévi-Provençal, 3 vols. (Leyden, 1932). [The English translation of the first edition is entitled R. Dozy, *Spanish Islam: A History of the Moslems in Spain*, trans. . . . by F. G. Stokes (London, 1913).] See also E. Lévi-Provençal, *Histoire de l'Espagne musulmane*, 3 vols. (Paris, 1950–53); Idem, *España musulmana hasta la caída del califato de Córdoba, 711–1031* (1950); Claudio Sánchez-Albornoz, *La España musulmana según los autores islamitas y cristianos medievales* (Buenos Aires, 1946). [A. Ashtor, *Koroth ha-Yehudim bi-Sefarad ha-Muslemith* (History of the Jews in Moslem Spain), I (Jerusalem, 1960).]

5. On the earliest contacts between Spanish Jewry and the centers of talmudic learning in the East see, S. Assaf in *Ha-Shiloah*, vol. XXXV; Eppenstein in *MGWJ*, LVI, 1912, p. 80 f.; J. Mann in *JQR*, n.s. vol. VII, p. 457 f.; J. Mann, *Texts and Studies in Jewish History and Literature*, vol. I (Cincinnati, 1931), passim; *Pirkei ben Baboi* (Chapters of Ben Baboi), edited by B. M. Lewin, in *Tarbiz*, II (1930–31), pp. 385, 396. Also J. N. Epstein in *Tarbiz*, III (1931–32), p. 435; S. Assaf in *Zion*, n.s. (quarterly), vol. VI (1940–41), p. 33 f.

6. For a discussion of the subject see the author's article in *Zion* (annual), vol. VI (1934), pp. 150–154.

7. In addition to the works listed in note 4 above, consult also Philoxene Luzzato, "Notice sur Abou-Jousouf Hasdai ibn Schaprout," in *Archives Israelites*, XIII (Paris, 1852). Since the publication of this small but exhaustive volume, nothing substantially new has been added to the subject. Jacob Mann, in *Texts and Studies*, vol. I, pp. 3–30, brings three fragments from the Geniza and ascribes them to Hasdai. However, only in the case of the first fragment does Mann's argument have any plausibility. As regards the letter of Hasdai to the king of the Khazars, I incline to the view of Abraham N. Poliak that this letter is not authentic. It is rather an item of religious and nationalistic propaganda, composed not long after Hasdai's time. See his article, "The Conversion of the Khazars to Judaism" (Hebrew) in *Zion*, n.s., vol. VI, pp. 106–112, 160–180, and his Hebrew book, *Khazaria*, 3rd edition (Tel Aviv, 1951), pp. 17–21. A definitive decision in this matter can be made only after a critical study

of the contents of the letter, which as yet has hardly been attempted. The analysis of its style, made by M. Landau in his article in *Zion*, n.s., VIII, pp. 94–106, serves, to my mind, to prove only that the author of the Hasdai letter had mastered well the language and style of Menahem ben Saruk. See also S. M. Stern in *Zion*, n.s., XI, 141–146.

8. For the career of Samuel ha-Nagid see the following articles by Hayyim (Jefim) Schirmann, "Samuel ha-Nagid: a Bibliographical Note" (Hebrew), in *Kiryat Sefer*, vol. XIII (1937); "The Wars of Samuel ha-Nagid" (Hebrew), in *Zion*, n.s., vol. I, pp. 261–83, 357–76; "Samuel ha-Nagid as poet" (Hebrew), in *Kneset* (in memory of Bialik), vol. II (1937), pp. 393–416; "Sammuel Hannagid, the Man, the Soldier, the Politician," in *Jewish Social Studies*, vol. XIII (1951), pp. 99–126; see also S. M. Stern, "Life of Samuel ha-Nagid" (Hebrew) in *Zion*, n.s., vol. XV, pp. 135–45. Recent editions of the poetry of Samuel ha-Nagid are: *Diwan of Shemuel Hannaghid*, edited by David Solomon Sassoon (Oxford, 1934); and a three volume edition published in Tel Aviv, divided as follows: *Diwan* (= Ben-Tehillim), ed. A. M. Habermann, 1947; *Ben-Mishlei*, edited S. Abramson, 1948; *Ben-Kohelet*, ed. S. Abramson, 1953.

9. Sentiments typical of Samuel ha-Nagid's religious and nationalist views are found in the following poems (Sassoon edition): *Ben Tehillim*, no. 143; no. 29; no. 105, vv. 1–8; no. 111, vv. 1–6. The verses cited in the text are, in order of their quotation, *Ben Tehillim*, no. 143, vv. 25, 44; no. 29, v. 62; no. 143, v. 18.

10. For additional information on Joseph ha-Nagid consult the material published by Levi-Provençal in *Al-Andalus* (Madrid), vols. III, IV, and VI. Also Schirmann, "Yehosef ha-Nagid" (Hebrew), in *Moznaim* (Tel Aviv), vol. VIII (1939), pp. 48–58.

11. I am familiar with the vast amount of material found in the responsa and the poetic literature. I have assembled as much of this material as I could. I have also read most of the Arabic sources that are available in translation. I refrain, however, from entering into a detailed discussion of the subject. I want, however, to call attention to responsum no. 131, of the Responsa of R. Isaac Alfasi. Not only are the historical facts contained therein (already cited by Graetz in vol. VI [3rd German edition, 1894], p. 77), important in themselves, but there is evidence there of Jewish ownership of villages and large estates, precisely the situation prevailing in Andalusia later, under Christian rule.

The first attempt at a sociological evaluation of the Hebrew poetry of Spain was made by Simhoni in his articles on Solomon ibn Gabirol in *Hatekufa*, vols. X, XII, and XVII.

See also B. Klar, "Ha-Shira we-ha-Hayyim" (Poetry and Life) in his volume of Studies, *Mehqarim we-'Iyyunim* (Tel Aviv, 1954), pp. 85–106; J. Weiss, "Tarbuth Hasranith we-Shira Hasranith" (Courtly Culture and Courtly Poetry), Jerusalem, 1948 (reprinted in the *Proceedings of the First Congress of Judaic Studies* [Hebrew], Jerusalem, 1952, pp. 396–403); J. Schirmann, "The Function of the Hebrew Poet in Medieval Spain," in *Jewish Social Studies*, XVI (New York, 1954), pp. 235–252. For the Hebrew poetry of Spain generally see the two-volume anthology, *Ha-Shira ha-Ivrit bi-Sefarad u-vi-Provence* (The Hebrew Poetry of Spain and Provence), edited with an introduction and illuminating notes by Hayyim (Jefim) Schirmann (Jerusalem/Tel Aviv, 1954–56). These volumes contain a number of well-known as well as little-known poems which have a direct relevance to the subject of this work. Consult also J. M. Millás Vallicrosa, *La poesia sagrada hebraico-española* (Madrid, 1940; 2nd ed. Madrid, 1948).

NOTES TO CHAPTER I

1. The reader will find most of the documents on which the subsequent account is based in my two volumes of source material, *Die Juden im Christlichen Spanien: Urkunden und Regesten.* I—Aragonien und Navarra; II—Kastilien/Inquisitionsakten (Berlin, 1929–1936). These will hereafter be referred to as Baer I and II. Wherever I give the date of the document in the body of the text, and no further elucidation of its contents is required, the references are not usually given in these notes.

For an interpretation of the general and social history of Spain see the writings of Claudio Sánchez-Albornoz and the following comprehensive work of his school of Spanish historians: Luis G. de Valdeavellano, *Historia de España* I: *De los origenes a la baja Edad Media*, 1–2, segunda edicion, Madrid, 1955. See also M. Vallecillo Avila, "Los judios de Castilla en la alta Edad Media," in *Cuadernos de historia de España* XIV (Buenos Aires, 1950), pp. 17–110.

2. Baer I, no. 1.

3. For Jewish ownership of landed property in Catalonia at this time see Baer I, p. 2 f., p. 1006 f., and the publications of Miret-Schwab and of Millás Vallicrosa, listed in Baer I, p. 1083. Cf. *Sefarad*, VII (1947), 123–136.

4. *REJ*, vol. 68, pp. 60 ff. For places called "villa judaica," "allodium judaicum," "mons judaicus," see Monsalvatje, *Colección diplomatica del condàdo de Besalu I*, no. 186. Carreras, *Lo Montjuich de Barcelona* (1903), pp. 210, 333. Balari, *Origenes historicos de Cataluña*, p. 475.

5. *Teshubot Hakhmei Tsarfat veLoter* (Responsa of the Rabbis of France and Lorraine) edited by Joel Müller (Vienna, 1881), nos. 13, 30.

6. Carreras, *La Ciutat de Barcelona* (1913).

7. See below, Chapter II, note 8.

8. Baer I, no. 7.

9. Cf. Baer I, p. 1045 f.

10 Baer I, p. 17.

11. P. Kehr, *Das Papsttum und der Katalonische Prinzipat bis zur Vereinigung mit Aragon* (1926), p. 27.

12. Baer I, no. 6; J. M. Ramos y Loscertales, "El fuero latino de Jaca," in *Anuario* V (1928), 408–411; J. M. Lacarra, "Desarrollo urbano de Jaca en la Edad Media," in *Estudios de Edad Media de la Çorona de Aragón* IV (Saragossa, 1951), 139 ff. See *ibid.* p. 140, note 1: "En documento sin fecha, pero que parece de la primera mitad, y tal vez del primer tercio del siglo XI, se citan unas compras 'ad Belito, iudeo maiore de kastro quod vocatur Jaka, frater enim fuit de iudeo qui vocatur Azaka.'" See also *ibid.* p. 146, and the map of Jaca on pp. 144-5.

12a. Baer I, nos. 11, 12, 568, 574, 575. Concerning Estella see also chapter II, note 14.

13. For Castrojeriz see Baer II, no. 2, and note. For Burgos see Baer II, nos. 5, 13. In 1032 the convent of Covarrubias purchased the villa Fontosio, "Sanctius Rex (Sancho III, el Mayor) confirmans . . . Testes . . .

Scape Levi, Bueno, Jacob." See Justo Perez de Urbel, *Sancho el Mayor de Navarra* (Madrid, 1950), pp. 187-8, p. 430, no. CXVI (from L. Serrano, *Cartulario del Infantado de Covarrubias*, Valladolid, 1907, p. 45.) For Nájera see Baer I, nos. 570, 578, 579, 583; Baer II, no. 11. See also Luciano Serrano, *Cartulario de San Millán de la Cogolla* (Madrid, 1930), nos. 178 (Baer II, no. 9), 249, 289, 297. No. 289, which is a decision rendered by Alfonso VI in 1099 concerning some real property belonging to San Miguel de Pedroso, reads in part: "Et ex iudeis fuerunt ibi testes Naamias maior testis, Naamias minor testis, Cide testis." No. 297, which is a charter granted by Queen Urraca to the monastery of San Millán in 1110, reads in part: "Cartam de illo foro quod solebant facere et ipsa matera, quod portabant per vim ad palatios de Nagera vestre ville pernominate . . . ut omnino ingenue permaneant . . . Totum concilium de Nagera et christiani et mauri et iudei testes."
13a. Baer II, no. 5, note. See also Serrano, *Cartulario de San Millán*, no. 287 (*anno* 1097): D. L. de Pontecurbo (Pancorbo) and his wife give to the monastery of San Millán "octo solares quos comparavimus de iudeis in Villanova de Pontecurbo . . . Hec predicte solares, sicut mos fuit iudeis ibi commorantibus, habeant communem pastum et exitum atque regressum cum Ponticurbo et cum aliis vicinis de Villanova."
14. Baer I, no. 1. For the political and social importance of the reign of Alfonso III, king of Asturias-Leon (866–910), see Valdeavellano, *Historia de España*, I, pp. 467–509.

Claudio Sánchez-Albornoz, in his "Serie de documentos ineditos del reino de Asturias," in *Cuadernos de Historia de España* I-II (1944), p. 346, no. XIV, publishes the following document (dated April 22, 905, from Archivo catedral de Leon, Tumbo Legionense, fol. 392 v.) dealing with the converted Jew, Habaz (see Baer II, no. 4, note): "Ego Lazarus presbiter tibi Cixilani presbiteri et fratribus Sanctorum Cosme et Damiani. Notum est quod Habaz, quondam judeus postea vero christianus et monachus, profiliavit me in omnem facultatem suam, quam dinoscitur habere, sive et terram et aquam cum adito suo pro molinos facere . . . Tradidit etiam et se ipsum mihi. Quam ob rem previdi et decrevi ego Lazarus offerre et donare illud ecclesie Sanctorum Cosme et Damiani . . . ut . . . abeant ipsam terram et aquam cum aditis suis et rivum quam ipse Nabaz cum suis operariis aperuit . . ." This document reveals the contribution of a Jew to the repopulation of the devastated territories during the reign of Alfonso III. See also *Archivos Leoneses* II, no. 2 (1948), p. 47-8, no. 4: "Ego Samuel ebreo et uxor mea . . . placuit nobis . . . ut faceremus vobis kartula venditionis . . . de hereditate nostra propria que habemus in territorio Legionense . . . terras cultas et incultas, arbores fructuosas vel infructuosas . . . aquas . . . ortos, pratuis, orgas, parietes et fundamentis, sautos et devesas, mulinos et mulinarias . . ." (*anno* 977). See Sánchez-Albornoz in *Cuadernos* I-II, 326-7. There are several possible reasons for either the forced or the voluntary conversion of the Jew Habaz to Christianity. It may be that the Christian community was determined not to allow the estate of the man to pass into the hands of his Jewish heirs, or that the Jew himself sought a home and repose in his old age within the walls of the monastery. But the distinguished Spanish historian, in his own observations on the matter, gives a rather unusual interpretation of the motives for the conversion of some Jews to Christianity. He speaks of "la particular tendencia [! !] de los conversos [*anno* 905!!] a ingresar en las jierarquías eclesiásticas, ingreso que había de inocular a éstas del espíritu hebraico." Cf. *ibid.*, p. 327, note 151: "Importará estudiar un dia la influencia de los conversos en la cuestión de la intolerancia hispana [!!!]."

14a. Baer II, no. 6.

14b. Baer II, no. 4: "Qui habuerit cassam in solare alieno . . . , si voluerit ipse sua sponte vendere domum suam, duo christiani et duo iudei aprecientur laborem illius." Cf. note 13, above.

14c. For the Jews of Leon generally see Baer II, nos. 3, 4 and note; Francisco Cantera y Burgos, "Nuevas inscripciónes hebraicas leonesas," in *Sefarad*, III (1943) 329 ff.; J. Rodriguez Fernandez in *Archivos Leoneses* I-II (1947-8). Claudio Sánchez-Albornoz in his *Estampas de la vida en Leon hace mil años* (1947 ed., Buenos Aires), pp. 32 f., 54 f., draws a somewhat fantastic picture of the commercial activities of the Jews at this time. On p. 54, in note 91, he writes, "Elijo como acreedor a un judio leonés, por la tradición de gentes dedicadas al negocio del credito que pesa sobre los hebreos [!!!]," etc. But this Jewish type did not exist in Spain at this time. On p. 55, in note 92, the author cites a document of the year 964 which tells of a Christian holding for several years the land of a fellow Christian to whom he had lent money *ad usuram*. I know of no similar document of that period, dealing with loans and security, involving Jews.

The noun אשכפת (אשכפה), found in a Hebrew legal instrument drawn up in the province of Leon in 1053 (*REJ*, IV, 227), became in the course of time a family surname (Escapat, Scapat, etc.), but was originally employed to indicate that a man was by occupation a shoemaker. We find some of the sages of the Talmud pursuing this occupation for a livelihood. Cf. *e.g.*, *Pesahim* 113b: "R. Hanina and R. 'Osha'ya were shoemakers (אושכפי) in *Eretz Yisrael*. They lived in the harlots' quarter and made shoes for the harlots which they would deliver to them. They (*i.e.*, the harlots) looked at them, but they (*i.e.*, the rabbis) would not raise their eyes to look at them." I mention this in order to allay the doubt expressed by Cantera Burgos in *Sefarad* III, 333, note 2. See also Sánchez-Albornoz, *Estampas* (1947), p. 69: "sillones de guadamecíes cordobeses, fabricados por los judíos del castro próximo a la ciudad." Cf. *ibid.*, note 58: "Juzgo a éstos fabricados por los judíos del castro próximo a Leon, porque según un documento de Alfonso IX, de 1197 (*España sagrada*, XXXV, 259), Fernando I estableció que dichos israelitas pagasen annualmente a la iglesia legionense doscientos sueldos, una piel y dos guadamecis." There is good reason for this assumption that the Jews residing in the citadel *(castrum)* of Leon engaged in specific handicrafts, as was the case in other localities.

14d. Baer II, no. 14. A similar document, dated about a year earlier (February 7, 1090), was published by Justiniano Rodriguez in *Archivos Leonenses*, año VII, número 14 (Julio-Diciembre, 1958), p. 55 f. (A. H. N. Cartulario de Sahagun). Cf. Rodriguez, *ibid.* p. 33, note 50.

15. See my Hebrew article on "The Political Position of the Jews of Spain during the lifetime of Judah Halevi," in *Zion*, I (1935-36), pp. 6–23. The definitive work on this period of Spanish history is Ramon Menendez Pidal, *La España del Cid* (Madrid, 1929). The English translation, by Harold Sunderland, is entitled *The Cid and his Spain* (London, 1934).

16. Menendez Pidal, *op. cit.*, p. 329.

17. Cf. Angel Gonzalez Palencia, *Los Mozarabes de Toledo en los siglos XII y XIII*, 4 volumes (Madrid, 1926–1930). See especially the Introduction, pp. 119, 151 f. Consult also my review of this book in *Tarbiz*, V (1934), pp. 228–236.

18. Baer II, no. 23, mentions a bathhouse in Toledo confiscated from the Jews. A charter granted in 1131 by Alfonso I of Aragon to the town of Calatayud provides that, in the event of a Moor or a Jew fleeing the city, the estate of the fugitive should be turned over to a Christian. Baer I, no. 17.

The charter granted by the archbishop of Toledo to the townspeople of Alcala de Henares, in the second quarter of the 12th century, allows for the free emigration of Jews from the town. Baer II, no. 20.

19. Baer II, no. 12. See my note there on the relation of El Cid to the Jews.

20. On Joseph Ferrizuel, surnamed Cidellus, see the note to Baer II, no. 29, as well as the note on p. 552 of Baer II. For the poems which Judah Halevi dedicated to Joseph and to his nephew Solomon see notes 51, 51a and 52 of this chapter. See also L. Serrano, *Cartulario de San Millán de la Cogolla* (Madrid, 1930), p. 298, no. 296 (June 26, 1110): "Ego Urraka, gr. D. Ispaniae regina, filia Aldefonsi regis, placuit mihi . . . ut faciam vobis Didaco Lopez cartam quod de isto die usque in perpetuum non intret saion in vestras hereditates." Among the *confirmantes*, "Citiello iudeo confir[mat]." The story of Cidellus' (Cidiello) services as intermediary for the Castilian nobles is told by Rodrigo Jiménez de Rada, archbishop of Toledo (*ob.* 1247), in his *De rebus Hispaniae*, VI, 34 (*Hispaniae Illustratae . . . Scriptores Varii*, ed. Schott, vol. II, p. 111), and also in the *Primera Crónica general de España*, published by Ramón Menendez Pidal, vol. II (1955), p. 644, cap. 963. See also the comments of H. Grassotti upon Baer II, no. 29, in *Cuadernos de Historia de España* XXIX-XXX (1959), 204.

21. Baer II, no. 18.

22. Baer II, no. 20. For the college of translators working at Toledo under the direction of Archbishop Raymond, and the work of Johanan ibn Daud (Joannes Avendeuth, Johannes Hispanus), see Friedrich Ueberweg, *Grundriss der Geschichte der Philosophie*, vol. II (11th edition, edited by B. Geyer, Berlin, 1928), p. 343. See also M. T. D'Alverny, "Avendauth?" in *Homenaje a Millás Vallicrosa* I (Barcelona, 1954), pp. 19–43.

23. Baer I, nos. 569, 570. See J. M. Lacarra, "La formacion de las familias de fueros navarros," in *Anuario* X (1933), p. 208. Lacarra in an article, "La fecha de la conquista de Tudela," published in the review, *Príncipe de Viana*, año VII, número xxii (Pamplona, 1946), argues for a later date for the conquest of Tudela. He concludes that Tudela was captured early in 1119, following the fall of Saragossa in December 1118. The article itself was not accessible to me. I rely on the summary of it by E. García Gómez in *Al-Andalus* XI (Madrid, 1946), 497 f. See also Lacarra, *"La conquista de Zaragoza por Alfonso I (18 diciembre 1118),"* in *Al-Andalus* XII (1947), 65 ff., as well as what Lacarra has written in *Estudios de Edad Media de la Corona de Aragón*, V (1952), 418–419. For the terms granted by the Cid to the Moslems of Valencia, and their historical significance, see Menéndez Pidal, *La España del Cid*, p. 519 ff.

24. Baer I, no. 570. I wish to call attention here to the activities of the brothers Don Abolfaçan (Abu-al-hasan) and Don Jucef, and the latter's

son, Don Muça, who were involved in financial and real estate transactions in Tudela and its vicinity in the second half of the twelfth century
—Baer I, no. 577. Noteworthy, too, is the policy of the then reigning king
of Navarre, Sancho VI (1150–1194) el Sabio, toward the Jews, as docu-
mented in Baer I, nos. 578–581. One interesting document is a royal order
to partition a disputed tract of land among several claimants, among
them the crown and two churches. Two men were charged with the actual
task of partitioning: one a monk, representing the two churches; and the
other, who was to represent the crown, a Jew named Jucef Abenpesat,
appointed by the aforementioned Don Abolfaçan. Baer I, p. 933.

25. Julian Ribera Tarragó, *Orígenes del justicia de Aragón* (Saragossa,
1897), 397 ff. See the note to Baer I, no. 27. See also Lacarra, "La
conquista de Zaragoza por Alfonso I," in *Al-Andalus* XII (1947), 65 ff.
For the location of the Jewish quarter in Saragossa consult Manuel
Serrano y Sanz, *Orígenes de la dominación española en América* (Madrid, 1918). Eleazar and his son-in-law Abulfat are named in Baer I, no.
21, as recipients of certain privileges from Count Ramon Berenguer IV,
of Barcelona. See also Lacarra, "Documentos para el estudio de la
reconquista y repoblación del valle del Ebro," in *Estudios de Edad
Media de la Corona de Aragón*, II, III, V (Saragossa, 1946, 1947–48,
1952), especially nos. 62, 76, 86, 108, 119, 134, 189, 194, 220, 232 (cf. Baer
I, no. 577), 272, 328, 351 (Baer I, *loc. cit.*), 372, 373, 380, 382, *et al.*
Alhaquim Benebenisti is named in nos. 76 (*anno* 1132), 90 (*anno* 1136),
220 (*anno* 1141). No. 220 reads, "Ego . . . Abenbenist Alhachim una
cum coniuge mea et filios meos . . . vendo vobis uno orto pauco de illas
uvas que est in via de Zaragoza . . . Et est fidiator de salvetate . . .
Jahie Abenbacoda, cognato de Jacob qui fuit leztero de Alagon . . ."
It may be assumed that the aforementioned Alhaquim Benvenisti was a
relative of Abu Ibrahim ben Benvenisti, the friend of the poet, Moses
ibn Ezra. See the latter's *Shirei ha-Hol* (ed. Brody, see note 36, below),
I, *Diwan* no. 33 (p. 34), and the note to the superscription of the poem
in vol. II, p. 69. See also my comments in *Zion*, I, p. 16, as well as my
remarks there concerning the Eleazar family of Saragossa. The Aben
Bacoda family, to which the famous philosopher, Bahye ibn Pakuda,
belonged, also resided in Saragossa. See also the remarks of Schirmann
in *Tarbiz*, IX (1938), 51 f., concerning the Kamaniel family, and cf.
Lacarra, *op. cit.*, no. 119, where mention is made of Jucef Alcumiel. Note
also the remarks of Lacarra in *Estudios*, V, 798: "La población judia
continuó viviendo en Huesca, Tudela, Zaragoza, Calatayud, Daroca y
Tortosa, y en otras poblaciones como Barbastro, Alagon, etc. Su situa-
ción jurídica fué la misma que en tiempos anteriores, ya que las
capitulaciones no les afectaron."

26. Baer I, no. 13.
27. Baer I, no. 10.
28. Baer I, no. 15.
29. Baer I, nos. 21, 23, 24, 25, 32, 33, 34, 35, 612.
30. Baer I, nos. 27, 28 (and p. 1020), 29, 30, 30a, 48, 48a, 112; *Responsa*
of Ibn Adret, vol. IV, no. 260.
31. Baer I, nos. 31, 37, 40, 42, 43, 50, 62.
32. This story is told in the "Poem of the Cid," vv. 78 f. Cf. the critical
edition of Ramon Menendez Pidal, *Cantar de mio Cid*, vol. III
(Madrid, 1911), and the same scholar's *Poema de mio Cid* (Madrid,

1923), p. 33, and also his *La España del Cid*, p. 299. It is difficult to accept this tale as the account of an event that could have happened in the Cid's own day. There were, no doubt, in the history of Spain instances of knights borrowing money from Jews in order to equip themselves for a campaign against the Moslems (see Baer I, no. 577, item 9, p. 925). At the time of the Cid, however, the Jews did not yet inhabit the citadel of Burgos (cf. Baer II, p. 39). They took up residence there later, close to the date of the poem's composition. One must therefore conclude that the poet tells a tale, possible in his own day, without possessing any evidence supporting such a possibility in the time of the Cid. See also E. García Gomez, "Esos dos judios de Burgos," in *Al-Andalus*, XVI (1951), 224-7. Cf. also the works of F. Cantera cited in Chapter VII, note 52.

33. See my article, "Eine jüdische Messiasprophetie auf das Jahr 1186 und der dritte Kreuzzug," in *MGWJ*, vol. LXX, p. 120. Millás published new material on Petrus Alfonsi in *Sefarad*, VII (1947), 136.

34. Cf. the well-known story concerning the Jewish merchant who wanted to ransom a Moslem captive girl from a Christian knight during the sack of Barbastro, told in Al-Makkari's *History of the Mohammedan Dynasties of Spain*, translated by Pascual de Gayangos, vol. II, p. 268. Lately this story was dealt with by R. Menendez Pidal in his *La España del Cid*, I, 165.

35. Cf. Graetz VI, 76, for the part taken by the Jews in the battle of Sacralias-Zallaka in 1086 and the proposal made by Alfonso VI to postpone the battle from Friday to Monday to avoid fighting on the holy days of the Moslems, Jews, and Christians, respectively. Compare with this account, however, the cautious words of R. Dozy in his *Histoire des musulmans d'Espagne* (second edition, revised by E. Lévi-Provençal, Leyden, 1932), vol. III, p. 127.

36. For the biography of Moses ibn Ezra see H. Brody, "Moses Ibn Ezra —Incidents in his Life," in *JQR*, n.s., vol. XXIV (1933-4), p. 309 f., and Brody's introduction to his edition of *Selected Poems of Moses Ibn Ezra* (with an English translation by Solomon Solis-Cohen; Philadelphia, 1934). For the year of Ibn Ezra's death see the article by Schirmann on the life of Judah Halevi in *Tarbiz*, vol. IX (1938), p. 233. The complete secular poetry (*Shirei ha-Hol*) of Moses ibn Ezra was edited, with commentary, by H. Brody in two volumes. Volume I (Berlin, 1935) contains the *Diwan* and other poetry, as well as two letters in rhyme. Volume II is an exhaustive commentary to the *Diwan* (Jerusalem, 1942). The liturgical poems (*Shirei ha-Kodesh*) were edited with commentary by Simon Bernstein (Tel Aviv, 1957). The publication of Ibn Ezra's poetic works makes it possible for us to examine at their source several items of information pertinent to our account. No. 199 of the *Diwan* is a laudatory poem addressed by the poet to the physician Joseph ibn Kamaniel upon the latter's marriage, following his return from a journey to Portugal. —See Schirmann in *Tarbiz*, IX, 51.—Now, in *Kobes Teshuboth ha-RaMBaM we-Iggrotaw* (Collection of Maimonides' Responsa and Epistles), ed. Lichtenberg (3 parts, Leipzig, 1859), no. 237, we have a responsum of R. Joseph ibn Megas (Migash) which quotes an official document of the community of Toledo (reprinted in Baer II, p. 10), dated 1112. It makes mention of a certain Isaac ibn Kamaniel who is later, near the end of the document, referred to as "Joseph," which ap-

pears to be the correct reading in the first instance as well. This Joseph seems to have been one of the wealthy members of the Toledo community. Very likely, he was sent by Alfonso VI of Leon on a mission to Portugal, then a county held in fief from the crown of Leon by the king's son-in-law, Henry of Burgundy, and Ibn Ezra wrote this poem—in which Joseph is highly praised as a man of social and professional distinction—upon the physician's return to Toledo. Such poetic tribute was customarily tendered by the Hebrew poets of the day to a Jewish diplomat upon his safe return home from a political mission, and the encomium was particularly appropriate in this case since the gentleman entered into marriage very soon after his arrival in Toledo. The event must be dated prior to 1112, since in the aforementioned document bearing that date Ibn Kamaniel is spoken of as a married man. It is evident from this poem that Moses ibn Ezra moved in the upper circles of the Jewish community of Toledo, a fact corroborated by other poems as well. Isaac ibn Ezra is mentioned in a business document of Toledo, dated 1119, cited in a responsum of Joseph ibn Megas, found in *Kobes Teshuboth ha-RaMBaM*, ed. Lichtenberg, no. 240.

37. *Shirei ha-Hol*, Letters, no. 262, lines 61 f. (p. 288); no. 263, 1. 41 f. (p. 292.)

38. *Diwan*, no. 153, lines 24–26.

39. *Diwan*, no. 175, lines 13–17.

40. *Diwan*, no. 36.

40a. *Diwan* of Judah Halevi (ed. Brody), vol. I, no. 66, p. 92 f.; see also no. 101, pp. 154-7, and Brody's commentary thereto; Schirmann, *Ha-Shira ha-Ivrit bi-Sefarad u-vi-Provence*, vol. I (Jerusalem-Tel Aviv, 1954), nos. 185a, b, pp. 459–462. See also Schirmann in *Tarbiz*, IX, 233.

40b. Moses ibn Ezra, *Shirei ha-Hol* (ed. Brody), vol. I, no. 186, and vol. II, p. 355; cf. vol. I, no. 187. For Estella see below, Chapter II, notes 14, 15.

41. *Shirei ha-Hol*, I, no. 164, lines 10–12.

42. There is, as shown above, good basis for the assumption that Moses ibn Ezra sojourned for a while in Toledo. From the superscription to no. 99 of the *Diwan* it would appear that he also lived for a time in Saragossa, among friends. We do not know where he made the acquaintance of Abu Ishak (Abraham) ibn Abulfaraj of Barcelona (no. 195). I could find no mention of this man in any of the documents which I collected. See also what I wrote in my article in *Zion*, n.s., vol. I (1936), p. 16, about Avubrahim Avenbenvenist and the family of Abenalazar. These were families which resided, according to existing documents, in Saragossa and Barcelona.

43. *Diwan*, no. 13, lines 17–26; no. 20, line 43; no. 67, lines 31–32; no. 112, lines 14, 29.

44. *Diwan*, no. 20, lines 31–37.

45. See Abraham ibn Daud's account of the persecution of the Karaites during the reigns of Alfonso VI and Alfonso VII, in his *Sefer ha-Kabbala*, in A. Neubauer's *Mediaeval Jewish Chronicles*, I (Oxford, 1887) pp. 79-81. For the persecution to which they were subjected in the reign of Alfonso VIII, in 1178, through the efforts of R. Joseph ibn Alfakhar and R. Todros Abulafia, see the testimony of R. Moses de Leon, cited by Abner of Burgos, and published by Isidore Loeb in *REJ*, XVIII, 62.

See also *REJ*, XIX, 207. Cf., too, the letter of R. Joseph Abulafia, son of the same R. Todros, in Kobak's *Jeschurun*, VIII (1872), p. 41.

46. See Jacob Mann's Hebrew article on the messianic movements during the Crusades, in *Ha-Tekufa*, XXIII (1925), p. 243 f. Cf. Maimonides' *Epistle to Yemen: The Arabic Original and the Three Hebrew Versions*, edited . . . with Introduction and Notes by Abraham S. Halkin, and an English translation by Boaz Cohen (New York, 1952), p. 101 f.; English translation, p. xix; Hebrew Introduction, p. xxix.

47. See my article in *MGWJ*, LXX (1926). For the life and thought of Abraham bar Hiyya see Leon D. Stitskin, *Judaism as a Philosophy: The Philosophy of Abraham bar Hiyya, 1065–1143* (New York, 1960).

48. Baer, "The Political Position of the Jews in Spain in the Time of Judah Halevi" (Hebrew), in *Zion*, I (1935/6); Schirmann, "Life of Judah Halevi" (Hebrew), in *Tarbiz*, IX (1938). See also Schirmann's note, "The Birthplace of Judah Halevi," in *Tarbiz*, X, 237, in which he seeks to prove that Judah Halevi was born not in Toledo, as is generally held, but in Tudela. For the purposes of our discussion, however, it is not very important whether Halevi was born in Toledo or Tudela, since the fact of his residence in Toledo and his close association with the Jewish courtiers of the Castilian court is well attested to. New and valuable material for the study of Judah Halevi's life is to be found in the following articles of S. D. Goitein, "The Last Phase of Rabbi Yehuda Hallevi's Life in the Light of the Geniza Papers," *Tarbiz*, XXIV (1954/5), 21 f., English summary p. iv; "Rabbi Yehuda Hallevi in Spain in the Light of the Geniza Papers," *ibid*. p. 134 f. and p. ii; *ibid*. p. 468 and p. vii; "Autographs of Yehuda Hallevi," *Tarbiz*, XXV (1955/6), p. 393 f. and p. iii; "The Biography of Rabbi Judah ha-Levi in the Light of the Cairo Geniza Documents," in *Proceedings of the American Academy for Jewish Research*, vol. XXVIII (1959), pp. 41–56. See also D. H. Baneth, "Some Remarks on the Autographs of Yehuda Hallevi and the Genesis of the *Kusari*," in *Tarbiz*, XXVI (1956/7), p. 297 f. and p. vii. For the most part, this new material which is brought to light in the above articles lies outside the compass of the present work. It does, however, point up the fact that Judah Halevi was held in reverence both within the Jewish community as well as outside of it. The documents published by Goitein in *Tarbiz*, XXV, throw new light on the composition of the *Kusari* and on the communal activities of Judah Halevi in Toledo under Christian rule. Three letters, written in Arabic in Halevi's own hand, deal with the efforts made by the Jews of Toledo to ransom a Jewess held captive by the "wicked woman," and to obtain her release, under bond, for the Sabbaths and holidays, while awaiting ransom.—*Tarbiz*, XXV, pp. 397, 404; XXVI, 301.—Temporary release from imprisonment for the Sabbath and holidays was a privilege sometimes accorded to the Jews by the crown. See Baer I, p. 93, paragraph 5.—Goitein suggests the identification of the "wicked woman" with Queen Urraca of Castile (1109–1126).

The *Diwan* of Judah Halevi was edited by H. Brody in four volumes (Berlin, 1894–1930), of which volumes I and II contain his secular poetry with commentary, and volumes III and IV his religious poetry, without commentary. A good representative selection of Halevi's poetry is to be found in *Jehudah Halevi: Selected Liturgical and Secular Poems*, edited and annotated by Simon Bernstein (New York, 1944), and in volume I of Schirmann's anthology, *Ha-Shira ha-Ivrit bi-Sefarad u-vi-Provence*.

Much has been written about the non-Hebrew verses in some of Halevi's poems. See S. M. Stern, *Les Chansons mozarabes*, Università di Palermo, Instituto di Filologia Romanza, 1953, and the earlier studies of Spanish scholars, mentioned by Stern in his work.

49. From Judah Halevi's letter to R. David of Narbonne, Brody, vol. I, p. 224. Schirmann, who hesitates to identify the city as Toledo (*Tarbiz*, IX, 221), is, to my mind, excessively cautious. "Babel" is used in medieval Hebrew literature as a symbol for Christendom. The Christian conquerors appeared to the Jews and Arabs as veritable "giants," and outside Andalusia there was no "large city" other than Toledo. None of the other cities of northern Spain approached Toledo in size.

50. Brody, I, no. 87, p. 303. Brody later included this poem in his edition of Moses ibn Ezra's poetry (*Shirei ha-Hol*, I, no. 92). However, I see no justification for denying Halevi's authorship of these verses, appearing as they do in the manuscripts of his *Diwan*.

51. Brody I, no. 102, pp. 157–8. My reasoned opinion that it was Cidellus who drew this praise from the poet (*Zion*, n.s., I, 17) has since been confirmed by Schirmann, who found a superscription to this poem, reading "by him, in praise of Cidello." See *Tarbiz*, IX, 219, note 3.

51a. The famous poem *Ba'alat Keshaphim* (The Enchanting One), Brody, I, no. 13, p. 14; Schirmann, *Ha-Shira ha-Ivrit*, etc., I, no. 184, p. 457.

52. Brody, II, nos. 11, 12; Schirmann in *Tarbiz*, IX, 220

53. Brody, IV, nos. 58, 59, pp. 131–4; Bernstein, nos. 62, 72, pp. 61, 74.

54. Brody, IV, no. 24, p. 67–8; Bernstein, no. 159, p. 175-6; Schirmann, I, no. 197, pp. 472–4.

55. Brody, III, no. 26, p. 49; no. 66, p. 125–6. Bernstein, no. 43, p. 40–41.

56. See B. Dinaburg's article, "R. Judah Halevi's Journey to Palestine" (Hebrew), in *Minha le-David* (David Yellin Festschrift, Jerusalem, 1935).

57. Cf. my article in *Zion*, n.s., I, p. 20.

58. Brody, III, no. 12 (p. 18–9), no. 114 (p. 207); Bernstein, no. 148 (p. 158), no. 78 (p. 80). See also *Zion*, n.s., I, p. 23.

59. Brody, II, p. 185; Bernstein, p. 252; Schirmann I, p. 498.

60. Brody, III, no. 102 (p. 187), IV, no. 4 (p. 7); Bernstein, no. 192 (p. 211), no. 167 (p. 184).

61. The philosophy of history expounded in the *Kusari* is treated by Dinaburg in his article in *Minha le-David* and in I. Heinemann's "R. Judah Halevi—the Man and the Philosopher" (Hebrew), in *Kneset* (in memory of Bialik), VII (1942), pp. 261–279, and in his "Judah Halevi's Conception of History" (Hebrew), in *Zion*, n.s., IX (1944), pp. 147–177. See also my remarks in *MGWJ*, LXX (1926), 121. Cf. my little Book *Galut* (German edition, Berlin, 1936, p. 20 f.; English edition, New York, 1947, p. 27 f.). A comparison of the *Kusari* with the *Sefer Megillat ha-Megalleh* (ed. A. Poznanski, Berlin, 1924) of Abraham bar Hiyya, who influenced Halevi, is illuminating. I am particularly impressed by the manifest influence of Christian polemical literature upon the *Kusari*. The formulation of the theological conception of Jewish history and of the doctrine of Israel's selection in Part One of the *Kusari* shows affinity with Christian apologia. Compare, for example, the discussion of the Jewish system of chronology, referring back to Creation (Part One, 44 f.), with a similar treatment of the subject in Augustine's *Civitas Dei* XI, 6; XII, 10; XVIII, 39 f. Compare too the *Kusari's* claim that learning and science came to the Greeks from the Hebrews

(I, 63; II, 66) with a similar statement in *Civitas Dei* XVIII, 37 f. Cf. David Cassel's edition—with German translation and notes—of the *Kusari* (Leipzig, 1853), p. 172, note 2.

62. Cf. Baer II, no. 34, note (p. 17).

NOTES TO CHAPTER II

1. See Baer I, Beilage 1, p. 1024 ff., and the remarks of Sánchez-Albornoz in *Anuario* VI (1929), 544. It is not my function to deal with the complex problem of the development of the various *fueros* (compilations of laws) of Aragon and Navarre, but rather to define the basic elements common to all twelfth century legislation dealing with the Jews. See in this connection *Los fueros de Aragón*, edited by Gunnar Tilander, Lund, 1937. For the *fuero* of Estella (*anno* 1164) see note 14, below.

2. Baer I, pp. 1035–6. The fact that Jews and Moslems are here mentioned together and the same law applies to both alike would indicate that these Jews were, like the Moslems, in a status of partial serfdom (*novenarii et tributarii*). Cf. also Baer I, no. 17, paragraph 7, and the quotation from the *fuero* of Viguera and Funes in Baer I, pp. 1036–7. From a number of Catalonian documents it appears that Jews often leased tracts of land from Jewish or Christian landlords and cultivated them themselves, with their own hands. However, one cannot deduce therefrom that these Jewish tenant-farmers were, like so many of the Christian peasantry, in a status halfway between serfs and freemen.

3. Baer I, no. 574—"illa populatione, que dicitur Elgacena (in Navarre), que fuit de illos judeis"; A. Herculano, *Historia de Portugal*, III (Lisbon, 1849), p. 210, note 5— "audivit dicere, quod popula de judaeis est facta extra terminos qui continentur in carta de Gardone."

4. Baer I, nos. 578, 579.

5. Baer II, no. 60, note, p. 39.

6. Baer II, no. 45. Cf. the references given there and also J. Catalina Garcia in *Memorial Historico Español*, vol. 43 (1905), pp. 116 f., 133 f. See also my note on "castra Judaeorum" in Baer II, no. 10. Consult also the important charter granted (*ca.* 1187) by Alfonso VIII of Castile to the Jews of Haro, in which he turned over to the Jewish community the citadel of the town and all the rights and privileges appertaining thereto. This document, published by Pilar León Tello in "Nuevos documentos sobre la juderia de Haro," in *Sefarad*, XV (1955), 161, reads: "Notum sit . . . quod ego Aldefonsus Dei gratia rex Castelle et Tolleti una cum uxore mea Alienor regina . . . dono et concedo castrum de Faro vobis toti aliame judeorum de Faro ad inhabitandum . . . cum omni hereditate qui est de via qua itur de Faro ad Biliuio ad juso usque ad Ebro . . . Ad hec dono et concedo uobis et (read: ut) uos et omnes posteri uestri secundum subscriptas consuetudines et foros in predicto Castello uiuatis: Judeus aut judea, qui in aqua aut oppressione petre aut parietis aut ligni aut alicuius ruppe mortua fuerit, libere sepeliatur, et nec homicidium nec calumpnia pro ea pectetur. Nullum pectetur a judeis homicidium aut calumpnia pro aliquo interfecto qui extra januas castelli inueniatur. Quicumque petra aut sagitta aut lancea aut aliquibus castellum impugnaverit, pectet mille aureos regi . . ." Compare the above privileges with those granted by Sancho VI, *el Sabio*, of Navarre to the aljamas of Tudela and Funes, in Baer I, nos. 578, 579. I would like to

call attention here also to the documents—among them Hebrew legal instruments—pertaining to the Jewish community of Calahorra, published in *Sefarad*, VI (1946); XV (1955); XVI (1956). Note especially document no. xi, in *Sefarad*, XVI, 79, according to which the entire population of the city—nobles, burghers, Jews and Moslems—in 1320 chose two Christians and two Jews to serve as a board of arbitration to deal with the problem of establishing mills within the limits of the city.

6a. Baer II, no. 60, p. 36.

7. Baer I, no. 31, and passim. Further details illustrating this development during the later stages of the Reconquest will be found in chapters III, IV and V.

8. I. Millás i Vallicrosa, *Documents hebraics de jueus catalans,* no. III (Institut d'Estudis Catalans: Memories, vol. I, fasc. 3, Barcelona, 1927). The marketplace was then outside the city walls of Barcelona, near the old castle (castrum vetus). See I. Balari y Jovany, *Origenes historicos de Cataluna* (Barcelona, 1899), p. 647.

8a. Baer I, no. 40.

8b. Baer I, no. 39.

9. Baer I, no. 52. See also nos. 74, 78, and the note to no. 39. The garden is referred to as "hortus de alchazeria," which means that the business quarter was already in existence prior to this transaction. The main highway touched this garden on its north and east sides. Among its neighbors were the garden of the Church of St. Vincent on the west, and the house of Xavaxorta on the north. The latter was apparently a Jewish notable and landowner, bearer of the title "Sahib-al-Shorta." David ibn Aldaian's son, magister Vitalis, was after his father's death placed under the jurisdiction of the convent of Sigena by Pedro II (Baer I, no. 74). The signature of Eleazar, in his capacity as royal steward (*repositarius*), appears on a number of documents from the reign of Pedro II (Baer I, no. 52, note, p. 44-5). It may be assumed that Joseph the physician is identical with Joseph ibn Shaprut, mentioned in Baer I, no. 78. Xavaxorta is undoubtedly the Abraham Çavi Xorta who appears in the same document. See also J. Bosch Vilá, "Escrituras Oscenses en aljamía hebraicoárabe," in *Homenaje a Millás* I, 183 ff., esp. p. 195, #5; Ricardo del Arco, "La aljama judaica de Huesca," *Sefarad*, VII, 271 ff.

10. Baer I, no. 83, and note. The reader will be able to find further references in the documents to Jewish-held stores and workshops by referring to the indices of Baer I and II. Cf. also the Arabic documents from Toledo mentioned in my article in *Tarbiz*, V, 235.

11. Baer I, pp. 1033-34, 1040-41.

12. Baer I, pp. 942, 958-59, 975, 976. A statute of the aljama of Tudela, of the year 1305, considers a quarrel among Jews taking place either in the synagogue or in the *alcaiceria* as an equally grave offense, and imposes identical penalties for assault committed in a quarrel there. Baer I, no. 586, paragraph 7 (p. 592). See also "alcaiceria" in the subject index of Baer II, p. 587.

13. See above, chapter I, note 41.

14. Baer I, nos. 568, 574, 575, and p. 1025 f. A new edition of the *fuero* of Estella (*anno* 1164) was published by J. M. Lacarra in *Anuario*, IV (1927), 404 ff.; IX (1932), 386 ff. See also Lacarra, "La formación de las familias de fueros navarros," in *Anuario*, X (1933), 202 ff., 219 ff. Cf. *ibid.*, p. 265 f., the permission granted in 1164 by Sancho VI, *el Sabio*, of

Navarre to the bishop and church of Pamplona, "quod populetis iudeos undecumque potueritis, et de mea terra et de altera, sive de Pamplona sive in Vharte (Huarte) . . . ad qualecumque foro vobis placuerit, tali modo quod sint iudei illi de Deo et de Sancta Maria de Pamplona et vestri . . . ad faciendam vestram propriam voluntatem sicut de nostra propria causa, solta et ingenua, libera et franca ab omni regali servitio, et sint securi et emparati in tota mea terra, sicut illi de Estella, et si quis homo turbaberit illos in ire aut in venire in tota mea terra usque VII annis, pectet mille solidos, et sint D vestri et D mei, et de VII annis in antea sint omnes calumpnie vestre et omnia iura illorum . . ."

15. See Abraham ibn Daud's *Sefer ha-Kabbala* in Neubauer's *Medieval Jewish Chronicles*, I, 83. The event occurred between 1134 and 1143. Cf. Régné, "Etude sur la condition des Juifs de Narbonne," in *REJ*, LVIII, 80. It is worthwhile to point out here that the Jewish woman could own landed property and be the beneficiary of royal protection in her own right. Cf. Baer I, no. 48a. In Balari's *Origenes*, p. 690, we are told of a Jewish woman named Druda who was invited to the queen's palace in 1158/59. The name, Druda, was common among the Jewish women of the time. Cf. Baer I, no. 33, note (p. 23); *REJ*, LXVIII, 78.

16. "Nam iudei servi regis sunt et semper fisco regio deputati"—Baer I, p. 1043. Cf. also the references given in Baer I, pp. 1037-38, and in the subject index of Baer II, p. 592, under "Staatsrechtliche Stellung der Juden." The English chronicler Roger de Hovenden (ed. Stubbs, III, 45), tells how the English crusaders in 1190 attacked the Moslems and the Jews in Lisbon, Portugal, and "paganos et judaeos servos regis, qui in civitate habitabant, fugaverunt." The theory that the Jews are the property of the crown (*servi camere*) was accepted as an established principle of law throughout medieval Europe. See my article in *Zion* (annual), VI, 153-4. See also *El Fuero de Teruel*, ed. M. Gorosch in *Leges Hispanicae Medii Aevi*, ed. G. Tilander (Stockholm, 1950).

17. According to Jose Yanguas, *Diccionario de antiguedades del reino de Navarra* (Pamplona, 1842), I, 389, Jewish slaves are spoken of in the *fuero* of Sobrarbe. We must, however, wait for a critical edition of this *fuero*. One is struck by the fact that in all the other collections of laws provision is made regarding Moslem captives and slaves, whereas Jews of these statuses are not even mentioned.

18. *Kusari* III, 10.

19. Isaac Arama, *'Aqedat Yishaq*, chap. 98 (the homily on Deuteronomy 28). An almost identical statement is found in Don Isaac Abravanel's commentary to the same chapter of Deuteronomy.

20. Thus, for example, in the municipal charter of Daroca, granted by Count Ramon Berenguer IV of Barcelona, "Christiani, judaei et sarraceni unum et idem forum habeant de ictibus et calumniis."—Baer I, no. 22. Similar provisions are found in other charters.

20a. Baer I, p. 1039.

21. See subject index in Baer I, p. 1161, *s.v. "alvedi,"* and in Baer II, p. 589, *s.v.* "Gemeinde." The same official existed also in the aljama of Toledo.— *Zikhron Yehuda* (Responsa of R. Judah b. R. Asher), no. 67 (והבדין הלך למשכנו), and *Tarbiz*, V, 231. Cf. also Régné, no. 2720, for Saragossa, and no. 752 for Calatayud. In the latter reference (no. 752) Régné's last phrase should be corrected to conform to the source, which reads, "et filium del alvedi judeum argenterium."

22. Baer I, p. 1039 f. and similar legislation discussed in Beilage I. Cf. the provisions of the *fuero* of Alba de Tormes governing collateral deposited to secure a loan, in Baer II, no. 59.

23. Baer I, p. 1026.

24. Baer I, p. 1029 f.

25. Baer I, pp. 1027, 1042. From a document of Leon, dated 1091, it appears that duelling might still be resorted to as a means of deciding disputes between Christians and Jews, at that time. However, in such an eventuality the Jew's side would be represented by a Christian proxy.— Baer II, no. 14. For similar procedures in other countries see Johannes E. Scherer, *Die Rechtsverhältnisse der Juden in den deutsch-österreichischen Ländern* (Leipzig, 1901), p. 305 f. (The author there adds some strange assumptions of his own.) The aversion of the Christian merchant class to duelling as a means of adjudication is well known. The contemporary Jewish attitude is expressed in this statement from an anonymous medieval Hebrew chronicle, "It is contrary to the law of Israel to engage in duelling in the manner of the Gentile population."—Page 51 of the Hebrew supplement (*Ozar Tob*) to Berliner's *Magazin fur die Wissenschaft des Judenthums*, IV (1877); A. M. Habermann, *Sefer Gezerot Ashkenaz-we-Sarfat* (Jerusalem, 1945), p. 14.

26. Baer I, no. 175, paragraph 23 (p. 221); Baer II, no. 58. It may be assumed that such exemptions appeared more frequently in the older charters. Compare, on the other hand, the statement of R. Eliezer b. R. Joel of Germany (12th–13th cent.), "It is still customary in Spain for Jews to accompany their king into war."—Victor Aptowitzer, *Mavo le-Sefer Rabiah* (Jerusalem, 1938), p. 10.

27. Consult Baer I, subject index, pp. 1162, 1169, *s.v.* "Busse," "Wergeld"; Baer II, p. 588, *s.v.* "Bussgelder."

28. F. Diez, *Leben und Werke der Troubadours* (second edition, Leipzig, 1882), p. 181 f.

29. See below, chapter VII, end.

30. Brief mention of this catastrophe is made in the chronicle of Joseph ibn Sadiq, in Neubauer's *Mediaeval Jewish Chronicles*, I, 95, and in Abraham Zacuta's *Sefer Yuhasin* (ed. Filipowski), p. 221, col. 1. These may be the persecutions referred to by the English chronicler Matthew Paris, *Historia Anglorum*, ed. Madden, II, 391: *Chronica Maiora*, ed. Luard, III, 369, "Illis quoque diebus facta est strages magna Judaeorum in partibus transmarinis, praecipue autem in Hispania." (Graetz's attempt [VI, 347] to emend this text is entirely unnecessary.) For the revolt which broke out in Leon upon the death of Alfonso IX see Antonio Ballesteros, *Historia de España*, III (Barcelona, 1922), pp. 3, 145.

31. Our source is the chronicle at the end of the *Shebet Yehuda*, ed. Wiener (Hannover, 1856 and 1924), p. 112 f.; ed. Shohet (Jerusalem, 1947), p. 146 f. It is discussed by Graetz in Note 1, at the end of volume VI. The entry for שנת קכ״ז (ed. Wiener, p. 113; ed. Shohet, p. 146) reads, "The king of Ishmael Emir Almanatuner (read "Almuminin") came and plundered the land of Castile, captured Calativa (*sic*) and other large cities and ravaged the entire district of Toledo. The Jews of the city went out to meet him and fought against him and killed many of their enemies." Graetz correctly emends קכ״ז to קנ״ז (=תתקנ״ו) or קנ״ז (=תתקנ״ו) See his discussion, vol. VI, p. 342. For "Calativa" read "Talavera," as is evident from the parallel entry, for the year 1196, in *Annales Toledanos*,

in *España Sagrada,* vol. XXIII, p. 393. The author of the Hebrew chronicle, like the Christian chronicler, describes here the advance of the Almohades into Castile in 1196–97 under Emir Almuminin Yakub Al-Mansur, and he stresses the participation of the Jews in the defense of Toledo. The entry for ב"קע שנת (=שנת תתקע"ב) in the same chronicle (ed. Wiener, p. 113; ed. Shohet, p. 147), discussed by Graetz on p. 345, reveals that the Jews were gravely threatened by the crusading fervor which ran high in 1212, at the time of the battle of Navas de Tolosa.

32. Baer I, p. 1025 f., p. 1039 f.; Baer II, no. 14.

33. See the references to the Leonese *fueros* in note 35 below.

34. Baer I, p. 1037 f.; Baer II, no. 56.

35. Baer II, nos. 56, 57, 59. Cf. also no. 125, which belongs to a later period.

36. Baer, II, nos. 24, 34, 35, 39; *Tarbiz,* V, 232; H. Brody, *The Poetry and Letters of R. Meir Halevi Abulafia,* in *Studies of the Research Institute for Hebrew Poetry* (Hebrew), vol. II (Berlin, 1936). See especially Brody's Introduction, and of the poems, no. 1, "in praise of the *almoxarife* Abu 'Amr (Joseph) ibn Shoshan," and no. 10, which is a eulogy of him after his death. Joseph ibn Shoshan is therein eulogized as the ever vigilant guardian of his coreligionists' welfare and honor (esp. vv. 24–34). Nos. 9 and 13 are requests addressed to Abu Ishak (Abraham) ibn Alfakhar and Joseph ibn Shoshan, respectively, asking for a reprieve from taxation for R. Abraham b. Nathan of Lunel. No. 5 bemoans the deplorable state of the times, in which the unscrupulous rise to power. In no. 37 the poet laments the recent assassination of his uncle, R. Zerahia Halevi (in 1215 or 1218), and extends consolation to the latter's son, Todros—further evidence of the dangerous situation prevailing at the time, as described in the text and in note 31 above. The responsa of R. Meir Halevi Abulafia, included in *Or Sadiqim* (Salonika, 1799), shed no additional light on the history of the Jews in Spain during his lifetime, but his description of himself at the close of one of his responsa (no. 247) as "the prisoner of toil and sighs" strikes a poignant note.

37. For the families Sheshet-Perfet, Benveniste, and Eleazar see Baer I, nos. 45, 46, 47, 48a, 52, 61, 63, 79, 86, 87; Aptowitzer, *Mavo le-Sefer Rabiah,* p. 209; Brody, op. cit., p. 9.

37a. For the *almoxarife* Abu Omar ibn Shoshan (Avomar Avenxuxen) see Baer II, no. 39, pp. 19–21, and note 36, above. He is without doubt the *almoxarife* Avomar named in the document published in L. Serrano, *El obispado de Burgos y Castilla primitiva,* III (Madrid, 1936), p. 315, no. 201.

38. Baer I, nos. 47, 65, 66, 74, 76, 77, 79, 80.

39. Baer I, nos. 21, 64, 65, 80. Such privileges were recorded in the registers of the proper royal officials and were inherited and exercised by the descendants of the original recipients through the thirteenth and fourteenth centuries. In the *Responsa* of R. Solomon ibn Adret, vol. II, no. 213, it is reported that the king had given a patent to a Jew of Saragossa authorizing him to receive two pounds of mutton from the Jewish slaughterhouse every Monday.

40. *Meshal ha-Kadmoni,* ed. Venice, 1546, fol. 10b; ed. Zemora (Tel Aviv, 1953), p. 46.

41. Baer I, no. 78; cf. also no. 76. In connection with the right given to the aljama of Huesca, "et etiam si volueritis, possitis in eum insurgere

et irruere ac eum lapidare" (Baer I, no. 78, p. 73), compare the right given in 1127 to the twenty "homines meliores" of the Christian municipality of Tudela, "et qui vos voluerit inde forzare, totos in unum destruite in suas casas et totum quod habet in Tutela, et ego ero inde vobis adjutor" (Yanguas, *Diccionario,* III, 402), and the provision of the *fuero* of Daroca, "Nemo vicinorum Daroce contra voluntatem concilii efficiatur merinus. Si autem effectus fuerit, ipse lapidibus lapidetur et domus eius funditus subvertatur" (*Anuario,* X, 243).

42. *Divre ha-Alah we-ha-Niddui* was published by Israel Davidson in Guenzig's *Ha-Eshkol,* VI (Cracow, 1909), p. 165 f. One of the men anathemized by the author of this little book is Abraham b. Samuel Lobel who, as scribe of the aljama of Saragossa, affixed his signature to deeds of sale of real estate, written in Judaeo-Arabic, dated 1217 and 1223. —Baer I, nos. 82, 84. Ibn Sabbatai also wrote *Minhath Yehuda Sone ha-Nashim* (The Offering of Judah the Women-Hater), which he dedicated in 1208 to Abraham Alfakhar, and *Milhemet ha-Hokhma we-ha-Osher* (The Conflict between Wisdom and Wealth) which, in 1214, he dedicated to the *Nasi* R. Todros Halevi. Both men were among the leading notables of Toledo. For Judah ibn Sabbatai and his works see Israel Davidson, *Parody in Jewish Literature* (N. Y., 1907), p. 7 f.; Schirmann, *Ha-Shira ha-Ivrit,* II, 67 f. and 689.

43. Correspondence dealing with this affair was found among the writings of R. Abba Mari, the author of *Minhath Kenaoth,* and was published in the periodical *Israelitische Letterbode,* IV (1878/9), pp. 162–168. The date of this correspondence is established by the signatures of R. David Kamhi (p. 167) and his contemporaries. R. Sheshet ben Benveniste is to be identified with the celebrated *nasi* who died in 1209 (Baer I, pp. 35 and 53). The name of the *Nasi* R. Makhir ben Sheshet appears in Hebrew documents from Barcelona, written between the years 1195 and 1230.— I. Millás i Vallicrosa, *Documents hebraics de jueus catalans,* nos. IV-VIII; Miret-Schwab, "Documents sur les juifs catalans," in *REJ,* LXVIII, 177. These documents also provide other data concerning the family of the *nasi.* Under the protection of Queen Maria (ob. 1213), consort of Pedro II and mother of James I, Samuel Benveniste was able to escape to Provence.

44. *Milhemet ha-Hokhma we-ha-Osher* (ed. Haberman, Tel Aviv, 1952), end.

45. See chapter I, note 45.

46. See my article, "The Religious and Social Ideology of the *Sefer Hasidim*" (Hebrew), in *Zion,* III, 1–50.

47. The letters of R. Meir Abulafia were published under the title *Kitab al Rasail* by J. Brill, Paris, 1871. See also N. Brüll's article in *Jahrbücher für jüdische Geschichte und Literatur,* IV (1879), and A. Marx in *JQR,* n.s., XXV, 414 f.

48. The controversy is treated in a number of modern works and articles. I call attention to the following: Abraham Geiger in *Wissenschaftliche Zeitschrift für jüdische Theologie,* V (1844); Graetz, vol. VII, note 1; Brüll, op. cit.; Joseph Sarachek, *Faith and Reason: The Conflict over the Rationalism of Maimonides,* Williamsport, Pa., 1935; B. Dinaburg, *Yisrael ba-Gola* (Israel in the Diaspora), vol. II, book 2 (Tel Aviv, 1936), p. 494 f.

The principal sources are:

A. The well-known collection of Maimonides' responsa and epistles entitled, *Teshuboth, She'eloth we-Iggroth* (*editio princeps*, Constantinople, *ca.* 1520–1540; see Steinschneider, *Catalogue Bodleiana*, cols. 1898–1902), which contains letters of the principals in the Maimunist controversy. This collection was reprinted several times. The references below are to the following edition: *Kobeṣ Teshuboth ha-RaMBaM we-Iggrotaw* (Collection of Maimonides' Responsa and Epistles), ed. Lichtenberg, three parts, Leipzig, 1859. Part III of this edition is entitled *Iggroth Kenaoth* and contains the letters pertaining to the controversy. The editorial method of the original compiler of this collection reveals him to have been one of the Maimunists.

B. The correspondence published by S. Z. H. Halberstam in Kobak's *Jeschurun*, VIII (1872). The editor of this compilation appears to have been a scholar close to R. Moses ben Nahman.

C. *Sefer Milhamoth Adonai*, by Maimonides' son, Abraham Maimuni (Hanover, 1840, and in *Kobes*, part III), written about 1235. Considerable light on the background of this controversy was shed by H. Brody's publication of the poetry of Meshullam ben Solomon da Piera in *Studies of the Research Institute for Hebrew Poetry* (Hebrew), IV (Jerusalem, 1938), and by Gershom Scholem's article, "A New Document for the study of the Origins of the Cabala" (Hebrew), in *Sefer Bialik* (Tel Aviv, 1934). See also Scholem's *Reshith ha-Kabbala* (The Beginnings of the Cabala), 1150–1250, Jerusalem/Tel Aviv, 1948; E. E. Urbach in *Tarbiz*, X, 35, and in *Zion*, XII, 149 f. For the conflict between philosophy and religion, in this and subsequent generations, see Isaac (Julius) Guttmann, *Ha-Pilosophia shel ha-Yahaduth* (The Philosophy of Judaism), Jerusalem, 1951, pp. 169–191. The entire episode calls for a fresh treatment, but I have to confine my remarks to only such matters as touch directly on the subject under our consideration.

49. *Jeschurun*, VIII, 100.

50. H. Brody, *Mivhar ha-Shira ha-Ivrit (Anthologia Hebraica)*, Leipzig, 1922, p. 281 f. The archival documents of this period yield nothing new of R. Moses ben Nahman and his circle. It is worth mentioning, however, that R. Moses' teacher, R. Judah b. Yakar, in the capacity of *dayyan* affixed his signature to a document executed in the *beth-din* of Barcelona in 1215.—Millás, *op. cit.*, no. X.

51. *Kobes*, III, fol. 4, column 4.

52. *Kobes*, III, fol. 8. This letter was critically edited by Joseph Perles in *MGWJ* IX (1860), 184–195.

53. The proclamation is published in *Kobes*, III, fol. 5b-d. For Bahye Alconstantini see chapter IV, note 2. His signature, in Hebrew, appears on a Latin document of 1238, published by Miret-Schwab in *REJ*, LXVIII (1914), 179. The correct reading there is בחיי בן אלקסטנטין. That the proper name is to be read Bahye is apparent from its Latin form "Bahiel," which appears there and in several other documents (cf. Baer I, p. 151). In a document dated 1229, the brothers Bahye and Solomon Alconstantini are listed among the recipients of certain grants from the crown, namely, specified revenues from the dyeing establishment of the city of Saragossa and two pounds of mutton from the Jewish slaughterhouse there, which is evidence of their position within their community. See *El Registro del Merino de Zaragoza*, ed. M. de Bofarull y de

Sartorio (Saragossa, 1889), p. 50; *CDIA*, XXXIX, 240. Graetz already noted that Solomon's name was not among the signatories to the proclamation of the ban. The omission is not, as Graetz thought, a copyist's error. Don Solomon, as royal *alfaquim*, accompanied James I at the time on his third trip to Majorca. See *Cronica de Jaime I*, ed. Aguilo (1873), p. 167, paragraph 118; I. Miret y Sans, *Itinerari de Jaime I el Conqueridor*, p. 99. Among the signatories there appears also the name of Abraham ben Judah aben Lavi, who was a member of the same family as Judah aben Lavi de la Cavalleria, the famous bailiff of James I (Baer I, 116). For the אלפואל and שמריאל families, whose members are among the signatories for Huesca, see Baer I, no. 52, and Index, p. 1099, *s. n.* "Alfavell," p. 1130, *s. n.* "Samarel."

54. This is clearly stated in the first letter of R. David Kamhi.—*Kobes,* III, 1c.

55. See my article in *Debir*, II (Berlin, 1924), p. 316 f.

56. For Abraham Maimuni's views on this subject see his *Responsa,* ed. Freimann (Jerusalem, 1938), p. 19 f.

57. *Kobes*, III, 6b–7a.

58. For the views of Judah Alfakhar see Julius Guttmann, *Philosophie des Judentums* (Munich, 1933), p. 209; *Ha-Pilosophia shel ha-Yahaduth*, p. 172. His letter to Kamhi is in *Kobes*, III, 1c–3b.

59. *Jeschurun*, VIII, 21 f.; Brüll in *Jahrbücher*, IV, 18 f. The modern scholars who discuss this letter believe its author to have been a resident of Burgos. However, this assumption is based on a very doubtful reading. In opposition to this view it should be pointed out that, since both R. Meir Halevi and his brother R. Joseph described the situation in their city in similar terms, they were apparently talking about the same community. If we grant that R. Joseph Halevi was in Toledo when he wrote his letter we must also conclude that R. David Kamhi, in his travels through Spain, actually reached Toledo at some time between the writing of his second and third letters. But, since the influence of the zealots was very strong there, he was compelled to leave the city without accomplishing his purpose, and he quite understandably passed over his experience there in silence.

60. Our sources of information are the following:

A. The third letter from R. David Kamhi to R. Judah Alfakhar, which Kamhi wrote after he returned to Narbonne.—*Kobes, III*, 4b.

Kamhi wrote, "The man whom you have favored and called righteous, wise, and pure (*i.e.*, Solomon of Montpellier), turned out to be a vicious fool, for he embarked upon a corrupt course and turned informer. . . . For when he saw that the rabbis of France turned their backs upon him, regarding him a fool and recognizing him to be a bearer of false testimony, he turned to the infidel and appealed to them for help in his actions against the Jews. He applied first to the Franciscan friars and said to them, 'Behold, most of our people are unbelievers and heretics, for they were led astray by the words of Rabbi Moses of Egypt, who wrote heretical books. Now, while you are exterminating the heretics among you, exterminate our heresies as well and order the burning of those books, namely, *The Book of Knowledge* and the *Guide.*' And he was not fully satisfied until he applied also to the Dominicans and to the priests, making the same request, until the matter ultimately reached the ears of the Cardinal, putting the

Jews of Montpellier and its satellite communities in great danger, and exposing them to the ridicule of the Gentiles." In his reply (*ibid.*, fol. 4c), Alfakhar did not deny the accusation against R. Solomon of Montpellier, but attempted to defend him by saying that whatever he did, he did in desperation brought about by the persecution he suffered from the Maimunists. However, this cannot be taken as corroboration of the testimony of R. David Kamhi, since Alfakhar's own, and only, source of information was this letter of Kamhi.

B. The letter of R. Joseph ben Todros Halevi to the scholars of Provence.—*Jeschurun*, VIII, 43.
Writing in the medieval euphuistic style, at the sacrifice of both precision and clarity, R. Joseph states, "It is not right to turn Israel over into the hands of Gentiles and to let our enemies be our judges, they who by word and deed seek to sully our honor and mar our glory, to denigrate our Torah and to harass and persecute our persons, and who regard us with derision and speak of us with contempt . . . and certainly [it is not right] to carry a matter in controversy for a decision to a Christian prelate, in whose hand our cherished Torah, abhorrent to him, is crumbled, and is consigned to the flames. This is what led to the burning of this book by the friars, and the blaspheming enemy was well pleased upon seeing God's word burnt, going up in smoke." R. Joseph also sought to defend R. Solomon of Montpellier.

C. The letter of R. Samuel b. Abraham (*Jeschurun*, VIII, 154), which states, "The abominable deed was done . . . the Divine Name was desecrated publicly . . . when these books were exposed in their public places and even judged by them in their courts."

D. The letter of Judah and Abraham ibn Hasdai to the communities of Castile and Aragon—*Jeschurun*, VIII, 49 f.—"People wayward and perverse banded together . . . and they handed the *Book of Knowledge* and the *Guide* over to the priests and the prelates and the Franciscan friars and they said to them, 'Why do you weary yourselves and travel to the ends of the earth and traverse the distant seas in pursuit of heretics in order to eliminate the evil from your midst? We too have heretical works, called the *Book of Knowledge* and the *Guide*, filled with devious error. . . .' They came to the Franciscans and to the high clergy with plaints and to the Dominicans with pleas . . . asking them to wreak judgment upon the surviving holy books. At their command a huge bonfire was built, and they took the 'bar of gold and the fine mantle' (see Joshua 7.21), the two exalted Tablets of the Covenant, and they broke them for the second time by burning them." In the same letter they also tell the well-known story of the excision of the tongues of the informers.

E. The statement of R. Abraham Maimuni in his *Sefer Milhamoth Adonai* regarding the burning of the *Book of Knowledge* and the *Guide* and the excision of the tongues of the informers.—*Kobes*, III, 17a. The testimony of a man so far removed from the scene of the events obviously does not have the validity of an eyewitness report.

F. The Letter of Hillel of Verona, written some sixty years after this controversy.—*Kobes*, III, fol. 13–15. This tract is a product of the biased imagination of the rationalist circles and is full of manifest lies, among them the account of the alleged repentance of R. Jonah Gerondi and his death in Toledo "in a manner unspeakable." Anyone who investigates the various reports will be able to trace the growth of this myth until it reached the absurdities reported by Hillel of Verona. The most reliable testimony is that of R. David Kamhi, and on the basis of his statements it cannot be established that the books were actually burned. The excision of the tongue was, to be sure, a common punishment for informers and blasphemers among the Christians. We do not know, however, if it was actually practiced in Montpellier. R. Jonah Gerondi died in Toledo, where he was held in great honor. His reformatory activity, directed toward the improvement of the religious and moral life of the community of Toledo, was carried on by others after him, and was directed, quite vigorously, against the rationalists. The memory of R. Solomon of Montpellier and his scholarship were held in reverence during the next generation.

NOTES TO CHAPTER III

1. See Baer II, nos. 53, 68, for the Jews in Cordova.
2. For Seville see Baer II, nos. 67, 76 note (p. 60), 216, 249; *Repartimiento de Sevilla*, Estudio y edición preparada por Julio Gonzalez, Madrid, 1951.
3. Baer II, no. 76.
4. Baer II, no. 81.
5. Justo Garcia Soriano, "La reconquista de Orihuela," in *BAH*, CIV (1934), 216. The name of the Jewish combatant was Jacob Avendino.
6. Baer II, nos. 18, 81.
7. Baer II, nos. 46, 47, 48, 53.
8. Baer II, nos. 65, 72, 78. See also my article in *Zion*, II, 24.
8a. Baer II, nos. 61, 63.
9. Baer II, nos. 64, 66, 69, 72, 73, 75, 78, 79.
10. Baer II, nos. 59, 62; cf. nos. 125, 142.
11. In addition to the references given above, see also Baer II, no. 52, and the decrees of the successors of Alfonso X.
12. See chapter V.
12a. Baer II, no. 62; no. 63, p. 44 (Las Siete Partidas II, 20, 8).
13. See *Zion*, II, 29 f.
14. Baer II, no. 67 and note, no. 76; M. Rico y Sinobas, *Libros de saber de astronomía del rey Alfonso el Sabio* (1863–1867); Steinschneider, *Die hebraeischen Uebersetzungen des Mittelalters* (Berlin, 1893), 388, 616 f.; *Primera Crónica general de España*, ed. R. Menendez Pidal (1955), pp. xv–lxii.
15. He is most probably the "Jucef Gironda," "Juceph fijo de rabbi Mosse de Gironda," mentioned in Baer no. 69 and note.
16. *Responsa* of R. Solomon ibn Adret, vol. I, no. 548.
17. Don Juan Manuel, *Libro de los estados*, I, cap. 93 (Biblioteca de Autores Españoles, vol. LI, p. 337 f.); *Libro de los castigos*, cap 13 (*BAE*, LI, 272).
18. Baer II, nos. 55, 82.
19. C. Michaelis de Vasconcellos in *Zeitschrift fur romanische Philologie*, XXV, 303, 314.
20. See my article, "The Life and Times of Todros ben Judah Halevi" (Hebrew), in *Zion*, II (1936/37), pp. 19–55. The references to the poetry

of Todros Halevi are to the edition of his *Diwan (Gan ha-Meshalim we-ha-Hidoth)* by David Yellin, 2 parts in three volumes, Jerusalem, 1932–1936.

21. *Gan ha-Meshalim* no. 570.

22. Baer II, pp. 51–52; *Zion*, II, 22–23.

23. Baer II, no. 84; *Zion*, II, p. 23 f. For the meaning of the name "de la Maleha" see *Gan ha-Meshalim*, part II, vol. II, p. XXXVII, note 5.

24. *Gan ha-Meshalim* no. 390 and the note thereto.

25. *Ibid.*, no. 393 and note. For the decrees referred to in these verses see *Zion*, II, 24. See also *Crónica de Alfonso X*, cap. 5 (*BAE*, vol. 66, p. 6); *Cortes de Leon y Castilla*, I, 54 f., 64 f.; A. Ballesteros in *BAH*, vol. 106 (1935), p. 136.

26. See *Zion*, II, 28.

27. Baer II, no. 84.

28. A copy of the *Cantigas de Santa Maria* by Alfonso X is not available in Jerusalem. Hence I convey only my general impression of them, drawn from memory, without going into detail.

29. See chapter VI.

30. See *Zion*, II, 33 f. A. Ballesteros, in his article, "Burgos y la rebelion de Infante Don Sancho," in *BAH*, CXIX (1946), offers new material relevant to our discussion.

31. The definitive work for the reign of Sancho IV is Mercedes Gaibrois de Ballesteros, *Historia del reinado de Sancho IV de Castilla*, 3 vols., Madrid, 1922–28. See also Baer II, nos. 87–101.

32. Baer II, p. 91. In Leon (p. 448) the tax collector "went from place to place in search of the Jews." The levy imposed upon Pennafiel (p. 445), undoubtedly a very small community, could not be collected because the agents "did not find a single Jew there." See Baer II, no. 96 for the tax distribution for 1290–91.

33. For Abraham el Barchilon see Baer II, no. 93. His name appears for the first time in the ledgers of the crown in 1284.—Baer II, no. 87.

34. For Abraham ibn Shoshan see the references given in Baer II, Index of Names, p. 549, *s.n.* "Abrahen Abenxuxen." Cf. particularly the end of the note on p. 69.

35. Baer II, no. 93.

36. *Zion*, II, 51 f.; Baer II, no. 98.

37. The verses are quoted from *Gan ha-Meshalim*, nos. 975, 642, 643, 644, 1039, 645, 765. Cf. *Zion*, II, 53.

38. Baer II, no. 100.

39. The names of these Jewish officials will be found in the material I assembled in Baer II, nos. 87, 93, 98. Don Joseph de Avila (Baer II, pp. 72, 104) is the famous magnate who offered to have his son marry the daughter of the indigent cabalist, R. Moses de Leon, if the latter's widow would turn over to him the manuscript of the *Zohar*. See Abraham Zacuta, *Sefer Yuhasin*, ed. Filipowski, p. 89; Gershom Scholem, "Did Moses de Leon write the *Zohar*?" (Hebrew), in *Mada'ei ha-Yahaduth*, I (Jerusalem, 1926), p. 16 f. I call attention to the designation of several of the men around Sancho IV by the title "el rab," viz. "el rab don Yuçaf" (Baer II, p. 72), "al rab don Samuel de Valladolid" (p. 91), and "al rab don Fanna" (90). In case of the last-named the correct reading is probably "Fanan," the equivalent of the Hebrew *Hanan*. These all appear to have been learned men who served the king in some official capacity; but I have not been able to find any further information about

them. Cf. in this connection "el rab don Yuçaf Çamanon, fisico de la infante" (Baer II, no. 108), who appears to have belonged to the cabalistic circle of Guadalajara. See also chapter VII, note 22. A number of other Jews are also designated by the title "rab," which probably identifies them as possessors of a rabbinic education.

40. See Baer II, p. 89, note 1; p. 91, note 2.

41. For the brothers Isaac and Abraham ibn Wakar see my remarks in Baer II, p. 89, note 3, and *Zion*, II, p. 50. In Régné nos. 2753, 2854 (read there "aben uacar"), Don Isaac is called the *alfaquim* of Don Juan Manuel. He was the recipient of estates at Elche long after the city was reconquered from the Moslems, for the apportionment of the conquered land there had not yet been completed in the early years of the fourteenth century. Don Isaac served as mediator between Castile and Aragon in matters affecting that city. As Don Çac Alfaquim he appears in documents cited in A. Gimenez Soler, *Don Juan Manuel* (Saragossa, 1932), pp. 24, 25, 61, 237, 297, 432, 669, 688.

42. *Gan ha-Meshalim* no. 632.

43. Todros Halevi's verses on the last illness and death of Sancho IV are in *Gan ha-Meshalim* nos. 637, 638. For Don Juan Manuel's account see his "Tractado sobre las armas," in *BAE*, LI, 262. [See also Castro, *The Structure of Spanish History*, pp. 383–86.] For the messianic episode which occurred at this time see chapter VI.

NOTES TO CHAPTER IV

1. See especially Baer I, nos. 85, 86, 87, 89, 90, 94.

2. Bahye (Bahiel) is mentioned as interpreter for the Arabic in *Crónica de Jaime I*, ed. Aguilo, par. 74, p. 119; English translation, *The Chronicle of James I, King of Aragon*, translated by John Forster, 2 vols. (London, 1883), p. 151. In December 1229, he was sent along with Don Nuño Sanchez and two other knights on a mission to the Moslems in order to negotiate their surrender. Bahye's brother, the *alfaquim* Solomon, fulfilled a similar function on the island of Minorca in 1232.—*Crónica*, par. 118, ed. Aguilo p. 167, tr. Forster, p. 212. For the role of the Jews in the conquest of the Balearic islands see M. Kayserling, *Die Juden in Navarra, den Baskenländern und auf den Balearen* (Berlin, 1861), p. 160 f., and J. Amador de los Rios, *Historia social, politica y religiosa de los Judios de España y Portugal*, I (Madrid, 1875). Additional documents dealing with the apportionment of the lands acquired by Count Nuño Sanchez in Majorca were published in *Bolleti de la Societat Arqueologica Luliana* (Palma, 1919). It is stated there in several places (pp. 251, 252, 255, 273) that the apportionment was made by a Christian official of the count with the consent, or counsel, and according to the wish (cum assensu et voluntate, cum consilio et voluntate) of a Christian monk and of the Jew Astrug (Astrugus Judeus). In several other places there is mention of "Samuel Abenvenist, judeus, noster alfaquimus." A number of Jews received houses and workshops in Majorca, among them several Jews from Marseilles and one from Alexandria. Reference is also made to a Jewish quarter and a synagogue. Certain other Jews received from the count a garden with a water conduit on the outskirts of the city. As far as I know, no other documents dealing with the share of the Jews in the apportionment of the island were found, so that our information remains

incomplete. In *CDIA*, vol. XI, there are a few scattered references to estates given to Jews in villages on the Balearics. See also the bibliography given in Baer I, p. 1087. Consult also J. Busquets Mulet, "El códice latinoarábigo del Repartimiento de Mallorca" (Texto arabe), in *Homenaje a Millás-Vallicrosa* I (Barcelona, 1954), p. 243 f.

The *Repartimiento de Valencia* was published in *CDIA*, vol. XI, and the French historian Régné summarized a few items from it in his *Catalogue*, nos. 13, 27, 31–34, 38–42. I want to call attention to a few other items from the same source. Among the recipients of houses and estates in this area we again find the *alfaquim* Bahye and his brother Solomon (pp. 153, 162, 258). The name "Alassar Alhufach (read, Abulfath), judeus Cesarauguste" (p. 175), reveals its bearer to be a member of the famous Eleazar family of Saragossa.—See above, Chapter II, note 37. Solomon Bonafos (p. 190) is undoubtedly the bailiff of Catalonia whose name and whose signature in Hebrew characters appear in several documents of the year 1233.—Baer I, no. 90. Magister David Abnadayan, *alfaquim* of Infante Fernando, the uncle of the king and abbot of the monastery of Montearagon in the province of Huesca (pp. 202, 239) must have been related to the *alfaquim* of Alfonso II bearing the same name.—Baer I, no. 74. These examples illustrate sufficiently the policy of resettlement pursued in Valencia, one which resembled in every detail the policy in effect about this time also in Andalusia. It was, in fact, the established policy of the Reconquest. Consult also the bibliography in Baer I, p. 1088, for other aspects of the history of the Jews in Valencia. See also Ch. de la Véronne, "La population musulmane de Valence en 1238 d'apres le *Repartimiento*," in *Bulletin Hispanique*, LI (Bordeaux, 1949), 423–6; L. Torres Balbás, "La población musulmana de Valencia en 1238," in *Al-Andalus*, XVI (1951), 167–8.

The *Crónica de Jaime I* in its account of the capture of Jativa in 1240 describes negotiations carried on by *alfaquim* Bahye (par. 325, ed. Aguilo p. 353, tr. Forster p. 441). Here too Bahye was rewarded with grants of land.—*CDIA*, XI, 356. The Repartimiento yields further information regarding the Jews in Jativa and Murviedro. Ninety-five Jews received estates in the city of Valencia.—*Ibid.*, p. 536. During the operations which led to the capture of Elche, in 1263, and of Murcia, in 1266, Astrug Bonsenyor served as interpreter for Arabic.—*Crónica de Jaime I*, paragraphs 422, 436, 437, 439; ed. Aguilo, pp. 431, 442, 444, tr. Forster, pp. 544, 559, 560, 562. Astrug Bonsenyor was a Jew of Barcelona and the son-in-law of Judah de la Cavalleria. For references to him see the index to J. Miret y Sans, *Itinerari de Jaime I "el Conqueridor"* (Barcelona, 1918). He is mentioned even in the last will and testament of James I, dated 1276.—Miret, *Itinerari*, p. 537.

3. Baer I, no. 91; Régné, nos. 31, 141, 142, 160, 161, 566, 652, 654. Several documents of this period, dealing with these matters, were published in Francisco de Bofarull y Sans, *Los Judios en el territorio de Barcelona. Reinado de Jaime I* (Barcelona, 1911).

4. Régné, nos. 580, 582.

5. Régné, no. 239.

6. Much relevant material on this subject is found in J. E. Martínez Ferrando, *Catálogo de la documentación relativa al antiguo reino de Valencia*, 2 v.: I—Jaime I, el Conquistador; II—Pedro el Grande (Madrid, 1934). See also the information gathered below concerning Jewish officials who came into possession of estates in this province.

7. Régné, nos. 43, 46, 432, 433.
8. Régné, no. 36.
9. See Miret, *Itinerari*, p. 188.
10. Pierre Vidal, "Les Juifs de Roussillon et de Cerdagne," in *REJ*, XV (1887), 19–55; XVI (1888), 1–23, 170–203; Régné, nos. 30, 178–180, etc. See also note 43 below.
11. See F. de Bofarull y Sans, "Jaime el Conquistador y la communidad judia de Montpeller," in *BABL*, V (Barcelona, 1910).
12. Régné nos. 21 (*MGWJ*, XV, 90), 273, 313 (cf. Baer I, no. 73); also Régné, nos. 259, 460, 476. "Suta" is not a "porcherie," as translated by Régné, in no. 460, but a fortress.
13. Régné, nos. 71, 91, *et al.;* Baer I, no. 73.
14. The reader will find many of the details by referring to Régné's *Catalogue*. For instances where permission was given by James I to build a synagogue see Régné, no. 208 (text in Bofarull's *Los Judios en el territorio de Barcelona*, p. 57, no. XXXIII), no. 290, no. 357 (Bofarull, p. 71, no. LXI), no. 389 (Bofarull, p. 75, no. LXX), no. 394 (Perpignan).
15. Charters embodying this privilege are extant only for Calatayud and Barbastro.—Baer I, nos. 88, 107.
16. Régné, no. 113. Bofarull, no. XVIII. See also chapter VI, note 13.
For similar action on part of the king consult the following items in Régné's *Catalogue:* No. 194—The king confirms the will of a Jew. No. 250—The king annuls in advance any penalty that the community of Tortosa might impose upon a certain Jew who spread the report that a certain young woman was his wife. No. 252—The king appoints a Jewish widow as guardian (*tutrix*) of her children on condition that she does not remarry. No. 352—The king gives a certain young woman in marriage to a Jew, and another Jew, who stated that the king exceeded his rights in so doing, has his penalty for making this statement waived by the king. No. 359—Since Jewish law does not forbid polygamy and holds all of a man's children by several wives to be equally legitimate, the king—in 1267—declared an orphan lad of Catalonia, the son of a Jewess of Barcelona, to be the legitimate son of his late father and a rightful heir of his estate. (Text in Bofarull, no. LXII.)
Nos. 526–531, 538–544, 587.—The king confirms the terms of a Jew's will, appoints executors, charges the widow with the support of the orphan son until the end of his eighteenth year, and forbids his marriage before he reaches that age.
Cf. also note 42 below for the case of the orphan whose interests were defended by R. Solomon ibn Adret.
17. See note 1 above. It is noteworthy that even in this period Jewish officials of the crown signed their names in Hebrew on official documents. Cf. particularly the document published by Miret-Schwab in *REJ*, LXVIII, 178, no. xxiv, dated 1235, in which the commander of the Knights Templar in Tortosa leases land to a Christian. This transaction is confirmed in writing by the *Nasi* Bonafos, through his agent Yahye, in the Arabic tongue, in Hebrew script. (Schwab's translation of the Arabic text is, according to my colleague, Prof. Baneth, inaccurate.)
18. L. Klüpfel, *Verwaltungsgeschichte des Königsreichs Aragon zu Ende des 13. Jahrhunderts* (Berlin, 1915), p. 4 f.
19. For Judah de la Cavalleria see Baer, *Aragonien*, p. 178. Consult also Bofarull's *Los Judios en el territorio de Barcelona*, and the indexes of

Miret's *Itinerari* and Martínez Ferrando's *Catalogo*. See also Baer I, no. 104, and the catalogue of the archives of the cathedral of Valencia, published by E. Olmos in *BAH*, vol. 103 (1933), nos. 305–307, 387, 404, 419, 434, 577. The warrant of his appointment to office in 1260 is printed in Bofarull, *op. cit.*, no. 21, and nos. 24, 28, 134 throw light on his financial dealings with the king. It seems that James I would undertake a military campaign or diplomatic journey, such as the trip—the last of his reign—to the Council of Lyon, France, in 1274, only after Don Judah provided him with the necessary funds. He was rewarded with very large estates in the province of Valencia. In the city itself he built several large houses near the city wall and close to the harbor, apparently for business purposes. In 1273 he obtained from the king for his tenants (*exariqui*) grazing rights for one thousand sheep.—Bofarull, *op. cit.*, no. 127.

20. For Benveniste de Porta see Baer I, no. 96; Bofarull, *op. cit.*, passim; Miret, *op. cit.*, passim.

21. For Astrug Jacob Xixon see Baer I, nos. 102, 112, and the indexes of the aforementioned works of Bofarull and Miret. According to Bofarull, no. 59, the king declared Astrug to be free from the jurisdiction of any of the Jewish communities and subject to none of their ordinances (*takkanot*) save the interdict against informing (*herem malshinut*), "Quod nulla aliama judeorum terre vel iurisdictionis domini regis non possit ipsum vel sua ponere in vet neque in tacana neque in aliquod stabilimentum neque in aliquam taillam seu questiam neque etiam in aliquid aliud nisi tantum in herem malsenuth." Compare *Responsa* of Ibn Adret, vol. V, no. 270, "the aforementioned bailiff is not subject to taxation in 'Babylon,' nor to any of their *takkanot*, because he was expressly exempted from their *takkanot*." See also Martínez Ferrando, *op. cit.*, nos. 804, 805, *et al.* for the estate and flour mills which Astrug Xixon owned in the kingdom of Valencia. He also owned land in Catalonia, which was confiscated after his death.—Régné, no. 1212. On one of his country estates (*mansus*) Astrug built a synagogue.—Baer I, no. 112, note, p. 125.

22. Vives f. Jucef aben Vives is mentioned in Régné, nos. 140, 466, 469, 576, *et al.* This man was accused of exploiting his Moslem serfs and of acts of sodomy, but the charges against him were dropped in 1274.—Régné, nos. 613, 617; Miret, *Itinerari*, p. 506. Consult also the index to Martínez Ferrando's work where details are given concerning Vives' administration of certain rural districts populated by Moslems. Similar service was rendered by Joseph ibn Shaprut, bailiff of Murviedro. The successors of these men, who served in similar capacities under Pedro III, will be discussed later in this chapter. There were also other men who rendered occasional service to the crown, the details of which need not concern us here.

23. Régné, no. 4; Cortes de Cataluna I, 120 f.

24. Régné, nos. 9, 10; Cortes de Cataluna I, 126, 131.

25. Régné, no. 28; Cortes de Cataluna I, 133.

26. See *Fueros de Aragon*, ed. Tilander, pp. 3–4.

27. O. Raynaldus, *Annales Ecclesiastici ad a. 1250*, no. 48; see also Vincente de la Fuente, *Historia eclesiastica de España*, segunda edicion (6 vols., Madrid 1873–5), vol. IV, p. 389.

28. The edict was published in full by R. del Arco in *BAH*, vol. 66 (1915),

p. 329, from a text in the municipal archive of Huesca. References to it are found in the documents digested in Régné, nos. 53, 54, 58.

29. The supporting documents are easily found in Régné's *Catalogue*. For the incident in Monzon, see Miret in *BABL*, VIII (1915/16), 373 f.

30. Cf. my article, "The Disputations of R. Yehiel of Paris and of Nahmanides" (Hebrew), in *Tarbiz*, II (1931/32), 172–187. See also J. Millás Vallicrosa in *Anales de la Universidad de Barcelona*, 1940 (where the Latin document should be corrected to read "DCCC vel D annis"); C. Roth in *Harvard Theological Review*, vol. 43 (1950).

31. Cortes de Cataluna, I, 217 f.

32. R. Jacob's polemic was published in Kobak's *Jeschurun*, vol. VI (1868), pp. 1–34. See also Jacob Mann—who contends that R. Jacob was a resident not of Venice but of Valencia—in *REJ*, vol. 82 (1926), 363 f., and in the Samuel Poznanski Memorial Volume (Warsaw, 1927), Hebrew section, p. 24.

33. See my aforementioned article in *Tarbiz*, II.

34. Régné, nos. 208, 209, 212, 215, 216, 217, 224, 225, 226, 249, 318. The text of Régné, no. 249, is published in *CDIA*, VI, 164–166. The summary of the contents of this document as given here by Régné, and elsewhere, is not precise.

35. Régné, nos. 262, 302, 303.

36. Régné, no. 323. See also my article in *Tarbiz*, II.

36a. I have already called attention in my *Aragonien*, p. 36, note 84, to the legends that were current in Jewish circles regarding the relations between James I and Nahmanides. I now find that Américo Castro (*España en su historia* [Buenos Aires, 1948], p. 483; *La realidad historica de España* [Mexico, D. F., 1954], p. 455; *The Structure of Spanish History* [Princeton, 1954], p. 478) accepts popular legend as fact.

37. For the investigation of the Christian merchant of Gerona, Berengarius Durandi, by the inquisitor Petrus de Cadireta see Miret, *Itinerari*, pp. 371, 376; Régné, no. 339.

38. Régné, no. 354; text in Bofarull, no. LX.

39. See A. Potthast, *Regesta Pontificum Romanorum inde ab a. 1198 ad a. 1304* (2 vols., Berlin, 1875), nos. 20081–2; T. Ripoll, *Bullarium Ordinis FF. Praedicatorum* (8 vols., Rome, 1729–1740), I, 487–8.

40. Régné, no. 377.

41. Régné, nos. 386–392, 394–400. The question of expenditures is dealt with in the *Responsa* of Ibn Adret, vol. V, no. 183 (cf. vol. I, no. 644); vol. III, no. 401 (cf. vol. I, no. 1091). In vol. III, no. 401, the following argument is quoted, "The rich man in the community argues that his contribution should be only in proportion to the number of souls in his household, since he does not buy any more bread and meat than do the other Jews of the town." This reveals that the Jews purchased bread and meat from forced converts, in spite of the attitude of the clergy. Rabbi Solomon ibn Adret also ruled that "a convert to Judaism who relapsed to his former faith out of fear, as well as a Jew who converted to another faith out of fear, though they sinned, are Jews. Even though they should, according to the law, have resisted apostasy, even at the pain of death ... nevertheless since they acted out of fear, that is, out of fear of death ... they are Jews, and meat ritually slaughtered by them and wine handled by them is ritually fit for consumption." This responsum is found in the *editio princeps* of Ibn Adret's *Responsa*, no. 41, and is quoted in the

Responsa of R. Isaac b. Sheshet Perfet, nos. 4, 11, 14. I did not find this statement in any of the common editions of the *Responsa* of Ibn Adret. A different attitude toward converts is expressed in Ibn Adret's *Responsa*, vol. I, no. 194.

42. This document is digested in Régné, no. 384, and is published in full by F. Valls Taberner in *Analecta Sacra Tarraconensia*, V (1929), p. 48 f., no. XXXIV. See also chapter VI, note 27.

43. *MGWJ*, XLII, 513; Régné, nos. 518, 564, 573, 605, 628, 630. See also my article, "Recent Books and Sources for the History of the Jews in Spain" (Hebrew), in *Debir*, II (Berlin, 1924), 313 f.

44. Pedro's policy in dealing with the Jews was the subject of a short monograph by Helene Wieruszowski, "Peter der Grosse von Katalonien-Aragon und die Juden, eine Politik des gerechten Ausgleichs," published in *Homenatge a Antoni Rubio y Lluch*, vol. III (Estudis Universitaris Catalans, vol. XXII, Barcelona, 1936), pp. 239–262. The author, who has written extensively on the foreign policy of Pedro III, revealed in this study some wise and original insights into the subject. I find it difficult, however, to agree with her general estimate of Pedro's policy as expressed also in the title of the monograph. She attempted to support her view by citing selected instances which, in my opinion, were not properly interpreted by her.

45. Régné, nos. 666, 667, 668, 672, 674, 675, 681, 687, 697, 700, 720, 763, 771, 851.

46. Cf. Régné, nos. 659, 662–666, 680, 704; Martínez Ferrando, *Catálogo* II, Pedro el Grande (Madrid, 1934), nos. 161, 472.

47. For Moses Alfaquim Alconstantini see Régné, nos. 680, 704, 709, and also no. 745, where he is called, in the original document, "Mosse Alcostanti, olim baiulus Cesarauguste." Consult also the index to Martínez Ferrando's *Catálogo*.

48. For Astrug Ravaya (also Ravaylla, Heb. רבאליה) and his two sons see Baer I, nos. 105, 109, 110, 111, 113, 120, 122; Régné, nos. 309, 310, 311, 340, 373 et al., 663, 677, 682 et al. The names of these men appear in innumerable official documents and they are discussed in all the modern monographs treating this period. It would be impossible to cite here all the known details of their activities. See especially L. Klüpfel's *Verwaltungsgeschichte des Königsreichs Aragon zu Ende des 13. Jahrhunderts* (Berlin, 1915), and Martínez Ferrando's *Catálogo*, index. The text of the privilege granted to Palamos is printed in *CDIA*, VIII, 148. See also H. Finke, *Acta Aragonensia* I (Berlin, 1908), Introduction, p. XCIX, for a study of the directors of the royal chancellery and their signatures on royal decrees.

The signatures of Joseph Ravaya and of other Jewish officials of the crown appear on a number of royal orders from this period preserved in the Archivo general de la Corona de Aragon (ACA) in Barcelona, especially in the Registers numbered 39, 40, 41. I will cite a few examples: 1. The royal order digested in Régné, no. 726, bears at the end the notation, "Juceffus Ravaya mandavit ex parte regis." 2. An order making attendance at any of the fairs of Catalonia compulsory for the inhabitants of the district in which the fair is held is signed, "Hanc mandavit ita expresse Juceffus Ravaya" (April 27, 1279—ACA, Reg. 41, fol. 63). 3. An order to the *vicarii* of Besalu-Gerona, commanding them to protect the countess of Ampurias against threatened harm by her husband the count, is signed, "Jucef Ravaya" (May 12, 1279—ACA, Reg. 41 fol. 76). 4. The municipality of Barcelona is informed that it must accept a certain appointee as royal vicar (*veguer*) in the city. The letter is signed, "P. de Santo Clemente pro Jucef." (June 23, 1279—ACA, Reg. 41, fol. 96). A detailed study of the activities of this family in the service of the crown is soon to appear under the title, David Romano, *Estudio historico de la familia Ravaya, bailes de los reyes de Aragon en el siglo XIII.*

The public career of Muça de Portella began under James I, whom he served as bailiff of his native Tarazona (Régné, no. 548 et passim). A royal decree exempted him from bearing more than twenty per cent of the tax burden of his small aljama, and this privilege was retained by his family even after it had become one of the wealthiest in the land (Régné, nos. 369, 672, *et al.*). Muça also exercised administrative jurisdiction in the province of Valencia. See Martínez Ferrando, *op. cit.*, no. 259 et passim (see index). For Aaron Abinafia (Ibn Yahia), a native of Calatayud, see Régné nos. 90, 125, 190, *et al.*; Martínez Ferrando, index.

49. For Samuel Alfaquim see Martínez Ferrando nos. 566, 808, 880, 1633, 2208, *et al.* In Régné, nos. 800 and 978 (Martínez Ferrando, nos. 1093 and 1595) he is called Samuel f. Abraham Abinnaxim (perhaps for Ibn Nahmias), and is spoken of as the secretary for Arabic correspondence. See also Régné, nos. 836, 978, 1020, 1117, where he is referred to as royal physician and secretary to the king's household. In 1283 he was commissioned to raise a levy from among the Moslems of Valencia for war against France. The full warrant of this commission is printed in *CDIA*, VI, 196. See also J. Carini, *Gli Archivi e le biblioteche di Spagna*, II (Palermo, 1884), 22, 111 f., 133. During the years 1292–94 he was sent by James II of Aragon and Sancho IV of Castile on diplomatic missions to the Moslem rulers of Granada and Morocco.—Régné, nos. 2513, 2524–27 (includes the instructions for his mission); *BABL*, III, 123–7; *BAH*, LXXVI (1920), 54, 72, 139. He is mentioned for the last time in 1300, in connection with his mission to Granada.—*JQR*, VIII, o.s. (1896), 491.

The Jews were very active as interpreters during this period. I offer a few facts concerning some of them. The brothers Abraham and Samuel Avengalel were sent by Pedro III and Alfonso III on missions to Granada and Morocco. Already in 1276 James I had, upon the request of the king of Tunis, given Abraham Avengalel, who was a resident of Valencia, an *operatorium* in that city.—Régne, no. 654; Miret, *Itinerari*, p. 531. Abraham utilized his diplomatic journeys also for business purposes. When his merchandise was impounded by the Castilian authorities, Pedro III retaliated, in 1280, by impounding the goods of Castilian merchants.—Régné, no. 810. In 1286 both brothers went on a mission to Morocco. The preparations for this journey were made in Majorca.—Régné, nos. 1514, 1701; L. Klüpfel, *Die äussere Politik Alfonsos III. von Aragonien* (Berlin, 1911/12), 107. On p. 168 of this work are given the instructions which Abraham Avengalel carried with him on this mission to the king of Morocco. In 1291 Abraham was sent by James II to the king of Tlemcen. On this trip the Jewish diplomat took his family along with him.—*MHE*, III, 451 f. He is identical, apparently, with the "don Abrahem aben Gilel" who in 1294 was in the service of Sancho IV of Castile.—See Baer II, p. 91, note 2.

A certain Abraham aben Nahmias (Abenamias) was in 1290–92 sent by the king of Aragon on a mission to Granada. His instructions are given in Klüpfel, p. 164 f.; Régné, no. 2386. In 1291 he was appointed by James II of Aragon as his secretary for Arabic correspondence ("scriptor noster arabicus et turcimanus").—Finke, *Acta Aragonensia,* I, p. LIX; Régné, no. 2387. He died in Granada in 1292, and the king of Aragon asked the emir of Granada to send him the effects of the deceased.—*BAH,* LXXIV, 526. See also the information given in Baer I, no. 144, and the note thereto concerning Judah aben Hacen (aben Facen). The instructions which Judah received in preparation for a diplomatic mission to Granada are printed in Klüpfel, p. 162. All these men were, apparently, residents of Valencia. Cf. also A. Gimenez Soler, *La Corona de Aragon y Granada* (Barcelona, 1908), 24, 333 f.; *Los documentos árabes diplomáticos del ACA,* ed. M. A. Alarcón y Santón y R. Garcia de Linares (Madrid, 1940), 15; J. Vernet in *Sefarad,* XII (1952), 125 f.; Ch. E. Dufourcq, "Nouveaux documents sur la politique africaine de la couronne d'Aragon," in *Analecta Sacra Tarraconensia,* XXVI (1953), 291 f.; D. Romano, "Los hermanos Abenmenasse al servicio de Pedro el Grande de Aragon," in *Homenaje a Millás-Vallicrosa* II (Barcelona, 1956), 243 f.

50. Martinez Ferrando, nos. 772, 784, 1512; Régné, no. 755. Cf. *Responsa* of R. Solomon ibn Adret, VI (Warsaw, 1868), no. 224, "Reuben was sent by the king on a mission from the kingdom of Murcia to the king of Tlemcen to serve as interpreter to the knights."

51. Cf. the following documents, digested by Régné, which bear, in the original, the signature or authorization of Joseph Ravaya: no. 819, "P. Marchesii ex parte Juceffi"; no. 845, "Juceffus mandavit"; nos. 866, 868, signed "Jucefus," "Jucefus Ravaya." See also Baer I, nos. 118, 121. Joseph also signed an order to the bailiff of Saragossa directing him to investigate the charges against Moses ben Solomon Alconstantini and Meir aben Eleazar, who were accused of having assaulted Yom Tob Asbili.—Régné, no. 841; see chapter V, note 33.

52. Régné, nos. 689, 695, 696; Wieruszowski, *op. cit.* pp. 245, 256.

53. See my *Aragonien,* p. 37.

54. See my article, "The Forged Midrashim of Raymond Martini" (Hebrew), in *Studies in Memory of (Sefer Zikkaron) Asher Gulak and Samuel Klein* (Jerusalem, 1942). Cf. also note 82, this chapter, below. See also Saul Lieberman in *Historia Judaica,* V (New York, 1943), 78 f., and A. Diez Macho in *Sefarad,* IX (Madrid, 1949), 165 f.

55. Régné, nos. 723, 731–36, 746–48; Baer I, no. 117; Wieruszowski, 245, 256 f.

56. See the letter of R. Solomon ibn Adret published in *JQR,* o.s., VIII (1896), 228 f.; Baer I, no. 116.

57. See the articles of Fr. Carreras y Candi, published in *BABL,* III, and in his book *Miscelanea historica catalana* II. (Bibliographical reference in Baer I, p. 1082)

58. Régné, nos. 781, 787, 788, 790, 791, 794, 799, 801, 802, 803, 805; Wieruszowski, 251.

59. Joseph Ravaya is called by Finke, in *Acta Aragonensia,* I. p. lx f., "Leiter der Rechnungswesens unter Pedro III," on the basis, apparently, of the documents cited above and below. The signature "Jucef Ravaya" appears in Régné, nos. 802, 803, 807, the last dealing with the appointment of Vives aben Vives "pro custode in opere regalis nostri Valentiae," *i.e.,* supervisor over the construction of fortifications around the royal

palace in Valencia. His signature also appears on orders dealing with the shipment of arms to Balaguer.—*BABL*, III, 138, 174. See also Baer I, 118–120.

I add herewith further data from the notes which I made in the course of my work in the Archivo general de la Corona de Aragon in Barcelona: 1. Joseph signed an order addressed to the judge of Morella, directing him to convoke a *curia* if the *comendator* of Cervera should fail to call one (ACA, Reg. 48, fol. 1 v.). 2. Joseph's signature appears on a document in which the king writes to the countess of Ampurias, "Noveritis nos vidisse quasdam litteras fidelis baiuli nostri Astruch Ravaya, per quas intelleximus negocium et tractatum inter vos et ipsum Astruch et Bng. de Toroella habitum super vicecomitatu de Bas." The king confirms the contract (May 4, 1280—*ibid.*, fol. 11). 3. The signature, "Juceffus Ravaylla," also appears on an order from Pedro III to the king of Majorca summoning his aid against the count of Foix (ACA, Reg. 48, fol. 51v), and on a letter of warning to the count of Urgel, requesting that the latter return to the king certain fortresses (*castra*) which he received in fief from the king (*ibid.*, fol. 86), and on similar royal orders. 4. A warrant of appointment for a judge in Egea also bears his signature (Reg. 48, fol. 177 v.). These documents prove that Joseph Ravaya's jurisdiction was wider than that of a financial agent or of a supervisor over the collection of taxes. However, he cannot properly be designated as *cancellarius* either. In all the aforecited instances he signs the document as the official who has jurisdiction over the matter dealt with in the particular document. The matters under his jurisdiction, however, appear to change from month to month. He himself, in fact, sometimes signs the warrants of his new appointments. Other Jewish officials are found doing the same thing. Thus, Aaron ibn Yahia (Abinafia) signs an order which directs him to establish a settlement in a certain locality (whose name I was unable to make out). "Quatenus in . . . populetis seu edificetis ad utilitatem nostram quandam populationem, nos enim condiciones seu pacta, que inita fuerint inter vos et populatores eiusdem loci confirmabimus" (ACA, Reg. 48, fol. 2). A related document is found on fol. 62 of the same Register.

60. Baer I, no. 121; Régné, nos. 819, 826, 827. Cf. in Régné also the other decrees issued by Pedro III about the same time (summer, 1280).

61. In addition to the works already mentioned, consult J. Carini, *Gli archivi e le biblioteche di Spagna,* II (Palermo, 1884). See Baer I, p. 1082.

62. Régné, nos. 888, 900, 933 *et seq.;* no. 981 *et seq.*

63. Carini, *De rebus regni Siciliae, Documenti inediti estratti dell' archivio della Corona de Aragona* (Palermo, 1882) contains a number of documents dealing with Joseph Ravaya's activities in Sicily. In no. 27 he is called "fidelis baiulus noster"; in no. 29 "thesaurarius nostre camere"; no. 245 speaks of him as "dilectus consiliarius familiaris et fidelis noster ac camere nostre thesaurarius." We have information only concerning Joseph's fiscal responsibilities during the Sicilian campaign. In no. 302, dated December 30, 1282, he is referred to for the first time as deceased. Other Jews were also summoned by the king to Sicily, among them Judah aben Vives (Régné, no. 1022) and Samuel Alfaquim (Régné, no. 1020, if exact; cf. Martínez Ferrando no. 1665).

64. Baer I, no. 122. Cf. also the excerpt from the Hebrew ledger of a

Jewish tax collector which I publish there. A directive to Moses Ravaya, giving him instructions regarding the farming of the taxes of Catalonia, was dispatched by the king from Messina, Sicily, on November 6, 1282.— Carini, *De rebus regni Siciliae*, p. 161.

65. Régné, nos. 1025, 1029, 1045, 1050. At the same time, however, Don Alfonso took steps to prevent attacks against the Jews on Good Friday and Easter Sunday.—Régné, no. 1034 *et seq.; Wieruszowski, p. 256.

66. Martínez Ferrando nos. 1285, 1504, 1766, *et al.* (see Index); Régné, no. 908.

67. That the property of Joseph Ravaya was impounded, at least temporarily, after his death, appears from Régné, nos. 1168, 1486, and other documents, while it is evident from the same sources that the king extended his patronage to the widow of the deceased official. For the removal of Moses Ravaya from his position see Carreras in *BABL*, III, 286. However, Carreras' statements are not altogether clear nor are they fully substantiated. Moses Ravaya participated for at least another two years in the administration of the state finances. According to Klüpfel (*op. cit.*, pp. 42, 161) he was still in the royal service early in the reign of Alfonso III. Nevertheless, a fundamental change did take place in 1283. In place of the various Jewish officials there now appears as auditor of the state finances the first Christian official of the burgher class, Bn. Scriva, concerning whom interesting information is to be found in the Introduction of Finke's *Acta Aragonensia*, I. Carreras claims that misdemeanors committed by regional tax collectors, among them Jews, prompted this change. However, the evidence which he cites is not convincing. While there undoubtedly were Jewish officials whose conduct was not entirely above reproach, it is clear that these administrative changes reflect a fundamental shift of policy. Carini offers some details concerning the removal of Jewish officials from their positions. See also Régné, no. 1120.

Several responsa of R. Solomon ibn Adret, in which the dismissal of a Jewish official (*gizbar*, usually the equivalent of the Latin *baiulus*, bailiff) is mentioned, relate, apparently, to the events of this period in Aragon:

1. Vol. I, no. 915—"Reuben and Simon both had property adjoining a certain garden. Reuben's property adjoined the garden along most of its periphery, whereas Simon's touched only a small portion of it. Simon went and bought the garden four years ago. At that time Simon's father was a royal bailiff, highhanded in his actions, and Simon himself, whenever his father went out of the country, exercised the prerogatives of bailiff in his father's name. The father has recently been removed from office, and now Reuben has summoned Simon to court demanding that Simon sell him a portion of the garden. Reuben bases his demand upon his right of preemption due to contiguity, and he claims that he failed to exercise this right and to buy a portion of the garden when it was for sale only out of fear of Simon and of Simon's father who was then bailiff, and he, Reuben, was afraid that he would create trouble for him with the crown, for he once despoiled two men by pressing false charges against them until they agreed to sell their property to him cheaply."

2. Vol. I, no. 941.—Simon's son in making a claim against Reuben's son states, "Your father was an official and a favorite of the king, and as such he was like an extortioner who does not establish a presumption of ownership by prolonged uncontested occupancy." Ibn Adret in his reply

says, "The argument of Simon's son, based on the fact that Reuben's father was a royal official, has no validity . . . for the Jewish official does not have lifelong tenure or arbitrary power like a king . . . and particularly in this case where Reuben was removed from office during Simon's lifetime."

3. Vol. I, no. 1159.—"Reuben was the king's bailiff, but in the end the king arrested and executed him and seized all his property. After the execution, a new king ascended the throne, and Reuben's son, Simon, entered the service of the new king and found favor in his eyes. The king returned his father's house to him and he occupied it for some years. Simon then went on a journey to another country and was killed. When news thereof reached the king he seized that house. Some time later, Reuben, son of the said Simon, deeded half the house to Samuel, son of Jacob." Ibn Adret states in his reply, "I do not wish to take a position with regard to the question whether the property of those who are executed by the kings of the Gentiles is rightfully the king's or not." I found no record, among all the Aragonese documents that I examined, of the execution of a Jewish official. Such executions did take place in Castile in 1280. But there is nothing in the words of Ibn Adret to indicate that the events referred to took place outside his own country, although there was good reason for mentioning such a fact.

The following responsa are also illuminating in this connection: Vol. I, no. 612.—"The government has a Jewish official who receives one-tenth of all the fines collected in the city." Vol. V, no. 270.—"The king had a Jewish bailiff in 'Babylon' . . . and the said bailiff is not subject to taxation in 'Babylon' nor to any of their ordinances (*takkanot*), because he was expressly exempted from their ordinances." Now Reuben claims "that the debt which the bailiff owes him remained uncollected because the bailiff is a powerful man and he could not collect from him." See also chapter VI, note 29, for Ibn Adret's attitude toward this type of official.

68. The constitutional changes which took place in the kingdom of Aragon in 1283 are well known. [See R. B. Merriman, *The Rise of the Spanish Empire*, I (New York, 1918), 434 f.] For their relevance to the Jews see my *Aragonien*, p. 180; *CDIA*, VIII, 166 f.; *Cortes de Cataluña*, I, 145 f.; Régné, nos. 1097, 1098, 1100–1103, 1133, 1169, 1185, 1232, 1402. For the Jewish oath see my *Aragonien* p. 80, note, and Klüpfel, *Verwaltungsgeschichte*, p. 130.

69. For Muça de Portella's activities in the last years of his life see Klüpfel, pp. 9, 39 f., 100 f.; Carini, II, 92, 102, 105, 118, 120, 127, 148 f.; *EUC*, IX, 167 f.; Régné, nos. 1129, 1134, 1135, 1175, 1208, 1389, 1406. ACA, Reg. 58. fol. 22 (the original of Régné, no. 1343), "Bernardo Scribe. Mandamus vobis, quatenus donetis fideli nostro Samueli, regis Castelle medico, vestes idoneas," is signed, "Muça," and similarly in letters on behalf of David Mascaran and others. Cf. Régné, nos. 1433, 1487, 1525, 1653, 1654, 1660, 1691, 1811, 1923. For Ibn Adret's relationship to "the exalted Don Muça" see *Responsa*, vol. V, no. 95. For his assassination see Klüpfel, p. 40. The last mention of him alive is of early November 1286, in Régné, no. 1690. For his brother Ishmael see Baer I, no. 153; Régné, no. 1691.

70. Upon complaint by the local Jews, Pedro III wrote to his *vicarius* and *baiulus* in Barcelona ordering them to restrain the Dominicans and others from investigating the Jews "super eo videlicet quod sustinuerunt judeos

aliquos qui facti essent christiani vel recolligerunt eos in domibus eorum ac aliud auxilium prestiterunt eisdem." Régné, no. 1206, Wieruszowski, p. 257. For other steps taken by Pedro III in defense of the Jews see Régné, nos. 1101 (Wieruszowski, pp. 254–5), 1309, 1310, 1336, 1408, 1430. For matters involving the Jews of Gerona see Régné, nos. 1390, 1394, 1407, 1468, 1469, 1470; also my *Aragonien*, p. 159, note 60.

71. For the predatory taxation of Pedro's last days see Baer I, nos. 126, 128, 129; Régné, nos. 1077, 1116, 1163, 1254, 1255, 1256, 1266, 1267, 1268, 1277–1282, 1292, 1293, 1294, 1339, 1340, 1341, 1362–1379, et passim.

72. Régné, nos. 1252, 1337, 1382.

73. Régné, no. 1278.

74. For David Mascaran see Régné, nos. 459, 464, 508, 574, 909, 1155, 1350, 1433, 1441, 1464, 1465, 1488, 1507, 1508, 1515, 1849. Documents bearing his signature are Régné, nos. 1433–1440. For his assassination in 1290 see Régné, nos. 2248, 2455.

75. See the decrees abolishing the use of the tax "coffers" (*arcae*), and also those offering other forms of relief to the Jewish communities weighed down by poverty and burdensome taxation, in Régné, nos. 1506, 1550, 1562, 1568, 1580 *et seq.*, 1711, 1788, 1868 *et seq.*, 1951, 2100 *et seq.*, 2203 *et seq.* The tax coffers (חיבות) are also mentioned in the *Responsa* of Ibn Adret IV, nos. 312, 313; V, no. 277. Several responsa of Ibn Adret, dealing with the recovery by Jewish communities of interest paid by them to Christian creditors, must also be assigned to these years. See vol. III, no. 416, "The *kahal* appointed men to demand and recover from the Gentile creditors of the *kahal* the interest which they were ordered by the king and the Pope to return," and also nos. 316, 405, and 415, where Ibn Adret concludes, "I have been asked the same question by other Aragonese communities." This order is, in my opinion, unique and without equal in the history of the Middle Ages. I have not found the text of the papal order anywhere. The king's concern with the burden upon the communities of the interest which they had to pay on the loans they made is revealed in Régné, nos. 1711 *et seq.*, 1788 *et seq.*, 2002.

76. For the decisions made by Alfonso III in 1286 and in 1289 see my *Aragonien*, p. 181 f.; Klüpfel, p. 106; Régné, nos. 2034, 2043, 2163, 2275.

77. For the taxes of the Jews of Castile see primarily Baer II, nos. 87, 96, 98. For Aragon see my *Aragonien*, p. 129 f.; Baer I, nos. 103, 108. I arrived at the ratio of 22% through computation based upon the data found in the tax ledger of the province of Aragon for the year 1294, published in *CDIA*, vol. 39. It is safe to assume that in Catalonia the taxes of the Jews accounted for an even larger percentage of the total revenues of the crown.

78. The reader will find the evidence for most of the statements made here in the other parts of this work.

79. See the references to converts in Ibn Adret's *Responsa* above, in note 41. Consult also Adret I, nos. 315, 661; III, 352; V, 66; VIII (*Teshubot ha-RaShBA ha-meyuhasot le-ha-RaMBaN*), no. 142. Material dealing with the ownership of slaves by the Jews of Spain, culled from the responsa, is presented by Simha Assaf in his article, "Slavery and the Slave Trade among the Jews in the Middle Ages" (Hebrew), in *Zion*, IV, 91–125, reprinted in his *B'Oholei Ya'acov* (Jerusalem, 1943), 223–256. Instances of the judaization of slaves are recorded in the *Responsa* of Rabbi Solomon ibn Adret. See vol. I, nos. 99, 328, 329. In Adret, III, nos.

191, 192, we read, "Leah, in her last bequest, made as she was dying, distributed all her property, with the exception of a Moslem slave girl which she had." "Leah directed that should the Moslem girl accept Judaism she would gain her freedom. Should she refuse to accept Judaism, yet wish to be set free, she may purchase her freedom for two hundred *solidi*. . . . The slave refused to be judaized, paid two hundred *solidi* to Reuben (Leah's brother and executor of her estate), and was manumitted."

Adret, IV, 139, tells of an incident in Tortosa: "The supervisor of the public oven had a Moslem woman in his employ and she accepted Judaism. It was then charged that he had caused her conversion. . . . I find no validity in any of his arguments, but the community ought to lighten his share of that which they undertook to pay to the lord of the land in order that the proselyte be permitted to remain in the Jewish faith." It appears from the foregoing that the proselytization of slaves in Catalonia at this time was already fraught with difficulties. In the kingdom of Aragon as a whole, with the exception of Majorca, the ownership and conversion of slaves ceased to be a problem after the end of the thirteenth century. (The situation was different in Castile.) For Majorca see Régné, nos. 46, 433, 562, 617, 1479, 1918; and see also chapter VIII below, note 44. Régné, no. 177, tells of a Jew who converted a Saracen slave girl and was exempted by the king from the punishment usual in such cases. A similar incident occurred in Huesca in 1286.—Régné, no. 1543. See also Régné, nos. 1617, 2516, 2528. In 1258 James I gave a Jew of Tortosa the franchise to transport Moslem prisoners of war to Africa for ransom, at a profit to the Jew.—Régné, no. 101. A similar franchise was granted at the time also to a Christian of Genoa and to another of Valencia.—Miret, *Itinerari,* 274. In 1277 Pedro III issued a decree favoring the Jews by providing that the master of any slave seeking baptism should receive compensation.—Régné, no. 687. An ordinance issued by Pedro III in 1285, governing the taxation of the Jews, still assumes the possibility that Jews might own slaves as domestics or for trade.—Baer I, no. 127, paragraph 7 (p. 144). Later tax ordinances no longer mention slaves. Pedro IV of Aragon, in May 1369, forbade the Jews of his realm to buy Tartar slaves since they intend to convert them. See J. Miret y Sans in *Revue Hispanique,* XLI (1917), 22. Two months later he reversed himself, and in July of the same year he permitted the Jews of Barcelona and of Majorca to purchase Tartar and Turkish slaves, provided they did not seek to convert them.—Fita-Llabrés, "Privilegios de los Hebreos mallorquines en el códice Pueyo," no. 85, in *BAH,* XXXVI (1900); Baer I, p. 546. However, this privilege was of practical benefit only to a small number of rich Jews, principally Majorcan. In Castile, the judaization of non-Christian slaves was already forbidden by the thirteenth century code of Alfonso X, *Las Siete Partidas,* partida VII, titulo 24, ley 10 (Baer II, p. 48). But this law remained unenforced for a long time. Only in 1380 were such conversions effectively prohibited by Juan I.—Baer II, no. 227.

Ch. Verlinden's study, "L'esclavage dans le monde ibérique médiéval," in *Anuario,* XI (1934–5), does not contain anything relevant to our problem. The work of J. M. Ramos y Loscertales, *El cautiverio en la Corona de Aragon durante los siglos XIII, XIV, y XV* (Zaragoza, 1915), does not, to the best of my recollection, contain any material pertaining to the Jews. The article of J. Miret y Sans, "La esclavitud en Cataluña en los últimos tiempos de la Edad Media," in *Revue Hispanique*, XLI (1917), in which a vast amount of material is assembled, cites only four instances of slaves in Jewish hands in Catalonia in the years 1252-1276, and one instance, from the year 1452, of a Moslem slave, owned by a Jew of Tortosa. In the study by J. Segura—in *Jochs Florals* (Barcelona, 1885)—based upon the records of the village of Santa Coloma de Queralt, I found among numerous instances of slavery, covering about fifteen pages, only one case of a slave passing into Jewish hands (p. 150).

In general we can say that Jewish ownership of slaves was a problem only in the periods of active warfare during the Reconquest and in later times only in the large commercial centers. There is no evidence of a slave trade carried on by Jews. A Jew occasionally buys a slave for domestic service, as the Christians frequently do, and he sometimes sells a slave whose services he no longer needs; but such instances do not add up to a slave trade. After the Reconquest the ordinary Jewish household had no slaves. In Castile we find slaves appearing principally in the homes of the Jewish notables of Toledo, and the reader will find the subject treated in several places in this work. I found one reference—in a fourteenth century document emanating from Portugal—to the sale and transfer of a slave by Jews from Seville to Lisbon in 1368. See P. A. d'Azevedo, "Os escravos," in *Archivo Historico Portuguez*, I, p. 299, no. 1.

Converts to Judaism (*gerim*) are mentioned in the *Responsa* of R. Asher ben Yehiel, XV, 1, 3, 4. In the *Responsa* of Ibn Adret, I found only one such reference, in VIII, no. 69. In the responsa of the later Catalonian Rabbis there is no mention of the matter at all, and certain inferences may be drawn therefrom. The Inquisition, already greatly dreaded in Aragon, no doubt moved the Jews to exercise strict caution. Cf. chapter VIII, note 16, below, for the activities of the Inquisition in Aragon during this period. Yet the treatment of this subject by Bahye ben Asher in his ethical encyclopedia, *Kad ha-Kemah, s.v.* "Ger," would seem to suggest that the question of proselytism was a living and vital problem in his time in his locality. He deems the acceptance of converts by the Jews inadvisable. Similar as well as contrary sentiments are also expressed in the *Zohar*. See *e.g.*, *Zohar* I, 95 f.; II, 95 f.

80. Baer II, p. 139 f. Cf. chapter III, note 43.

81. Ramón Lull, *Libre del gentil e dels tres savis*, in *OBRAS*, ed. Rossello (1896), I, pp. 64 f., 93 f., 103, 118; M. Menendez Pelayo, *Origines de la novela*, I (Madrid, 1925), p. 74. Ramon Lull (Raymond Lully) devoted most of his life to the propagation of Christianity, and in his later writings clearly advocates the use of religious repression against the Jew as well as against adherents of other faiths. In this connection see B. Altaner, "Glaubenszwang u. Glaubensfreiheit bei R. L.," in *Histor. Jahrbuch* for 1928. Cf. also O. Keicher, "R. L. u. seine Stellung zur arab. Philosophie," in *Beitr. z. Gesch. d. Philosophie des Mittelalters*, 1909, pp. 32 f., 90 f., 144 f., 341, 344. It is evident from Ramón Lull's treatment of the question of resurrection among the Jews that he was aware of the controversy which raged around the teachings of Maimonides. Ramón Lull's attitude toward Judaism deserves a special study, but the necessary books are not available here in Jerusalem. For the patent granted by James II to Lull on October 30, 1299, authorizing him to preach to the Jews, see Régné, no. 2719. See also *El "Liber predicationis contra Judeos" de Ramón Lull*, edited with introduction and notes by J. M. Millás Vallicrosa (Madrid-

Barcelona, 1957). On p. 21 Millás reports: "En el inventario (21 febr. 1526) de Mn. Joan Bonllavi . . . el primer editor de la obra *Blanquerna* (Valencia 1521), se registraba una obra, en catalán, desconocida al parecer, con este incipit: 'Als savis jueus de Barcelona, Mestre Abram Denanet e Mestre Aron i Mestre Bon Jue Salamon i altres savis que son en la aljama, Ramón Llull, salut.' " Millás correctly points out that instead of "Denanet" the reading should be "Ben Adret" or "Den Adret." The three Jewish scholars to whom the Christian mystic addressed himself were, most certainly, R. Solomon ibn Adret, R. Aaron Halevi de na Clara, and R. Judah Solomon, all of Barcelona. See about them below, chapter V, note 33, and chapter VI, note 27. It is a pity that the text of Ramón Lull's letter did not survive.

82. For Raymond Martini see this chapter, note 54, above, and the literature cited in my article referred to therein. Martini influenced Arnaldo de Villanova, who was close to the Spirituals whom we will discuss in chapter VI. Cf. note 8 *ibid.*

NOTES TO CHAPTER V

1. Baer II, no. 96. This register, and any similar tax register, cannot in itself serve as a basis for computing the size of the Jewish population. See my remarks in Baer II, p. 88. The tax registers provide data for an estimate of the wealth of the Jews; but there is, of course, no direct relationship between the wealth of the Jews in a community and their number. However, the tax figures, taken in conjunction with available authentic statistical data, can be useful in determining the relative sizes of the various communities, large and small, and fantastic estimates, such as still appear in the modern literature on the subject, may thus be avoided. The reader, I trust, will correctly understand my position. He who is not conversant with the problem of statistics as it applies to the Middle Ages, and does not appreciate how small the population of Europe was in those days, should consult the following volumes in the series *Histoire Générale*, edited by Gustave Glotz: *Histoire du Moyen Age*, vol. IV, part 2: Ch. Petit-Dutaillis, *L'Essor des Etats d'Occident* (Paris, 1937), p. 15 f.; vol. VIII: Henri Pirenne, *La Civilisation Occidentale au Moyen Age* (Paris, 1933), p. 148 f., English translation, *Social and Economic History of Medieval Europe* (London, 1936; New York, n.d.), p. 172 f. My method of estimating the size of the Jewish population will be demonstrated in the notes which follow.

2. M. Kayserling, in his *Die Juden von Toledo* (1900), p. 8, makes some sound comments concerning the number of Jews in Toledo. Abraham Zacuto in his *Sefer Yuhasin* (ed. Filipowski), p. 221, states that R. Abraham ben Nathan of Lunel reports in his work, *Ha-Manhig*, that he saw in Toledo more than twelve thousand Jews. The same notice, in corrupt form, is found in the chronicle of Joseph ibn Sadik in Neubauer's *Mediaeval Jewish Chronicles*, I, 95. Both writers copied the information from an earlier chronicle, now lost. The printed edition of *Ha-Manhig* does not contain this statement. According to the Franciscan Aegidius de Zamora, who wrote late in the reign of Alfonso X, there were in Toledo seventy thousand Jewish taxpayers, not counting women, children and the indigent. See F. Fita in *BAH*, V (1884), 138; *REJ*, IX (1884), 136. Such numbers are obviously unreliable. According to the *Crónicas*

of Pedro Lopez de Ayala, twelve hundred Jews—men, women and children—were killed in Toledo in 1355. These resided in the Jewish quarter called *el Alcana,* which was in the center of the city. The larger quarter, which was surrounded by a wall, was not taken by the rebels. See *Tarbiz,* V (1934), 236. It does not seem likely that so large a group of Jews had their permanent residence in the Christian part of the city, and it would be unreasonable to assume that these Jews gathered in the Alcana in wartime rather than seek refuge within the fortified quarter. According to Menahem ben Zerah, about eight thousand Jews, of all ages, perished in Toledo in 1368, when the city was besieged by the forces of Henry of Trastamara (Neubauer, *op. cit.,* II, 244). Samuel Çarça gives the number as "more than ten thousand" (Graetz, VII, 372). I would oppose to these estimates some more realistic considerations. The Jewish community of Avila had at the end of the thirteenth century about fifty families, perhaps a few more.—See note 5, below. This community paid, according to the tax roll for 1290, a stated annual tax of 59,592 *maravedis* (Baer II, p. 81). The community of Toledo, where the Jewish magnates of the realm lived, paid—together with the smaller aljamas in its district— 216,505 *maravedis (ibid.), i.e.,* nearly four times as much. Now, it seems to me, that the ratio of the populations of the two communities could not exceed the ratio of their respective tax payments. This comparative method, which can provide us with statistics more reliable than those found in the estimates of the aforementioned authors, is the one which I intend to use. I also wish to make it clear that the numbers given here and on the following pages are of families, not of souls. We have no way of determining the average number of children and servants per household, or the number of the needy—they must have been numerous—who were supported by communal funds and by the tax-paying members of the community. One cannot apply to the solution of these problems methods used elsewhere, where circumstances were different, especially since the situation in Spain itself varied from place to place and changed with the times.

3. For the decline in the population of Seville see R. Carande in *Anuario,* II (1925), 249. For the decline of the population of the country as a whole see *ibid.,* p. 267. Consult also the index to Baer II, *s. v.* "Sevilla." For exaggerated statements concerning the size of the Jewish community of Seville in 1391 see Baer II, p. 233. For Jerez de la Frontera see Baer II, no. 76. The tax burden of all the Jews of the Frontera (virtually identical with Andalusia) amounted in 1290 to 191,898 *maravedis* (Baer II, p. 81), which was less than the sum paid by Toledo together with the rural communities attached to it. Seville contributed the greater part of this levy, and Jerez only 5,000 *maravedis* (Baer II, p. 92).

4. Baer II, p. 91.

5. The tax of the aljama of Burgos amounted in 1291 to 87,760 *maravedis* (Baer II, no. 96, p. 82). The composition of the aljama of Avila can be studied in greater detail. Judged by the amount of her tax, as given in the same document, she would rank third among the communities of Old and New Castile, following Toledo and Burgos. A register of the houses standing on land belonging to the local cathedral, compiled in 1303, contains the names of about forty Jewish householders.—Baer II, no. 117. The full register is published in the quarterly *Cuadernos de Historia de España,* XII (Buenos Aires, 1949), 151 f. On the basis of the other sources cited in my note to the above document (no. 117) we can name another

ten families. There is no ground for assuming that many Jews lived in other parts of the city, outside the holdings of the cathedral. For the economic structure of this community see note 12, below. For Segovia, it is possible to extract from similar registers for the year 1389-90, which Fita published in *BAH*, IX (1886), 344 f., the names of fifty-five Jewish householders. It is safe to assume that the situation in Segovia was substantially the same as in Avila, and that its aljama experienced little change in the course of the fourteenth century. The prayer of R. Jacob Gikatilia is cited by Gershom Scholem in *Mada'ey ha-Yahadut*, II (Jerusalem, 1926), 225. R. Jacob was, according to a prevalent tradition, born in Soria, and he was buried in Segovia shortly before 1270. A population of sixty-five families seems reasonable for a large community, situated in the area between Toledo and Burgos. Consult Rabal's *Soria* (1889), p. 204, for the Christians residing at the foot of the citadel in Soria. For the size of the Jewish populations of Sahagun, Palencia and Villadiego see Baer II, nos. 31, 37, 50. In the light of these statistics the statement of Samuel Çarça (Baer II, no. 209) that there were two hundred Jewish families in Briviesca in 1366 is open to doubt. To this day Briviesca remains a very small town. There is no information available at the present time on the size and composition of the Jewish community of Guadalajara during this period. According to Baer II, no. 282, 122 Jews were there converted to Christianity in 1414. Such a number is in line with the conclusions arrived at in this discussion. This document was published from the original manuscript by J. E. Martinez Ferrando in *Analecta Sacra Tarraconensia*, XXVI (1953), 70. Peñafiel, a mere village, had a very small Jewish population. See chapter III, note 32. According to Zacuto, *Sefer Yuhasin* (ed. Filipowski), p. 224, R. Joseph Gikatilia the cabalist, was buried there. The ordinances of the local Christian municipality, drawn up by Don Juan Manuel, mention the house of Don Çag, who is none other than Isaac ibn Wakar (chapter III above, note 41). See A. Gimenez Soler, *Don Juan Manuel*, p. 669.

6. Tudela in 1391 had ninety Jewish taxpayers.—Baer I, p. 977. The community was hard hit by the persecutions of 1328 and continued to suffer from the economic decline of the fourteenth century. One cannot, therefore, say with certainty whether this number is applicable also to the earlier period. Compare *ibid.* the statistics for the other Navarrese communities for the year 1391. Pamplona, according to this list, had fifty-eight taxpayers and Estella fourteen. In 1367 there were sixty houses occupied by Jews in Pamplona, and the situation appears to have been the same in 1328.—See Baer I, p. 973 and my note *ad locum*. In 1265 there were twenty-nine houses in Estella occupied by Jews (Baer I, p. 941 f.), but a few years later, in a document of 1279, we already find evidence of a decline.—Baer I, p. 947.

7. For the data pertaining to Aragon see my *Aragonien*, p. 128 f. For taxes paid by the Aragonese aljamas see principally Baer I, no. 108; *CDIA*, vol. 39. I quote here a few statistics that are well authenticated. Manuel Serrano y Sanz, in his *Origenes de la dominación española en América* (Madrid, 1918), p. 10, estimates, on the basis of fifteenth century material which he studied, that there were in Saragossa two hundred Jewish families. In the tax ordinance of the aljama of Saragossa for 1331 —published by Serrano in the periodical *Erudición Ibero-Ultramarina* (Madrid, 1930), and again, with philological notes, by Gunnar Tilander

in *Studia Neophilologica*, XII (Uppsala, 1939/40)—it is stated near the end of the document that in case of necessity a surtax, in the form of a poll-tax, may be imposed upon 100 to 150 members of the community.

In Huesca, "the majority of the *kahal*, about one hundred and fifty people," agreed upon the appointment of a cantor, and only a minority of ten was opposed (Adret, I, 300). According to the tax ordinance of that community for 1340, a poll-tax was imposed upon every male Jew, fifteen years old and over, according to the following schedule (Baer I, no. 210); eighty taxpayers—20 *sueldos* each, eighty others—10 *sueldos* each, and the rest—5 *sueldos* each. The *adelantados* of the *kahal* were permitted to choose fifty men whose property did not exceed 50 sueldos in value, and to exempt them from the payment of the poll-tax. Likewise exempted were the men "who study day and night and have no other occupation," and also beggars and servants. The communal officials were also empowered to exempt, according to their judgment, other needy persons, up to a total exemption of 200 *sueldos*. On the basis of these data it is safe to estimate that in Huesca there were about three hundred males, aged fifteen years and above, entered in the poll-tax rolls. This number would represent approximately two hundred families. We do not know how many there were who made study their sole occupation. Scholars were found on all economic levels. There were not many wealthy people, but the number of professional beggars must not be exaggerated. The Jewish community of Huesca must, therefore, have numbered between a thousand and fifteen hundred souls, no more. The same situation obtained in most of the Jewish communities of Spain.

Calatayud, one of the larger communities in the province of Aragon, is discussed in my *Aragonien*, p. 147. Its Jewish quarter was large, and spread over so wide an area, "that many of the residents of the streets far removed from the synagogue attended communal worship only on the Sabbaths and the Festivals."—See *Responsa* of R. Isaac Perfet, no. 331. One must, however, take care not to exaggerate the number of Jews in Calatayud on the basis of this statement. Medieval man's conception of distance was different from ours. According to Klüpfel's *Verwaltungsgeschichte*, p. 137, Calatayud had at this time a population of 7,500. The size of the Jewish population should be estimated correspondingly.

Of special interest is the information available concerning the Jewish community of Alcañiz. Early in the fourteenth century thirty Jewish families settled there under the jurisdiction of the order of Calatrava. Near the end of the fourteenth century a number of Jewish families, scattered in the surrounding villages, were attached to this small aljama. The original community had not grown any larger, its possibilities for growth apparently limited by the terms of the agreement between the king and the Order.—See Baer I, no. 340. In the *Responsa* of R. Isaac Perfet, no. 405, there is some information on the topography of the city.

8. For Barcelona see the beginning of Chapter I above, and below, Chapter VIII. For the bases for the estimates of two hundred families in Barcelona and of one hundred families in Lerida see below, Chapter IX, notes 20, 22. For Perpignan, see my *Aragonien*, p. 142 f. Cf. also Richard W. Emery, *The Jews of Perpignan in the Thirteenth Century* (New York, 1959), Chapter I. For Gerona we have no statistics. The following statistics are available for some of the smaller communities of Catalonia:

Santa Coloma de Queralt—7 families in 1328, 30 families in 1347; Vich—15 families in 1277, 10 families in 1318; Manresa—16 families in 1342; Fraga—40 families at the end of the fourteenth century. The sources of the above information are found in the books and articles listed in the bibliography at the end of Baer I, pp. 1083–1086.

9. I derived the number of Jews in the city of Valencia from the tax rolls published by J. Millás in his article, "Un manuscrit hebraic-valencià," printed in *Buttletí de la Biblioteca de Catalunya*, VI, 1920–1922 (Barcelona, 1923), pp. 341–357. For Murviedro see *Aragonien*, p. 153. A register dated 1348 lists the names of forty-seven householders who appear to have constituted the better part of the community. See Antonio Chabret, *Sagunto (Murviedro), su historia y sus monumentos* (Barcelona, 1888), II, 429.

10. See my account of the aljama of Majorca during its most flourishing period, the latter part of the fourteenth century, in Chapter VIII.

11. Light is shed on the social-economic structure of the Jewish community of Toledo by certain Arabic documents, as I pointed out in *Tarbiz*, V (1934). Add thereto Baer II, nos. 262, 390. We will also show later how the Hebrew poetry of this period reflects social conditions. For Jewish cloth merchants in Castile who sold their fabrics in shops see the index to Baer II, p. 590, *s.v.* "Handel"; *Responsa* of R. Asher, *kelal* 78, responsum 2. *Kelalim* (groups) 88 and 89 of R. Asher's *Responsa* contain references to other commercial enterprises. See especially *kelal* 88, resp. 6, for the purchase of scarlet cloth, silk and garments for sale in a shop; *kelal* 89, resp. 11, for the manufacture and retail sale of pack-saddles; *kelal* 104, resp. 2 and 5, for textiles.

12. For the structure of the Jewish community of Avila consult Baer II, nos. 88, 117, and note 5 above. No. 117, which is an excerpt from the property-book of the cathedral chapter of Avila, contains approximately fifty Jewish names. Seventeen of the men named are artisans, three of them blacksmiths. The only rich man seems to have been Don Joseph of Avila. We must add thereto our information concerning the cabalist Moses de Leon and his circle. The names of scholars and preachers of his type are not likely to be found in the ledgers of church chapters. A similar picture unfolds itself in Segovia as one examines the material assembled by Fita in *BAH*, vol. IX (1886).—See note 5, above. Of the fifty-five householders living there, twenty-three are artisans—weavers, shoemakers, tailors, and a few other craftsmen. Only one man stands out above all the others, and he is Don Moses Çarça (the court physician ?). The publication of the complete register of houses in Avila in *Cuadernos de Historia de España* XII (1949)—see note 5, above—makes it possible to add to the extracts from it, given in Baer II, no. 117, the following items: no. 94, La tienda que tiene Don Yague alfayate en que mora e cosen los costureros; no. 95, La tienda en que tiene Don Yague los pannos con una camareta etc.; no. 100, La tienda en que mora Semuel çapatero; no. 115, En la rua de los çapateros ante las casas que fueron de don Yague fijo de donna Adena; no. 120, En la otra tienda y luego mora Y. N., e en la otra que se tiene con ella mora Yunto (*i.e.*, Yomtob) texedor . . . Rinde la que tiene el judio XXX *maravedis* . . .

12a. For Guadalajara see Baer II, nos. 95, 108; cf. also nos. 282, 391, 420. On Ibn Sahula see G. Scholem, *Perakim le-Toldot Sifrut ha Kabbala* ("Studies in the History of Cabalistic Literature," Jerusalem, 1931),

p. 59 f.: see also chapter II, note 40, and chapter VI, note 17. Interesting data on one of the small communities of Castile is found in F. Cantera, "La juderia de Miranda de Ebro," in *Sefarad*, I–II (1941–42); L. Huidobro, "La juderia de Pancorbo," in *Sefarad*, III (1943). A document of 1294 (*Sefarad*, I, 112) tells of a number of Jews of Miranda who went out to work in the fields. A document of 1296 (*ibid.*, 118) names a "don Esias de Burgos" among the royal tax collectors. A text of the year 1312 (p. 130) speaks of six indigent Jewish artisans who pay their taxes through the municipality (*conceio*), and not through the local Jewish community. On pp. 132–140 are some general orders of Alfonso XI, and other valuable material further on.

13. Baer II, no. 86. The extent of Christian participation in the exploitation of the salt mines is made clear by a number of other documents in Toribio Minguella y Arnedo's *Historia de la diócesis de Siguenza* (2 vols., Madrid, 1910–12). For salt mines in Aragon operated by Jews see Régné 2341, 2643.

14. Baer II, no. 313. In my note to this document I cite further information derived from the work of Domingo Hergueta, *Noticias historicas de la ciudad de Haro,* 1916. There are a few more items worth adding here. Particularly interesting is the contract of the year 1403 (*ibid.*, p. 207) which obligates the Jewish community—whose representative is R. Yom Tob—to pay to the local church the "first fruits" of the fields which they own within the "Jewish precinct (termino que se llama de los judios, termino de los judios)." This area lay close to the city, on the right bank of the Ebro river. The Jews owned land also on the other side of the river. Unfortunately, Hergueta's work does not have a map showing the topography of the city and its environs. For the nature of the inhabitants of this town see *ibid.*, pp. 203, 267.

15. See, in addition to the enactments of the Cortes, also Baer II, nos. 151, 174. For contracts of purchase on credit which included an interest charge, see Baer II, no. 177, #4; no. 186, note; no. 299. The discussion which follows herewith is based on the *Responsa* of R. Asher, *kelal* 6, responsa 4 and 10. Responsum 4 deals with the taxation problems of an unnamed Castilian aljama:

> The king imposed a levy of one thousand silver *maravedis,* to be raised in the following manner. Everyone who owns 120 *mrs.* shall pay 8 *mrs.* The difference between the sum so collected and 1,000 *mrs.* shall be paid by those members of the community who own more than 120 *mrs.*, each one contributing according to his wealth. Now there are men against whose names no entry was made in the 8 *maravedi* tax roll, but the notation was made that the assessors did not know the worth of these people and therefore left a blank after their names. Now the assessors of the surtax due from those who own more than 120 *mrs.* taxed them according to their estimation. But these men argue that they do not have to pay this levy, since the first assessors did not tax them and the king has exempted anyone who does not possess 120 *mrs.* . . . The *kahal,* on the other hand, argues that the first assessors did not exempt them but merely indicated that they did not know their financial status. . . . Furthermore, there were only three concerning whom the first assessors wrote that they did not know, whereas the others, whose worth they did know be-

cause they taxed them, were a hundred or more. . . . Also, the royal
order does not exempt those whose wealth the first assessors didn't
know, but only those who haven't any.

The text of the responsum is somewhat corrupt, but it does seem to
mean that a hundred or more men were found by the first group of
assessors to own 120 *mrs.*, and that they were uncertain about three
others. This means that a hundred or more members of the community
owned 120 silver *maravedis* and that there were perhaps ten who owned
a little more. This is a very modest amount and it is difficult to accept
that there were many Jews in this community who did not even possess
this sum. The *maravedi* (*zahuv*) in R. Asher's responsa is a silver *maravedi*, and for 120 silver *maravedis* one could purchase a small wardrobe.
See *e.g.*, Baer II, no. 177. It follows, then, that all the members of the
community were not well-to-do. It may be assumed that most of them
were artisans. For Valdeolivas see the references given in Baer II, no. 240.
The last name on the list referred to is that of Solomon Curiel, a tailor,
whose capital amounted to 100 silver *maravedis*. See also Maria del
Carmen Carlé, "El precio de la vida in Castilla del rey Sabio al Empla-
zado," in *Cuadernos* XV (1951), 132–141.
16. For Talavera in the thirteenth century see *Tarbiz*, V (1934), 236; *Zion*
II (1937), 46. For the same community in the fifteenth century see Baer
II, no. 288, and the interesting material published by Fidel Fita in *BAH*,
II (1882), 309 f. (ref. in Baer II, p. 323, note 4). Regarding Fita's statement about the wealth of the Jews of this community, it must be stressed
that his assumptions do not consider the value of the coinage of that
period. Even the well-to-do people in the community were of decidedly
modest means, and most of the community was far from well-to-do. The
tax-roll does not, of course, list the poor, the scholars and those who
boarded at the tables of the householders.
17. For Jewish artisans in Castile see the index to Baer II, pp. 590–1,
s.v. "Handwerker." Cf. too *Responsa* of R. Asher, *kelal* 8, resp. 18 (ap-
prenticeship to a tailor); *k.* 18, resp. 14 (a blacksmith); *k.* 104, resp. 3
(a tailor); *k.* 89, resp. 12 (a leather worker and tanner). In *Zikhron
Yehuda* (responsa of R. Judah ben Asher), no. 50, we read of "a tanner
whose wife assists him at home." Note also the situation described by
R. Asher in his *Responsa, kelal* 43, resp. 7: "It happens here that a worthless scamp among the artisans will marry a woman here today and then
become enamored of another and go and marry her elsewhere and return
brazenly to his home town." Consult also the information assembled in
the last chapter of this work concerning Marrano artisans. As a general
statement one would have to say that the Jews in Castile—and also in
many places in Aragon—could be found engaging in all the handicrafts,
the light ones and the heavy ones. They served a clientele consisting of
both Jews and Christians, of high rank and low. Sometimes these Jewish
artisans were the only practitioners of their particular craft in their locality. See, for example, the case of the Jewish braziers (*latoneros*) who in
1403 were commissioned by the bishop and municipality of Burgos to
repair the town well.—Baer II, no. 253, note, p. 239. This occurred during
a period of severe persecution and in a place traditionally hostile to Jews.
Yet Jewish artisans were hired to do this work, apparently because qualified Christian workmen were not available. The charge that the Jews

do not engage in occupations requiring hard labor was made at the time of the Expulsion by a fanatical priest, the historian Andrés Bernáldez, in his *Historia de los reyes católicos,* but it is pure libel. The Jew as a blacksmith (*ferrero*) is mentioned in several documents. See Baer II, index, p. 591. Only masonry seems to have been the monopoly of the Moslems in many places. The artisans among the exiles from Spain were later the mainstay of their communities in Turkey. In the responsa of the rabbis of these communities we find mentioned the same occupations in which the Jews had engaged earlier, while still in Spain. See S. A. Rosanes, *Divrei Yemei Yisrael be-Togarma* (History of the Jews in Turkey), III (Jerusalem, 1938), p. 293 f. Also among the exiles who in 1492 sought refuge in Portugal the handicraftsmen were among those who received special consideration. See chapter XIII, note 98.

18. For Tudela see Baer I, no. 587; for Pamplona, no. 596. The aljama of Pamplona had among its members in the fourteenth century a famous jester (*juglar*). A Jewish jester (*ioculator*) is also mentioned in Régné, no. 2732. There is also a record of one in Sicily, in B. and G. Lagumina, *Codice diplomatico dei Giudei di Sicilia* (Palermo, 1884–95), I, 37, et passim. The tax ledgers are given in Baer I, no. 588. The quotations are from Falaquera's *Ha-Mebakesh* (Josefow, 1881), pp. 10, 13, 15, 16, 20, 23. For the role of the Falaquera family in the communal affairs of Tudela see Baer I, pp. 953, 957, 984, 985. The name of R. Joseph b. Shem Tob ibn Falaquera heads the list of three judges named in 1287 as a court to deal with cases of informing (*malshinut*).—Baer I, p. 593. Another member of this family, Naçan del Gabay (= Nathan Falaquera), rendered valuable service to the crown of Navarre from 1391 on.—Baer I, pp. 980, 996, 997, 1000. For the author of *Ha-Mebakesh* himself see Henry Malter's article, "Shem Tob ben Joseph Palquera, a Thinker and Poet of the thirteenth century," in *JQR*, n.s., I (1910), 151–181; also Habermann's edition of Falaquera's *Iggereth ha-Musar* (Treatise on Ethics) in *Kobez-al-Yad*, n.s., I (1936), 45–90; II (1937), 231–36. One can learn much about the social problems of the time from works such as these, but one must first analyze the Arabic literary sources which served their authors as models. See also M. Plessner, "The Importance of R. Shem Tob ibn Fala-quera to the Study of the History of Philosophy" (Hebrew), in *Homenaje a Millás-Vallicrosa* II (Barcelona, 1956), 161 f.

19. For the workshops (*operatoria*) and stores (*tendae*) devoted to the manufacture and the sale of cloth—some of it imported from France—in Saragossa, Huesca and elsewhere see Régné, nos. 235, 571, 1664, 1936, 1953, 2017, 2054, 2210, 2793, and others. Cf. also Ibn Adret, III, no. 142 (Huesca): "Reuben, Simon, Levi, and Leah opened a store for the sale of cloth in partnership." Other Jewish merchants with stores in Saragossa are mentioned in Adret, III, 135; IV, 125; V, 263. Of special interest is Adret, II, no. 3, where the litigation is over a store selling cloth from Paris and Muret(?). The mention of a *senescal* in this responsum indicates that the incident took place in Navarre, for this title was not in use elsewhere in Spain. For cloth merchants and artisans in Saragossa in the fourteenth century see also chapter VIII, note 49. The Ibn Azfora family was prominent both in the cloth trade and in communal affairs in Saragossa See, for example, Baer I, no. 147. Manuel Serrano, *Origenes,* p. 38, note, describes a contract of partnership between a Christian brass worker (*oripellero*) and a Jewish sheet-metal worker (*batifulla*).

They agree to work together, and each to teach his trade to the other. In a contract dated 1406, a Christian dyer of Saragossa agrees to teach a Jewish rug-weaver the art of dyeing, but reserves for himself the secret of producing certain specified dyes.—*RABM*, vol. 37. There are also extant a number of contracts between master craftsmen and apprentices who seek to learn their trades. For example, in 1386 an adolescent Jew from the village of San Martin in Catalonia apprenticed himself to a Jewish tailor of the village of Verdù. The young man promised to serve the tailor faithfully for one year. The tailor, in turn, undertook to teach the boy his trade and to provide him with board and shoes. Both swore on the Torah. The contract was drawn up in Latin by a Christian notary. —*BAH*, vol. 65 (1914), p. 252. Similar contracts are recorded by Juan Segura y Valls in his article in *Jochs florals de Barcelona* (1885), p. 148. These contracts are drawn up in accordance with the practices prevalent in Barcelona. For further information concerning Jewish artisans in Aragon see Baer I, index p. 1164, *s.v.* "Handwerk"; Serrano, *Orígenes*, passim. Conspicuous in Aragon are Jewish bookbinders, scientists who devise scientific instruments, and gold- and silver-smiths. One of the latter even made the vessels used in Christian ritual. See Baer I, p. 415, top. Cf. also chapter VIII, note 35.

20. Baer I, no. 535. For land owned and cultivated by Jews in Aragon in the second half of the thirteenth century see Régné, nos. 264, 265, 271, 789, 950, 952, 964, 1049, 1078, *et al.* See also Adret, II, 229; III, 148, *et al.* In 1459 the Jews of Borja were accused of bringing home secretly from their fields their produce, their flax and hemp (*fruges, linum et canapum*), as well as their sheep and goats, so as to avoid paying the tithes and "first fruits" due the Church.—*España sagrada*, vol. 49, p. 483 f. In an account of the crown's income for the year 1294 (*CDIA*, vol. 39, p. 222, 252), we find the names of isolated Jews who lived in the villages of Fariza and Rueda. Their livelihood was undoubtedly derived principally from agri-culture. In Rueda (p. 252) most of the population were Moslems and the Jews paid their taxes—with the exception of the land tax—along with them. In Barbastro (*ibid.*, p. 296) the Jews paid two loads of grapes (*dos cargas de vino*) for the services of "the scribal office for Jewish notes" (*escrivania de las cartas de los judios*). This was apparently the office where promissory notes for loans extended by Jews to Christians were written. This would mean that the local Jews, while they engaged in moneylending, also cultivated the vine for a livelihood. See also my *Aragonien*, p. 165.

21. Baer I, no. 210.

21a. The statute of Murviedro is printed in Antonio Chabret, *Sagunto* (*Murviedro*), *su historia y sus monumentos*, II, 408 f. One comes across such statutes frequently in the volumes of registers of the *Archivo general de la Corona de Aragon* in Barcelona, and their like may very well exist in other archives. Cf. also the statute of Saragossa cited in note 7 above, and the statutes of the aljama of Majorca of the year 1315, published in *REJ*, IV (1882), 43 f. The royal tax decrees, however, are of a different character. See Baer I, no. 126 and esp. no. 210, where the principal tax levy is upon loans. These were not, however, a major source of income for the Jews.

22. See Pierre Vidal, "Les Juifs de Roussillon et de Cerdagne," in *REJ*, XV (1887), p. 22.

23. For the Ascandrani family see *REJ*, vol. 68 (1914), pp. 182, 184; Régné, nos. 72, 679, 705, 739, 785, 883. For other Alexandrian Jews with contacts in Aragon see Régné, nos. 443, 2003. For Isaac b. Samuel Cap see REJ, vol. 68, p. 184 f; Régné, nos. 804, 857, 1464, 1496, 1534. For commerce carried on by Jews of Barcelona in Alexandria and elsewhere in the eastern Mediterranean in the beginning of the fourteenth century see Baer I, nos. 158, 212. In chapter VIII I shall deal in greater detail with the marine commerce of the Jews of Barcelona and Majorca. Consult also my *Aragonien*, p. 170 f. See also the interesting document in Baer I, no. 130, and the references in the index to Baer I, p. 1164, *s.v.* "Handel, Seehandel." Régné, no. 577 (Miret, *Itinerari*, p. 492) digests a document dealing with Jews who were detained on board a ship in the harbor of Cartagena. In the reign of Pedro III of Aragon, a Jew in Tunis received half the revenues which accrued to the king from the sale of franchises in the merchants' exchange (*alfondech*) of that city (Régné, no. 1381). Pedro III made it a point to stress that this concession did not carry with it the power of jurisdiction over the exchange. This arrangement is related to the Aragonese occupation of Tunis. After Pedro's conquest of Sicily commerce between the island and Jews of Barcelona, and of Aragon generally, became more brisk. See for example Régné, no. 1382. For the commercial activities of Abraham Avengalel, a resident of Valencia who served as interpreter to several Spanish monarchs, see above, chapter IV, note 49. We do not have much detailed information concerning the economic activities of the Jews of Valencia. No less than 43 Jews were functioning there as brokers in 1315 (Régné, no. 3023). Brokerage appears to have been a virtual monopoly of the Jews. According to A. Schaube, *Handelsgeschichte der romanischen Völker des Mittelmeersgebiets* (Munich, 1906), p. 762, the number of brokers in Pisa was limited to 60 in the thirteenth century, and in Venice there were at the beginning of that century 40 brokers.

24. Information concerning these aljamas will be found in the monographs listed in the bibliography in Baer I, pp. 1083–86, and in the additional documents which I have published in the same volume. These documents reveal a number of interesting facts which it is not necessary to detail here. In the writings of this period one finds statements extolling country living above life in the cities. See my article, "The Religious and Social Ideology of the *Sefer Hasidim*" (Hebrew), in *Zion*, III (1937/8), 47; Kalonymos ben Kalonymos, *Even Bohan* (The Touchstone), ed. Wolff (Lemberg, 1865), p. 76; ed. Habermann (Tel Aviv, 1956), p. 78; and the testament referred to in Baer I, no. 190. On the other hand, the poet Solomon Bonafed complains profusely of the coarseness of the Jews in the small towns. See about him in Schirmann, *Ha-Shira ha-Ivrit bi-Sefarad u-vi-Provence*, II, 620 f. and 699–700. See also Adret, VIII, nos. 217–18: "There are Jews living in a town, within its wall, which has gates that they lock whenever they so desire. There are about 60 or 70 [families of] Gentiles living there and 21 to 24 [families of] Jews. The Jews want to rent all the houses in order to create a 'common court' (*'erub haserot*) Kalonymos. . . . Will it suffice if they rent all the houses, for an annual fee, from the lord of the town, or must the houses be rented from the tenants who occupy them?"

25. For the forms of Jewish communal organization in Castile see Baer II, nos. 60, 62, 63 (p. 44), 70; Adret, II, no. 290 and V, nos. 238–243. The

comment of Todros Halevi, the poet, is in his *Diwan* (ed. Yellin), no. 739. The admonitory sermon of the *rab* Don Todros Halevi Abulafia of Toledo and the strictures of the *Ra'aya Mehemna*, both discussed in the next chapter, also throw light on the state of communal affairs in Castile. Consult also the responsa of the fourteenth century cited below, in chapter VII, notes 9, 10.

26. Baer I, nos. 104, 136, 153.
27. See chapter IV, above, note 69, and Baer I, nos. 136, 153.
28. Francisco de Bofarull y Sans, *Los Judios en el territorio de Barcelona* (Barcelona, 1910), no. XCV. Cf. Adret, I, 475 (= VIII, 245), where Adret's correspondent, in his question, states, "In our country there are rabbis appointed by the crown who possess no learning."
29. Adret, III, no. 411.
30. Baer I, no. 88.
31. Adret, III, nos. 394, 399, 428.
32. The statutes of the aljama of Tudela, Baer I, no. 586. See also *Zikhron Yehuda* (*Responsa* of R. Judah b. Asher), no. 81.
33. Documentary evidence for this controversy is found in Baer I, nos. 98, 99; Régné, nos. 244, 245, 248, 253, 255; Adret, III, nos. 394, 402, and V, no. 279. (Space does not allow us to offer detailed proof of the relevance of these responsa to the events of 1264.) For parallel tension in the rest of the city see M. Mora y Gaudó, *Ordinaciones de la ciudad de Zaragoza* (Saragossa, 1908), 135 f. For incidents that occurred in Saragossa in subsequent years see Régné, nos. 458, 461; Bofarull, op. cit., nos. CII, CIII; Baer I, no. 104. For significant events in that community that occurred during the reign of Pedro III see Régné, nos. 666, 667, 668, 680, 704, 709-711 (= Baer I, no. 114). (In Régné, no. 668, instead of "Abindeunich" read "abin dehut" or "abin deuuit," *i.e.*, ibn Daud or ibn David. In no. 704, instead of "Abuffach" read "Abulfath"). For the appointment of R. Solomon ibn Adret and R. Aaron de na Clara—both of Barcelona—to adjudge the dispute between Joseph ibn Baruch and the *kahal* of Saragossa see Baer I, no. 115 = Régné, nos. 712, 713. Responsum Adret I, no. 617, may very well be concerned with this litigation. See further Baer I, no. 118; Régné, nos. 780, 796, 813, 816, 829, 830, 831 (inaccurately digested), 832, 833. For the attack on R. Yom-Tob Asbili see Régné, No. 841, which is a royal order on the matter, dated August 26, 1280, and signed on behalf of the king by Joseph Ravaya, the famous royal bailiff, who, apparently, supported Asbili in this matter. Concerning R. Yom-Tob Asbili see *Zion*, II, p. 45, note 59. Cf. Régné, nos. 925, 926, 927. No. 927 is an order to R. Yom-Tob (Jentono Asibili, judeo Caesarauguste) to adjudge a dispute between two Jews of Saragossa. See also Régné, no. 947. For the assassination of Solomon ibn Baruch see Baer I, no. 127. For further information concerning R. Aaron de na Clara (R. Aaron b. Joseph Halevi) see Régné, no. 1237, where he is called "Aaronum filium Clare, judeum Barchinone." He helped draw up the statutes cited in *Responsa* of R. Isaac Perfet nos. 388 (= Baer I, no. 143, #14), 389, 390. He later took up residence in Toledo, but returned after a short while to his native Barcelona. See *Zion*, II, p. 44, note 58.
34. Baer I, nos. 93, 106. For the various *berurim* see *ibid.*, index, p. 1162.
35. Adret, V, 284 (= Baer I, no. 143, #11). For the development of the communal council (*'etza*) of Barcelona see chapter VI, note 61, and chapter VIII, note 27. Additional information concerning the public

careers of R. Solomon ibn Adret and R. Judah Solomon will be found
in chapter VI, note 27.
36. See what I have written about the distribution of taxes in my *Aragonien*, p. 95 f. For the conflict between the upper and lower classes see
Adret, III, 380; Bahye ben Asher, *Kad ha-Kemah, s.v. Gezel.*
36a. Baer I, no. 146.
37. On the exercise of capital jurisdiction generally see Simha Assaf,
Ha-'Onshin aharei Hathimath ha-Talmud (Criminal Jurisdiction since
the Conclusion of the Talmud) (Jerusalem, 1922). For details see below,
esp. chapter VIII. See also the case of criminal jurisdiction in the *kahal*
of Behar (Castile), treated in the *Responsa* of R. Yom Tob b. Abraham
Asbili (*RYTBA*), ed. Joseph Kapah (Jerusalem, 1959), no. 131.
38. Adret, III, 318, replies to the following question from Jaca: "In this
city they decided, by statute, to punish transgressors of the law and they
appointed *berurim* to enforce this decision. The *berurim* have the power
to impose a monetary fine upon the transgressor and to keep for themselves the fines that they collect. Now Levi had a Jewish wet-nurse to
nurse his child, and this wet-nurse went to bathe in the river on the last
day of Passover. The *berurim* demand from Levi a fine for the transgression committed by the nurse in his employ. Levi swore by the Torah
that he knew nothing of the matter. Furthermore, the nurse, he alleges,
is not a member of his household but came with her daughter from another city to spend the holiday in his house. In the meantime the nurse's
daughter fell ill and a woman 'healer' told the mother to rub the child
down with a mixture of oil and salt and then to throw it into the river,
and this will cure her. The nurse took the daughter herself down to the
river in order to avoid the suspicion on part of the Gentiles that she
threw a magical object into the river, casting a spell upon it. Is he to be
fined or not?" This incident is of cultural as well as historical interest.
For one thing, it is evidence to the currency of the libel that the Jews
poison the waters.
      In Adret, IV, 315 R. Solomon is asked the following question:
"A wealthy man of excellent reputation and meticulous in his observance
of the commandments contracted with some [non-Jewish] masons for
the construction of a court for a specified price, with the stipulation that,
if the operation brought a loss to the builders they should bear the loss
themselves. When they began the work, they would work on Saturdays
and holidays on their own premises, cutting and dressing the stones in
houses of non-Jews, two or three courts removed from the one under
construction. One Saturday they began to work in this court, building a
stone wall. When the man first noticed this he was uncertain whether this
was permitted or not. After he returned home, he, fearing that it might
be forbidden, sent word to the masons to stop their work. When the
messenger arrived there he found Jews already gathered there, preventing
the masons from working. On Sunday, the Council of Twelve, which
governs the community, called him before them and asked him to explain
the matter. The man swore a solemn oath that he did not know that the
men had been working there. He promised to abide by the law and offered to pay a fine to purge himself of any fault in this incident. The
kahal officials were not satisfied and they put him under ban (*niddui*),
and fined him besides. This ban angered him greatly. He remained under
ban for five days, and after it was lifted he swore solemnly that he would

abstain from meat and wine and that he would refuse to pay the fine until an answer arrived to this question, informing us whether the ban was legally justified or not. Inform me, please, whether it was lawful to impose the ban upon him or whether the fine would have sufficed."

Ibn Adret had a good word for both parties in this controversy and sought to mollify the offended man while supporting the officers of the *kahal*. He replied,

"Inasmuch as it is not established that the masons were working with his knowledge, and since he did send a messenger to halt them, he was, perhaps, not liable to the ban. However, there is also this to be said in favor of the communal officers who imposed the ban upon him. Since most people today are not learned, a matter of this sort can lead to a great disaster and the desecration of the Divine Name. And this worthy gentleman is none the worse for his experience. It is better that he fell under the ban innocent than that he should have suffered it because he was guilty and deserving of the penalty. It behooves him to consider and obey what erudite Jews tell him, in order to stem this thing for the sake of Heaven."

[For the force of the *niddui* see Abraham A. Neuman, *The Jews in Spain* (Philadelphia, 1942), I, chap. IV.] For the other fines see Baer II, no. 60, # #62, 216, 217, 219, 220; Baer I, nos. 163, 584, 585.

39. I offer herewith—in addition to the statutes which I discussed in several other places—a selection of communal ordinances preserved in the *Responsa* of R. Solomon ibn Adret and in official documents of the Crown.

Adret, I, 590–92. "The *kahal* ordained that one may not sell wine for more than eight *denarii* per measure. If, however, the wine is of an inferior grade and is not worth eight *denarii* the measure, then it shall be sold for a price fixed by the inspectors of measures. . . ." Adret, III, 325: "The townspeople decided not to drink the wine produced in a certain locality. However, in order not to give that particular locality any notoriety, they forbade, for a limited time, the consumption of all wine produced outside their own city." We do not know the reason for this prohibition. Such a decision might be influenced not only by religious motives, but by economic and political considerations as well.

The *mukademin* and the *kahal* of Alagon decided to expel six butchers from the city for a period of four years and to forbid them to practice their trade during those years. All the members of the community were forbidden, under pain of *herem*, to eat meat purchased from these butchers. Infante Don Alfonso (later Alfonso III) intervened on behalf of these butchers in 1283, and again in 1286, after he had already become king, and annulled the prohibition of the *kahal* (Régné, nos. 1066, 1561). According to the document the *kahal* punished these butchers because on a certain day, which happened to be a Christian holiday, they brought meat to Saragossa and sold it there. But the exact nature of their offense is not clear. We do not know whether they were punished because they sold meat to Christians and on a Christian holiday, or whether they incurred the displeasure of the *kahal* in some other way, and the mention of the Christian holiday is here incidental, serving only to fix the date. It may be that the reasons were economic or political and had something to do with the rebellion that had broken out in Aragon at this time. Cf. Adret, V, 235: "The *kahal* forbade, under pain of *herem*, travel to a cer-

tain place because the roads were dangerous. This prohibition was to be
in effect until the first of Nisan, with its possible extension to the first of
Iyyar, depending upon the judgment of the *berurim.* If they find that
conditions on the roads have improved they will permit travel, otherwise
they will not."

See also Adret, VIII, 257: "The *kahal* ordained that no one shall take
up residence in a certain district prior to a given date. This man rented a
house there prior to that date and it served him as a store for the sale of
bread and as a workshop. Now the lord of the town demanded that he
pay a penalty for violating the prohibition."

Adret IV, 268:—"The *kahal* of Estella had long been enacting statutes
governing the welfare of the community. One of these statutes orders all
the inhabitants to close the privies which had been constructed close to
the city wall on the outside of it, to remove the beams which protrude
beyond the wall, and to cut down the trees growing outside the wall as
far as the tree called 'asta.' They may not construct a canal within two
cubits of the wall, neither inside nor outside, and they may not carry
any beams outside the wall."

The statutes of Huesca, forbidding the opening of textile shops outside the Jewish quarter, in the Christian part of town, are cited in Régné,
nos. 2017, 2054. The statute of Jativa is in Régné, no. 1021.

40. For Jewish education in Spain consult the material assembled by
Simha Assaf in his *Mekoroth le-Toldoth ha-Hinukh be-Yisrael* (Sources
for History of Jewish Education), II (Tel Aviv, 1930), 12–91, esp. 52 f.
Add thereto Adret, III, 319 (Tudela):—"A man had solemnly promised
another to teach him Halakha, three times, and the student in turn
pledged to minister to the teacher throughout the period of their study.
Should either one of them fail to keep his commitment he was to abstain
from meat and wine. Now the student was rather hard of comprehension
and he could not bear the burden of study. He left his teacher, and he
now abstains from meat and wine, and he has grown weak as a result.
A certain scholar heard of his condition and told him that he would
absolve him of his vow. . . ." This question, which I cannot quote
here in its entirety, expresses such beautiful and delicate sentiments, that
it reads like an excerpt from a pietist work like the *Sefer Hasidim,* rather
than an account of an actual occurrence. Cf. a similar document from
Barcelona, dated 1374, published in *Sefarad,* XVI (1956), 60; cf. also *ibid.,*
p. 69.

In a document dated 1327, published by Joan Segura in *Jochs florals
de Barcelona,* 1885, p. 248 (Assaf, *op. cit.,* II, p. 60, no. 46), Aster (Esther), the widow of Moses Cabrit, and her daughter, Astrugona of Santa
Coloma, the widow of Isaac Zaporta, declare that they will assume full
responsibility for the maintenance of the two sons of Astrugona and the
late Isaac Zaporta and that they will provide for their instruction "in
lege hebraica" and will pay the fees of their teachers. According to
another document, also of the 14th century, published by Segura in
Revista de ciencias historicas, V (Barcelona, 1887), p. 334 (Assaf, *loc. cit.,*
no. 47), a Jewish woman of Santa Coloma engaged a teacher to teach
her grandson "las letras hebreas . . . segun costumbre de los otros rabinos"
between Passover and Tabernacles. See also J. M. Madurell Marimón,
"La contratación laboral judaica y conversa en Barcelona (1349–1416),"

in *Sefarad*, XVI (1956), p. 60, no. 13; p. 69, no. 25. In the work *Hukkei ha-Torah* (Laws of Learning), as quoted in Assaf, I (1925), 15, we read: "When a boy reaches the age of five his father should put him under the care of a teacher for instruction, to begin on the first of Nisan. . . . The father should stipulate clearly the program of study, as follows, 'I am advising you that you are to teach my son during this first month to recognize the letters; during the second month, the vowels; in the third month, the combination of letters into words. Thereafter . . . let him study the book of Leviticus.'" I already described the extent of illiteracy in Spain, on pp. 214–219 above. See also the comment of R. Isaac Perfet in his *Responsa*, no. 37, upon the custom in the province of Aragon where on Rosh ha-Shana the cantor leads the congregation in the recitation of the *Musaf* aloud. "It seems to me that this practice was introduced in those territories because most of the people there are ignorant and find great difficulty even in the reading of the prayer book." The level of religious culture in the small provincial towns is revealed in the following responsum, Adret, I, 487 (= VIII, 199), "The Jews who live in the small towns in our vicinity are accustomed to reading the prescribed portion of the Pentateuch out of codices bound like our books, and to recite the benedictions before and after the reading." I have dealt in the text itself in several places with prevalent heresy and laxity in religious observance. See also Adret, IV, 105: "There is someone here who harangues the people and tells them that the evening prayer (*'arbith*) is not obligatory . . . and that the obligation of morning prayer may be met by the recitation of the brief supplication, *Habinenu*, and he permits them the consumption of cheese bought from Gentiles." See also the heresies of the German cabalist R. Dan, to which I call attention in *Zion*, V, 41, n. 87.

For the status of the woman in the Jewish society see my discussion of the statutes governing marriage and inheritance in Baer I, p. 1067 f. In the review published by the Escorial monastery, *Religion y Cultura*, XIX (1932), 263–276, there is an article by P. J. Llamas, entitled, "Documentos para la historia jurídica de las aljamas hebreas de Toledo y Molina." This article contains a description and a Spanish translation of several pages from a Hebrew manuscript in the Escorial monastery. Opposite p. 264 is a facsimile of the first of these pages (Codex G-I-9, p. 215 r.), headed *Dinei Takkanot Toletula u-Molina*. The text translated is, according to the author, a discussion by a fifteenth century scholar of these *takkanot* which deal with inheritance and dower rights. For the effectiveness of the *Herem* of Rabbenu Gershom in Spain see chapter VI, note 13.

41. See my article, "The Life and Times of Todros ben Judah Halevi" (Hebrew), in *Zion*, II (1936/37), 19–55.
42. Adret, I, 610.
43. *Diwan* of Todros ben Judah (ed. Yellin), no. 656, By way of balance, one must also mention the pietist of Toledo who would have liked to fast every day of the year.—Adret, IV, 262.
44. For the courtesans in the judería of Saragossa see Régné, no. 1053; for those in Toledo see *Zikhron Yehuda* (*Responsa* of R. Judah b. Asher), no. 17. See also Isaac Arama's *'Aqedat Yishaq*, chap. 20. For the high-handed Jewish bailiffs see above, chapter IV, note 67. Cf. Régné, no. 1316.

45. Gershom Scholem, *Perakim le-Toldoth Sifruth ha-Kabbala* (studies in the History of Cabalistic Literature), (Jerusalem, 1931), p. 13. See also the quotation given by Adolph Jellinek in his edition of R. Shem Tob Falaquera's *Iggereth ha-Vikkuah* (Vienna, 1875), note 1, as well as the interesting quotation from Moses de Leon's *Sefer ha-Rimmon* (Book of the Pomegranate) in G. Scholem's *Major Trends in Jewish Mysticism* (New York, 1941), p. 391; 2nd ed. (N. Y., 1946), p. 397. Similar statements are found in most cabalistic writings of the thirteenth century. R. Joseph Gikatilia, in his *Ginnath 'Egoz* (The Nut Garden), complains frequently of widespread heresy. People accept astrology and natural science, but deny Torah and Prophecy. The man of reason, they believe, can dispense with ritual observance.

45a. See above, chapter IV, note 74.

NOTES TO CHAPTER VI

1. A full bibliography of Gershom Scholem's publications would not be in place here. The reader will find much valuable information and bibliography in his *Major Trends in Jewish Mysticism* (New York, 1941; 2nd, revised edition, New York, 1946). See also note 17 below.

2. Nahmanides' commentary to Exodus 13. 16.

3. *Zohar*, I, fol. 177b–178a (based on *Mekhiltha*, tractate "Vayhi Beshalah," chapter III, ed. Lauterbach [Philadelphia, 1933], p. 207); III, fol. 112a; II, fol. 188b.

4. *Vikkuah ha-RaMBaN* (Disputation of Nahmanides), ed. Moritz Steinschneider (Stettin, 1860), p. 13.

4a. See G. Scholem, *Sabbatai Zevi* (Hebrew, Tel Aviv, 1957), p. 14; *Major Trends* (1941), pp. 225–27 (2nd ed., 1946, pp. 229–32); and his article, "Zur Konzeption der Schechina," in *Eranos-Jahrbuch*, XXI (Zurich, 1953).

5. *Vikkuah ha-RaMBaN*, p. 12; *Sefer ha-Ge'ula* (Book of Redemption), ed. Lipschitz (London, 1909), p. 20; ed. I. M. Aronson (Jerusalem, 1959), p. 43; ed. S. N. Marat (New York, 1904, *sub titulo, Sefer Heshbon Kes ha-Ge'ula*), p. 20.

6. Nahmanides' commentary to Leviticus 18. 25.

7. Nahmanides' commentary to Genesis 2. 3.

8. *Vikkuah ha-RaMBaN*, p. 10 f. Gershom Scholem—in his works—did not, in my opinion, give sufficient consideration to the place of eschatology in the cabala of Spain. For eschatology in the *Zohar* see *Major Trends*, p. 183 (2nd ed. p. 186). Bahye b. Asher in his *Kad ha-Kemah*, directs interesting criticism, beautifully expressed, against those who do not accept the belief in the Messiah literally. See his homily on *Nahamu* ("Comfort, comfort my people," Isaiah 40. 1) and another in honor of a bridegroom (*s.v.* "Hathan"), in which he states, "God will give a banquet for the righteous, and at that banquet—we are to believe—a real, material repast will be served, but the food will be of a delicate substance, ready and prepared since the beginning of Creation." In the homily, *Ner Hanukkah* (The Hanukkah Lamp), he exhorts his contemporaries to endure the tribulations of the *Galut*, which were growing more severe at the time.

Examples of contemporary Christian eschatology may be found in

Heinrich Finke, *Aus den Tagen Bonifaz,* VIII (Münster i/W., 1902), p. 210. The Pseudo-Joachimite work, *De semine scripturarum,* foretold that the end of the world would come in the year 1315, at the very latest. An eschatological tract, emanating from Christian Spiritualist circles, published in *Notices et Extraits des Manuscrits de la Bibliothèque Impériale,* t. 20 (Paris, 1862), 2e partie, p. 235, foresees the "end-of-days" tribulations beginning in 1287, and continuing until 1320, with the Antichrist appearing in Jerusalem in 1316. Arnaldo de Villanova, also, in his eschatological speculations, gave 1307 as the year of the "end." See H. Finke, *Papsttum und Untergang des Templerordens,* II (Münster i/W., 1907), 93 f. The Spanish scholar, J. Carreras y Artau—who has made a study of the personality of Arnaldo de Villanova and of his relationship to the Jews and Judaism and to the mystic movements of his day—published in full Villanova's tract, *Allocutio super Tetragrammaton,* in *Sefarad,* IX (1949), 75 f.; cf. *Sefarad,* VII (1947), 49 f.; *Revue de Synthese,* vol. 64 (1948), 22 f. Villanova wrote this little work in 1292, and submitted it to Pope Clement V in 1305. I believe—contrary to the opinion of Carreras—that Villanova derived his knowledge of Judaism principally from Raymond Martini's *Pugio Fidei,* and not from Hebrew sources. This is a problem which requires further investigation. I call attention here to the article by Miguel Batllori, "La documentacion de Marsella sobre A. de Villanova y Joan Blasi," in *Analecta Sacra Tarraconensia,* XXII (1948), 57 f. This study, which is based on notarial documents in the municipal archives of Marseilles, deals with events in the lives of Villanova and his kinsman, Joan Blasi. Both of them were physicians and also merchants. Because of their Spiritualist leanings they were forced to flee from Montpellier to Marseilles in order to escape the Inquisition. The author is inclined to assume that Villanova was of Jewish descent, and he offers as support for this assumption certain unique traits of Villanova's personality(!) and the fact that both men had business dealings with Jews.(!) Be that as it may, the author did bring to light certain materials that deal with Jews. Among the effects of Villanova (*ibid.,* p. 90) was the *Almanaque de Profach de Marsella,* whose author was the well-known Jacob b. Makhir.

9. *Sha'arei Teshuba,* part III, #43. Cf. Adret, III, 5; and Adret, I, 915, which was discussed above, chapter IV, note 67. On R. Jonah see A. T. Shrock, *Rabbi Jonah ben Abraham of Gerona, his life and Ethical Works* (London, 1948).

10. *Sha'arei Teshuba,* III, #88. For other rabbinic opposition to imprisonment for debt see Adret, I, 1069; Asher, *kelal* 68; Jacob b. Asher, *Tur Hoshen Mishpat,* sect. 97, 99. I also dealt with this matter in Baer I, Beilage 2, p. 1057 f.

11. *Sefer ha-Yir'a,* end; *Sha'arei Teshuba,* III, ##70–73.

11a. *Sha'arei Teshuba,* III, ##159–168, 59.

12. Adret, II, 279. Cf. my article on *Sefer Hasidim* in *Zion,* III, 43, n. 58. I did not interpret Ibn Adret's responsum correctly there.

13. Adret, III, 446 (no. 280 in the *editio princeps* of Adret's *Responsa*), and Adret, I, 1205. The contradiction between the two responsa was already pointed out by Isidore Epstein in his, *The Responsa of Rabbi Solomon ben Adreth of Barcelona (1235–1310) as a Source of the History of Spain* (London, 1925), p. 87, and p. 120, note 63. Epstein believes that Adret, III, 446, which mentions a scholar from Germany who went to

Montpellier in order to circumvent the *Herem* of Rabbenu Gershom, is earlier than Régné, no. 113, a document from Montpellier dated 1259. However, all that Régné, no. 113, proves is that there were individuals in Montpellier who felt that the *Herem* of R. Gershom was binding upon them, but it does not prove that the entire community shared their view and accepted the *Herem*. In a document dated 1267 (Régné, no. 359) James I of Aragon states that Jewish law permits bigamy. He deals with a case that occurred in Barcelona, and it is reasonable to assume that the king made his decision after consultation with the local Jewish religious authorities, among them Ibn Adret. Cf. above, chapter IV, note 16.

Adret, IV, 314, discusses the following case: "Reuben took Dinah, daughter of Joshua, into his house as a maid to work for him, with her consent and the consent of her parents. Now Reuben had been married for over ten years and his wife bore him no children. Since Dinah was in his house he seduced her and she conceived. When Reuben became aware of her pregnancy he married her formally, and her parents agreed to the marriage." Ibn Adret's correspondent inquired whether the child was legitimate or not. R. Solomon replied that the child was, without doubt, legitimate. But he prefaced his decision with the following remonstrance, which leaves no doubt concerning his position.

> First of all, I must say that this thing is prohibited and vile besides. The prohibition is clearly biblical, for such action violates the biblical injunctions, "There shall be no harlot among the daughters of Israel" (Deut. 23. 18), and "Degrade not thy daughter by making her a harlot" (Lev. 19. 29). It is also a vile practice, for this reason. Before the Revelation of the Torah a man might meet a woman in the street, and if they pleased each other he would have carnal relations with her, and then he would either keep her as his wife or else pay her the price of her favors and go his way. But the Torah has consecrated marriage and established the legal and ritual procedures for such a union. In many places there is even a communal statute which provides that a marriage ceremony can take place only in the presence of ten men, and that the bride's father and mother, or other relatives of hers, and the *hazzan* of the *kahal* must also be present. Certainly marriage by seduction is utterly forbidden, and it is all the more reprehensible when done by a man who already has a wife; for bigamous marriage, even when properly contracted, was banned by Rabbenu Gershom, of blessed memory, except that Maimonides was inclined to permit polygamy, as practiced by the Moslems.

It is evident that Ibn Adret changed his position in the course of his lifetime, responding to the trend of the times. For documents of a later date dealing with this subject see Régné, no. 3102; Baer I, index, p. 1162, *s.v.* "Bigamie." See also Kayserling in *JQR,* o.s. VIII (1896), p. 493. Particularly noteworthy is the fact that the philosopher Hasdai Crescas, in middle age, took a second wife while still married to the first, in order to beget children.—Baer I, no. 452. On the general subject of polygamy see Epstein, *op. cit.,* chap. VIII; Abraham A. Neuman, *The Jews in Spain,* II, chap. XIV. In most of the extant medieval business contracts and similar documents of a private nature, both those of Aragon and those of Castile, the husband and wife appear as a couple, both of them with equal legal status, and one can find no evidence of polygamy in them. See also chapter II, note 15. Perfet, no. 199, records a case of a Jew living in a village in Catalonia who had two wives. I have not found a similar case, however, in the many official documents from the small Catalonian towns that I have examined. Except for the rare instances where talmudic tradition require a man to take a second wife as a matter of conscience, the practice of polygamy was regarded as a sign of excess, both of wealth and of passion.

14. *Sha'arei Teshuba, III,* ##94, 131–33. Although Nahmanides supported R. Jonah's campaign of moral reform he was not fully in accord with his views on concubinage. The issue between them, however, was a purely legalistic one. Nahmanides wrote to R. Jonah (Adret VIII, no. 284): "I received your request for my opinion on the subject of concubinage. . . . I do not think that there can be any doubt that a man may keep a concubine whom he has espoused. . . . If she lives in his house, and is known to be exclusively his, her children bear his name, and the relationship is a licit one. We find that King David took one; and neither Scripture nor the Talmud make any distinction between a king and a commoner in this matter. . . ." Nahmanides, however, concluded his letter with these words of encouragement, "May God keep you well, Rabbi. Warn them, in your community, against concubinage, for if they learn that there is no prohibition, the door will be opened to lewdness." These words were addressed to R. Jonah during the latter's tenure as rabbi in Toledo. R. Solomon ibn Adret, as can be seen from the preceding note, agreed with R. Jonah.

15. Nahmanides' epistle is in *JQR,* o.s. V (1892), 116. See also *Zion,* II, and above, chapter III, note 15.

16. The sermon of R. Todros is printed in *Zikhron Yehuda* (Berlin, 1846), no. 91. The influence of R. Jonah is clearly discernible in it. R. Todros not only mentions R. Jonah and his *Sha'arei Teshuba,* but also some of his admonitions are identical with those made by Rabbi Jonah in his work, and are similarly phrased, as the quotations in the text show. R. Jonah's recommendation to appoint "supervisors in every street and square of their quarter (*Sha'arei Teshuba,* III, 73)" must have been written during his rabbinate in Toledo, for to a large community like Toledo, with its streets and squares, it would apply well, and not to a small town like Gerona. [For the meaning and force of *herem* and *niddui* see A. A. Neuman, *The Jews in Spain,* I, chap. IV.] For Ibn Adret's advice see his *Responsa,* V, nos. 238–243. It appears from the end of the responsum that at this time Ibn Adret had not yet arrived at the extreme position on concubinage which he took in *Responsa,* IV, 314. See note 13, above. Also relevant to the situation in Toledo at this time is the poem of the younger Todros Halevi, in his *Diwan,* no. 595.

17. For the structure of the *Zohar* and the date of its composition see Gershom Scholem, *Major Trends in Jewish Mysticism* (New York, 1941; 2nd ed., 1946), Fifth Lecture; I. Tishbi, *Mishnath ha-Zohar* (The Lore of the *Zohar*), I (Jerusalem, 1949; 2nd ed., 1957), Introduction. According to Scholem (*Major Trends,* p. 185; 2nd ed., p. 188), "the *Midrash ha-Ne'elam* (The Mystic Midrash), the forerunner of the *Zohar* proper, was written between 1275 and 1280, probably not long before the latter year, while the bulk of the work was completed in the years 1280–1286." Scholem has already shown, in *Tarbiz,* III (1932), 181–183, that in Isaac ibn Sahula's *Meshal ha-Kadmoni,* composed in 1281, there is a quotation

from the *Midrash ha-Ne'elam*. The *Meshal ha-Kadmoni* itself is fundamentally a collection of ethical homilies, composed under the impact of the shattering events of 1280–81, and saturated with the contemporary mystic ideology. Its belletristic form veils but thinly its moralistic purpose. See S. M. Stern, "Rationalists and Kabbalists in Medieval Allegory," in *Journal of Jewish Studies*, VI (1955), 73 f.; cf. J. G. Weiss, "A Contemporary Poem on the Appearance of the Zohar," in *Journal of Jewish Studies*, VIII (1957), 219–221, who attempts to interpret a poem of Todros Halevi, *Diwan*, no. 797. [In the second Hebrew edition of this book (Tel Aviv, 1959), p. 509, I have collected additional evidence of Ibn Sahula's dependence upon the *Midrash Ha-Ne'elam*.]

18. *Zohar* I, fol. 93a, 189b.

19. *Zohar* II, 3a, b. I was informed by Prof. Scholem that the *Zohar* recognizes only monogamous marriage. See also what K. Preis wrote in *MGWJ*, vol. 72 (1928), 167 f. about the inclination of the *Zohar* toward monogamy. Consult in this connection *Zohar* I, 85b, 91b; III, 7a, 19a, 44b.

20. *Zohar* III, 46a.

21. *Zohar* III, 157b.

22. *Zohar* III, 8b–9a; *Midrash ha-Ne'elam* to Ruth in *Zohar Hadash* (Zolkiew, 1804; Livorno, 1866), 94b; *Zohar* I, 168b; II, 61a, 86b; III, 85a; II, 198a. For the symbolism of the "broken vessels" cf. *Pesikta di-Rab Kahana, piska* 25 (ed. Buber, fol. 158b); *Vayikra Rabba*, sect. 7 (ed. Margulies, p. 152).

23. "Sithrei Torah" in *Zohar* I, 88a, b.

24. For the real-life setting of the *Zohar* see Scholem's *Major Trends*, Lecture V, and also his article, "The *Zohar's* Knowledge of the Geography of Palestine: A Problem of Zoharic Criticism" (Hebrew), in *Zion* (annual), I (1926), pp. 40–55. In connection with the water clock described in *Zohar* I, 92b, see *Libro del relogio del agua*—prepared by Isaac of Toledo at the behest of Alfonso X of Castile—in Manuel Rico y Sinobas, *Libros de saber de astronomia del rey don Alfonso el Sabio*, IV, 24 ff. The account of the deliverance of a village from a plague is in *Midrash ha-Ne'elam*, *Zohar* I, 101a. I found a similar account, involving the expulsion of a devil, in the legendary life of St. Francis of Assisi by Thomas of Celano, *Vita Prima*, cap. XXV, in *Analecta Franciscana*, 1926, p. 51; *The Lives of St. Francis of Assisi*, by brother Thomas of Celano, translated by A. G. Ferrers Howell, New York, 1908, p. 66 ff. Specialists in this literature can, no doubt, provide additional parallels. The story of the devils gathered in a house is in *Zohar* III, 50b. For the travels of the fellowship of mystics and their closeness to nature see especially *Zohar* II, 39a, 126a ff.; III, 20b ff., 200b ff. The reference to King David as "the King's minstrel" (*bediha de-malka*) is in *Zohar* II, 107a. Compare the story about St. Francis who was walking in the forest chanting the praises of the Lord, and he encountered a band of robbers who asked him what his occupation was, and he replied, "I am the herald of the great king (praeco sum magni regis)."—*Vita Prima*, cap. VII, p. 15; trans. Ferrers Howell, p. 16 ff. See also in *Speculum Perfectionis* (The Mirror of Perfection), ed. Paul Sabatier (Paris, 1898), IX, 100, p. 197, St. Francis' final charge to the brethren, "ut irent . . . per mundum, praedicando et cantando laudes Domini . . . et post praedicationem omnes cantarent simul laudes Domini tanquam ioculatores Domini." [There is a recent translation of the *Mirror of Perfection* by Leo Sherley-Price in his *St.*

Francis of Assisi (London, 1959). The above passage is on p. 124.] The Franciscan poet, Jacopone da Todi, also designated himself as the "Lord's minstrel." For eschatology in the *Zohar* see primarily *Zohar* I, 116b ff.; II, 9b; *Zohar Hadash* (Livorno, 1866), 69. For muleteers as prophets see *Zohar* III, 22b–23a. For prophecy in the mouths of children see *Zohar* II, 170a.

25. The discussion of the *Ra'aya Mehemna* in the text is a summary of my article, "The Social Background of the *Ra'aya Mehemna*" (Hebrew), *Zion*, V, 1–44, where I give full references. On Joachim of Fiore and the Spiritualist movement see H. Grundmann, *Studien über Joachim von Floris, 1927;* E. Benz, *Ecclesia Spiritualis: Kirchenidee und Geschichtstheorie der franziskanischen Reformation,* 1934. For the symbolism of the Raven and the Dove as used by Joachim himself to denote different tendencies in the Benedictine Order see E. Buonaiuti, *Scritti minori di Gioacchino di Fiore* (1936), 60; C. Baraut, "Un tratado inédito de Joaquin de Fiore: De vita S. Benedicti etc.," in *Analecta Sacra Tarraconensia,* XXIV (1951), 16 ff. See especially *ibid.*, p. 19, where Benedict is presented as the symbol of the spiritual truth (*spiritualis veritas*) which rose from its tomb, that is, the Scriptures, and *ibid.*, p. 72, where the author speaks of the approaching Flood which will engulf the souls of those human beings who remained outside the "spiritual Ark." See also *Abbatis Joachim divina prorsus in Jeremiam prophetam interpretatio* etc., Colonia, 1577 (written in Italy about 1240), and my references to this work in my article in *Zion*, V (1939), p. 4.

I believe that it is possible to establish an affinity between the cabalist Abraham Abulafia and the Christian Spirituals. Such a study, however, must await the publication of a definitive edition of Abulafia's writings. The opinion has been ventured that Joachim was himself born a Jew and was educated in the Jewish faith in the early part of his life. See H. Grundmann in *Archiv für Kulturgeschichte,* vol. 37 (1955), p. 157. The matter calls for investigation. The crucial question is whether it is possible to detect in the writings of Joachim traces of a direct influence of Jewish tradition.

25a. *Ra'aya Mehemna* in *Zohar* III, 153a. See *Zion*, vol. II, p. 24, note 17; vol. V, p. 6, note 8. See also *Crónica de Alfonso X*, cap. 7. Antonio Ballesteros, in his "Itinerario de Alfonso X, rey de Castilla," in *BAH*, vol. 106 (1935), p. 136, writes: "Más exacta es la Crónica (cap. vii) al asegurar que en este año (1258) Alfonso X mandó labrar la moneda de los dineros prietos y mandó *desfacer* la moneda de los burgaleses. Los dineros prietos o negros, de los cuales quince valían un maravedí." Ballesteros in "Burgos y la rebelión del infante Don Sancho," in *BAH*, vol. 119 (1946), p. 118–9, quotes a letter of Alfonso X to the *concejo* of Burgos, dated December 23, 1275: "Sobre el conseio que me dieron, tanbien los de Castilla como los de Extramadura. Mandaron me en Ayuda, tanto auer quanto podria montar una moneda cadanno, e esto fata tres annos. Et que se diesse in esta guisa, que el que ouiesse ualia de diez maravedis de los prietos que diesse diez sueldos de los buenos burgaleses que se fazen cinco maravedis e tercio de la moneda blanca. Et el que ouiesse diez maravedis dé los blancos que de diez sueldos de los blancos."

25b. *Ra'aya Mehemna* in *Zohar* III, 153b. See above, note 25.

25c. *Tikkunei Zohar*, chap. 20; *Zion*, V, 17. Cf. Scholem, *Major Trends*

(1941), 229–30 (2nd ed., 1946, p. 234): "The Zohar . . . lays special stress on the glorification of poverty as a religious value . . . In the *Ra'aya Mehemna* . . . these tendencies are systematized . . . The Shekhinah is poor for 'she has nothing from herself,' but only what she receives from the stream of the Sefiroth. The alms from which the poor live symbolically reflect this mystical state of the Shekhinah."

26. Adret I, 548; Graetz VII, 196 ff., 437, 443; *Zion*, V, 40 ff. See also H. Finke, *Aus den Tagen Bonifaz VIII* (Münster i./W., 1902), p. 209 ff., pp. cxvii ff., cxxix ff., clxxix ff.; Pou y Marti, *Visiones, beguinos y fraticellos catalans* (Vich, 1930), especially p. 54. The letter of Olivi was edited by Ehrle in *Archiv für Literatur—und Kirchengeschichte des Mittelalters*, vol. III; cf. Benz, *Ecclesia Spiritualis*, p. 258 f.

27. For the life of Rabbi Solomon ibn Adret see Josef Perles, *R. Salomo ben Abraham ben Adereth* (Breslau, 1863); Isidore Epstein, *The Responsa of R. Solomon ben Adreth of Barcelona (1235–1310) as a source of the History of Spain* (London, 1925). I should like to elucidate certain events in the career of Ibn Adret with the help of information drawn from documents in the Aragonese archives. I have already utilized some of these documents in my *Aragonien*, pp. 42–43, to which I refer the reader. The first mention of Ibn Adret in this literature is in a document dated early in 1263, a few months before the Disputation at Barcelona. Ibn Adret is therein named as the recipient of a fee from the royal household.—Régné, no. 182. The earliest of his responsa to deal with communal problems belong to the year 1264.—See note 33, ch. V. According to a document dated September 3, 1268, R. Solomon defended the interests of a Jewish orphan against the actions of high officials of the crown, Jews and Christians, and pled the child's case before the palace court.—See reference in chapter IV, note 42. From the contents of this document one may safely conclude that Ibn Adret knew Latin and was versed in the secular jurisprudence of his day, a fact borne out by some of his responsa. That same year the ailing R. Moses b. Isaac de Tolosa designated R. Solomon and several other relatives as guardians of his family and property. The designation was made in a Hebrew warrant, published in J. Millás-Vallicrosa, *Documents hebraics de jueus catalans*, no. XXV. For responsa of Ibn Adret belonging to this period which throw light on the situation of the Jews in Aragon at this time see chapter IV, note 41. For his activities during the reign of Pedro III see above, ch. IV, notes 56, 67 (his attitude toward the Jewish bailiffs), 75 (recovery of interest paid by Jews to Christians), and note 33 of chapter V, which documents the conflicts within the aljama of Saragossa. I call attention also to the following items:

1. Régné, no. 873:—Ibn Adret was attacked at night in Villafranca, where he was on a mission for the king.
2. Régné, no. 881 (anno 1281): Pedro III refers a divorce case to R. Solomon ibn Adret and R. Judah Solomon of Barcelona.
3. R. Solomon ibn Adret is mentioned as one of the *neëmanim* of the *kahal* of Barcelona in 1282.—Régné, nos. 915, 917; cf. no. 1391.
4. Régné, no. 998: R. Solomon, his son, and the latter's sons are named as the creditors in a financial transaction early in 1283. Even if we assume that the grandsons were still minors and are named only as a formality, Ibn Adret must have been at least fifty years old at this time. If, however, we assume that they were already of legal age,

then R. Solomon must have been at least sixty years old at the time and therefore about ninety at the time of his death.

5. Baer I, no. 127: This letter, written by Pedro III to Ibn Adret in 1284, shows how cautious he was in rendering a decision in capital cases.

6. Régné, no. 1196: In 1284 R. Solomon interceded at the court on behalf of a Jewish tax-farmer of Barcelona in connection with the salary due this man from the crown. The rabbi must at this time have been at the royal court in Teruel.

7. Régné, no. 1464: In 1285 Pedro III referred to Ibn Adret a serious case affecting the notoriously high-handed courtier, David Mascaran.

8. Régné, nos. 1507, 1508: In 1286 Ibn Adret and two other Jews of Barcelona were appointed to sit as judges in a trial growing out of the offenses of the aforementioned David Mascaran.

9. The case referred to Ibn Adret for adjudication in 1286, according to Régné, no. 1597 (cf. nos. 1056, 1181), is the one treated in the *Responsa*, vol. II, no. 229.

10. Régné, no. 2310: In 1291 a civil suit between private individuals was referred to R. Solomon ibn Adret and Solomon Gratiani.

11. Régné, no. 2329: Ibn Adret was directed to render a decision in the dispute between the *kahal* of Gerona and the small neighboring communities over the distribution of taxes.

12. Régné, no. 2859: In 1306 Ibn Adret interceded with James II on behalf of the *kahal* of Montblanch.

The references, full of reverence, to Ibn Adret in documents of Jewish origin attest to the esteem in which he was held by his coreligionists. In a petition addressed by a Jew of Valencia to James II, he is called "maestre Salomo den Adret."—Baer I, no. 144, pp. 164–5. A Hebrew legal instrument of 1293 stresses the "concurrence of our teacher and master (*haskamath morenu ve-rabbenu*) Rabbi Solomon ben Abraham ibn Adret."—Miret-Schwab, "Documents sur les juifs catalans," no. XXXVI, in *REJ*, vol. 68, p. 197. A survey of all the available documents shows that R. Solomon's public career covered a period of approximately forty years, beginning in the early 1260s. He is referred to in all the documents as a resident of Barcelona.

This is the place to offer some information about R. Judah Solomon of Barcelona who sometimes served in a judicial capacity alongside Ibn Adret. In 1268 he represented the *kahal* of Barcelona in negotiations with the king over taxes.—Régné, no. 399. In 1281 he was designated, as an expert in Jewish Law, to deal with a problem of divorce, together with Ibn Adret.—Régné, no. 881; item 2 above. We hear of him several times, between 1285 and 1289, in connection with financial matters.—Régné, nos. 1359, 1676, 1686, 1706, 1941. He was, apparently, one of the wealthy members of the Barcelona community. A Hebrew document, embodying the judgment of a court pronounced in 1292 and approved by Ibn Adret, carries R. Judah Solomon's signature ahead of those of the other members of the court.—Miret-Schwab, *Documents . . .* , no. XXXVI. There is reason to assume that he was the celebrated teacher of Abraham Abulafia.

28. Adret, II, 219.

29. For Ibn Adret's relations with the Ravaya family see above, chapter IV, note 56; for his high regard for Don Muça de Portella see note 69;

for his opinion of the high-handed Jewish bailiffs see note 67. The following responsa will serve to elucidate further Ibn Adret's attitude toward Jews who held office under the crown and their relations with their co-religionists:

Adret I, 637: "Any Jewish officer (*shilton*) appointed [by the crown] in his city to exercise authority in his locality, his decision is law. As long as his action accords with the local ordinances he is covered by the principle of *dina de-malkhutha dina* (the law of the realm is law), even as the king himself."

Adret I, 612: Ibn Adret's correspondent wrote, "A Jew who was arrested by the officer (*shilton*) [of the crown] on a false charge was able to settle the matter with him for specified sum. This officer has a Jewish official under him to whom he has allotted one-tenth of all the fines collected in the city. When the officer reached the settlement with the accused Jew he said to him 'I am settling with you for this amount on the condition that you pay one-tenth to the Jewish official.' The accused Jew admits to this arrangement. Please advise me whether or not the Jewish official may accept that portion from the accused inasmuch as he conceded this voluntarily." R. Solomon replied, "If this officer has the power to ordain laws for the government of his city his decision is law, in accordance with the established talmudic principle, 'The law of the realm is law [unto us].' Whoever is empowered to punish criminals such as robbers, thieves, murderers and the like in accordance with the laws of the realm and of the sovereign power belongs to this category and his decision in these and like matters is law. Therefore, whether the officer himself collected the fine, or the tithe thereof, and gave it to the Jewish official, or whether he told the accused to give it, the Jewish official may accept it.... I have already written to you several times on something similar to this. The Jewish official, however, must not cause or bring about any losses to Jews under accusation. But these are matters vouchsafed only to the Blessed One, to Whom all thoughts are known, and he who would save his soul will keep far from them." It is regrettable that the responsa to which Ibn Adret refers have not survived. Perhaps they are still in manuscript somewhere.

30. See principally Adret, III, 394, 399, 428.
31. Adret, III, 428, end.
32. Adret, IV, 311.
33. Adret, VIII, 240.
34. Baer I, no. 144, p. 164.
35. Adret, V, 287–289. See also III, 384, 385, 388; II, 84. See also II, 239–244, where Ibn Adret remarks, near the end of his discussion (no. 244), "Anyone against whom a suit has been filed in a secular court, and he spent large sums of money in bribes in order to avoid going to trial, is a fool."
36. The responsum of Nahmanides is found in the work of his contemporary, R. Samuel b. Isaac ha-Sardi, *Sefer ha-Terumoth*, chapter XLVI, section 8, and in Adret, V, 198. It was included by Simha Assaf in his *Sifran shel Rishonim*, Jerusalem, 1935, 87 ff., and annotated by him. Cf. *Los fueros de Aragon*, ed. Tilander, p. 3 (*Prologo*): "Como de los Fueros de Aragon nenguna scriptura cierta o autenticada fuesse trobada, en tanto que los foristas . . . iutgandò de coraçon, menos de libro los fueros, los iudicios diessen . . . , el piadoso Rey don Jayme . . . fizo

et estableó aquest libro, por el qual libro des de uuey de más todas las iusticias iudguen, assí como fuero manda . . ." It seems to me that the different viewpoints of the French and German *Tossafists* on the one hand and of Nahmanides and his disciples on the other in the interpretation of *dina de-malkhutha dina* are related to the different political philosophies operative in their respective countries in the Middle Ages. It was the same in later periods as well. A monograph giving a comprehensive treatment of this important subject is a desideratum. [A study of this subject, confined to Ashkenazic Jewry, is included among the posthumously published *Mehkarim* (Studies) of Israel M. Horan (Tel Aviv, 1951), pp. 41–134.] The rabbis of Catalonia ruled—following the progressive notarial regulations of their country—that the record books of the crown-appointed notaries are as valid proof of indebtedness as the notes of indebtedness themselves. See Adret, I, 982; III, 15, 16; Nahmanides in Assaf, *op cit.*, p. 103. Consult also Joseph Karo, *Beit Yosef, Hoshen Mishpat,* #68; Adret, VIII, 74–78.

37. Adret, VI (Warsaw, 1868), no. 257.

38. Adret, I, 98; similarly in *Minhath Kenaoth,* letter 14.

39. See chapter II, note 48.

40. *Minhath Kenaoth* (Pressburg, 1838), passim. The denial of personal immortality is reported in a small work by a disciple of R. Abba Mari, R. Simeon b. Joseph, entitled *Sefer Hoshen Mishpat,* published in *Zunz Jubelschrift* (Berlin, 1884), Hebrew section, pp. 155–174.

41. *Minhath Kenaoth,* letter 1.

42. *Ibid.,* 2.

43. *Ibid.,* 5.

44. *Ibid.,* 7.

45. *Ibid.,* 10, 11. Bonafos Vidal is mentioned in Régné, nos. 1634, 1709, 1932, 2034, 2048, 2122, 2330, in connection with loans and taxes. He was, apparently, the son of Vidal Solomon, the bailiff of James I (Baer I, no. 94). Already in 1258 he was connected with the fiscal administration of Aragon (Régné, no. 107). Crescas Vidal is mentioned with Bonafos in Régné, no. 1932. See also Régné, nos. 2344, 2416. Crescas was apparently still a resident of Barcelona in 1291.

46. See about him Henri Gross, *Gallia Judaica* (Paris, 1897), 431 ff.

47. *Minhath Kenaoth,* 12.

48. *Ibid.,* 13.

49. *Ibid.,* 14.

50 *Ibid.,* 20.

51. *Ibid.,* 39.

52. *Ibid.,* letters 25–31.

53. *Ibid.,* 44–53.

54. *Ibid.,* 52.

55. *Ibid.,* 51. Cf. the letter of R. Asher b. Yehiel, *ibid.,* 99.

56. *Ibid.,* 61.

57. *Ibid.,* 67.

58. *Ibid.,* 68, 69; see also no. 70.

59. The text of the *herem* is printed in the editions of the *Responsa* of R. Solomon ibn Adret, vol. I, no. 415. The letter in which R. Solomon declared, "We have expressly exempted etc.," is printed in *Israelitische Letterbode,* vol. V (1879/80), p. 55. See also vol. IV (1878/9), pp. 123, 124 ff., and *Minhath Kenaoth,* letters 82, 83, 84, 89.

60. *Minhath Kenaoth*, letter 81; Adret, I, 417. The authors of the *herem* acted wisely in introducing the quotation from Maimonides' *Guide*. This is sufficient evidence that the reformers had no intention to forbid the study of the *Guide;* in fact, they found in it support for their aims. See also Ibn Adret's letter in *Minhath Kenaoth*, no. 79.

60a. Adret, I, 416. B. Halper, *Post-Biblical Hebrew Literature* (Philadelphia, 1921), I, 137–141, English translation in vol. II, 176–182.

61. *Minhath Kenaoth*, letter 71.

This is the place to add a few known facts concerning some of the signatories of the *herem* whose names appear at the end of Adret, I, 415.

1. Solomon b. Moses Hen (Solomon Gratiani) served as a judge in Barcelona alongside Ibn Adret.—Régné, no. 2310.
2. Moses b. Isaac Halevi (Escapat-Malet) is the author of *Minhath Kenaoth*, letter 84. He is mentioned in connection with financial matters in Régné, nos. 2594, 3039. He was the brother-in-law of the *nasi* of Narbonne. See *Israelitische Letterbode*, IV, 160 ff.
3. The brothers Jacob b. Sh'altiel (Bonafos Saltell) and Sheshet b. Sh'altiel (Perfet Saltell) are identified as merchants engaged in marine commerce in Baer I, no. 152, and as leaders of the *kahal* of Barcelona, *ibid.*, no. 169. At the time of his death in 1326, Bonafos Saltell was one of the *neëmanim* of Barcelona.—Régné, no. 3406. The poet Kalonymos b. Kalonymos, at the end of his *Even Bohan* (ed. Habermann, Tel Aviv, 1956, p. 121) names him among his benefactors and heaps lavish praise upon him. Perfet Saltell is mentioned as one of the leaders of the *kahal* also in Régné, no. 2931.
4. Isaac b. Todros was a well-known cabalist.
5. Isaac b. Solomon b. Abraham ben Adret, the son of the rabbi, is named among the leaders of the *kahal* of Barcelona in Baer I, no. 169.
6. Isaac b. Samuel Cap was one of the foremost merchants of Barcelona. See chapter V, note 23, above.

Many of the signatories of the *herem* also signed the responsum printed in *REJ*, XII (1886), 88. Most of the men who signed the *herem*, and they constituted a majority of the lay leaders of the *kahal*, were scholarly men. Nearly all of the signatories belonged to the old established Jewish families of Barcelona. No physicians were included in this group. Apparently they were excluded from the leadership of the *kahal* (cf. chapter VIII, note 45), which was firmly in the hands of the wealthy and learned aristocracy.

62. *Minhath Kenaoth*, letters 99, 101.

NOTES TO CHAPTER VII

1. Baer II, no. 115.
2. See Antonio Benavides, *Memorias de D. Fernando IV de Castilla* Madrid, 1860, I, 99 ff., 114 ff., 124, 140; II, 383. Baer II, p. 89, note 1.
3. Baer II, nos. 122, 128, 132.
4. Baer II, no. 121.
5. Baer II, nos. 133, 138, 139, 142, 144.
6. Baer II, no. 146.
7. The sources of this information may be traced by referring to Baer II, Index, p. 585, *s.v.* "Sevilla." See especially Baer II, nos. 163, 249. Baer II, p. 89, note 1. R. Carande, "Sevilla, fortaleza y mercado," *Anuario* II,

233–401. *Barraganas* and wailers are mentioned in Baer II, no. 163. Cf. *Responsa* of R. Isaac b. Sheshet (*RIBaSH*) Perfet, no. 508, for the employment of professional wailers by the Jews of Saragossa.

8. *Zikhron Yehuda*, no. 61. For the other data consult Baer II, Index, p. 586, *s.v.* "Toledo." For Christians of possible Jewish descent see Baer II, no. 190.

9. For the development of the *concejo cerrado* in the cities of Castile see Ramon Carande in *Anuario* II (1925), 278 ff., 312. For the *veedores* in Castilian municipalities see Timoteo Domingo Palacio, *Documentos del archivo general de la Villa de Madrid* I (1888), 273 ff.; A. Salvá, *Cosas de la vieja Burgos*, p. 37 ff. For *me'aynim* in the aljamas see *Zikhron Yehuda*, nos. 51, 52; Asher, *kelal* 13, no. 20; consult also Baer II, Index p. 589, *s.v.* "Gemeinde." For the *almahona* and *alancel* see Asher, *kelal* 13, no. 20, and my notes to it in Baer II, no. 136, p. 125. The *almahona* is mentioned in a number of R. Asher's responsa. The complaint of the Cortes is given in Baer II, no. 132. For the manner of selecting judges see *Zikhron Yehuda*, nos. 45, 46, 47, 52, 70. No. 52 describes the following arrangement. Of the three judges to be chosen, two were to be "men who pay the annual tax (*cabeza del pecho*) in the city," and the third "a man who does not pay the tax in the city," or "a man who pays his tax outside the city," that is, either a beneficiary of special privileges or a resident of a neighboring rural community. [Cf. A. A. Neuman, *The Jews in Spain*, I, 115–6.]

10. Cf. for all these matters the famous statute of 1432 (Baer II, no. 287), which is based on fourteenth century precedents. Information concerning the communal *haskamoth* (statutes) and the position of the *rab de la corte* during this period will be found in the documents dealing with Molina which I published in Baer I, no. 292. *Haskamoth* are mentioned also in Asher, *kelal* 6, no. 14, and *kelal* 13, no. 20; *Zikhron Yehuda*, nos. 52, 74; Perfet, no. 232. For the functions of the *rab* see also the references given in Baer II, Index, p. 589, *s.v.* "Gemeinde." The meaning of the Hebrew title *rab* as used in the responsa of this period is not always clear. See the statement at the end of *Zikhron Yehuda*, no. 82 (fol. 38a), "he obtained . . . a decision (*pesak din*) from the distinguished Don Çag ibn Wakar who was *rab* at that time," meaning the crown-appointed *rab*, who later resigned that position. See also in *Zikhron Yehuda*, no. 77, the mention of "the *rab* Don Moses ibn Zargil" (read Zaradiel, see note 23 below), and the statement, "this kind of punishment is meted out by the rabbis of the crown—who have the power and the authority—according to the exigencies of the hour."

11 For judges who dealt out draconic sentences and for attempts upon the lives of judges see *Zikhron Yehuda*, no. 75 (fol. 55); Perfet, no. 251. The cruelty of some of the elders of the *kahal* of Toledo may be inferred from the statement of R. Abraham Shoshan, quoted in Asher, *kelal* 68, no. 27, "I know the character of the elders of the city, who are likely to say, 'Anything is permitted.'"

12. For the lives of R. Asher and his sons see Alfred Freimann's studies, "Ascher ben Jechiel: Sein Leben und Wirken," and "Die Ascheriden (1267–1391)," in *Jahrbuch der jüdisch-literarischen Gesellschaft* XII (1918), 237–317; XIII (1920), 142–254. See also their ethical wills in Israel Abrahams, *Hebrew Ethical Wills* (Philadelphia, 1926), I, 118–125; II, 163–205. The spirit of German-Jewish pietism which permeated R. Asher's circle is reflected in the commentaries to the Pentateuch ascribed to

R. Asher, in *Da'ath Zekenim* (Livorno, 1783), and *Hadar Zekenim* (Livorno, 1840). See M. Liber in *REJ*, vol. 54 (1907), 64 ff. The most complete and authoritative edition of the responsa of R. Asher is the one published in Venice, 1607.

13. Asher, *kelal* 107, no. 6; Baer II, no. 135.

14. Asher *k.* 55, no. 9. This conflict is treated in J. L. Teicher, "Laws of Reason and Laws of Religion, A Conflict in Toledo Jewry in the Fourteenth Century," in *Essays and Studies Presented to St. A. Cook* (London, 1950).

15. Asher, *k.* 18, no. 17 = *k.* 99, no. 1; *k.* 84, no. 1; *k.* 68, nos. 10, 11 (Jacob b. Asher, *Tur Hoshen Mishpat,* #99).

16. Asher, *k.* 43, nos. 6, 8, 9.

17. Asher, *k.* 78, no. 3. This responsum was written in the spring of 1315.

18. Asher *k.* 21, no. 8. The locality was Paredes de Nava in the bishopric of Palencia.

19. Asher *k.* 18, no. 13; *k.* 17, no. 8. See Baer II, no. 146.

20. Asher *k.* 17, no. 1.

21. Asher, *k.* 17, no. 6. The cancellation of debts must be the one discussed above, note 4. R. Joseph Halevi might be Don Yuçaf de Ecija; see note 22 below. In another case of informing (*kelal* 6, no. 21), R. Asher merely congratulated the afflicted community upon their success in eliminating the evil from their midst. See also *Zikhron Yehuda,* no. 75 (fol. 55) for a case of informing in which proceedings apparently began while R. Asher was still alive. See also *ibid.,* no. 58, on the criminal jurisdiction of the Jews.

22. On Don Yuçaf de Ecija see Baer II, no. 150, and the sources cited in my note thereto. The most important are the *Crónica de Alfonso XI* (*BAE,* vol. 66; Madrid, 1875), and Solomon ibn Verga's *Shebet Yehuda* (The Rod of Judah), Chapter X (ed. Shohet, Jerusalem, 1947, p. 52 ff.), whence the quotation in the text is taken. See also Baer I, no. 193; Baer II, nos. 157, 167. The distinguished historian Antonio Ballesteros, in his article, "Don Juçaf de Ecija," in *Sefarad,* VI (1946), 253–287, offers new and noteworthy material, important for the history of Spanish Jewry during this period. The order of Alfonso XI, dated in April 1324, and addressed to certain Jewish "farmers of the harbor tithes" of the entire realm, is, apparently, the same one which was published in a better text by F. Cantera Burgos in his article, "La Judería de Burgos," in *Sefarad,* XII (1952), 70. In Cantera's text the name of the first tax-farmer is given as "el rab don Yuçaf aben gamanon (read "çamanon"), medico del rey." See the reference to Don Joseph Çamanon in Chapter III, note 39. Along with him the document of 1324 names Don Joseph b. Don Todros Halevi, and Don Joseph's son, Yaffiel.

The rivalry between Don Yuçaf de Ecija and Don Samuel ibn Wakar drew comment in verse from the pen of a minor Hebrew poet of that period, Samuel b. Joseph ibn Sason. See my article in *Minha le-David* (David Yellin *Festschrift*), 197 ff. For more information about Samuel ibn Sason and selections from his poetry see Schirmann, *Ha-Shira ha-Ivrit bi-Sefarad u-vi-Provence,* II (1956), 524 ff.; H. Hamiel, "Sefer Eben ha-Shoham li-Shmuel b. Yosef ibn Sason," in *Sinai,* XXXV (1954), 45–54, 134–142, 199–206, 353–356.

23. For R. Moses Abzaradiel see Baer II, pp. 142–4. He is mentioned in *Zikhron Yehuda,* no. 77 (see note 10 above), in *Shebet Yehuda,* chap. X,

and in the commentary of R. Joseph aben Nahmias to Jeremiah—M. L. Bamberger, ed. (Frankfurt, 1913) p. 8. also Einleitung. p. 4.

24. On Abner of Burgos see my articles, "Abner von Burgos," in *Korrespondenzblatt der Akademie fur die Wissenschaft des Judentums*, X (Berlin, 1929), 20–37; "Abner of Burgos' *Minhath Kenaoth* and its Influence on Hasdai Crescas," (Hebrew), in *Tarbiz*, XI (1940), 188–206; "Cabalistic Doctrine in the Christological Teachings of Abner of Burgos," (Hebrew), in *Tarbiz*, XXVII (1958), 278–289. [In his article in *Tarbiz*, XI, the author describes the extant manuscripts of the works of Abner: 1. The Paris manuscript, a Spanish fourteenth century manuscript of 338 folia, consisting entirely—except for the first few pages—of the *Mostrador de Justicia*, which is a Spanish translation of Abner's Hebrew work, *Moreh Zedek* (Teacher of Righteousness); 2. The Parma manuscript, a Hebrew manuscript, containing polemical tracts of Abner and Isaac Policar; 3. The Vatican manuscript, a Spanish manuscript of the fourteenth century, containing a Spanish translation of the *Minhath Kenaoth* (Offering of Zeal), followed by a Spanish translation of the contents of the Parma manuscript.]

25. The introduction to *Mostrador de Justicia*, Paris Ms., fol. 12. The Spanish text is given by Isidore Loeb in *REJ*, XVIII (1889), 54–56.

26. Parma Ms., fol. 6b.

27. Moses Narboni *Ma'amar ba-Behira* (Treatise on the Freedom of the Will), published in *Dibrei Hakhamin*, ed. by Eliezer Ashkenazi (Metz, 1849), pp. 37–41. Abner's major work on Determinism is his *Minhath Kenaoth*, which he wrote after his conversion. He himself refers to two other works of his on the same subject, one of which was written before his conversion. See my article in *Tarbiz*, XI (note 24 above), and I. Guttmann, *Ha-Pilosophia shel ha-Yahaduth* (The Philosophy of Judaism, Jerusalem, 1951), p. 187 ff. For the life and works of Moses Narboni, see S. Munk, *Mélanges de Philosophie Juive et Arabe* (Paris, 1859), p. 502 ff.; M. Steinschneider, *Die hebraeischen Uebersetzungen des Mittelalters* (Berlin, 1893), pp. 185 f., 191 f., 209, 311 f., 424.

28. Paris Ms., fol. 29 ff.

29. Parma Ms., fol. 2–6. Policar later on repeated the same words, with some additions and changes, in the first chapter of his *'Ezer ha-Dath* ("The Support of Faith," ed. by George S. Belasco, London, 1906), with the obvious intention of refuting the arguments of Abner, and of modifying to some extent his own rationalist outlook. It is difficult to say that he succeeded.

29a. See G. Scholem in *Tarbiz* VI (1935), 90–98.

30. Parma Ms., fol. 8–13.

31. See my article in *Tarbiz*, XXVII (see note 24 above), where I treated the subject more fully. [For the theory of *Sefiroth* see Scholem, *Major Trends in Jewish Mysticism*, Sixth Lecture.]

31a. See G. Scholem, *Jewish Gnosticism, Merkabah, Mysticism, and Talmudic Tradition*, N. Y., 1960.

32. Parma Ms., fol. 21–27. I give here only brief excerpts from the works of Abner. It is impossible for me to treat the subject exhaustively within the confines of this work. [For the meaning of *shi'ur koma* (measure of the body) see Scholem, *Major Trends* (2nd ed., 1946), p. 63.]

33. Paris Ms., fol. 88–89. Abner's own words are as follows (fol. 89): "Among them was the heretic Elisha, the teacher of R. Meir, one of

the great sages of the Talmud. We are informed in tractate *Haggiga* (fol. 14b) that this Elisha was one of the four who entered the 'orchard' (*pardes*), meaning that they entered the study of theosophy, desirous of learning the nature of afterlife and Paradise. We are told that Elisha pruned the tender shoots, meaning that Elisha, in his conception of this lore, denied the several aspects (*personae*) of the Divinity, believing them to be separate entities, like the tender shoots which serve as saplings and are planted in the soil so that they might grow into tall trees. So he too believed that these aspects were separate entities, and that the Divinity was composed of them."

34. Parma Ms., fol. 54.
35. Paris Ms., fol. 292 ff.
36. Parma Ms., fol. 58.
37. Parma Ms., fol. 66 ff. See in this connection Joseph Albo, *Sefer ha-'Ikkarim* (Book of Principles) Book IV, Chap. 42 (ed. I. Husik, Philadelphia, 1930, vol. IV, part 2, p. 413 ff.). This entire chapter is, in essence, a refutation of Abner.
38. Parma Ms., fol. 47b. See Augustine's *City of God*, XIX, 27.
39. Paris Ms., fol. 335-337.
40. Parma Ms., fol. 58 f.
41. See the references to the sources in note 22 above.
41a. In Valladolid, on August 20, 1335, Alfonso XI granted to all the Jewish communities of his realm important privileges, published by Fr. Cantera in *Sefarad* I (1941), 132-137. The Jews had complained, "en como son pobres e estragados por muchos daños e perdidas que an recebido en sus faziendas . . ." (*ibid.*, p. 133).
42. See my article in *Minha le-David*, pp. 198-9. Graetz, VII, 444, note 13.
43. See what I wrote in *Minha le-David*, p. 201 ff.; *Tarbiz*, XI, p. 205. A critical edition of the *Proverbios morales*, based upon several manuscripts, of which the oldest and most significant is the Cambridge ms. of the early 15th century, in which the Spanish text is given in a Hebrew transliteration, was published not long ago. It is, Santob de Carrión, *Proverbios morales*, edited, with an introduction, by Ignacio Gonzales Llubera, Cambridge Univ. Press, 1947. The Cambridge ms. was edited by Llubera in *Romance Philology*, IV (1950), 217-256. See also E. Alarcos Llorach, "La lengua de los Proverbios Morales de don Sem Tob," in *Revista de Filologia Española*, XXXV, 3-4 (1951), 249-309. [For an account of Shem Tob's Hebrew poetry and the text of his *maqama*, *Milhamoth ha-'Et ve-ha-Misparaim* (The Dispute between the Pen and the Scissors) see Schirmann, *Ha-Shira ha-Ivrit* . . . , II, 529-540.]
43a. See the order of Alfonso XI, dated December 8, 1340, published by Cantera in *Sefarad* I, 138 f., "et como quier que nos tovimos por bien de nos servir de los judios del nuestro señorio con una grand quantia de aver para este mester que avemos de la guerra, que avemos con los moros, et nos finco que avemos de cobrar la mayor parte dello et los judios nos dizen que estan muy afincados que lo no pueden conplir . . ."
44. Baer II, no. 167. For other Jews who maintained relations with the court or held high office in the state during the reign of Alfonso XI see Baer II, nos. 150 (end of note, p. 144), 166, 169, 171, 174, 175; Baer I, no. 237. For R. Shemarya of Negroponte see the report of him by R. Jacob b.

David Provenzali (*Dibrei Hakhamim,* ed. Eliezer Ashkenazi, p. 69), "He stayed in Spain and he was highly esteemed by the king, Don Alfonso, as a great astronomer and expert physician. The king rewarded him with many gifts and with fine garments on the day he disputed mystic lore with the scholars of Salamanca." This report, except the statement concerning the disputation with the scholars of Salamanca, seems credible. See also A. Neubauer in *REJ,* X (1885), 86 f.; H. Vogelstein and P. Rieger, *Geschichte der Juden in Rom,* I (Berlin, 1895), 446 f.; H. Vogelstein, *Rome* (Philadelphia, 1940), 212 f. For the critique of Alvarus Pelagius I am indebted to R. Scholz, *Unbekannte kirchenpolitische Streitschriften aus der Zeit Ludwigs des Bayern,* II (Rome, 1914), 493 ff.; see also I, 197 ff.

45. Baer II, no. 178. Compare the English document published in *Statutes of the Realm,* I (1810), 221. See also J. M. Rigg, *Select Pleas, Starrs, and Other Records from the Rolls of the Exchequer of the Jews, 1220–1284,* London, 1902, p. xxxviii ff.; Georg Caro, *Sozial- und Wirtschaftsgeschichte der Juden,* II (Frankfurt am Main, 1920), 40–42, 286.

46. Baer II, no. 181.

47. See Charles Verlinden, "La grande peste de 1348 en Espagne; Contribution à l'étude de ses conséquences économiques et sociales," in *Revue Belge de Philologie et d'Histoire,* XVII (1938), pp. 103–146. Cf. the transactions of the Cortes of Valladolid of 1351, in Verlinden, *op. cit.,* pp. 138–9; Baer II, no. 181; Carande in *Anuario* II, 268. Only in the texts of the tombstones of the Jewish cemetery of Toledo do we find any detailed information concerning Jews of Castile who died in the plague. See Cantera—Millás, *Las inscriptiones hebraicas de España* (Madrid, 1956), nos. 65–89, pp. 113–148. For the effect of the plague on the Jews of Aragon, see the next chapter.

47a. This occurrence is only incidentally referred to in the Hebrew document embodying the decisions of the conference of Aragonese aljamas held in 1354.—Baer I, p. 352, #2. See also A. Pons, "Los judios del reino de Mallorca durante los siglos XIII-XIV," in *Hispania,* XVI (1956), 335.

528. On May 15, 1354, Guillem de Lagustera wrote to the officials of Majorca ordering them to take measures to prevent disturbances leading to possible attacks upon the Jews, upon the arrival of reports of attacks upon Jews in Seville: "Per algunes noves que sic recomten d'un excés, que's diu esser esdevengut en Xibilia contra los jueus."

48. For Don Samuel Halevi see the material assembled in Baer II, no. 187. See also nos. 171, 205 note, 223 (p. 218). For the synagogue which he built in Toledo and its inscriptions see M. Schwab, *Rapport sur les inscriptions hebraiques d'Espagne,* 1907, p. 47 ff.; Francisco Cantera Burgos, *Sinagogas Españolas,* Madrid 1955, pp. 65–149. A document of 1371 mentions a house in Toledo which had belonged to Don Samuel.—Baer II, p. 180. Another document of the same year refers to stores that he had owned in Seville. —Baer II, no. 223 (p. 218). The account of Don Samuel's death, as told by Ayala in his *Crónicas,* had already taken on the form of legend in the chronicle which R. Menendez Pidal calls *Cuarta Crónica General,* in *Colección de documentos ineditos por la historia de España,* vol. 106, p. 92 ff. The story told by Elijah Capsali, in M. Lattes, *Likkutim Shonim mi-Sefer Debei Eliyahu* (Excerpts from the Chronicle of Elijah Capsali), Padua 1869, p. 48 f., is mostly legend. The Spanish historian, Juan Catalina Garcia, in his *Castilla y Leon durante los reinados de Pedro I, Enrique II, Juan I, y Enrique III,* I (Madrid, 1892), 227, concluded, on

the basis of the material at his disposal, that Samuel's death must have occurred after the middle of 1361. Unfortunately, a comprehensive study of the documents relating to this period has not yet been made.

49. Baer II, nos. 189, 197, 202, 207, and the other documents belonging to the reign of Pedro I.

50. Baer II, nos. 190, 191. Pedro Lopez de Ayala, *Cronica de Don Pedro*, ano VI, cap. 7 (*BAE* vol. 66, p. 462): "E el Conde (Don Enrique) e el Maestre (de Santiago) despues que entraron en la cibdad (Toledo) asosegaron en sus posadas; pero las sus compañas comenzaron a robar una judería apartada que dicen el Alcana e robaronla e mataron los judios que fallaron fasta mil e dozientas personas, omes e mugeres, grandes e pequenos. Pero la juderia mayor non la pudieron tomar." Moses Narboni was at this time residing in Toledo and writing his commentary to Maimonides' *Guide*. But he was compelled to interrupt his work, "for I had not the strength to continue the work for many reasons, among them the pillage and the plunder which I suffered on the second day of Shabuoth, in the year 5115 (May 18, 1355)." He moved to Soria and completed his commentary there in 1362, shortly before his death. See *He-Halutz* XI, (1880), 88–90; Munk, *Mélanges*, p. 505; Steinschneider, *Hebr. Uebersetzungen*, p. 424. Cf. note 27 above.

51. For the condition of the Jews during the civil war in Castile see Avala's *Crónicas* and Baer II, nos. 205 ff. The treatment of this war in French literature of this period mirrors the anti-Jewish feeling current in Europe at that time but does not throw any valuable light on the condition of Spanish Jewry. See also P. E. Russell, *The English Intervention in Spain and Portugal in the time of Edward III and Richard II* (Oxford, 1955).

52. See the quotation from the epilogue to the *Mekor Hayyim*, by Samuel Çarça, in Baer II, no. 209. In describing the troubles of the aljama of Burgos as a result of the demands made upon it by Henry II, Çarça tells that "in order to complete the payment they sold all the silver crowns and ornaments of the Torah scrolls, except the case of the Torah scroll of Ezra, which they did not sell." At a later date (Sept. 9, 1391) the representatives of this aljama swore upon the Torah scroll of Ezra (*en la tora de yzra*) to abide by certain emergency regulations proclaimed by the municipal authorities. See J. Teofilo Lopez Mata, "Morería y Judería (de Burgos)," in *BAH*, vol. 129 (1951), 335 ff.; Fr. Cantera, "La Judería de Burgos," in *Sefarad*, XII (1952), p. 77; Idem, *Alvar Garcia de Santa Maria: Historia de la Judería de Burgos y de sus conversos mas egregios* (Madrid, 1952), p. 23. Samuel Çarça's *Mekor Hayyim* (Fountain of Life) is a commentary to the Pentateuch, printed in Mantua in 1559. Writing of the obligations of Yom Kippur, in his commentary to Leviticus, chapter 23 (*ibid.*, fol. 80b), he stresses the urgent need for repentance. "We are obligated to repent at all times, and especially in this generation. For, because of our sins, all Israel finds itself in distress, surrounded by lions whose teeth are spears and arrows and whose tongue is a sharp sword. It was, no doubt, of such a time that the prophet (Jeremiah 30.7) spoke when he said, 'It is a time of distress for Jacob, yet he shall be saved therefrom.'" In the epilogue to the work the author gives detailed information of the suffering of the Jewish communities of Castile in the years 1366–68. See also the introduction to the same author's book, *Mikhlal Yofi* (The Perfection of Beauty), in

Graetz VII, p. 374. Consult also Menahem ben Zerah's *Zeda la-Derekh* (Sabbioneta, 1567), fol. 16 (Neubauer, *Medieval Jewish Chronicles*, II, 244), where the author recounts the events of his own life and gives a history of his times up to the year 1368. See also the short and partially confused notes in Isaac Lattes' *Sha'arei Zion*, ed. Buber (Jaroslaw, 1885), p. 48, and the chronicles of Joseph ibn Zaddik and Solomon b. Abraham Ardutiel in Neubauer's *Med. Jew. Chronicles*, I, pp. 97 and 109. See, in general, Graetz VII, chapter XI. Menahem ben Zerah was living in Alcalá de Henares at the time of the persecutions of 1368, and he fled from there to Toledo with the aid of one of the leading Jewish courtiers of the time, Don Samuel Abravanel. Don Samuel, who was a resident of Seville, later converted to Christianity, but at this time he was a loyal Jew It was for him that Menahem ben Zerah wrote his *Zeda la-Derekh* (Provisions for the Road), a book of laws, precepts and homilies, in which he expounded, for the benefit of courtiers like Don Samuel, the fundamentals of the religious tradition, and at the same time made an effort to lighten for them the burden of religious observance, to the extent to which it was possible to do so without infringing upon the prescriptions of the Halakha. See on that A. Freimann in *Annuario di Studi ebraici*, I (1934), 147–167.

52a. See Fr. Cantera, "La judería de Calahorra," in *Sefarad*, XV (1955), p. 363: "El 30 de Marzo de 1370, la reina de Navarra, doña Juana, tomaba desde Olite bajo su protección a los judios de la ciudad de Calahorra y del reino de Castilla que hubieran ido o tuvieran el proposito de marchar al reino navarro (Jose Ramón Castro, *Archivo de Navarra*, Comptas, siglo XIV, tomo VII, Pamplona 1954, doc. num. 119)."

53. For Joseph Picho see especially Baer II, nos. 211, 223; Baer I, no. 281. It is evident from these documents that his character was not above suspicion, and it was not without good reason that he was later executed as an informer. For the office of *contador mayor* which he held see C. Espejo in *Boletin de la Sociedad Castellana de Excursiones*, vols. III and IV (1907–1910); L. M. de la Torre de la Hoz, Conde de Torreanaz, *Los concejos del rey durante la edad media*, II (Madrid, 1892), 118 ff. In the reign of Pedro this office was held by a Jew by the name of Don David.— Baer II, no. 207, p. 199. The man whose illegible signature is reproduced in Baer II, p. 204, appears to have held a similar office. For Joseph ibn Wakar see M. M. Antuña in *Al-Andalus*, I (1933), 105 ff. (He is not, apparently, identical with the philosopher and mystic, Joseph ibn Wakar, about whom G. Scholem wrote in *Kiryath Sefer*, 1954, p. 153, and Georges Vajda in *Sefarad*, vols. IX and X, 1949–50.) Antuña (p. 114) argues that Ibn Wakar's journey to Granada must be placed in the reign of Pedro and not Henry II, since the latter is not known to have entrusted political missions to Jews. Antuña's assumption, however, is not correct. On p. 144, Antuña tells of a well-known Jew by the name of Ibn Zarzar who went on a diplomatic mission for Pedro. For other Jewish courtiers and officials active during the reign of Henry II see Baer II, no. 223.

54. See the interesting information concerning Samuel Abulafia of Molina, which I published in Baer I, no. 292.

55. See *Poesias del canciller Pero Lopez de Ayala*, ed. Kuersteiner (Madrid, 1920), vol. I, verses 244 ff., 463 ff.

56. *Sefer ha-Kanah*, Cracow, 1894; *Sefer ha-Peliah*, Przemysl, 1883. See

S. A. Horodetzky, "Ha-Peliah ve-ha-Kanah" (Hebrew), in *Ha-Tekufah,*
X (1921), 283–329; G. Scholem, *Major Trends in Jewish Mysticism*, p.
207 (2nd ed., p. 211); Scholem, *Sabbatai Zevi* (Hebrew), I (1957), p. 93–
4; G. Margoliouth, *Catalogue of the Hebrew . . . Manuscripts in the
British Museum,* Part III, Section I (1909), p. 95 f., no. 789 (a manuscript of the *Sefer ha-Peliah* of the year 1415).
57. *Sefer ha-Kanah,* Part II, fol. 11b, 38b.
58. *Sefer ha-Kanah,* Part II, fol. 145a–b.
59. *Sefer ha-Peliah,* Part I, fol. 35a.
60. *Sefer ha-Kanah,* Part II, fol. 105, 114. Compare the position of
Menahem ben Zerah in *Zeda la-Derekh, ma'amar* III, *kelal* 1, where he
praises monogamy but is inclined to permit concubinage (*barraganeria*),
which was in vogue at the time. Cf. note 7, above.
61. *Ha-Kanah,* Part II, fol. 6b–7b; *Ha-Peliah,* Part II, fol. 27b–28b.
Compare *Zeda la-Derekh, ma'amar* I, *kelal* 4, chapter 21.
62. *Ha-Kanah,* Part II, fol. 6b–7; *Ha-Peliah,* Part II, 27b–28b, 29–33.
63. R. Israel al-Nakawa, *Menorath ha-Maor,* edited by H. G. Enelow,
4 vols., New York, 1929–1932.
64. *Ezer ha-Emunah,* manuscript of the Jud. Theolog. Seminar of
Breslau, fol. 36. See I. Loeb in *REJ,* XVIII (1889), 227.
65. Baer II, no. 220.
66. See Luis Suarez Fernandez, *Juan I, rey de Castilla,* Madrid, 1955.
67. The enactments of the Cortes of Soria of 1380 are given in Baer II,
no. 227, where I give Ayala's opinion in the note. On Jewish ownership
of slaves see chapter IV, note 79 above.
68. Baer II, no. 230.
69. For Don Meir Alguadex and the other Jewish courtiers of John I, as
well as other high Jewish officials of that reign, see Baer II, no. 246.
For Samuel Matut (Matud) see Steinschneider, *Hebr. Uebersetzungen,*
no. 156, p. 287; no. 212, p. 370; and S. M. Schiller-Szinessy, *Catalogue
of the Hebrew Manuscripts Preserved in the University Library* (Cambridge, 1876), p. 136 f. See also Baer II, p. 278, for mention of Samuel
Matut and other Jewish notables of Guadalajara. For Samuel Abravanel,
see Baer II, p. 246, note 2.

INDEX

461